The Making of American

PHYSICAL EDUCATION

SERIES IN HEALTH, PHYSICAL EDUCATION, PHYSICAL THERAPY, AND RECREATION

Charles A. Bucher, *Editor*

ARTHUR WESTON
Rice University

The Making of American
PHYSICAL EDUCATION

New York
APPLETON-CENTURY-CROFTS
Division of Meredith Publishing Company

TO MY WIFE

Corinne Comstock Weston

FOREWORD

A LONG established need in the field of physical education has been for some person to meticulously go through the outstanding speeches, articles, and other literary contributions of professional leaders in our field of endeavor and select those which have proved to be historical milestones. Dr. Arthur Weston undertook this Herculean task and has carried it out in a scholarly and effective manner. He spent years going through the archives and carefully examining every professional piece of literature available. Then, he selected those contributions which met his high literary standards and which have been most effective in shaping our profession. In addition to selecting the most important documents, Dr. Weston has also done a yeoman's service in outlining the historical foundations for American physical education by analyzing its European background and then tracing the history of physical education through colonial days, the "battle of the systems," and up to the present.

I am confident this book will make an outstanding contribution to the professional literature in our specialized areas of endeavor and be "must" reading for all students preparing for physical-education work as well as for leaders in the field.

CHARLES A. BUCHER
Professor of Education
New York University

PREFACE

The Making of American Physical Education is a concise history of American physical education with interpretive documents. The history has been written so as to keep the main lines of historical development constantly before the reader. It begins with the European background of American physical education and moves from Colonial America through the span of American history to the early months of the Kennedy administration. Attention is given to the milestones in the making of American physical education such as the now-famous Battle of the Systems; the ultimate triumph of the "new physical education" following the First World War; the continued professional growth of physical education as it was affected by the Industrial Revolution, the Great Depression, and two World Wars; and, finally, the emphasis on physical fitness provoked by the exigencies of the Cold War and the revelations of the Kraus-Weber tests.

The making of American physical education is also narrated through interpretive documents, selected from the speeches and papers of outstanding leaders in physical education, whose influence has shaped the course of modern American physical education. The first document illustrates, for example, the development of the first academic program of physical education in American education. Similarly, other appropriate documents have been selected to illustrate other important historical developments in American physical education, concluding with the timely document "What is Physical Fitness?" by the well-known research professor of physical education, Dr. Charles H. McCloy. The documents are accompanied by brief biographical sketches of their authors and have been linked with the historical account to give it depth at vital points. Through the documents the readers may learn directly from the leaders who have shaped physical education in the United States rather than solely from those who have written about past developments. The documents embody the ideas, motives, attitudes, and spirit of an age and of the people who were a part of the age. Here is an opportunity to interpret more objectively the major issues, controversies, and historical developments in the making of modern American physical education.

The Making of American Physical Education has been written primarily for courses in the history and philosophy of American physical education and may be used in courses in principles and foundations of physical education to give the reader greater insight, in a convenient way, into the deeper meaning of American physical education. Other special uses may be in seminar and research courses to introduce the fundamental documents in American physical education and to provide a ready access to primary source materials which are difficult to secure.

ARTHUR WESTON

CONTENTS

CHAPTER

DOCUMENTS

Chapter 1

THE EUROPEAN BACKGROUND

To GAIN a clear insight into the values of modern physical education, it is necessary to have an historical perspective with regard to the place of organized physical activity in the lives of people through the ages. Even before civilization arose and recorded history existed, men engaged in physical activity determined by the needs of daily living; and physical-activity programs have had almost as long a history.

Physical-activity programs have evolved under many different names. Such varied titles have been used as physical activity, body training, physical training, military training, gymnastics, calisthenics, hygiene, physical culture, physical fitness, sports and games, recreation, health education, athletics, and physical education. It will be seen in the course of this chapter that each physical-activity program, regardless of the name applied to it, has grown out of a complex of social, economic, and political conditions in areas as varied as the city states of ancient Greece, the Roman Empire, and modern national states like Prussia and England. This complexity can only be suggested in this sketch of the European background of physical education as it evolved in modern America.

In early societies there were few organized physical-activity programs even though every day brought the need for vigorous physical activity in the search for food, clothing, shelter, and protection against a hostile environment. In so far as early programs existed, they centered on feats of strength, running and jumping events, boxing, wrestling, climbing, swimming, and dancing. Primitive ceremonies contained dance routines that aimed to purge body and soul of evil spirits. It was only as civilizations became more complex, with more opportunity for leisure, that physical-education programs were organized to meet the needs and interests of a given society.

The earliest physical education considered educational in nature according to present-day standards was that of the ancient Greeks, the people of predominantly Indo-European strain who inhabited the Balkan peninsula, the islands of the Aegean Sea, and the west coast of Asia Minor from approximately the eighth century B.C., or earlier, to the end of the ancient world in the late fifth century A.D. They called themselves Hellenes rather than Greeks, and their country Hellas rather than Greece. Nor was Hellas a national state in the sense of the nation

1

states of the modern world but rather an agglomeration of small, independent city states, of which Athens and Sparta were the leaders in the troubled years of the Persian Wars (499–480 B.C.) and the Peloponnesian War (431–404 B.C.). A small country with rocky soil and a beneficent climate, jutting into the blue Mediterranean, Greece was the center in the fifth and fourth centuries B.C.—the Golden Age of Greece—of an artistic and intellectual output that dazzles the mind of modern man.

A discussion of physical education in ancient Greece may be divided conveniently into three phases: (1) Homeric Greece as manifested in the *Iliad* and the *Odyssey*, usually attributed to the poet Homer; (2) Athens during the Golden Age of Greece; and (3) Sparta during its entire history.

Homeric Greece

The oldest literary sources of early Greece are the *Iliad* and the *Odyssey*, which were the products of Greeks, it is thought, of the ninth and eighth centuries B.C. Controversy exists about their authorship: some scholars believe that Homer wrote the epic poems while others attribute authorship to numerous ministrels who preserved legends in a poetic form. The life of early Greece was reflected in the *Iliad*, which is usually interpreted as the story of a war waged by the Greeks under the leadership of Agamemnon against Troy, and in the *Odyssey*, the story of the adventures and travels of Odysseus, who was returning from Troy to his native Greece. Society was primitive, families were self-sufficient, and even the nobles worked. In the absence of writing there were no formal educational institutions. Whatever education existed was the responsibility of the family and the clan. The epic poems reveal the role of sports in this society. In the *Iliad*, for example, the funeral of Patroclus, the great friend of the Greek hero Achilles, is followed by funeral games of a chariot race, a boxing match, wrestling, a foot race, and javelin throwing. In the *Odyssey* Odysseus is challenged to display physical prowess during a visit to the land of the Phaeacians, and he responds by casting a heavy weight beyond that of his opponent and by challenging, in his turn, the Phaeacians to contests in boxing, wrestling, or in a foot race, saying: "I am no weakling in all sports." No one steps forward so the Phaeacians please Odysseus with an exhibition of their dancing.

Athenian Ideals and Physical Education

When one thinks of physical education in ancient Greece, there comes to mind not the role of sports in Homeric Greece but rather the physical education in Athens during much of the Golden Age of Greece. Particularly during the years before and after the Persian Wars the Athenians carried physical education to the highest degree of perfection of any people before or since. Though only a small proportion of the population participated, it was a limited group who gave Athenian culture as a whole its distinctive flavor.

It has been suggested that the *Iliad* and the *Odyssey* illustrate two ideals of human development highly prized by later Greeks. Achilles, the hero of the *Iliad,* personifies "the man of action," while Odysseus, the hero of the *Odyssey,* personifies "the man of wisdom." The Athenians favored blending the two ideals to achieve excellence in the individual and the harmonious personality that is free from the blemishes accruing from more limited ideals of development. The sensitivity of Athenians to beauty and harmony that was reflected in their public art also extended to physical beauty and harmony; they admired skill and grace in athletic performance more than the establishment of records of strength and endurance.

Physical education flourished in Athens as an integral part of the educational process. The first seven years of a child's life was spent at home under the guidance of the mother, who instilled a respect for elders, a knowledge of the gods and heroes, and some familiarity with games. The education of the girls was limited to the home; but the boys, severing at the age of seven their home ties, studied reading, writing, some arithmetic, music, literature, and gymnastics. Gymnastics were learned in the privately run *palaestra,* in its beginnings a wrestling ground near a stream, which naturally provided swimming and bathing facilities, but later an elaborate structure equipped with bathing facilities, rooms for oiling and sanding the body and for recreation, and an open court for wrestling, boxing, jumping, and gymnastics. Playing fields for throwing the discus and javelin were also available. Physical-education programs in ancient Athens emphasized such physical activities as hunting, fishing, swimming, running, throwing the discus and javelin, boxing and wrestling, dancing, and military maneuvers.

At the age of eighteen the Athenian boy left the palaestra for two years of military training; and in later life, whether he became a philosopher, an artist, or an ordinary citizen, the state-supported gymnasium gave him the opportunity to continue, if he wished, the activities learned in the palaestra. Serving the men of Athens of all ages were three great gymnasiums: the Academy, the Lyceum, and the Cynosarges, the first two being associated with the names of Plato and Aristotle, respectively. In their writings, and earlier, in Socrates', there appeared strong emphasis on physical-education programs for the attainment of courage and strength, for the symmetry of body development, and for complete physical development as the foundation for mental development. By the fourth century the memory of the Persian Wars had receded. Plato and Aristotle were writing when Athenian education had become intellectualized and professionalism in athletics was on the rise. The great days of physical education were over, and Plato, at least, was seeking its return for the good of the city state.

The Spartan Régime

Democratic, highly individualistic, civilized Athens was not the only voice of ancient Greece. There was also the totalitarian, garrison state of Sparta, devoted to the single ideal of "the man of action" rather than the blend of action and wisdom sought by Athens in its best days. Ruling in southern Greece a subject population twenty times their number, Spartans were virtually compelled to give their attention to military training and an educational program organized to create citizens who would devote their lives to the service of the city state.

The education of the Spartan child was the exclusive responsibility of the city state. Early in life he was examined by a council of examiners to determine whether he was strong and healthy enough to grow into a valuable citizen-soldier. A child classified as too weak was left exposed on the countryside. If one qualified he left his home at the age of seven to enter the barracks, where he stayed until he was thirty. At that age he was allowed to marry but continued to take his meals in the common mess until he was sixty. The training of the Spartan youth was composed of a military conditioning program of gymnastics, swimming, wrestling, boxing, running events, and the throwing of the discus and javelin. Dancing was prescribed for the warrior as a means of welding soldiers into military units through rhythmic patterns of attack movements. At the age of twenty the Spartan emerged as a trained soldier, famed for his laconic speech and his capacity to endure pain and hardship. Intensive military maneuvers followed until he was thirty, and during this period exercises were still prescribed. After that he continued in military service, perhaps training others under the same system. In the result Sparta had the best military machine in Greece, emerging victorious over Athens in the Peloponnesian War. Her subsequent inability to rule Greece despite undoubted military strength opened the way, however, for the conquest of the country by Macedonia in 338 B.C. and then by Rome in 146 B.C.

The Olympic Games

Both Athens and Sparta participated in the numerous Greek festivals, of which the Olympic Games were the most famous. "At their height," wrote an historian of the Olympic Games, "the games were the embodiment of all that made Greece the mistress of the Mediterranean." The origin of the Games is obscure. Beginning as a simple religious festival, they continued to have ceremonies in honor of Zeus but became also a great athletic spectacle to which travellers came from all over the Greek world, even from distant Marseilles in the western Mediterranean. The victor found his name among the immortals, his fame celebrated in verse by a Pindar or Euripides. The first recorded Olympic Games were in 776 B.C.; they lasted until their abolition by the Emperor Theodosius in A.D. 394. They took place at the sacred spot of Olympia, located near Elis in the western Peloponnesus not far from the Ionian Sea. The events included racing, wrestling, boxing, and the pancratium (a mixture of boxing and wrestling). The Spartans may have been responsible for bringing in the famous pentathlon, which has been aptly denominated an elimination contest. The order of events cannot now be determined precisely, but it may well have been like this. All the entrants participated in a broad jump; those who cleared a certain distance qualified for javelin throwing. The four winners of this event engaged in a sprint the length of the great stadium. The three best sprinters twirled the discus, and the two surviving athletes participated in a wrestling match, the winner receiving the coveted palm branch. In the later stages, especially from the second century B.C. on, the Olympic Games fell victim to the professionalism that had penetrated Greek physical education generally. The Games were one of the few visible signs of unity among the highly individualistic city states.

Interaction between Greece and Rome

After the Macedonian conquest of 338 B.C., Greece became part of a much larger empire created by Alexander the Great, an empire that stretched from Macedonia to Egypt and from Egypt to the gates of India. Following his death in 323 B.C., the empire broke up into independent kingdoms. The civilization flourishing there for the next two hundred years was composed of Greek and oriental elements and is called Hellenistic. This term should not be confused with Hellenic, which refers to Greek civilization. It was in the Hellenistic form that Rome, turning eastward in the second century B.C., encountered the civilization of Greece, long after the passing of the Golden Age. Greek slaves and freedmen poured into Rome, the Greek tongue became a second language for the educated Roman, and his culture was built upon the Hellenistic foundation.

Rome: Republic and Empire

Like Athens and Sparta, Rome began as a small city state, but, unlike them, it demonstrated the political and legal capacity to rule larger political units, expanding from a small republic on the Tiber to a great Empire embracing the civilized lands bordering the Mediterranean Sea. The Republic, which had been established about 509 B.C., was destroyed by the expansion. After a period of civil war Octavian, better known as Augustus, emerged in 31 B.C. as master of the Roman world. Though he called himself the first citizen of the Republic, the Republic was, in fact, dead, and his successors were emperors. However, the emperor did not become completely autocratic, ruling like an eastern potentate and worshipped as a god, until the rule of Diocletian (A.D. 284–305). Diocletian carried autocracy to a new high in a desperate effort to stop spreading decay in the Empire. His successors bound their subjects into hereditary castes as to class and occupation.

The seeds of decay had been present since the late years of the Republic when the policy of imperialism led not only to the creation of great professional armies to hold in thrall the conquered provinces but also to the inflow of wealth and slaves that demoralized Roman society. Small landowners in Italy, unable to compete with large estates worked by slave labor, were compelled to leave the countryside; they swelled the city population that the rulers after Augustus fed and entertained with magnificent spectacles in a policy of bread and circuses. The seeds of decay were held in check for a time by prosperity and good government; but after the end of the second century A.D. there set in the economic and cultural decline of three centuries, culminating in the collapse of the Roman Empire in the West sometime around the end of the fifth century A.D.

Physical Education in Rome

Numerous attempts have been made to explain the sources of Roman strength that created the Roman Empire, as well as the weaknesses that led to its ultimate collapse. Success in war in the early history of Rome may be attributed in part at least to the severely practical character of physical education under the Republic. It ignored the aesthetic ideals cherished by the Athenians and the Hellenic concept of the harmonious personality in favor of rigid standards in ethics and physical training that exclusively emphasized health and physical fitness. The results were readily apparent as the Roman youth, who served in a citizen army, developed strength through physical conditioning and also the marching stamina and fighting ability by which they became the pride of the Republic. Even this avenue to physical education was closed after the army became professional in the late years of the Republic and under the Empire. By the time that the Romans turned eastward, the physical-education programs of the Greeks were in decline; and the palaestra and the gymnasium never won Roman support despite the assimilation of other aspects of Greek education. The Romans, though they were no more responsive to the ideal of competition than to aesthetic beauty in physical activity, did continue the Greek tradition of the Olympic Games in a "Romanized version"; these existed precariously until their abolition in A.D. 394.

Professionalism under the Empire

The Romans were not attracted sufficiently to sports and games to participate in public festivals. Except in the early days of the Republic they left participation to professionals and slaves; and after the establishment of the Empire, inactivity and complacency accentuated the trend. Signs of professionalism in athletics were everywhere. One needs only to view the elaborate public baths, the chariot-racing grounds, and the stadiums for gladiatorial combat that flourished in Rome and became the symbol of physical education throughout the Empire. The prime example of the public baths was the Baths of Caracalla (220 meters long by 114 meters wide) which could accommodate 3200 participants at one time for bathing and exercising. The baths were used extensively by professional athletes and the general public. When the Romans participated in exercises, it was usually there. Professionalism in chariot racing reached such heights that the famous Circus Maximus under Augustus accommodated 150,00 spectators. The brutality of the gladiatorial combats became so appealing to the bloodthirsty public that huge stadiums were built to provide a better view of the gory exhibitions. The most famous of the Roman stadiums was the Colosseum, which seated 90,000 spectators and had subterranean dens for animals and quarters for gladiators as well as facilities for flooding the arena for water battles.

Professional athletic events and festivals were promoted for political purposes and as spectator attractions. Influential politicians maintained schools for gladiators to supply men for the local arena and for use as private armies. By A.D. 354 professionalism had reached a peak with more than half the days of the year devoted to holiday festivals. Modern historians are agreed that professionalism in physical education was an important sign of social decay in the late centuries of the Roman Empire.

Medieval Society

The disappearance of the Roman Empire in the West was hastened by the Germanic invasions that began with the successful revolt of the Visigoths in A.D. 378. Two centuries of invasions followed in which the Germanic tribes overwhelmed without destroying Roman civilization. The thousand years from approximately A.D. 500 to A.D. 1500, usually called the Middle Ages, were spent in painfully rebuilding western civilization from Roman and Germanic elements under the directing influence of Christianity. The difficulty of the task was compounded when the rise of

Islam in the seventh century and after, closed the Mediterranean Sea to trade between western Europe and Constantinople and the devastating raids of the Northmen in the ninth century battered the northern coast of Europe. By A.D. 1000 western civilization had reached a nadir. The economy was overwhelmingly agricultural, the mass of the population consisted of serfs bound to the soil, town life was virtually extinct, whatever trade existed was by barter, and government had passed into the hands of the ruling feudal aristocracy. Even by A.D. 1100 economic conditions had begun to improve, however; and as trade resumed and swelled in volume, a money economy returned and the middle class began the rise that ultimately destroyed feudalism and helped produce the modern state.

The institutions of medieval society were those of the church, the castle, and the manorial village before the resumption of town life. Of the three only the institutions of the castle were receptive to any kind of physical education. The ascetic temper of Christianity, which looked to life beyond this world and viewed the body as evil when contrasted with the divinity of the soul, militated against an educational concept that stressed the development of the body. Typical of the attitude of the church was the view taken by its clergymen toward sports of the peasants in the manorial villages. Practically all modern sports in a simple form were known in the Middle Ages. A list of those played in medieval England would include, for example, archery, bowling, Morris-dancing, football, and wrestling; and sometimes whole villages engaged in rivalries in football, wrestling, and archery with neighboring villages. The attitude of the church can be gleaned from the comment of the English Bishop Brumpton, who wrote in the fourteenth century: "Such folk go willingly to a long day's occupation, to wrestling and fairs and spectacles, and vain bodily recreations, while they will scarcely trouble to go one mile to hear a sermon." Not only was play seen as carrying the temptation to miss church services, it was also disliked by the ruling authorities as socially disruptive. In Germany the village dance was repressed and playing at ball was forbidden. Other reasons also entered, as when Edward III in 1337, having in mind military needs for his war with France, forbade engaging in other pastimes so as to leave the time free for archery.

The Knight and Physical Education

Although the institutions of the castle were conducive to some kind of physical education, the goals of the feudal aristocracy were limited to meeting the military obligations involved in self-preservation and to acquiring the skills needed for a successful showing in tournaments or jousting or for fighting in behalf of the church, as in the crusades, for example. As he passed through the stages of training from page and squire to knighthood and entrance into the brotherhood of chivalry, a member of the feudal aristocracy learned boxing, wrestling, fencing, dancing, and horsemanship in military maneuvers. The most essential was horsemanship learned in conjunction with the adroit use of shield and lance and with wearing heavy armor. The brilliant tournaments in which the knight displayed publicly his skill were as characteristic of the Middle Ages and medieval society as the Olympic Games were of the city states of Greece and the huge spectacles in the Colosseum were of ancient Rome.

Emergence of Modern Society

During the centuries between the waning of the Middle Ages and the era of the French Revolution and Napoleon (1789–1815), the history of physical education was fundamentally influenced by the nationalism generated by the modern state system. Vast social, economic, cultural, and political changes at this time resulted in the secular or worldly outlook on the part of modern man which distinguishes him from his medieval forbears. A new Europe was in the process of formation during the Renaissance and Reformation (c. 1340 to 1648), the Age of Louis XIV, which saw the crystallization of the doctrine of royal absolutism (1661–1715), and the Age of the Enlightenment (c. 1740 to 1789).

The Renaissance and Reformation, viewed as an historical period, was one of the great creative eras in history. It was marked by a whole series of developments which eventually ushered in the modern world. Some of these include: (1) the rise of national states, usually governed by absolute monarchs; (2) the transition to urban, town life as the center of national affairs; (3) the revolutionary voyages of discovery and exploration of distant lands that widened European horizons; and (4) the intellectual quickening that was manifested in the invention of the printing press and the consequent speedier diffusion of knowledge, the more pronounced interest in the classical learning of ancient Greece and Rome, and the flowering of literature, the fine arts, and science. The breakup of the church universal coincided with the later stages of the Renaissance and resulted in the multiplicity of religious groups: the Roman Catholics, the Lutherans, the Calvinists, and the Anglicans. In the long run this variety promoted religious toleration and greater individualism in religion as well as increased secularism as the state took over functions formerly belonging to the church, such as charity and education, for example. The trends begun during the Renaissance and Reformation continued into the eighteenth century when men in the Age of the Enlightenment, which grew out of the science of Sir Isaac Newton and the psychology of John Locke, sought to develop scientific laws to serve as a basis for progress in all areas of human experience.

The emphasis upon Greek and Roman classics during the Renaissance was attended by "humanism," a new emphasis upon the cultivation of humanity or humanness through reading the writings of the ancients, who were presumed to have had a deeper insight into the meaning and value of life than the now discredited exponents of medieval philosophy. After reading the classics humanists in Italy glorified man while the humanists of northern Europe accepted man in less esctatic terms as a human being with successes and failures. In either case, individualism was clearly on the rise. The art of the Renaissance reflected the dawning realization of the individualism of man. For the first time since the days of the Romans the artist could render a live, human figure in painting, and a new realism entered as the artist centered his attention on details that recreated the uniqueness of the individual being painted. Thus the "Mona Lisa" and the "Last Supper" of Leonardo da Vinci (1452–1519) are psychological studies, and Michelangelo (1475–1564) before painting his great athletic figures dissected bodies to discover the mechanical secrets of movement.

The new outlook had repercussions in education. It could be said that Italian humanists had welcomed the return of education on the model of ancient Athens when Vittorino da Feltre (1378–1446) opened a school, for the sons of noblemen and others, where the study of Latin, Greek and classical learning was combined with characteristic features of knightly education. Special teachers taught dancing, fencing, riding, swimming, etc. A similar ideal of education was reflected in the famous treatise on manners, *The Courtier,* written by Baldassare Castiglione (1478–1529), who combined the tradition of knighthood with humanist culture. The perfect gentleman should be, preferably, of noble background, athletic, skilled in war, courageous in all situations, and able to speak and write well with a knowledge of literature. The Athenian ideal was also contained in the concept of the universal man—the man of many-sided talents and interests—who was the Renaissance ideal of a great man. Perhaps the best example was supplied by Da Vinci who combined personal qualities of courtly manners, great physical strength, and scientific curiosity with the study of architecture, mathematics, sculpture, anatomy, poetry, music, botany, hydraulics, and all manner of engineering problems.

Modern Educational Principles in Physical Education

The teachings of the humanists with regard to education were translated into practice only in some schools for the sons of noblemen, and it was not until the eighteenth century that Vittorino had a worthy successor in Johann Bernhard Basedow, whose "Philanthropinum" was opened in 1774. In the intervening centuries some thought was given, nevertheless, to the place of physical education in education as a whole. Instru-

mental in ushering in modern educational principles in physical education were John Milton (1608–1674) and John Locke (1632–1704), two
luminaries in seventeenth-century England whose lives span the century,
and Jean Jacques Rousseau (1712–1778), a brilliant figure in the Enlightenment in eighteenth-century France. Milton published in 1644 a
Tractate on Education, in which he outlined a curriculum for the well-
educated man. He included a program of physical activity that had a
Spartan ring in its emphasis on military training and wrestling but ap-
proached a more comprehensive view of education in his definition of
education when he declared: "I call, therefore, a complete and generous
education, that which fits a man to perform justly, skillfully, and mag-
nanimously all the offices both private and public, of peace and war."

Locke's views on physical education were expounded in *Some Thoughts
concerning Education* (1693), which passed through fourteen editions
and was translated into French, German, and Italian. The philosopher,
who was also a physician, considered that children's bodies would have
to be tended if their minds were to be trained at all usefully. Desiring
that English children should have bodies inured to the assaults of wind
and weather, he recommended a regimen of open air, plenty of washing
and bathing in cold weather, a simple diet, exercise, and sleep. Clothing
should be kept loose. In this way the body would be better able, in
Locke's words, "to obey and execute the orders of the mind."

The foundation for modern programs of physical education was laid by
Jean Jacques Rousseau in his *Émile,* published in 1762. In this book,
which reflected Locke's influence, Rousseau described what he believed
to be the ideal education for the boy Émile from birth to adulthood. His
premise was that education should be in accordance with the dictates of
nature and free from the hampering influence of society and the existing
systems of education. Émile was to grow up in the country under simple,
healthful conditions; and his personality was to mature in a completely
natural way. The guiding concern during the first five years was his
growth and physical welfare. Even in the years from five to twelve, Émile
was to have no teaching but was to learn naturally from a developing
curiosity about flowers, the rocks, the heavens, and other phenomena of
nature. After the age of twelve the boy would turn to learning a trade
and still later to the study of social, moral, and religious problems. Besides stressing the role of nature in education, Rousseau contributed
markedly to making popular the concept that intellectual and physical
growth were intertwined and interacting. He gave much attention to the
means of building a vigorous body, saying, "The weaker the body, the
more it commands, the stronger it is, the better it obeys." Though Rousseau recommended a variety of physical activities to strengthen the body
and improve agility of movement, he was content in the main to enun-
ciate theory while leaving practical application to his disciples.

The Philanthropinum: Naturalistic Education in Practice

One of the staunchest advocates of Rousseau's naturalism in education was Johann Bernhard Basedow, a German schoolteacher impressed with the importance of physical activity. After reading *Émile*, Basedow began the first modern physical-education program by using Rousseau's educational principles in the famous Philanthropinum School that he founded in Dessau, Germany, in 1774. It was the first school of modern Europe that admitted all classes of people while giving physical education an integral place in its curriculum. Basedow formulated a physical-education program known as the "Dessau System of Physical Training" that included fencing, riding, dancing, wrestling, running, jumping, and climbing events. Intrusting these activities to regular staff members, Basedow set aside certain hours of the day for gymnastics and sports, for study, and for manual labor. The staff member who was assigned physical training as part of his duties was Johann Friedrich Simon. He is regarded as the first teacher of modern physical education. The experiment aroused much interest, and other schools in the late eighteenth century patterned their curriculum after that of the Philanthropinum.

One of the most famous of these schools was the Schnepfenthal Educational Institute, where Johann Friedrich Guts Muths was a teacher. Guts Muths (who has been called the grandfather of present-day physical education) organized his physical-education program to include gymnastic exercise, manual labor, and social games. For fifty years he taught and wrote in the field of physical education, and among his many publications were *Gymnastics for the Young* (1793) and *Games* (1796). He also edited 53 volumes of the *Library of Pedagogical Literature*. The physical-education program of Guts Muths bore a striking resemblance to those of present-day United States.

The Era of the French Revolution and Napoleon, 1789–1815

Up to this point in this account of the European background of modern American physical education, physical education has been viewed within the context of the city states of ancient Greece, the Mediterranean Empire of the ancient Romans, the medieval society of the Middle Ages, and the nation states that emerged during the Renaissance and Reformation. A comparative latecomer to the historical scene is the nation state in which a sense of national unity has fused with a fervent patriotism to produce modern nationalism. Modern nationalism dates from the French Revolution (1789–1799); and, as Carlton J. H. Hayes, a distinguished historian of nationalism, has written: "The sudden rise of modern nationalism was one of the most impressive features of the French Revolution."

Hayes pointed out that modern nationalism was encouraged in France by the sweeping away of class privileges during the French Revolution so that all Frenchmen became equal before the law, by the conversion of the historic Estates General into a *National* Assembly, by the army at home being named the *National* Guard, and by the nationalistic statement in the "Declaration of the Rights of Man," the best expression of the philosophy of the French Revolution, that "the principle of all sovereignty resides essentially in the *nation*—no body nor individual may exercise any authority which does not proceed directly from the *nation*." Nationalism underlay the eagerness with which French leaders organized a system of national education (on which Napoleon later erected the modern educational system of France) and a system of national military conscription, novel in history, that provided for drafting Frenchmen between the ages of eighteen and twenty-five for military service. Patriotic rites were also established and celebrated. In the name of nationalism French armies were used to incorporate territories with French populations into France without regard for long-accepted treaties and the protests of their rulers. Nationalism also helps explain the success with which French citizen armies, in the international conflict that began in 1792, turned back the Austrian and Prussian armies from French soil and destroyed by the early nineteenth century two coalitions of great powers organized by Prime Minister Pitt of England to bring France to her knees. Members of these coalitions, besides England, were, at one time or another, Russia, Austria, Prussia, Spain, and others.

By 1799 the French Revolution was over and Napoleon, France's most successful general, had control of the state. He always called himself the son of the French Revolution, although he emphasized equality at the expense of liberty in his championship of the French revolutionary motto of "liberty, equality, and fraternity." Napoleon's seizure of power brought a temporary peace; but after he became emperor in 1804, a decade of war began in which the nationalistic armies of France brought that country to the very pinnacle of power before Napoleon's abdication in 1814. By 1810 he controlled, for example, all of Europe either directly or indirectly except for the areas on the periphery of the continent such as the British Isles, Portugal, and Turkey. The final defeat when it came was due in large measure to the counter nationalism created by French power in countries like Russia, Prussia, and Spain. Everywhere that the French armies went, they sowed the dragon teeth of nationalism.

The downfall of France was also due to English persistence. After Trafalgar in 1805 the English fleet was mistress of the seas and in position to blockade the European ports under Napoleon's control, thus shutting him off from colonial products. English gold, accumulating from the workings of the Industrial Revolution, paid the coalitions of Napoleon's enemies that finally defeated him. And after 1808 an English army under the Duke of Wellington waged in Portugal and Spain the famous Peninsular Campaign. When Napoleon invaded Russia in 1812, Wellington's veterans moved into southern France; and Napoleon was caught between his enemies when his forces, still suffering from the Russian invasion, were overwhelmed at Leipzig in 1813. His only course, as allied armies crossed the Rhine, was abdication. The return from exile on Elba in the spring of 1815 was a last desperate bid for power which ended with the defeat of the French army at Waterloo (June, 1815) administered by the allied armies under Wellington and the Prussian General Blücher. Napoleon was once more consigned to exile, this time to distant St. Helena, where he died.

Physical Education in the Era of Revolution and War

Organizational changes in physical-education programs in modern Europe reflected the political changes set in motion during the era of the French Revolution and Napoleon. It is of great importance to note the differing response in England from that of the continental countries. Whereas England continued to cherish the tradition of sports and games with their medieval, if not earlier, origins, the continental countries turned to systems of gymnastics as their response to the challenge of Napoleon and foreign domination. The reasons for the divergence are to be found in the very different historical backgrounds and geographical locations of the continental countries as contrasted with England. They were exposed to military invasion by Napoleon; England, sheltered by the wooden walls of her navy and protected also by the English Channel, was free to follow an independent course. Then, too, England had long had political unity; and the same need did not exist there for programs of physical education that encouraged nationalism. It will be seen in Chapter 2 that even the United States was affected in this period by the nationalism engendered by the Wars of the French Revolution and Napoleon. The War of 1812, fought between the United States and Great Britain, took its course in the shadow of the great events that brought Napoleon's downfall. The nationalism created in the United States by what some have called the Second War for American Independence gave rise, it will be seen, to early American programs of physical education.

Jahn's Turnvereins

The rise and spread of the *Turnvereins,* or German gymnastic societies, were inextricably bound up with the nationalism created in Germany by the Napoleonic Wars. At the very beginning of the nineteenth century Germany, or more properly the Germanies, consisted of approximately three hundred independent states loosely bound together by a common cultural tradition. The spirit of nationalism required to fuse the separate states into an organic whole was supplied by Napoleon when the citizen army of France administered a thoroughgoing defeat to the professional army of Prussia at the Battle of Jena (1806). Prussia was the leading state of north Germany. Prussian humiliation was deepened by the Peace of Tilsit (1807), which provided in its terms for the dismemberment of Prussia, for limiting its army to 42,000 men, and for French troops being placed in Prussia until a war indemnity had been paid. The degradation of Prussia led to a far-reaching program of national reforms, reminiscent in their scope of the changes in France after 1789. Under the leadership of the government serfdom was abolished and land ownership opened to the middle classes and the peasants; the army was reorganized and a system of national conscription supplemented by reserves was introduced; and the foundations were laid for a system of national education. Reformed Prussia led Germany in the rising known as the War of Liberation that climaxing in the Battle of Leipzig (1813) led to Napoleon's first exile.

One of the Prussians who through individual initiative and zeal played an important part in the national regeneration of Prussia even as he sought to realize the larger ideal of a united Germany was Friedrich Ludwig Jahn (1778–1852). Prussian by birth, he saw Germany as his fatherland; and he devoted his life to securing political unification. He had witnessed the rout of the Prussians at Jena, and he later volunteered for service in the War of Liberation. Jahn had done his part to prepare Germany for it. Beginning in 1810 he developed the program of gymnastics outside the schools with which his name is indelibly associated. Its objective was a free, united Germany; the means was the strengthening of Prussian youth and the creation of unity among them by common participation in athletic activity. Its effect was to make physical education for the first time an institution for all the people of Germany.

Jahn was a teacher in Plamann's School for Boys and also the Graue Kloster in Berlin when he began in 1810 the activities from which the formation of the German turnvereins flowed. Jahn was intrusted with expeditions of schoolchildren into the country; and the practice arose of going regularly to the Hasenheide, a hilly and wooded area, where his charges competed in running, jumping, and wrestling and played popular games. Sometimes they hiked or sang folksongs. From this beginning came the out-of-doors gymnasium known as the *turnplatz* (exercising ground), a democratic version, it has been suggested, of the Greek palaestra. When the turnplatz became too small for the growing volume of participation, a new and larger area at the Hasenheide was found where as many as five hundred competed on a single day.

During the years of expansion the amount and variety of apparatus grew apace, and gymnastic exercises and games were formulated. Making use wherever possible of the trees, Jahn first set up jumping standards and horizontal bars, which were soon supplemented by balance beams, vertical ropes, and ladders. In the new quarters vaulting bucks or horses without pommels were made from tree trunks, and parallel bars were improvised. The favorite pieces of apparatus were the parallel bars and the horizontal bar. Jumping ditches and running tracks were also in use. As individuals competed with each other, the gymnastic exercises and games evolved that Jahn later described in his very influential *Die Deutsche Turnkunst* (*German Gymnastics*), which, published in 1816, became the handbook of the turners throughout Germany as the Jahn system spread from the youth to the older classes of the country. In it were chapters on such exercises as walking, running, jumping, vaulting the horse, balancing, the horizontal bar, the parallel bars, climbing, throwing, pulling, pushing, lifting, carrying, holding the body outstretched horizontally, wrestling, and jumping with hoop and rope; and six games (prisoner's base, the hunt, etc.) were described.

Jahn's Influence

By the time of the War of Liberation Jahn was receiving financial assistance from the Prussian government, and his work was visited with official approval when General Blücher and members of the royal family reviewed his turners. The turnen spread like wildfire throughout Prussia and into other German states. Its spread was aided by the formation of the student societies in the universities called *Burschenschaften,* who seeking German unification, promoted physical education to foster the physical and moral vigor of their members. But by 1819, the year of the Carlsbad Decrees, the temper of the Prussian government had altered radically. Europe itself was in the grip of a reaction, of which the prime source was Prince Metternich, the leading minister of Austria. He had shaped importantly the Vienna peace settlement in 1815 that thwarted the hopes of German nationalists by erecting in place of a united Germany a German Confederation of thirty-nine states with Austria at its head. The assassination of one of Metternich's agents (Kotzebue) was the signal for the Carlsbad Decrees that stifled political activity in Germany for thirty years. Jahn himself was arrested, and after his release he participated no more in the movement that he had created. Three liberal Germans who had been Jahn turners—Charles Follen, Carl Beck, and Francis Lieber—emigrated to the United States, where they introduced German gymnastics into American physical education and laid out the first gymnasiums. (See Chapter 2.) Follen was for a short time superintendent of the gymnasium at Harvard, and on his resignation the post was offered to Jahn who refused it. On his refusal the post was accepted by Lieber, whose credentials included a certificate attesting his merit as a gymnast signed by Jahn.

After the liberal Revolution of 1848–1849 signaled the downfall of the Metternichean system Jahn's ideas were revived in the Turnvereins that existed, it will be remembered, outside the schools. They were modified before they passed into the schools through the work of Adolf Spiess, who strongly believed that German gymnastics should be incorporated into the school curriculum. He had read Jahn's *Die Deutsche Turnkunst* and had visited the master in his retirement, but experience in teaching led Spiess to develop methods related to the age and sex of children. His *Turnbuch für Schulen,* of which the first volume was published in 1847, contained a graded series of exercises for young children. That his ideas favored a disciplined response to commands may help account for his success in introducing physical education into the schools of modern Germany.

Swedish Gymnastics: Per Henrik Ling

Another program of gymnastics that proved to have world-wide repercussions was developed in Sweden, where military defeat had also created the desire for a program of military fitness. After a disastrous war with Russia in the early eighteenth century, Sweden lost most of her southern and eastern provinces. Her remaining possessions south of the Baltic were lost during the Napoleonic era. The severest setback of all was administered, however, when Russia conquered all of Finland in 1808.

Under these circumstances the time was ripe for programs that would help Sweden regain her lost prestige. One of these was a physical-education program stressing medical gymnastics that developed under the leadership of Per Henrik Ling (1776–1839). Ling, who had studied and travelled extensively in Europe, had been much influenced by the gymnastics of Jahn in Germany and that of Franz Nachtegall in Denmark. While studying abroad he had also become engrossed in Norse literature. In 1804 he returned to Sweden to assume duties as fencing master and lecturer in Norse literature at the University of Lund, and while there he also undertook the study of anatomy and physiology. Out of the curious amalgam of Swedish nationalism, his interest in the Norsemen, and his study of the human organism came Ling's program of gymnastics, based on military, aesthetic, medical, and educational values, which had as its aim the instilling in Swedish children and youth a spirit of nationalism reminiscent of their Norse forebears. A central feature of the program was medical gymnastics, centering on the therapeutic effect of physical activity, which Ling had noticed when his defective arm seemed to improve with the exercise involved in fencing. His Swedish gymnastics were based on apparatus work that included swinging ladders and rings, rope climbing, vaulting bars, stall bars, booms, and complex swinging exercises based on the principles of medical science. As Baron Nils Posse, the chief interpreter of Swedish gymnastics to the United States in the late nineteenth century, declared: "The Swedish system of gymnastics, devised by . . . Ling . . . was . . . founded upon . . . the laws of the human organism."

In 1814 Ling became Director of the Royal Central Institute of Gymnastics in Stockholm, which he had helped found; and until his death he was the guiding influence in Sweden's military and medical gymnastics. He was succeeded by Lars Gabriel Branting, who, since the threat of war had abated, emphasized medical gymnastics for school children as well as for youth of military age. The medical gymnastics program, which was highly controversial, was finally accepted in the Swedish schools and in many other countries of the world including the United States.

Sports and Games in England

While the countries of western Europe wrestled with the problems imposed by the demands of nationalism and physical fitness, the tradition of sports and games remained very much alive in England. Love of athletic sport was deeply ingrained in the English national character. Sports and games were flourishing in the great public schools like Eton, Harrow, and Rugby—the name *public schools* is misleading in view of their private, aristocratic character—and have persisted to the present although Swedish gymnastics were introduced in the twentieth century as a supplement to traditional forms of recreation. Curiously, the opposite process has been at work in the state-supported schools that were erected by the Education Acts of 1870 and 1902 and shaped by that of 1944. In adopting physical-education programs for the state-supported schools in the early twentieth century, the authorities turned to Swedish gymnastics as a result of disclosures during the Boer War (1899–1902) of deterioration in national health. But since then the traditional sports and games have moved to the front in the programs of physical education. They are today an integral part of the physical-education programs of the state-supported schools. The objectives of physical-education programs in England may be listed as the acquisition or formulation of approved social qualities, physical fitness and health, leadership ability, sound character, poise, and graceful body movements. The sports and games in these programs include cricket, football, tennis, golf, archery, hockey, bowling, wrestling, boxing, fencing, and track and field events.

The Tradition

The tradition of sports and games is sturdy and because of its implications for the making of American physical education should be briefly reviewed. That sports and games have a long history in England can be seen from a remarkable description of the pastimes of the London people in the late twelfth century, written by the chaplain of Thomas Becket. His comments, as translated by a sixteenth-century historian, were as follows:

Let us now come to the sports and pastimes, seeing it is fit that a Citie should not only be commodious and serious, but also merrie and sportful. . . . Every yeare . . . the schoole boyes do bring Cockes of the game to their Master, and all the forenoone delight themselves in Cockfighting: after dinner all the youthes go into the fields to play at the bal. The schollers of every schoole have their ball . . . in their hands: the auncient and wealthy men of the Citie come foorth on horsebacke to see the sport of the yong men, and to take part of the pleasure in beholding their agilitie. Every Fryday in Lent a fresh company of young men comes into the field on horsebacke, and the best horsm[a]n conducteth the rest. Then march forth the citizens sons, and other yong men with disarmed launces and shields, and there they pratise feates of warre. Many Courtiers likewise, when the king lieth nere, and attendants of noblemen doe repaire to these exercises. . . . In Easter holydayes they fight battailes on the water. . . . In the holy dayes all the Somer the youths are exercised in leaping, dancing, shooting, wrastling, casting the stone, and practising their shields: the Maidens . . . daunce as long as they can well see. . . . When the great fenne . . . is frozen, many yong men play upon the yce; some, striding as wide as they may do, do slide swiftly: others make themselves seates of ice . . . : one sits downe, many hand in hand doe draw him, and, one slipping on a sudden, all fall togither: some tie bones to their feete, and under their heeles, and shoving themselves by a little picked staffe, doe slide as swiftly as a bird flieth in the ayre, or an arrow out of a Crossebow. . . . Many of the Citizens doe delight themselves in Hawkes, and houndes. . . .

Impediments to Sports and Games

Sometimes sports and games encountered impediments in the hostility of the church, which was mentioned earlier, or in hostile legislation. But that the church had some understanding of the place of sports and games in the lives of the people is suggested by the granting of papal dispensations after mischance in a game had led to the death of a participant. The frequency of mischance is apparent from an old ballad that goes:

They warstled up, they warstled down, till John fell on the ground;
A dirk fell out of Willie's pouch, and gave him a deadly wound.

Sometimes the government legislated against particular sports when their popularity threatened to impair the practice of archery, which was cherished by the authorities for its usefulness in war. This view lasted until the introduction of small firearms at the end of the Middle Ages lessened

the need for longbowmen in English warfare. As late as 1477 the House
of Commons petitioned the king to enforce strictly the laws of the land so
that no person should use "dice, quoits, football and such like plays, but
that every person mighty and able in body should use his bow, because
the defence of this land standeth much by archers." And during the Renaissance football fell into disrepute at times because of its violence and
brutality.

Sports and Games on the Eve of Colonization

Since English sports and games played an important part in the life
of colonial America, it is worthwhile to notice the nature of the games
played in England on the eve of colonization by the common people, who,
in the final analysis, were the ones who migrated. Light is thrown on their
pastimes by the well-known *Declaration of Sports* (1617), issued by James
I a few years before the *Mayflower* sailed. The King had discovered, so he
said, that much discontent existed because of Puritan interference with
the playing of games on Sunday; and he had drawn up, accordingly, a
list of sports that could be played on Sunday after church was attended.
King James gave his approval to dancing on the green, the festival of the
Maypole, leaping, vaulting, wrestling, pitching the bar, throwing the
sledge, and archery. Bull baiting and bear baiting were acceptable only
on the weekdays that were not holy days, and bowling was prohibited at
all times to the lower classes. Since it was they to whom the King was
addressing his remarks, he made no mention of the more aristocratic
hunting and falconry.

Football

Nor did King James mention football, a leading game of the day with
the common people and the oldest of England's national sports. It appears
to have been introduced into western Europe by the Roman legions.
Football was played by villagers during the Middle Ages, and sometimes
a whole village was pitted en masse against another. The game during
the Renaissance was viewed as bloody and brutal, and both Henry VIII
and Queen Elizabeth legislated against it. Football persisted, nevertheless, among the common people and, in a less brutal form, entered the
sports programs of the public schools during the eighteenth century. The
continuing evolution of the game was recorded in a commemorative tablet
at Rugby, which read: "The stone commemorates the exploit of William
Webb Ellis who, with a fine disregard for the rules of football as played
in his time, first took the ball in his arms and ran with it, thus originating
the distinctive feature of the Rugby game A.D. 1823."

Football passed into colonial America in the eighteenth century. The first picture of a football game in the United States, dated 1806, showed some Yale students, at the college, kicking the ball. Watching the game was the Yale president, who probably disapproved of what he saw. But the game had been played at Yale for some forty years, and a few frowns would not have deterred the students. It will be seen in the discussion of American physical education that sports and games were long played by students before becoming part of the college curriculum.

Sports and Games in the Peninsular Campaign

One of the most illuminating examples of the role of sports and games in the lives of Englishmen can be seen in their contribution toward making Wellington's army contented during the Peninsular Campaign. For six years, from 1808 to 1814, the British army under his command was quartered on foreign soil; and in these years sports and games helped ward off homesickness and irritation. The officers, many of whom may have been of public school background, enjoyed football, cricket, fishing, fox hunting in particular, horse racing, and even English country dancing. Much less is known about the rank and file. Some officers organized games for their men. In the 95th regiment the officers joined their men in all kinds of athletics including cricket, football, leaping, running, and dusting the stone. Before Santarem one officer had the most alert men run races; rum was their reward. In another regiment the men were said to have been encouraged by prizes to leap and run. The historian Godfrey Davies concluded in *Wellington and his Army* (1954) that the effect of outdoor recreation was to help transfer the army from a collection of units into an harmonious whole. Officers were given more opportunity than usual to study one another and their men without the barriers imposed by rank and sharp class distinctions, and Wellington was able to appraise his subordinates on the hunting field. Under the circumstances it is no surprise to discover Wellington at Waterloo describing his officers under fire in these words: "Young ensigns and lieutenants, who had never seen a battle before, rushed to meet death as if they had been playing at cricket."

Gymnastics in England

It was noted earlier that gymnastics entered the physical-education programs in English schools in the early twentieth century. After 1815 gymnastics also made gains in the programs of the army and navy when they were brought in for the purpose of supplementing the traditional sports and games. In 1822 Phokion Clias, a Swiss army officer adept in German gymnastics, came to England to organize the program but stayed only a short while. A second major attempt was made in 1860 when

Archibald Maclaren, who was anxious to place gymnastics on a scientific basis, was intrusted with the task of formulating a system of physical education for the British army. The Maclaren system, for which he was indebted to Jahn and Ling, was introduced into the physical training programs of both the army and navy to supplement sports and games. In the early twentieth century it was largely replaced in the army by Swedish gymnastics and wholly in the navy.

The Revival of the Olympic Games

The revival of the Olympic Games was due to the aristocratic Baron Pierre de Coubertin (1863–1937) of France. It sprang from his deep concern over the lack of an athletic spirit in France. Disturbed by the weakness of France that had been displayed in the Franco-Prussian War (1870–1871) and impressed by the vigor of England, which was the center of a stable, far-flung empire, he decided that the secret of the English success might lie in its educational program. Travelling in England, he saw youth emerging from the schools, well-prepared, in his judgment, to meet the problems of society. He was particularly impressed by the formative effects of English sports and games on English character, and he attributed to sports and games the honor and integrity of Englishmen that had made them respected all over the world. He also travelled in the United States, where he studied athletic competition and organization. Returning to France, Coubertin sought to revive French games and formed athletic clubs like those that he had seen in the United States. Under his leadership a national organization of two hundred athletic clubs were formed in France. Coubertin also fostered international competition between France and England and brought a team of American university athletes to Paris. He was led in his thinking to the idea of international competition among all the countries of the world. Besides his desire to encourage athletics in France, Coubertin was inspired by the faith that international sports, played by young amateurs from all over the world, would be a major force for world peace. Sports, an integral part of the culture of all people, would serve as the means of overcoming the barriers to communication imposed by so many differing races, creeds, languages, and customs. The revival of the ancient Olympic Games, which occurred at Athens, Greece, in 1896, stands as a monument of the vision of one man, Baron Pierre de Coubertin.

The European Background: A Summary

With the re-establishment of the ancient Greek games at Athens in 1896, it is as though this account of the European background of American physical education has come full circle. It has been seen that long before the western hemisphere was discovered, western man engaged in organized physical-education programs. The Greeks, whose achievements were superlative in so many areas of human endeavor, excelled all others in the quality and comprehensive ideals of their programs of physical education though it must be remembered that this comment applies primarily to ancient Athens in the Golden Age of Greece. Very different was the Roman interest in physical education. Under the Republic the emphasis was on the physical fitness and endurance needed for successful imperial expansion; under the Empire the Romans were spectators at magnificent spectacles, in which professionalism was rife. The Romans did perpetuate, however, the Olympic Games, inherited from the Greeks, until the late fourth century A.D. The influence of the church in the Middle Ages was hostile to organized physical activity, which was practiced, nevertheless, by the feudal nobility. Sports and games also persisted in manorial villages.

The Renaissance radically altered the climate of opinion, and the new view of man and his world was carried still further during the Enlightenment. Humanism paved the way for the return of programs of physical education to education. But the humanist Vittorino's school, combining classical learning with instruction in organized physical activities, was chiefly for the sons of noblemen; and a program of education, in which physical education occupied an important place, was available to all classes only in the eighteenth century when Rousseau's principles of naturalistic education influenced Basedow and Guts Muths. In the meantime both Milton and Locke had publicly expressed views that recognized the need for physical activity in education. The advent of the French Revolution in 1789 opened a new era in physical education. The impact of nationalism led both Jahn and Ling to develop programs of gymnastics to strengthen the vitality of their respective nations, and Jahn was also inspired by the vision of a united Germany. In England, on the other hand, the tradition of sports and games that had descended from the Middle Ages shaped a program of physical education different in kind from that of the continental countries. By the end of the nineteenth century the Olympic Games were revived as Baron Pierre de Coubertin sought to demonstrate that nations could compete internationally in the modern era without the bane of professionalism that had helped bring the ancient games to an end.

Chapter 2

THE BATTLE OF THE SYSTEMS

THE ORIGINAL thirteen colonies, from which the United States grew, were founded in the years from 1607 to 1732 in what is called the *colonial period* (1607–1775). During these years the colonies were confined to the narrow area between the Appalachian Mountains and the Atlantic Ocean although penetration of the mountain barrier was underway by the time of the American Revolution (1775–1783). The new nation established at the peace table reached the mighty Mississippi River; and with the addition of territory acquired through purchase, diplomacy, and war in the first half of the nineteenth century, beginning with the magnificent Louisiana Purchase, the United States reached its present continental limits in the decade before the Civil War (1861–1865). "The rise of the new West," remarked the historian Frederick Jackson Turner, "was the most significant fact in American history in the years immediately following the War of 1812." Another important current in American history was, of course, the realization of the democracy implicit in the Declaration of Independence and the Constitution during the era of Jacksonian democracy, a term comprising not only political advances but also an intense interest in social reform. The latter extended to promotion of public education. And still another current was the nationalism released by the War of 1812, which, crossing with the countercurrent of sectionalism and states' rights, played a part in precipitating the tragic sectional conflict known as the Civil War.

In the years after the Civil War the United States filled out its continental limits by completing the westward movement and by building the transcontinental railroads that tied the nation together. During the unparalleled industrial expansion of these years the names of Vanderbilt and Stanford in railroads, McCormick in farm machinery, Carnegie and Morgan in steel, and Rockefeller in the oil industry became household words. With increasing urbanization—New York City quadrupled in population in the years from 1850 to 1900, for example—society became more self-conscious and more aware of the rift widening between the classes and the extremes of wealth and poverty that made this the Gilded Age. Meanwhile, the farmer, who had faced hard times in the years after the prosperity created by the Civil War had passed, attributed his difficulties to the money system and the growing monopoly in American business.

24

The result was the astonishing Populist Revolt that spread like fire over the prairies and culminated in the election of 1896, in which the eloquent William Jennings Bryan, voicing the Populist protest, was defeated by William McKinley. Despite its seeming failure, Populism had paved the way for the reform movements of the twentieth century. The outcome of the Spanish American War of 1898 revealed that a new world power had risen like a phoenix from the ashes of the Civil War; and by 1900, the end of the period under discussion, the United States, aided by an influx of twenty million immigrants between 1870 and 1900, had reached a population of 76,304,799 people.

Though the important foundations of modern physical education in America were laid during the Gilded Age, an historical account of American physical education must take cognizance of the colonial past in which the first beginnings were made. As the colonies passed through the primitive struggle for existence to the more leisurely society of the eighteenth century, the colonists turned to the sports and games indigenous to the country from which they had migrated. The prevailing pattern in the almost two centuries before the American Revolution was English, although beginning in the late seventeenth century there had been added to the numerous English such western European elements as the Dutch of New York, Germans of Pennsylvania, the Swedes of Delaware, the Swiss of North Carolina, and the Huguenots found in New York and South Carolina. The prevailing English pattern meant that English sports and games were found throughout the colonies.

After the war of 1812 many more Germans were added to the population, and in these years new seminal influences affected American physical education. In addition to the English system of sports and games which had been securely established in the colonial period there now existed the German gymnastics advocated by Charles Follen, Charles Beck, and Francis Lieber. Another element appeared when the wave of nationalism released by the War of 1812 gave rise to the early American systems associated with Catherine Beecher and Dioclesian Lewis, usually referred to as Dio Lewis. After the Civil War the system of German gymnastics and the systems of Catherine Beecher and Dio Lewis encountered rivals in the form of Swedish gymnastics and what contemporaries were calling a new physical education found in the systems of Dr. Edward Hitchcock at Amherst, Dr. Dudley A. Sargent at Harvard, and Dr. Edward M. Hartwell at Johns Hopkins. The outcome of the ensuing "Battle of the Systems" was to determine the nature of modern American physical education.

To reflect the phases of American physical education in the years from 1607 to 1900, this chapter has been divided into three periods: (1) the colonial period in which English sports and games became firmly rooted; (2) the period following the War of 1812, distinguished by the introduction of German gymnastics and the early American systems of physical education; and (3) the all-important post Civil War period, during which competing ideas in physical education engaged in the Battle of the Systems.

The English Background

The colonial settlements took shape in three distinct geographical areas: New England, the middle colonies, and the South. There soon developed in the interior of each colony a frontier region that remained throughout the colonial period more primitive than the seaboard. Differing in many ways from each other, these sections shared in common the predominantly English culture. The social and political traditions of the English settlers had prepared them for civic responsibility in the new world. In their former towns and villages they had been called upon to fill offices of local government since the Middle Ages. Even members of the lower classes assumed duties as church wardens and constables. Positions considered relatively unimportant on the English scene provided an education in self-government that proved of great value in the origin and growth of American institutions.

The English who migrated to the colonies carried in their intellectual baggage the common law and the jury system, belief in the rights of Englishmen as against the king, and recreational pursuits based upon the sports-and-games programs in England. Some of them, though the numbers can be easily exaggerated, bore the legacy of cruel religious and political oppression. One thinks here, in particular, of the Puritans. With all their handicaps the colonials looked neither to the English king nor to the Pope for direction. Ultimate truth for them lay in the Bible. It was these tough and serious-minded settlers who laid the foundation upon which modern American society has grown. It was a foundation built upon religion and education.

Colonial Education

Education in early Colonial America was left to parents and friends. Frequently a local housewife would volunteer to teach a group of neighborhood children. Early elementary education was supposed to stress reading, writing, arithmetic, and religion, though generally writing and arithmetic were neglected. Health and physical education were not included since a frontier society little understood their values. The meeting place in the early years was generally the teacher's home, the local church, or the town meeting house. This system of education came to be called "Dame Schools" and "Kitchen Schools." The earliest attention to education by civil authorities was taken by the towns and gradually by the colonial legislatures.

From the humble beginnings just described, a more elaborate system of education developed, especially in New England. In 1635 Boston established an elementary school, and by the end of the century thirty New England towns had similar schools. The schools were financed from tuition and income from town lands, fisheries, tolls, fines, licenses, and property taxes. The colonial secondary schools of the period followed the English models and became known as "Latin grammar schools," their major function being the teaching of Latin grammar. These were relatively restricted in their purpose and appeal since the only occupations where Latin was needed were the ministry, the magistery, and the teaching of Latin in a school or college. One of the most famous of these schools was the Boston Latin School founded in 1635. In the first century of settlement two colleges were founded: Harvard in 1636, William and Mary in 1693. Others appeared in the eighteenth century; about 1750 there were established Princeton, King's College (later Columbia University), Brown, Rutgers, and Dartmouth. Their curriculums were reminiscent of the Middle Ages. The foundation was provided by the study of Greek and Roman classics, supplemented with mathematics, some logic, a minimum of science, and what was called "moral philosophy." It was not to be expected that health and physical education would form part of such curriculums, but vigorous physical activity played an important role in the daily lives of the students.

Recreation in Colonial America

In the seventeenth century the settlers (composed mainly of farmers, European craftsmen, and seafaring men) were involved in conquering a wilderness on the Atlantic seaboard. They faced a formidable task on an inhospitable continent. Physical activity was an integral part of the struggle for existence, and pleasures from physical activity had to come almost wholly from productive efforts in their daily routine. On the continuous frontier the more pleasurable physical activities were barn raisings and husking bees, log rolling, planting and harvesting exploits, hunting and fishing, and fighting a hostile environment that frequently aroused the sporting instincts of the pioneer. In these pursuits were found the elements of competition and co-operation so essential to the development of the frontier.

The tone of the eighteenth century was different. A colonial aristocracy was in the process of formation with large houses equipped with fine furniture and china, and sometimes even with libraries; newspapers multiplied, and other professions grew up besides that of clergymen. Society became less provincial and more cosmopolitan. After a century of building a new country the colonials found more leisure time available for sports and pastimes, the diversity of which can only be suggested.

In New England, even though the Blue Laws of the Puritans curtailed many of the popular recreational activities, there was considerable participation in cricket, fives, marbles, rounders, hopscotch, kites, and water and racing events. The game of self-preservation known as Leap the Bush remained popular. It had developed from the continuous struggle with the Indians. On a signal the participants ran at full speed and leaped over the nearest bushes and hedges and settled down, perfectly silent, in the underbrush.

The Dutch of New York—an important part of the middle colonies—placed greater emphasis on recreational activities than the Puritans of New England. The Dutch, who were not subject to severe religious pressures, enjoyed a greater variety of sports and games. They danced and played cards, enjoyed boating and sleighing, engaged in ball games and sports, and frequently took part in hunting, fishing, and camping expeditions. Skating was introduced by the Dutch, but the climate and religious pressures in the colonies generally prevented this sport from gaining popularity. The game of ninepins was also added by the Dutch and soon became so popular that Bowling Green was built in the present New York City area in 1732. Ninepins acquired the name *bowling* and became so popular with the gambling interests that a law had to be passed to prohibit bowling. Responding to the challenge, sportsmen on the Hudson developed a new tenpin game which allowed bowling to continue within the framework of the laws.

There flourished in Virginia, the leading southern colony, nearly all the early sports and games including the early variations of football. It was a rough and tough game bearing very little resemblance to present-day football. And in the southern colonies, where a new leisure class had grown up around the plantation system, the English sports, especially fox hunting, were extremely popular. Throughout all the colonies there were settlers who enjoyed the sports of cockfighting, boxing, wrestling, and a variety of racing events.

Voices for Physical Education

Among the first to voice the need for physical education as essential to physical development were Benjamin Franklin before the American Revolution and Noah Webster in the years after the American Revolution. Franklin's interest in education led him to establish the Philadelphia Public Academy (1749), which later became the University of Pennsylvania in 1791. Earlier he had set forth his views on physical activity in *Proposals Relating to the Education of Youth in Pennsylvania* (1749), in which he advocated a strenuous program of running, leaping, wrestling, and swimming to harden the constitution. Noah Webster, perhaps best known for his dictionary, presented his views on physical education in an *Address to Yung (?) Gentlemen* (1790), in which he urged participation through organized physical activities to strengthen the growing body. Webster is usually credited with being the first to recommend required physical education as an essential part of American education.

Early German Gymnastics

From the War of 1812 to the Civil War, emphasis on physical education programs was for the development of health and the physical condition of the people in the new Republic. In these years a great variety of physical-education programs were instituted, but none proved capable of meeting the cultural needs of the people as a whole. The first attempt that was made in New England with German gymnastics proved unsuccessful except with German-American communities. In 1825 Dr. Charles Beck, German refugee and student of Jahn's German gymnastics, was appointed an instructor in Latin and in German gymnastics at the Round Hill School in Northhampton, Massachusetts, where he had the first gymnasium in America. Seeking valiantly to get German gymnastics accepted throughout New England, Beck even translated into English Jahn's *Treatise on Gymnastics*. At the same time Dr. Charles Follen, German refugee and the advocate of Jahn gymnastics, organized a gymnastic program for the students at Harvard University. Follen started the first college gymnasium in a dining hall at Harvard University in March, 1826, and later the same year moved to the Delta, a playground at Harvard University, where he set up his gymnastic apparatus. He, too, made a strong if unsuccessful attempt to get German gymnastics accepted in the schools, colleges, and communities of New England.

For a few years after 1825 German gymnastics programs flourished in New England and New York; but as soon as the newness wore off, the programs largely died out. German gymnastics received a new accession of strength in 1848 when the failure of revolutionary movements in Germany sent a wave of liberal Germans to the United States. By 1860 there were more than one hundred and fifty German Turnverein Societies in the United States. The program of these Societies followed the orginal plan of Jahn with exercises on parallel bars, ropes, masts, ladders, the wooden horse, running, vaulting, and leaping events. At the Chicago World's Fair in 1893 four thousand German-American members of the national *Turnerbünd* performed in unison. Despite this limited success German gymnastics were considered too strenuous and uninteresting for the general public, and the door remained open for the entrance of other types of physical-education programs.

The Beecher System

One of the physical-education programs introduced to take the place of German gymnastics for girls was the calisthenics program of Catherine E. Beecher, daughter of Lyman Beecher and sister of Harriet Beecher Stowe. She was the Director of the Hartford Seminary for Girls and later founder of the Western Female Institute in 1837. Her physical-education program for girls was based on the premise that calisthenics and gymnastic programs for men demanded so much strength and vigorous physical activity that they were unsuitable for girls. Accordingly she formulated a physical-education program for girls adjusted to the needs of the body with many of the physical movements set to music. Exercise plans for the girls stressed posture exercises, light chest weights, wand drills, archery, swimming, and horseback riding to develop beauty and health and to increase the life span. In 1859 she published *Physiology and Calisthenics for Schools and Families.* Her activity was premature in American history, for her program conflicted with the feminine ideals of the period and failed to win wide acceptance.

The Dio Lewis System

Another physical-education program, tailored to meet the needs and interests of the youth of the period, was the "New Gymnastics" of Dioclesian Lewis (1823–1886). He was a radical with a magnetic personality, exceptional ability in public speaking, and a strong interest in becoming a leader. Lewis grew up in America during the period when temperance, phrenology, hygiene, and educational reforms were in vogue. An all-consuming interest in exercise and hygiene overcame Lewis when his wife became seriously ill with tuberculosis. His untiring devotion to physical education enabled him to make worthwhile contributions in physical education for girls, preparation of physical-education teachers, and programs of physical education for schools.

Dio Lewis is credited with bringing about a revival of light gymnastics and calisthenics. The measures that catapulted him to fame were his opposition to German gymnastics and his decision to combine the most effective units of Catherine Beecher's calisthenics program with features of the Swedish gymnastics of Per Henrik Ling. A variety of exercises, bean bag, and ball games was used to lend constant variety to each class period. Music was frequently used to provide a tranquil setting for graceful exercise movements, social games, and dance routines. This program of physical education was accepted immediately into the more progressive schools (first in West Newton, Massachusetts, in 1860) and appeared to be the panacea for the difficulties troubling physical education in this period. But the Civil War brought an end, temporarily, to this new program as it became the fashion to emphasize military fitness and drill. Dio Lewis must also be given credit for popularizing light gymnastics for school children, the founding of the Boston Normal Institute for Physical Education (1861), for the preparation of teachers of physical education, and the publishing of the first American physical-education periodical called *Gymnastic Monthly and Journal of Physical Culture,* which was first published in December of 1861, in Boston, Massachusettts. The new program was beginning to be accepted into the curriculum of selected schools at a time when the principle of public education had won wide acceptance, and American education was on the threshold of an astonishing expansion.

Education in the Nineteenth Century

In the years when Follen, Beck, and Lieber were busily promoting German gymnastics and Catherine Beecher and Dio Lewis were formulating the early American programs of physical education, radical changes took place in American education that fundamentally altered its nature. The most far-reaching was the adoption everywhere outside the South by 1860 of the principle of free public education, which was accepted also by the South at the end of the century. This was due in the main to the tireless advocacy of Horace Mann of Massachusetts, the most famous educational reformer of his day, and Henry Barnard of Connecticut, editor and publisher of the *American Journal of Education.* Mann was also responsible for founding in Lexington, Massachusetts, the first normal school for the training of teachers in the United States.

The great growth of the public school system began in the years after the Civil War. By 1900 public high schools with their wide and varied offerings had pushed aside the private academy, teacher training had been further strengthened, and the pattern of eight years of elementary school plus four on the secondary level was set. The number of school childern rose from five million in 1865 to fifteen million in 1900, the rate of illiteracy meanwhile tumbling from 17 to 11 per cent. As an agency for popular education outside the schools, the lyceum, the means for lectures on a variety of topics, gave way late in the nineteenth century to the Chautauqua, which in turn lasted until the advent of movies and the radio.

Accompanying the spread of the public schools was an attack upon the narrow curriculum of the colleges as reformers insisted that courses in modern languages, English literature, history, physics, etc. be added to the more traditional trinity of classical languages, mathematics, and philosophy. It was only after the Civil War that the classical curriculum gave way to the broader system. As one modern historian has pointed out: "If universities were to be opened to the masses, then a university education must be charted in terms of its meaning to the masses." The change was also due, in some measure, to the influence of the state universities that had been established before the Civil War. As early as 1817 the territory of Michigan planned a system of public education running from primary public schools to a publicly supported state university; and after admission to the union, the state university was founded. Similar plans were adopted by other western states.

The Morrill Land Grant Act

The federal government also gave support to education and the rise of public institutions of higher learning when President Lincoln signed into law the Morrill Land Grant Act of 1862, which offered to each state public land for a state university. For some time the effect of the Morrill Act was detrimental, however, to school and college physical-education programs. One of the conditions of the land endowment was the institution of a program of military science and drill for all male students. As the system of land-grant colleges and universities arose, military drill was substituted in large measure for gymnastics and physical training; and the trend thus begun was followed by a large number of schools and colleges. Even the abundant evidence of poor physical condition among the soldiers during the Civil War only sparked a more intensive drive for military drill. Gradually the insistence on military drill declined in the schools and colleges outside the state university systems, and physical education began to return to the school curriculum.

The Variegated Pattern of Physical Education
in the Post-Civil-War Era

In the years from the Civil War to the end of the nineteenth century, the pattern of American physical education in schools and colleges became variegated as the older systems in existence before the Civil War persisted into the postwar years and new systems were added. In the result a variety of physical-education programs competed for supremacy in the Battle of the Systems. Among the systems that had survived from the prewar years were the German gymnastics and modified forms of the Catherine Beecher and Dio Lewis systems of calisthenics and light gymnastics. Into the competition in the postwar years were injected Swedish gymnastics and the American systems associated with the names of Dr. Edward Hitchcock, Dr. Dudley A. Sargent, and Dr. Edward M. Hartwell. There continued to exist in the background, and in a sense on the periphery of physical education, the popular sports and games brought from England in the colonial period and continuing now in the informal play of students. Also present, especially right after the Civil War, was the element of military drill. It will be seen that in the great Boston Conference of 1889, representative spokesmen for the various systems assembled to learn about other systems; and while no doubt, after leaving the Conference, each continued his own system, still, from this time on, they were aware of national developments in physical education. The only missing element of great importance from the Boston Conference was a prominent spokesman for the popular sports and games and the omission was of fundamental importance.

The Hitchcock System

Just before the Civil War broke out a program of physical education was formulated that proved to be the beginning of the foundation of twentieth-century physical education. In 1861 a physician, Dr. Edward Hitchcock, became the Director of the Department of Hygiene and Physical Culture at Amherst College. He is recognized as the first college director in his field to have full faculty status. Dr. Hitchcock's position resulted from an appeal by President Sterns of Amherst to the Board of Trustees for action to correct the poor state of health and physical development of the students. The result of this appeal was the Hitchcock system which emphasized instruction in the laws of health and required physical exercise for all students. Marching and class calisthenics were also stressed as a result of the military influence of the Civil War and the passage of the Morrill Land Grant Act.

After military drill had been de-emphasized at Amherst, Dr. Hitchcock revised his physical-education program and added horizontal and rack bars, vaulting horses, ropes, ladders, rings, weights, Indian clubs, and selected sports and games. This program went far beyond exercising as he experimented with anthropometric testing to facilitate the development of a physical-education program that would promote the physical development and health of the students. Because of an interest in scientific measurement he became one of the pioneers in anthropometrics. In the years from 1861 to 1881 he administered a battery of anthropometric tests to Amherst students and established standards for comparative purposes. For nearly twenty years the Hitchcock program stood alone as a symbol of progress in American physical education. (*See Document 1.*) This lonely eminence was ended with the appearance of the Sargent system.

The Sargent System

In 1879 Dr. Dudley A. Sargent was appointed Assistant Professor of Physical Training and Director of the Hemenway Gymnasium at Harvard University. Earlier in his career he had gained valuable experience as an instructor in gymnastics at Bowdoin College and at Yale University while studying for his medical degree. At Harvard University he developed a physical-education program based upon selected activities from German and Swedish gymnastics, calisthenics, and special strengthening exercises; he constructed some forty types of machines to aid in the development of the body. The Sargent program placed special emphasis on educational, recreational, hygienic, and remedial values, while an interest in scientific measurement led to an anthropometric testing program.

Even though the Sargent program of physical education was called the "Sargent System" in the late nineteenth century, it was much more comprehensive than the term implied. For he drew from all the existing programs of physical education and included his own principles and techniques. A distinctive quality in his program was the pronounced use of a thorough medical examination as the essential preliminary on which participation in his program was based. (*See Documents 2 and 7.*)

Recognizing a definite need to prepare teachers of physical education if his program was to be included in school and college curriculums, Dr. Sargent organized in 1881 the Sanatory Gymnasium in Cambridge, Massachusetts. This school became later the Sargent School of Physical Education and is now the Sargent College of Boston University. In 1887 he introduced physical-education courses at the Harvard University summer session. Through public lectures, professional publications, and an effective program of physical education, Dr. Sargent became a key figure in the development of twentieth-century physical education.

The two systems of physical education associated with Hitchcock and Sargent were the principal American programs of physical education after the Civil War. Another leader who borrowed from their programs and also from the German and Swedish gymnastics was Dr. Edward M. Hartwell of Johns Hopkins University, a former student of Hitchcock.

German Gymnastics

The late nineteenth century, which saw the entrance of the physical education of Hitchcock and Sargent, was also marked by a resurgence of interest in German gymnastics. Their strongholds were the Middle West and New England. Largely because of the location and pressure of the Turnvereins, German gymnastics were established in the public school systems where there were large settlements of German families including newly arrived German immigrants. Perhaps the development of the American public school system is the major reason why the German gymnastics forged ahead rapidly in this period. A large number of German youth were in the high schools by the 1870's, bringing German gymnastics that they had perfected in the local Turnvereins. The acceptance of German gymnastics in the public schools of the Middle West may be seen, for example, in the establishment of German gymnastics in the public school systems of Milwaukee in 1876, Chicago in 1885, Kansas City in 1885, Cleveland in 1888, St. Louis in 1888, and Dayton in 1892.

Swedish Gymnastics

The national scene was further complicated by the new interest in Swedish gymnastics that began when Dr. Hartwig Nissen introduced Swedish gymnastics in Washington, D.C. in 1883. Dr. Nissen, Vice Consul for Norway and Sweden, opened the Swedish Health Institute in the nation's capital and promoted Swedish gymnastics for the schools and colleges and Swedish medical gymnastics among the physicians. But the strong beginning of Swedish gymnastics in the United States was due to another source. They were introduced into the schools of Boston largely through the strenuous activity of Mary Hemenway, Amy Morris Homans, Baron Nils Posse, and Dr. Edward M. Hartwell. It was in particular the interest of Mary Hemenway, widow of a wealthy Boston ship owner, that promoted the growth of Swedish gymnastics. In 1887 she invited Baron Nils Posse to Boston to give a demonstration and series of lessons in Swedish gymnastics. Posse was a graduate of the Royal Central Institute of Gymnastics in Stockholm and one of the first to bring Swedish gymnastics to America. He organized the Posse Normal School in Boston in 1890. The demonstrations aroused so much enthusiasm that Mary Hemenway agreed to finance a program of teacher preparation if the Boston Public School System would introduce Swedish gymnastics on an experimental basis. There was immediate agreement, and the Boston Normal School of Gymnastics was organized in 1888 to give a two-year course of study. It became the Department of Hygiene and Physical Education at Wellesley College in 1909. Barson Nils Posse and Amy Morris Homans were employed to assist with the preparation of teachers. Miss Homans, a former teacher and principal, was a special friend of Mary Hemenway and had been in charge of much of the detail for her educational philanthropy. To complete the agreement with the Boston Public School System Dr. Edward M. Hartwell was appointed Director of Physical Training for the Boston schools in 1890; he organized a program based upon Swedish gymnastics that was used as a model for many years.

Founding a National Association

Even as the elements of the Battle of the Systems were taking shape, progress was also being made in the founding of a physical-education profession by the formation of a national association. It was William G. Anderson, a young medical doctor, who set in motion the sequence of events that ended in the founding of the Association for the Advancement of Physical Education, which evolved into the American Association for Health, Physical Education, and Recreation. After completing his medical degree at the Cleveland Medical College in 1883, he decided that his professional interests were in the field of physical education. Widely read in physical-education literature and a highly skilled gymnast, he lacked, nevertheless, an understanding of teaching methods and techniques in gymnastic activities. Teachers of physical education at the time were called, in most cases, gymnastic teachers; and the only professional gymnastic training available on the East coast was in private gymnasiums. When Anderson accepted a position as instructor in physical training at Adelphi Academy in 1885, the only extensive school of teacher preparation in gymnastics was the Normal School of the North American Gymnastic Union in Milwaukee. The Sargent teacher-education program in Cambridge was in the process of being organized.

Anderson concluded that the best way to establish a common ground in physical education was to assemble the leaders in the field for a complex evaluation of the place and values of physical education in education. In his now-famous letter of November 17, 1885, Anderson invited these leaders to a meeting at Adelphi Academy on November 27, 1885. (*See Document 3.*) Sixty people came to the meeting. The only group directly concerned with physical education who lacked representation was the German Turnverein.

As the meeting got underway it became apparent that the leader of this group was Dr. Edward Hitchcock of Amherst College. He directed the meetings to methods of instruction, systems of measurement, teacher preparation, and the manufacture of apparatus. When the group decided to form a permanent organization, Hitchcock was chosen president. Three vice-presidents were elected: they were Dr. Dudley A. Sargent, Director of the Hemenway Gymnasium at Harvard University; Helen C. Putnam, Director of the Gymnasium at Vassar College; and the Reverend P. Thwing. Dr. William G. Anderson was elected secretary, and T. D. Andrews of the Brooklyn YMCA was elected treasurer.

This group meeting at Adelphi Academy founded the Association for the Advancement of Physical Education and invited those present to become charter members. This Association, which is now the AAHPER, has become the spokesman for the physical-education profession in the

United States. Forty-nine of the sixty members present became charter members. In the group of charter members were three practicing physicians, two ministers, an anthropologist, eleven college teachers, thirteen academy and seminary teachers, six YMCA directors, and an apparatus manufacturer. At the conclusion of the first meeting they agreed to meet again the next year at Adelphi Academy.

At the meeting of 1886 a formal constitution was adopted and the name of the organization changed to the American Association for the Advancement of Physical Education. The members resolved to support teacher education, to publicize the values of physical education, and to urge all people interested in physical education to gather at conventions periodically. The current officers were re-elected with two exceptions. Dr. Edward M. Hartwell of Johns Hopkins University was elected treasurer, and Dr. H. J. Starkloff, President of the North American Turnerbund, became the only new member of the council. It should be noted that the election of Starkloff placed a German turner in an official capacity with the new organization.

The formation of the American Association for the Advancement of Physical Education was one of the avenues that led to the Boston Conference of 1889.

The Boston Conference of 1889

The climax to the long critical period of evaluation in physical education in the post Civil War years was reached with the Boston Conference of 1889, which was held in Huntington Hall at the Massachusetts Institute of Technology. The Conference was promoted and financed by Mary Hemenway, with the able assistance of Amy Morris Homans, and presided over by Dr. William T. Harris, United States Commissioner of Education. In November, 1889, Mary Hemenway was inspired by the influence of Amy Morris Homans to make a masterful attempt at bringing Swedish gymnastics to the attention of the general public as well as to the leaders in physical education. She hoped that Swedish gymnastics would be incorporated into school systems throughout the country. So great an interest was aroused in physical education, by the publicizing of the Conference, that the American Association for the Advancement of Physical Education cancelled its scheduled convention in 1889 and entered enthusiastically into the Boston Conference.

The Boston Conference of November 28–29, 1889, has always been considered by leaders in physical education as one of the most important physical-education conferences ever held in the United States. Speakers at the Conference included such leaders in physical education as Edward Hitchcock, Dudley A. Sargent, Edward M. Hartwell, Claes J. Enebuske,

Jay W. Seaver, Baron Nils Posse, William G. Anderson, and M. de Coubertin.

Dr. William T. Harris, stating at the opening session that the Conference would be devoted to an evaluation of physical-exercise programs that develop the body, requested a comprehensive discussion of the entire subject of physical education, rather than an exposition of the merits of any single system. This was an opportunity for presenting all views, he pointed out, so that everyone may "supplement his own deficiencies." Whereas the old physical education, which prevailed up to about 1860, had stressed only muscular education in the physical training of the body, he noted that a "new physical education" was now on the scene—taught by such men as Dr. Hitchcock at Amherst, Dr. Sargent at Harvard, and Dr. Hartwell at Johns Hopkins—that centered attention upon "the total development of the vital organs." (The new physical education to which Dr. Harris referred should not be confused with the "new physical education" formulated by Dr. Thomas D. Wood and Clark W. Hetherington at the turn of the century, which evolved into the present-day programs of physical education.)

Amidst the many speeches and discussions, the views expressed by Hartwell, Metzner, Posse, and Sargent may be singled out to illustrate the main lines of the Conference.

The keynote speaker was Dr. Edward M. Hartwell who delivered a paper titled "The Nature of Physical Training and the Best Means of Securing its Ends." He discussed the special values of physical training and set forth the principles of the European systems, especially the German and Swedish gymnastics. He also recognized that American physical-education programs offering sports and outdoor pastimes were performing a valuable service to children and youth. (*See Document 4.*)

A paper on German gymnastics, called "The German System of Gymnastics," was prepared by Henrich Metzner of the New York Turnverein and was read, in his absence, by Carl Eberhard, who was Superintendent of the Boston Athletic Club Gymnasium. In it stress was placed on the fact that through many years of scientific research the German system of gymnastics had been perfected to "develop all bodily faculties in an agreeable manner." German gymnastic exercises placed, it was said, special attention upon health, strength, courage, and self-reliance. (*See Document 5.*)

Swedish gymnastics provided the main interest at the second session of the Conference. Baron Nils Posse delivered a paper on the values of Swedish gymnastics titled "The Chief Characteristics of the Swedish System of Gymnastics." The values of Swedish gymnastics, he said, were known all over the world by "gymnastically learned men;" this system had been adopted in every country where its principles had been carefully tested, including sport-minded England. (*See Document 6.*)

At the third session of the Conference a paper was presented on the

Sargent system, one of the two most important American systems of the period. It was written and presented by the influential Dr. Dudley A. Sargent, who spoke on "The System of Physical Training at the Hemenway Gymnasium." He posed for the consideration of his listeners the following question. Why should not a physical-education program, conducted in a gymnasium, produce through the use of especially designed machines physical results similar to those attained through physical labor? Dr. Sargent had developed at Harvard University a number of machines that involved chest weights, pulley weights, and a great variety of machines to strengthen special muscle groups in the body. These were used after a student had a medical examination to determine his specific needs. Concluding his address, Dr. Sargent said with prescience:

What America most needs is the happy combination which the European nations are trying to effect: the strength-giving qualities of the German gymnasium, the active and energetic properties of the English sports, the grace and suppleness acquired from French calisthenics, and the beautiful poise and mechanical precision of the Swedish free movements, all regulated, systematized, and adapted to our peculiar needs and institutions. (*See Document 2.*)

At this national conference there was no prominent spokesman for sports and games, which had existed since the days of colonial America and were then in the schools and colleges as student-sponsored programs. Sports and games existed almost wholly outside the organized programs of physical education. References to sports and games at the Conference were made only in passing by the leaders who evaluated the major physical-education programs of the day. But it will be seen that in the "new physical education" of Wood and Hetherington, which was at that time just over the horizon, sports and games were the medium of the physical-education program. Their program lies at the center of present-day physical education.

The Boston Conference of 1889 enabled the leaders in physical education to make a comparison of the values of these systems to see if some agreement could be reached on the type of physical-education program that would meet the needs and interests of the American people. At the conclusion of these meetings it was the feeling, by the more neutral leaders, that each program had major weaknesses and that no *one* program was acceptable. The most valuable outcome of the Conference was a wholesome and enlightened attitude on the part of the leaders toward all the physical-education programs considered important at that time.

Early State Legislation in Physical Education

The battle between the German, Swedish, and American systems of physical education coincided with the beginning of state legislation in physical education. The early laws were due mainly to the efforts of the American Association for the Advancement of Physical Education, German Turnvereins, Swedish gymnastic leaders, and the Women's Christian Temperance Union. As the values of physical education became more widely known, interest mounted in organized physical-education programs in the public schools. State legislation was passed to require programs of physical education that would increase the health and vigor of the mind and body. (*See Document 7.*) The first states to pass such legislation were California in 1866, Ohio in 1892, Wisconsin in 1897, North Dakota in 1899, and Pennsylvania in 1901.

Terminology in Physical Education

This was the era when medical doctors were pioneering in physical education. Physicians were applying the known principles of medicine to each system of physical education. Physical education was variously denominated drill, gymnastics, hygiene, physical culture, and physical training. Only at the close of the nineteenth century did the term *physical education* appear to any large degree in the literature of the profession.

The subjects most widely discussed in physical education in the last decade of the century were anthropometry, gymnastics, hygiene, drill, and athletics, which were once more analysed in 1890, this time at the convention of the American Association for the Advancement of Physical Education in Boston. At the conference Dr. Dudley A. Sargent and Dr. Luther Halsey Gulick were leading speakers. As his presidential address Sargent presented a paper titled "Is the Teaching of Physical Training a Trade or a Profession?" Dispelling many misconceptions about the field of physical education, he presented reasons for calling physical education a new profession, although the main content of this paper concerned the manufacturing of equipment for use in physical-education programs. Dr. Gulick, Director of Physical Education at the YMCA College in Springfield, spoke on the subject "Physical Education—A New Profession." In this paper he stated that physical education could be a new profession in its own right if outstanding people entered the field and established a foundation based upon scientific principles. (*See Document 8.*)

Physical Education and the National Education Association

The new profession had its first contact with the National Education Association in 1893 when the Board of Directors of the Chicago World's Fair asked the National Education Association to sponsor an International Congress on Education. Accepting the invitation, the National Education Association organized a temporary department of physical education and hygiene as one division of the Congress. Since Dr. Edward M. Hartwell was president of the American Association for the Advancement of Physical Education at the time, he was asked to become chairman of the division. Dr. Hartwell was also well known in educational circles for a number of reasons, one of them being a survey on physical education in America that he had completed in 1885 for the U. S. Bureau of Education.

Following this venture into the field of physical education, the National Education Association organized a Department of Child Study in 1894 and a Department of Physical Education in 1895. The two departments were combined in 1924 into the Department of School Health and Physical Education. It was not until 1937 that the leaders in physical education entered, however, into a direct relationship with the National Education Association. In that year the American Physical Education Association— which in 1903 had replaced the American Association for the Advancement of Physical Education—merged with the National Education Association's Department of School Health and Physical Education.

Professional Publications

As physical education became more important in education, considerable interest developed in research and professional publications. (*See Document 9.*) There were numerous books published on hygiene, physiology, gymnastic exercises and tests, physical examinations, and sports rules. Of special significance among the periodicals were *The Triangle* (1891) and *Physical Education* (1892) edited by Dr. Luther Halsey Gulick; *Posse Gymnastic Journal* (1892) established by Baron Nils Posse; *Mind and Body* (1894) published by the North American Gymnastic Union; and *The American Physical Education Review* (1896), the official publication for over thirty years of the American Association for the Advancement of Physical Education.

Sports and Games

While the organized physical-education programs, consisting largely of gymnastics, were gaining a foothold in the educational programs of schools and colleges, the sports and games were becoming enjoyable, leisure-time community activities and student-sponsored school and college activities. The popular sports-and-games programs of the nineteenth century, which were rooted in the culture and folkways of the American people, provided the framework for physical-education programs in the twentieth century. The tempo of the period, combined with the national impact of the Industrial Revolution, introduced a new degree of leisure among the American people that contributed immeasurably to the foundation of present-day physical-education programs. Physical-education programs first arose in the areas where the Industrial Revolution had its greatest effect. The urbanization of communities brought the nervous tensions of city life, while the restfulness of the countryside was denied to most people until Henry Ford made the automobile available to large numbers in the early twentieth century. The desire to engage in wholesome recreational activities and to gain relief from the pressures of industrialization led to a systematic organization of sports and games.

Progress was striking. In 1864–1865 German-Americans organized their national Turnerbund. In 1867 the first conference of the National Association of Baseball Players was held. In 1868 the New York Athletic Club was formed. In 1869 Princeton and Rutgers engaged in the first American intercollegiate football game. In 1869 YMCA gymnasiums were built in New York and San Francisco, and by 1887 there were 348 YMCA gymnasiums in America. In 1875 the National Bowling League was organized. In 1879 the first national archery tournament was held in White Stocking Park, Chicago. In 1880 the League of American Wheelmen was formed. In 1881 the American Lawn Tennis Association made its appearance. In 1882 the first national tournament in croquet was held in Norwich, Connecticut. In 1886–1887 the first country clubs appeared in New York and Boston. In 1891–1892 Dr. James A. Naismith invented the game of basketball at the YMCA Training School in Springfield, Massachusetts. And in 1896 America won new laurels at the rebirth of the Olympic Games in Athens, Greece.

Student-Sponsored Athletic Programs

The sports-and-games programs, long popular in American communities, became prevalent in schools and colleges in the nineteenth century, especially in the years following the Civil War. The athletic movement in educational institutions was sponsored largely by students, who were living away from home and enjoyed sports competition in their leisure hours. There was very little publicity about these athletic programs, and it was not until 1895 that the sports page appeared when William Randolph Hearst established a section devoted to sports in the *New York Journal*.

From the beginning the student-sponsored athletic programs developed in the face of opposition by educational authorities. The programs resembled, in many ways, present-day intramural sports programs; but as competition became more intense, athletic associations with a faculty sponsor took shape and the program became gradually more acceptable in education. It was soon evident that football was the most popular competitive sport, and, since the 1870's, it has been the sport that has aroused the greatest concern about the place of athletics in education. Much credit is due to Walter Camp, Fielding H. Yost, and Amos Alonzo

Stagg for guiding and directing, with a measure of success and respectability, these athletic programs during the crucial years of their formal entrance into the schools and colleges.

Athletic Organizations

The programs of competitive sports among the students gained such a foothold that regulatory measures were adopted. In 1879 the National Association of Amateur Athletics of America was formed; this organization evolved into the Amateur Athletic Union (AAU) in 1888. Also organized in this period were the Intercollegiate Association of Amateur Athletics of America in 1885; the Intercollegiate Football Association in 1876; the Intercollegiate Athletic Conference in 1883, which was formed to help regulate sports competition through faculty control; the Football Rules Committee in 1893; and in 1895–1896 the Western Conference, which later evolved into the "Big Ten." The high schools did very little in this period to control interscholastic sports competition. The only reasonably effective attempt was made in 1896 when a group of Wisconsin teachers organized a committee to control competition in sports between their schools.

Organized Recreation and Camping

The Industrial Revolution stimulated the growth of the playground and recreation movement in the late nineteenth century. It grew directly out of deepening concern about the ill effects of city slums on children and youth inhabiting crowded, unsanitary tenement buildings. The first organized playground in the United States appeared in Boston in 1885. Dr. Maria Zakerzewska, who had seen the beneficial results of strategically located sand piles for childen in parks in Berlin, suggested a similar plan to a philanthropic group in Boston. The plan was tried in the Parmenter Street Mission in Boston and proved successful. The plan quickly spread to New York and three years later to Chicago. New York enacted the first state legislation leading to an organized play area for children in 1888. In the same year in Chicago, Hull House—the most famous American settlement house—constructed an organized playground that gave rise to the Chicago playground system. The playground movement, progressing slowly in the late nineteenth century, picked up momentum in the early twentieth century and in time became part of the highly organized recreation programs.

The organized camping movement in the United States developed on the whole after the Civil War even though as early as 1861 the students of the Gunnery School for Boys in Connecticut carried out an organized camping expedition. In 1876 organized private camping started with a program centering upon sports and games, hiking and nature study, and outdoor pastimes. Four years later church organizations undertook similar programs, followed by the YMCA in 1885. While the values of organized camping were perceived in these years, an extensive movement in camping came only with the greater leisure and affluence of twentieth-century society.

Physical Education in the YMCA

Parallel with the rise of interest in sports and games was the expansion in the programs of physical education found in the Young Men's Christian Association (YMCA). The movement had started in England in 1841 through the efforts of George Williams, who was a London dry-goods salesman, and had crossed the Atlantic before the Civil War. The early programs consisted of Bible reading and prayer meetings as Williams sought to provide moral and spiritual benefits to those around him who, in many cases, were involved in questionable activities. As the group increased in number, its members organized as the Young Men's Christian Association, which became a model for similar programs throughout the world. Ten years after the founding of the YMCA in England the movement reached Boston, and within a few years there were some 200 YMCA's established in the United States. The American version of the YMCA soon incorporated a physical-education program. A national convention of the YMCA in 1856 decided, after a discussion of the flourishing sports and games, to "establish gymnasia and baths" for the young men of the growing cities.

The first American leader of the YMCA in physical education was Robert J. Roberts, a product of the Tremont and Winship gymnasiums in Boston. His interests in physical activity plus his faith in Christian ideals made him the logical choice as superintendent of the Tremont gymnasium in 1879. Experimenting with all the known physical-education systems, he constructed a program which he said was "short, safe, easy, pleasing, and beneficial." Based upon the ideals of Christian manhood and character, the program comprised physical exercises with a liberal sprinkling of dumbbell drills, followed by bathing.

To provide the necessary leaders for the YMCA movement, the International Training School of the YMCA was founded in Springfield, Massachusetts, in 1885; two years later what was called a Physical Department was added. By 1887 there were approximately 170 YMCA gymnasiums in the United States with some fifty paid leaders. Robert J. Roberts was employed to direct the program of the new physical department; but concluding that he preferred the YMCA work in Boston, he resigned after two years with the YMCA School in Springfield. He was succeeded by Dr. Luther Halsey Gulick, an instructor at the Springfield YMCA

School, who was appointed Director of the Physical Department and remained in that capacity until 1900. Soon after Dr. Gulick was established in his new position the International Committee of the YMCA established an International Department of Physical Training. Dr. Gulick was chosen secretary, a position he held through 1903.

The keen mind and efficiency of Dr. Gulick enabled him to formulate a program of physical education that served as a model for the YMCA throughout the world. He developed a program of physical education to "promote by means of exercise, recreation, and education the highest physical, mental, and moral efficiency of men and boys essential to the development of the best type of virile Christian manhood." Within the program he placed a strong scientific interpretation on physical education, especially in the area of medical examinations, anthropometric measurement, and personal hygiene. Special attention was given to a well-ventilated gymnasium with shower baths and the maintenance of sanitary conditions. Sports and games and hiking became an essential part of the program during the 1890's as a wave of sport enthusiasm swept across the United States. The YMCA, with encouragement and direction from Dr. Gulick, promoted sports and games in an amateur setting. In 1895 the Athletic League was organized to promote, within the YMCA, amateur sports and the standardizing of policies and procedures for competition.

With the resignation of Dr. Gulick at the close of the century, the Springfield YMCA School chose Dr. James Huff McCurdy to direct the Physical Department.

The YWCA

Generally speaking the Young Women's Christian Association has followed the same pattern for girls and young women as the YMCA has for boys and young men. The YWCA, which was founded in England, materialized from an "outgrowth of a religious and social service work" for girls and young women. The YWCA was started in the United States in Boston in 1866 through the efforts of Mrs. Henry Durant. The ideals, purposes, and programs are similar to those of its counterpart, the YMCA.

The Dance in Physical Education and Education

Although several forms of the dance were popular in the communities of early America, there were only a few traces of dance in physical education and education before Melvin Ballou Gilbert introduced the aesthetic dance into these programs in the late nineteenth century. Gilbert stimulated an interest in the aesthetic dance, which was a modified form of the ballet, when he taught in the Harvard Summer School of Physical Education in 1894. So popular did this form of the dance become that he was asked to teach it at the Boston Normal School of Gymnastics and at Vassar College. Within a few years the aesthetic dance had become popular in physical-education programs throughout the country.

The Panorama of American Physical Education: 1607–1900

It is helpful at this point to summarize the conclusions of this survey of physical activity and physical education in the settlement and growth of America from 1607 to 1900. From the first, settlers had engaged in the physical activity called forth by a hostile environment and the challenge of settling a new country. In the early colonial period, physical activities were rooted in the daily routine of the people; they engaged in pastimes such as barn raisings, husking bees, hunting, and fishing. By the next century there was more leisure time, and they turned to sports and other diversions, engaging in cricket, fives, marbles, and numerous ball games. It has been noticed that activity of this type varied from region to region, depending upon the nature of the colonies themselves. Thus the Dutch placed greater emphasis upon recreational activities than the Puritans of New England. As early as the eighteenth century there were voices raised to tell of the importance of physical education to education as a whole; among them were the influential suggestions of Benjamin Franklin and Noah Webster, both of whom expressed publicly the view that physical activity, on a more than casual basis, was needed for optimum development of the growing body.

In the years after the War of 1812 and before the outbreak of the Civil War, a number of attempts were made to introduce physical-education programs into the schools and colleges, but none of them proved entirely successful in meeting the cultural needs of the people. Thus Dr. Charles Beck and Dr. Charles Follen, both Jahn disciples, brought German gymnastics to the new American republic and tried, unsuccessfully, to secure their acceptance in the schools and colleges of New England. Their influence persisted, nevertheless, in the Turnvereins, which numbered about one hundred and fifty on the eve of the Civil War. For their membership they drew heavily on German immigrants. Another important strand in physical education in this period was supplied by the physical-education program that Catherine Beecher developed for women first at the Hartford Seminary for Girls and later at the Western Female Institute. But the program that she developed conflicted with the feminine ideals of her time and hence did not secure widespread acceptance.

Still another physical-education program in these years was the "New Gymnastics" of Dio Lewis, who combined Catherine Beecher's program with the Swedish gymnastics associated with Per Henrik Ling. The coming of the Civil War, which brought a marked emphasis on military fitness and drill, brought to an end, for the time being, the revival of gymnastics, although not before Lewis had popularized light gymnastics for school children and had made beginnings in the training of gymnastic teachers. Since the period of Dio Lewis's activity coincided with the acceptance in the northern states of the principle of public support for education, a vehicle was at hand, after the Civil War, for the programs of physical education that arose in the late nineteenth century.

The years between 1865 and 1900 were a period of change and ferment in the United States, and the activity in industry and society was matched by advances in the field of physical education. Just as before the Civil War there existed, however, a variety of programs, no one of which had achieved supremacy when the period closed. Thus there existed, side-by-side, the foreign-born programs of German and Swedish gymnastics, the modified programs of Catherine Beecher and Dio Lewis, and the new American programs of physical education taught by such leaders of the new profession as Edward Hitchcock, Dudley A. Sargent, Edward M. Hartwell, and William G. Anderson. The values of the competing systems were examined at the Boston Conference of 1889, and the more neutral leaders present concluded that no one physical-education program in existence met as fully as was desirable the needs and interests of the American people.

Still the period was one of progress in physical education. Leadership was provided for the developing profession by men like Hitchcock, Sargent, Hartwell, and Anderson. The American Association for the Advancement of Physical Education had been organized in 1885; and in 1896 this Association started publishing the *American Physical Education Review*, which was the official organ of the new profession for nearly thirty years. A whole series of organized physical activities now existed that either formed a part of physical-education programs in the schools and colleges or else were found in closely allied areas. The beginnings of the dance in education have been noted; and the YMCA had, especially under the leadership of Dr. Luther Halsey Gulick, developed its own physical-education program in accordance with advanced ideas in physical education and education. And just before the turn of the century the playground and camping movements laid the foundations for new fields. About that time, too, one-third of the high schools were teaching hygiene; recreation and camping movements had been started; national organizations had been formed in such sports as archery, bowling, croquet, tennis, football, and baseball; Dr. James A. Naismith had invented the game of basketball; and Americans had participated in the modern Olympic Games in Athens in 1896.

Chapter 3

PHYSICAL EDUCATION
IN TRANSITION

THE PERIOD from 1900 to 1918, which ended in the shadow of the cataclysmic First World War (1914–1918), was marked by the emergence of modern American society. A fundamental factor in this development was the revolution in transportation and communication that broke down old barriers of isolation and left the American people more interdependent in their personal relationships and more national in their outlook. The era of building the great transcontinental railroads was over, but to their unifying impulse was added another when the gasoline engine was applied to transportation. As factories with their mass-production methods went into operation, the million automobiles were produced that were travelling the nation's rather primitive highways when the First World War came. Among them was, of course, Ford's utilitarian Model T, which surprisingly large numbers of people could afford to buy. In these years the Wright brothers were experimenting with airborne flight on the dunes of Kitty Hawk, but the air age was still beyond man's reach.

As a result of the revolution in communication, telegraph and telephone lines linked together all parts of continental United States, and a beginning was made of the motion picture that was to make entertainment and sports of national interest. The demand for electricity was also heightened by the trolley cars in the fast-growing cities, fed by streams of immigrants as well as people from the country, and by the use of Edison's incandescent lamp to light the urban areas. The construction of giant hydroelectric plants and the rise of great electrical firms such as General Electric and Westinghouse completed the picture. The revolution in transportation and communication in turn made business and markets more national; their interrelationship opened up new fields of industry and enterprise, encouraged the movement to the cities, gave millions a taste for leisure hitherto thought accessible only to the wealthy, and changed the living habits of a whole nation.

The chief political interest of these years was the amazing Progressive Movement that flourished in the first two decades of the twentieth century and left its imprint on the policies of the two great parties in the Square Deal of Theodore Roosevelt and the New Freedom of Woodrow Wilson.

The Progressive Movement arose in response to the ills of an industrialized democracy and was a powerful protest against a federal government responsive to the privileged few in finance and industry, the corruption and bossism in city government, the social ills festering in the slums of the cities, the child labor in the factories, etc. Solutions offered by Progressives varied from a greater dose of democracy in the political machinery through wider use of the referendum, for example, to the adoption of public health measures and educational reform.

It is a leading thesis of Lawrence Cremin in *The Transformation of the School: Progressivism in American Education* (1961) that the progressive movement in education which ended, he thinks, in transforming the American school, "began as part and parcel of that broader program of social and political reform the Progressive Movement." In a detailed discussion of the leading ideas of William James, G. Stanley Hall, Edward L. Thorndike, John Dewey, and William Heard Kilpatrick, Cremin demonstrates how directly or indirectly they contributed to a Progressive crusade to reform the schools in the interests of a free democratic society. The first three —James, Hall, and Thorndike—supplied the psychological foundations on which Dewey, Kilpatrick, and others built. James's contribution is perhaps less obvious than the others. His *Principles of Psychology* (1890) contained an essentially behaviorist psychology, developed from applying the theory of evolution to man and his mind as James sought to make psychology a science. A writer in 1910 estimated that probably nine-tenths of the teachers who read psychology at all did so in the *Principles of Psychology* though Cremin thinks the estimate somewhat high. In other writings James seemed to ask the school to produce individuals bold and brave enough to shape society; and this was his most direct contribution to the progressive movement in education. G. Stanley Hall's contribution, expressed in works such as *Adolescence* (1904) and *Educational Problems* (1911), was more direct. His studies in child psychology substantiated the feasibility of a curriculum rising out of data on the child and suited to his nature, growth, and development. Edward L. Thorndike's studies on the transfer of learning, by discrediting the idea that certain subjects had an innate disciplinary value capable of transfer, opened the way for a broader, more utilitarian curriculum, while his research in heredity gave rise to studies of individual differences, intelligence testing, classroom grouping, etc.

From John Dewey and William Heard Kilpatrick came the view that the school should be centered on the child, and from Dewey, in particular, the view that the school should reflect the larger life outside it. In two seminal and vastly influential books, *School and Society* (1899) and *Democracy and Education* (1916), Dewey established for himself a secure place in the history of American education and thought. Schools should be organized, he contended in *School and Society,* to reflect the life of the larger community outside; and the child, trained in a variety of social situations within the school, should leave with a spirit of service and intellectually equipped to improve that society, making it "worthy, lovely, and harmonious." The school, in short, was the lever of social change. The same ideas were expressed in the later *Democracy and Education* when he wrote that progressive societies should "endeavor to shape the experiences of the young, so that instead of reproducing current habits, better habits shall be formed, and thus the future adult society be an improvement on their own." To carry out these objectives the curriculum should be broadened to include scientific and industrial subjects; and teaching methods should draw on the natural resources of the child, his natural impulse to conversation, inquiry, and expressions. The popularizer of Dewey's theories was William Heard Kilpatrick, who through his lectures at Teachers College, Columbia University, influenced a whole generation of teachers. Cremin concludes that Kilpatrick carried the idea of a child-centered school beyond Dewey's conception when in his *Foundations of Method* (1925) Kilpatrick waged war on subject matter "fixed-in-advance," which Dewey would have preserved in the curriculum along with new materials accruing from the experience of the child.

Even without the Progressive Movement the schools would have changed rapidly in these years, for the drive for free public education aimed earlier at the elementary schools now extended to the secondary level. Whereas in 1895 there were approximately 350,000 in the high schools, the number had doubled ten years later, and by 1915 had reached 1,300,000. In 1900 there were 15,503,110 in the public schools; by 1918, the end of the period under discussion, there were 20,853,516.

In the years before the First World War the advances in education and psychology influenced a "new physical education," which entered the Battle of the Systems that had been so much in evidence since the Boston Conference of 1889. It will be seen in the course of this chapter that the "new physical education" relied upon sports and games, long favored by students as their recreational outlet, as a means of attaining educational goals more comprehensive than those set by the supporters of formal gymnastics. The system of formal gymnastics continued to hold its predominant position in these years; but it now had, in the form of the "new physical education," a formidable rival with which it would have to deal.

In the resulting period of transition in physical education, as the various elements contended for supremacy in the physical-education program, sports and games, the medium of the "new physical education," became part of the program. As though preparing itself for the day when the Battle of the Systems would be over, physical education itself moved into new channels. A number of physical-education leaders received important positions in education, teacher preparation for physical education was improved and strengthened, advancements were made in tests and measurements as physical education became more scientific, health education gained stature in some school systems, and a professional literature flourished that made the profession more aware of progress in the field and the history of physical education. Other central themes in the years from 1900 to 1918 were provided by the growing popularity of sports and games, in the hands of students, which were in the process of becoming the interscholastic and intercollegiate programs of the twentieth century and by the role of physical education during the First World War. Attention will also be given to developments in areas allied to physical education at this time, such as recreation, camping, the YMCA, and the dance.

A New Philosophy Creates a New Program

The early twentieth-century programs of physical education were still dominated by formal gymnastics, the German and Swedish in particular. They were rivalled, however, by a new concept of physical education, known variously as the "new physical education," "natural program," and "natural gymnastics," which was in the process of formation largely through the efforts of a trinity of outstanding leaders in physical education: Dr. Thomas D. Wood, Clark W. Hetherington, and Dr. Luther Halsey Gulick. It was they who broke with the tradition of formal gymnastics and gave shape and content to a distinctively twentieth-century program of physical education, which centers upon the physical as an avenue for promoting education. This was in sharp contrast to the view distinguishing most earlier programs of physical education, namely, that the physical body should be developed as an end in itself.

This gifted group of men, who were distinguished by courage, insight, and gifts for teaching and writing, were strongly convinced that a new program of physical education would have to be formulated, and their qualities of perseverance and leadership meant that they would be the central guiding force in its evolution. Dr. Thomas D. Wood, while at Stanford University and later Teachers College, Columbia University, developed the natural program of physical education based upon sports and games, outdoor activities, and selected gymnastic progressions related to educational needs; the entire program centered upon the age, needs, and interests of those concerned. (*See Document 10.*) Clark W. Hetherington, known as the modern philosopher of physical education, believing in a program that would contribute to the total education of the student, emphasized that a program of physical education to do this satisfactorily must be rooted in American society so as to help train children for democratic citizenship. This result was impossible to obtain if one relied upon German and Swedish gymnastics which, he implied, drew their life blood from a radically different culture. (*See Document 11.*) Dr. Luther Halsey Gulick, one of the foremost leaders in physical education, recreation, and camping, placed great emphasis upon social values in physical education. An eloquent lecturer and prodigious writer, he worked to promote programs of physical education and recreation in education, community organizations, and youth groups that would encourage healthy relaxation and recreation free from the tensions of a highly industrialized society. (*See Document 12.*)

The leaders of the new physical education knew full well that the more sedentary life, with an increasing amount of leisure time available, carried with it a greater responsibility for the teacher of physical education and health education with regard to his students than had been the case in the past. A new era had dawned. They were also aware that the complexity of their task had been heightened by the adoption of a new philosophy of physical education, which had as a leading doctrine that physical education possessed inherent educational values capable of transforming the mental, physical, emotional, and social qualities of an individual to approach more closely the ideal of an educated man. Among the educational values that they cited as usually accruing from physical education were an understanding and respect for the human body as a means of expressing the development of the fundamental skills of movement so necessary in all daily activity; the physiological development of the human body; an understanding and knowledge of the care needed by the human body to enable it to function at peak efficiency; the development of interests and playing skills in a variety of wholesome leisure-time activities; and the realization that physical education could serve as one of the best avenues for group understanding and co-operation. With the development of the new physical education came an increasing emphasis upon health education and personal hygiene. (*See Document 13.*)

The new physical education posed a serious challenge to German, Swedish, and other types of formal gymnastics, which tended to ignore over-all education in their preoccupation with corrective and postural exercises that concentrated on developing the physical body. Its affects were felt only gradually, however, for the time lag between the formulation of a sound program and the placing of it in operation meant that the new physical education was slow in finding its way, on a large scale, into schools and colleges until after World War I. Remarkable progress in promoting the new physical education, with which the names of Dr. Thomas D. Wood and Clark W. Hetherington are indelibly associated, came in the 1920's as their disciples, Dr. Jesse Feiring Williams and Dr. Jay B. Nash, carried the movement vigorously forward.

Physical Education in Transition

As sports and games made inroads into the programs of formal gymnastics, many physical-education instructors yielded to the trend by revising their facilities for formal gymnastics to provide playing areas for sports and games. These changes frequently led to a physical-education program that combined sports and games and formal gymnastics, although formal gymnastics continued, nevertheless, to serve as the foundation of physical-education programs until after the First World War. Thus the Battle of the Systems in physical education, which had held the center of the stage at the Boston Conference of 1889, continued with unabated fury through the first two decades of the twentieth century.

In the new gymnasiums that were being built large open spaces were provided for the playing of sports and games, and the seating capacity was also increased. The gymnasiums were adaptable for numerous student and adult activities. An unexpected by-product occurred when community leaders, impressed by the extensive use being made of the gymnasiums and playing facilities, became willing to support financially the new construction.

Even the terminology in physical education was changing. Sociological and psychological objectives were being stressed in education through the efforts of such men as John Dewey, Edward L. Thorndike, and G. Stanley Hall. The new approach to education brought an understanding of the vital contribution that physical education could make to education generally, and by the early 1920's *physical education* had become the accepted term. The nineteenth-century terminology of *physical culture, physical training,* and *gymnastics,* which had carried over into the early twentieth century, gradually disappeared in most schools and colleges.

The early years of transition found many physical-education teachers being appointed to important positions in education in the schools and colleges. A few examples will suffice: Dr. Luther Halsey Gulick was appointed Director of Physical Education for the New York City Public School System in 1903; in the same year Dr. Delphine Hanna was appointed full Professor of Physical Education at Oberlin College (In appointing Dr. Hanna to this position, Oberlin College became the first college in the United States to have a woman in the position of full Professor of Physical Education.); Dr. R. Tait McKenzie was appointed Professor and Director of the Department of Physical Education at the University of Pennsylvania in 1904; five years later Ethel Perrin was appointed Supervisor of Physical Education for the Detroit Public School System; and Amy Morris Homans was appointed full Professor of Physical Education at Wellesley College in 1910, the first Women's College in the United States to appoint a woman full Professor of Physical Education.

Teacher Education in Physical Education

The teacher of physical education required in the early twentieth century a more comprehensive academic preparation than the undiluted medical background or the formal gymnastic training that had distinguished leaders of the earlier era. The urgency of the situation was recognized by Dr. Jay W. Seaver and Dr. Dudley A. Sargent. Dr. Seaver stressed the need for a thorough academic background in his thoughtful address "A Plea for More Theoretical Instruction in our Normal Schools of Gymnastics." (*See Document 14.*) Dr. Sargent urged a broad and liberal education in his memorable address "Should the Teacher of Physical Education in Public Schools Have the Training of a Physical Director and Instructor in Hygiene or That of a Physician?" (*See Document 15.*) A change followed in the professional preparation of the physical-education teacher as is evidenced by a survey taken in 1927 of the degrees held by physical-education directors in colleges. It revealed that whereas college directors of the earlier period usually held M.D. degrees, now 87 per cent held either the Ph.D. or Ed.D. degree; only 27 per cent held the M.D. degree, in some cases along with the Ph.D. or Ed.D. degree.

Teacher Education Schools and Colleges

Another noteworthy change in teacher education took place when the private, noncollegiate, teacher-education schools of physical education affiliated with colleges and universities and public normal schools. Their academic status rose appreciably as they merged with the better-known academic institutions. An interesting status report on the early teacher-preparation schools of physical education, before affiliation took place, was compiled in 1903 by Dr. Delphine Hanna. She gave the name and location of the schools involved and specific information about the directors, number of graduates who were teaching, and the type of diploma or degree granted. (*See Document 16.*)

Several of the outstanding mergers were the Anderson School of Physical Education, which moved to New Haven in 1901 to become the New Haven Normal School of Gymnastics, later Arnold College, and finally affiliated with the University of Bridgeport; the Boston Normal School of Gymnastics which became the Department of Hygiene and Physical Education at Wellesley College in 1909; the Bouvé School of Physical Education which became a part of Simmons College; the Posse School of Physical Education which affiliated with Tufts College; and the Savage School of Physical Education which became a part of New York University. Two of the early famous private schools of physical education that continued their independent status were the Sargent School of Physical Education, which did not become an official division of Boston University until 1929, and the Normal School of the North American Gymnastic Union, which continued as a private school until 1941, becoming in that year a part of the University of Indiana.

There was also a movement to establish departments of teacher education in physical education, and graduate instruction was introduced. Among the colleges and universities establishing departments of teacher education in physical education were Illinois in 1905, Oregon in 1907, Wisconsin in 1911, Missouri in 1914, Iowa in 1918, Indiana and Minnesota in 1919, and Michigan in 1921. Graduate instruction in physical education was begun in 1901 at Columbia University with the instituting of a program leading to the Master's degree. And Columbia University, along with New York University, also had the first graduate program leading to the Doctor's degree when this began in 1924. By 1930 twenty-eight colleges and universities were offering graduate preparation in physical education, and with this development there came simultaneously a more pronounced emphasis on research, on tests and measurements, and on professional literature.

Research and Tests and Measurements

Progress in research and tests and measurements, which was started principally by Dr. Edward Hitchcock and Dr. Dudley A. Sargent in the second half of the nineteenth century, became an integral part of the academic work of the young profession in the early twentieth century. The research emphasis changed. Whereas it had earlier been largely anthropometric measurement and strength testing, it now became principally physical-achievement tests and cardiovascular research, for the mushrooming sports-and-games program encouraged the type of test that would measure physical efficiency.

Among the notable physical achievement tests were these. Dr. Dudley A. Sargent revised his research program in 1902 and developed a Universal Test for Strength, Speed, and Endurance. In 1904, Dr. Luther Halsey Gulick developed the first athletic achievement tests, which were adopted in the Public School Athletic League in New York City. Nine years later Athletic Badge Tests denoting standards of athletic achievement were developed by the American Playground Association. Dr. George L. Meylan produced in 1907 a college achievement test for grading students in physical education; it was based upon an examination of posture, physical efficiency, swimming, and a written examination in health and physical education.

As advances took place in the area of medical research, more tests were added. Following research on heart and blood pressure changes in adolescents, Dr. James H. McCurdy set up standards in 1910 for measuring blood pressure and heart rate. A Blood Ptosis test meanwhile had been constructed in 1905 by Dr. Ward Crampton, that proved of special value in cardiovascular research. By 1913 Dr. George L. Meylan had constructed cardiovascular efficiency tests. And so it went as medical research provided the specific information needed for the emerging health-education programs that were in the process of becoming an integral part of the education program.

Medical Research Leads to Health Education

The foundation of school health education in the United States was due in large measure to the tireless efforts of Dr. Thomas D. Wood, who brought to leaders in education a keen awareness of the need for health. Dr. Wood stressed the value of good health as being of the utmost importance to everyone at all times, emphasizing that it is the keystone upon which man builds for the future. Without good health man cannot profit to the maximum from all his great worldly accomplishments. Since the health of the people is the most important resource of a country, it followed, in Dr. Wood's view, that it is the business of the schools to protect and improve the health of the children. (*See Document 10.*)

To improve the general health of the students, it was necessary to have a comprehensive health examination administered to the students at appropriate times to determine health status. The health examination had hitherto been largely a medical check-up to detect communicable diseases. But as it became evident that health defects affected academic progress, the health examinations were revised and a much more complex examination was used. New Jersey moved to strengthen school health education in 1903 by passing state legislation that compelled all students to have a complete health examination. A complete medical examination was required in Massachusetts for all children in towns and cities. And Vermont passed state legislation requiring an annual health examination of the eyes, ears, and throat of all school children.

The early school health examinations encountered vigorous opposition from groups in the community on the grounds of their interference with the right of parents, with private medical practice, and with the school program. After much debate school authorities continued, nevertheless, to employ the services of school physicians and nurses. By 1910 sixty-seven cities employed nurses for health instruction and guidance, for visits to homes to check on medical difficulties, and to check on medical cases as directed by school physicians.

Clearly progress had been made by 1915, for by that time twenty-six states had passed state legislation concerning the personal health of school children. There were in these years two professional organizations that were remarkably successful in promoting school health education. The National Congress of Parents and Teachers, created in 1897, worked to secure health examinations, sanitary conditions, proper heat and ventilation, and proper food and diet. The United States Children's Bureau of the Federal Security Agency, founded in 1912, prepared health-education materials such as reports, bulletins, posters, and exhibits concerning the health of children. But it remained for the draft statistics on the health of World War I service men to provide the stimulus for a national emphasis on health education.

The more professional approach in health education and physical education flowered into the professional literature of the period.

Professional Literature

Many of the pioneers in physical education were completing a lifetime of professional service in the years before the First World War. They saw the need and possessed both the interest and ability to present in writing their specific knowledge and findings, which were embodied in a whole series of publications. Some of the most important were *School Gymnastics and Light Apparatus* (1900) by Jesse Bancroft; *Physical Education* (1907) by Luther Halsey Gulick; *Folk Dance Tunes* (1908) by Elizabeth Burchenal; *Normal Course in Play* (1909) edited by Clark W. Hetherington; *Play in Education* (1910) by Joseph Lee; *Exercise in Education and Medicine* (1909) by R. Tait McKenzie; *Health Education* (1910) by Thomas D. Wood; *Action of Muscles* (1912) by Wilbur P. Bowen; and *Pioneers of Modern Physical Education* (1919) by Fred E. Leonard.

New professional journals were started in this period. Of special significance were *Physical Training* (1901), published by the YMCA, and *Playground* (1907), published by the Playground and Recreation Association of America. Two of the most important professional journals of this period were somewhat older; they were the *American Physical Education Review* (1896) and *Mind and Body* (1894). Thus physical education was becoming more professional at a time when the United States was posed on the threshold of a great rise of interest in sports and games.

New Laurels in Sports and Games

The sports-and-games program, indigenous to the American people, gathered momentum in the first two decades of the twentieth century, bringing the pleasure involved in sports participation to greater numbers than ever before (*See Document 17.*) and enjoyment to millions of spectators. Though the program was known as athletics to millions of spectators, the sports-and-games movement was more comprehensive than the term *athletics* by itself implies. It meant not only interscholastic and intercollegiate athletics, but also the sports and games that were soon an essential part of basic instruction and intramural programs in physical education, YMCA and camping programs, and other youth organization programs. Athletics, which from the beginning were student sponsored, began to gain some acceptance as a part of the school and college program by 1910; by 1914 the sports-and-games movement in the United States had begun to replace formal gymnastics as the medium for physical-education programs.

Contributing factors to the success of the sports-and-games movement were an increase in leisure time, more spending money, sports publicity, the development of the automobile and paved roads, child labor laws, earlier retirement policies, and active public support from the energetic President Theodore Roosevelt.

Athletics had a stormy passage in the United States in the nineteenth century, and the early twentieth century was no exception. Athletics came to be symbolized by football, which the students generally preferred over other types of physical activity on the college campus. Even though there were constant protests against its brutality, the game was played in high schools and colleges throughout the land. Its critics sometimes spoke of it as a religion with huge stadiums for its shrines.

President Theodore Roosevelt Extols Football

The reasons for the overwhelming popularity of football over other sports in the United States have been debated incessantly. Those who support football for the youth of America often insist that it provides a training ground for the preparing of leaders in the highly industrialized society in the United States. President Theodore Roosevelt, who in his personal and public activities symbolized the strenuous life, believed that football was a moral force capable of preparing young men for civic responsibilities. His public support of football, while he was President of the United States, did much to promote the sport in schools and colleges. It could hardly be otherwise.

Roosevelt's view of football was reminiscent of those who evaluate football in terms of the evolution of man. This school of thought urged that football has much in common with the early struggle of mankind, symbolizing survival through the swift, deft movements of running, dodging, blocking and tackling, and the escaping from pursuing opponents. The opposing linemen battling each other on the scrimmage line resemble man's military exploits throughout the ages. The spectator also shares in the exploits. He sheds the cares and tensions of society and relaxes as his pent up emotions find vent in castigating opponents and referees. Frequently the spectator, including the mature and highly intelligent, reverts to adolescence or appears to recover his lost youth at one of these contests.

By the first decade of the twentieth century football had become an integral part of campus life, and a concerted effort was made to weld it securely to educational goals by leaders of the athletic movement such as Walter Camp, Amos Alonzo Stagg, and Fielding H. Yost. Soon the stadiums were filled across the land with college alumni who found in the football spectacular a pageant of campus splendor that seems to draw them closer to their alma mater; and although educators frequently seem to regret it, to this day athletics provides apparently the most enduring bond between an institution and its alumni.

Football at the Crossroads

Increasing emphasis on athletics soon called for organizations to control the sports program. Football was the first to need control. At the end of the football season of 1905 the *Chicago Tribune* reported that eighteen high school and college football players had been killed and 159 were seriously injured. President Roosevelt, moved by rampant brutality and foul play, called together representatives of Harvard, Yale, and Princeton to discuss means of saving the game. Columbia University deemed the situation so serious that it abolished football temporarily while many colleges substituted other sports. But a solution that proved in the long run more acceptable to most institutions was adopted with the formation of the National Collegiate Athletic Association (NCAA).

The National Collegiate Athletic Association

Under the leadership of Henry McCracken, Chancellor of New York University, the Intercollegiate Athletic Association of the United States was organized in December of 1905 to govern the conduct of college athletics. In the first year of operation to help control college athletics, thirty-eight colleges and universities became charter members. Palmer E. Pierce of West Point served as the first president. This association evolved into the National Collegiate Athletic Association. The major contributions of the National Collegiate Athletic Association to the colleges holding memberships have been in the area of requiring faculty control of athletics, guiding the development and operation of conferences, standardizing rules, exercising control over tournaments, regulating recruitment and subsidization of athletes, and serving as a service bureau to schools and other organizations directly concerned with athletics.

Unethical Practices in Football

An evaluation of intercollegiate football revealed to the public the facts known all along to adherents of the game. Football had grown up in the colleges in the second half of the nineteenth century as a student-sponsored sport with very little direction and sponsorship from faculties, trustees, and others who were primarily interested in scholastic affairs. Undesirable elements became connected with college football, and deplorable practices arose that affected recruiting, eligibility standards and amateur status, and game behavior (*See Document 17.*) The football crisis of 1905 illuminated the evils that were becoming rooted in athletics and led to a clarification of policies and procedures that enabled the athletic program to proceed on a more favorable basis. Even so, the athletic program has periodically faced crises, especially in football and basketball. Meanwhile, despite the difficulties, sports such as baseball, track and field, swimming, and winter sports were gaining stature in suitable geographic areas.

Expanding Vistas in Sports and Games

The sports-and-games movement expanded rapidly in this period. Schools and colleges began to include the various activities in their physical-education programs, intramural programs, and general recreation programs. The first to organize a new sport in its program was generally the college or university, followed by the local high schools. Many of the students would learn to enjoy these activities and would continue participating in them as adults in their respective communities.

The sports program grew in complexity. Girls' field hockey was brought to the United States from England by Constance Applebee in 1901. After demonstrating the game at the Harvard Summer School, she later published a book on field hockey that insured its popularity. In 1907 playground ball, renamed softball in 1930, was invented and played on the Chicago South Park Playgrounds; the National Recreation Association standardized the playing rules for the game in 1923. Outing clubs started in 1910 with the development of the Dartmouth College Outing Club. Golf continued to be the sport of the wealthy at exclusive country clubs; but the picture gradually changed so that by 1910 there were twenty-four public golf courses throughout the country. The Olympic Games fired the imagination of the sport-minded American people. They were both spectators and participants in the Olympic Games in Paris in 1900, in St. Louis in 1904, in London in 1908, and in Stockholm in 1912. Interest in swimming assumed new proportions as cities began to invest in municipal swimming pools. Among the new additions were Syracuse in 1900, Kansas City in 1901, and Pittsburgh in 1903. The first high school swimming pool was constructed in Detroit in 1908. An interest in keeping the water sanitary in swimming pools led to the organization of the American Association of Hygiene and Baths in 1912, followed by the establishment of swimming pool sanitation standards in 1915. Sports and games became very popular general recreation activities in the local communities, as well as in the schools and colleges, and created the need for appropriate recreation facilities and equipment.

The Playground Movement

The Playground Association of America was founded in 1906 under the guidance and direction of Dr. Luther Halsey Gulick, Dr. Dudley A. Sargent, and Dr. Henry Curtis. Dr. Gulick, Supervisor of Physical Education for the New York City Public School System, saw an urgent need to provide adequate physical-activity programs in the schools and communities of the great urban centers. The effects of a sedentary way of life on the youth in American cities are well portrayed in his address "The Problem of Physical Training in the Modern City." (*See Document 12.*) Dr. Sargent helped developed playground equipment, and Dr. Curtis brought to the new organization the experience of a pioneer recreation specialist in Washington, D.C.

The Playground Association of America grew out of an informal meeting of playground and recreation groups held in Washington, D.C. (Dr. Gulick was elected president and Dr. Curtis secretary at the first annual meeting of this new Association, which was held in Chicago in 1907.) At the Washington meeting the main issues discussed were the play interests of the country, the best way to provide playgrounds, and the proper procedure to be used to arouse public interest and support for a playground program. The last problem moved toward solution when President Theodore Roosevelt, hearing of the meeting, arranged for one session to be held at the White House, which resulted in his being elected honorary president. His immediate interest and support for adequate playgrounds throughout the country augured well for the success of the new Association and immeasurably facilitated the growth of the movement.

The Playground Movement now expanded rapidly. Dr. Gulick arranged for the publication of an official monthly magazine called *The Playground.* Making a first appearance in 1907, it provided an excellent medium for bringing to the public the purposes and values of an adequate system of playgrounds that could give children a wholesome and safe program of physical-education activities. To meet the need for trained leaders in this new program, Clark W. Hetherington supervised the preparation of a professional training syllabus for recreation leaders called a *Normal Course in Play;* this professional material was prepared by the Association in 1909–1910.

Joseph Lee, who became President of the Playground Association of America in 1910, stressed a much more comprehensive understanding of the function and value of play and recreation. His book *Play in Education* (1910) developed the concept that play and recreation is a constructive and creative way of life and absolutely essential for people of all ages. The far-reaching effect of Joseph Lee on play and recreation gained for him the affectionate title "father of the playground movement." His influence led to a reorganization of the Association in 1911, and it became known as the Playground and Recreation Association of America.

The National Education Association supported a resolution in 1911 to use school buildings as recreation centers after school hours. By 1917 over 600 cities supported school recreation centers. So successful was the program that numerous school boards requested recreation centers in the construction plans for new school buildings. Thus there began a close and fruitful association between education, physical education, and recreation specialists.

During the First World War (1914–1918) the Playground and Recreation Association of America, at the request of the War Department, organized the War Camp Community Service to provide recreation for both military personnel and civilians in communities near military camps. The staff in this wartime program were, by and large, specialists in physical education and recreation.

Camping

The twentieth-century concept of physical education found a new field of expression in the camping movement, which was established in the first two decades of this century. Much of the early advancement in camping was due to the far-sightedness of Dr. Luther Halsey Gulick. Through his pioneering, he laid the foundation upon which present-day private and school camping is based. He was personally responsible for the Gulick Camps on Lake Sebago, Maine, which were a model of their kind, and the organization of the Camp Fire Girls of America, of which he became President in 1913. The recreation programs of the camps made much use of the medium of twentieth-century physical education: namely, sports and games, swimming and waterfront activities, and rhythmic activities.

The Camp Directors' Association was organized in 1910 with twenty camp directors as charter members. The number of camps increased to approximately one hundred by the First World War, largely through the efforts of teachers interested in camping who needed summer employment. In addition to the Camp Fire Girls of America, there were organized the Boy Scouts of America in 1910 and, two years later, the Girl Scouts of America. The camping movement also drew strength from the stalwart support soon forthcoming from the YMCA and YWCA, settlement house groups, church organizations, and the National Park Service.

The YMCA Movement

This period saw the Young Men's Christian Association extend its program of physical education to include more comprehensive recreation and playground activities, swimming and waterfront activities, athletic leagues, and camping programs. One facet of the program supplemented the formal gymnastic programs of the schools by providing light gymnastics, exercises in the skills of sports and games, running events, and bathing and massage.

Imprinted upon the philosophy of the entire YMCA program was the indelible mark of Dr. Luther Halsey Gulick. His interest in the philosophy of the movement was manifested in an address in which he urged the desirability of physical education forming a vital part of the Association's program for young people because its aim was, in his words, "the salvation, development, and training of the whole man complete as God made him." Even after he resigned in 1900 from the position of Superintendent of the Physical Department at the Springfield Training School, the principal training center of the YMCA, the movement continued largely in the direction he had imparted to it during the formative years.

The Springfield Training School underwent metamorphosis a surprising number of times before becoming Springfield College. A milestone in the history of the institution and physical education was reached when it gained professional status in 1905 by receiving authority, from the Massachusetts legislature, to grant bachelor's and master's degrees in physical education. To further its purposes and ideals, the YMCA began publication of the journal *Physical Training* in 1905, which became the official organ of the YMCA movement.

The Dance

The field of the dance became an integral part of physical education and education in the early twentieth century. Of the many types of dance practiced, two were foremost: natural dance, sometimes characterized as interpretive dance, and folk dance.

The creative gifts of Isadora Duncan were responsible for what is known as the Romantic Revolution in the dance as she achieved international recognition with a new form of the dance concerned primarily with expression. Inspired by nature she emphasized graceful movements that took full advantage of space while resisting effortlessly the force of gravity. At the age of twenty-two, influenced by the classic Greek style and attired in Greek costume and with bare feet, she interpreted the various forms of the Greek dance in the effort to gain greater expression of emotions. Brief though her dance career was, she, nevertheless, influenced greatly the dance in education. One of her legacies was a lasting influence on Gertrude Colby and Bird Larson, who were inspired by her theories to break with tradition and develop a form of the dance that met more closely the interests of the period.

Gertrude Colby and Bird Larson are celebrated for their work in the natural dance. The latter's brilliant career ended abruptly with her sudden death but not before her influence had carried the natural dance to the concert stage and into religious events. Gertrude Colby, on the other hand, made her contribution by bringing dance into education through inspired teaching and by her application of the principles of education to the dance. She introduced the folk dance into education and gained national fame in developing the natural dance. The natural dance was quickly accepted and became an art based upon "music, drama, design, color, and pantomime," using graceful anatomical and kinesiological movements of the body. Of special significance in this type of dance were natural body movements to express ideas and emotions through rhythmic movement involving the entire body. In education the natural dance was the intermediary between the aesthetic dance of the late nineteenth century and the modern dance of the 1930's.

Strong competition to the aesthetic dance and natural dance came from the popular folk dances. Folk dances commanded attention after Dr. Luther Halsey Gulick in 1904 arranged for the noted Russian ballet teacher, Louis Chalif, to teach a course in the dance at New York University. Chalif, highly skilled in aesthetic, ballet, national, and folk dances, popularized the dance through his teaching skill and through numerous publications. His influence helped to spread the dance to the concert stage and to school and college education programs. The task of bringing folk dances upon the national scene was left to Elizabeth Burchenal, who was aided by the interest aroused by Louis Chalif.

In bringing folk dances to education and recreational centers, Elizabeth Burchenal made an intensive study of this form of dance in Europe and the United States. She was able to contribute social and cultural enrichment to the people of many countries through her lectures, publications, and folk song recordings. The Burchenal collection of folk songs is in approximately fifteen volumes and is one of the best primary sources of folk songs available. In a very active professional career, she served as chairman of the American Folk Dance Society and chairman of the National Folk Dance Committee of the Playground and Recreation Association of America. It was ironic that her professional efforts with the

European and American folk dances, which were helping to break down
national barriers and gain an understanding of European traditions,
should have been reaching new heights of popularity just as the First
World War darkened the horizon.

Physical Education in the First World War

Military conflicts, in which the participating countries become involved
in a life and death struggle, have in the past brought marked emphasis
upon the formal type of military drill and physical-fitness programs, and
to this observation the First World War was no exception. When the
United States entered that great conflict in April of 1917, the development of a military-fitness program was of primary concern. Since the
military services did not have an established specific physical-fitness plan,
two basic programs were developed: namely, a formal conditioning program of combative activities, marching, drill, and calisthenics, and a
physical fitness and recreation program consisting largely of sports
and games. Gradually the two programs merged and eventually formed
the physical-fitness program of the allied forces. As a result of combining
the two basic programs, the troops gained precision of movement through
military drill even as they acquired the physical fitness and recreational
skills that emanate from sports and games.

The First World War posed a great challenge for physical education,
sometimes seeming to hold it back, sometimes encouraging its forward
thrust. Schools and colleges began to substitute military fitness programs
and drill in place of physical education, especially in those programs in
which the surging sports and games had so recently become dominant.
On the other hand, physical education emerged with enhanced prestige
as physical educators, with their superior background for war work
in the medical field, in physical fitness and sports and games, in recreation and camping, and in leadership training, did valuable work in the
military program at home and in Europe.

The type of military work carried out by physical-education specialists was of a scope and variety not seen in earlier wars but which became
the order of the day in wars of the twentieth century. Examples of the
responsible posts for which their special skills uniquely qualified them
are readily cited. Dr. R. Tait McKenzie joined the Royal Army Medical
Corps in England and did pioneering work in rehabilitation and plastic
surgery. Dr. George L. Meylan served as Director of Recreation for the
French army and, as one part of his program, established some two-
hundred rest camps for soldiers near the trenches. Dr. James H. Mc-
Curdy was Director of the Recreation and Athletic Program conducted
by the YMCA for the United States forces in France. Dr. James Naismith
worked in the Social Hygiene program of the American Expeditionary

Forces in France. Walter Camp became Chairman of the Athletic Division of the Navy Department; Dr. Joseph M. Raycroft, Chairman of the Athletic Division of the War Department Committee on Training Camp Activities; Jesse Bancroft, Chairman of the Government Commission on Training Camp Activities and President of the War-Camp Service; and John L. Griffis, Chairman of the Athletic Division of the War-Camp Community Service.

Their performance in responsible and skilled positions was extremely important in the retention of the new physical education after the war. The threat that military training might replace physical education in the schools and colleges receded into the background when peace came. In a memorable address The Honorable Newton D. Baker, Secretary of War, paid tribute to the work of physical educators in the war when he declared: "We carried with us, when we went to France, American recreational ideals, and we played ball from Paris to the Rhine." He concluded by saying that the United States had learned from the war that wholesome activity was a substitute for the things that get young men into trouble and was consequently all that was needed, in his words, "to keep them moral and upright, as well as to make them strong and valuable." The remarks of Secretary Baker were set forth at length in an article written by Dr. James H. McCurdy of Springfield College. In it he reprinted the opinions on physical education expressed by interested persons in the United Kingdom, France, and the United States. (*See Document 18.*)

Following the war there was a tendency on the part of many schools and colleges to keep military training programs in place of physical education. The physical-education teachers, who were returning from the battle fronts, were usually able, however, to demonstrate the need for a sound physical-education program involving all students, of which Secretary Baker had spoken. The public was prepared, after seeing approximately one-third of the young men of draft age classified as physically unfit for military service, to accept and support the twentiety-century concept of physical education. (*See Document 19.*)

Summary

By 1918 the picture in physical education was much more complicated than it had been when the century opened. Sports and games had arisen to a position within the physical-education program sufficiently strong to challenge the dominance of formal gymnastics while outside the physical-education program the sports and games, long in student hands, were passing under faculty control. Whenever the process should be complete, sports and games would prove too powerful for formal gymnastics, but such was not generally the situation in 1918. In these years from 1900 to 1918 programs which later became very closely associated with, if not part of, physical education were taking shape. Health education, which Dr. Thomas D. Wood had described as the keystone upon which man builds for the future, had clearly made gains. An increasing number of physicians and nurses were employed by the schools and colleges and a beginning was made, slight though it was, in introducing the compulsory medical examination. Recreation aided by Dr. Luther Halsey Gulick and Joseph Lee was moving toward professional status. The natural dance evolved by Getrude Colby and Bird Larson and the folk dances of Elizabeth Burchenal were fast becoming an integral part of physical education and education. Above all, physical education had passed the exacting test of the First World War when it had shown sufficient strength to prevent the substitution of military drill for physical education in American schools and colleges in the postwar years.

The essence of these changes was caught and recorded by Dr. George L. Meylan, an early leader in the profession, in his historical survey of twenty-five years of physical education, from 1885 to 1910. (*See Document 20.*)

Chapter 4

SHAPING A PROFESSION

A RECENT writer commented that "in the past sixty years the world has been turned upside down and inside out. New ways of making things, of doing things, of transporting our thoughts and ourselves have dislocated all the old familiar arrangements." Back of these changes were the dynamic ideas of Marx, Freud, Keynes, and Einstein and the vast dislocations created by two World Wars, a Great Depression, and since the Second World War (1939–1945) an almost continuous state of Cold War as the United States and Russia became the two superstates in a world where the traditional balance of power has been destroyed. All of this, happening in a little over half a century, has made the twentieth century, as far as it has unrolled, an age of unprecedented crisis and unrest.

Many of the changes date from the end of the First World War. It appeared for a time that there would be a return of normalcy, as Warren Harding said in an often-quoted phrase, when the United States refused to sign the Treaty of Versailles with Germany in 1919 that carried membership in the League of Nations and returned to its former preoccupation with peacetime profits. The great outstanding fact about the 1920's—the "Golden Twenties," as they are called nostalgically—was that the country literally rolled in money. European productivity had been reduced by the war while the American economy, unhampered by war damage, improved in efficiency and production. The national economy, despite the trouble spots in agriculture and textiles, reached the highest level in profits as yet recorded in American history. Installment buying brought new purchasers into the market, and new industries such as the motion picture, the radio, and the automobile—to which after the Second World War television would be added—heightened employment. Though business leaders, with sympathetic Republican administrations in the White House, thought that prosperity would be permanent, some signs indicated that economic health was not perfect. One of these was the feverish stock market speculation, heightened or encouraged by remarks of business leaders. John Raskob of General Motors predicted, for example, that any man who invested $15 a week would have within twenty years $80,000 in cash and a monthly income of $400.

These dreams were rudely smashed when the stock market crash of

1929 inaugurated the Great Depression, which ended a decade later when the Second World War began. Leadership in the crisis was provided by President Franklin Delano Roosevelt, who was four times elected President. He carried through a program of reform legislation known as the New Deal, which was infinitely complicated but contained such outstanding measures as the Social Security Act of 1935, the most extensive piece of social legislation in American history. It provided old age pensions, unemployment insurance, and public health benefits but not health insurance, which has remained into the 1960's a subject of contention. Direct relief to the unemployed was provided through the Civilian Conservation Corps, the Works Progress Administration, and the National Youth Administration, the latter providing part-time jobs for students. The unionization of labor was encouraged through the passage of the Wagner Act of 1935; and though Roosevelt sought to lessen the movement toward consolidation of business that had existed since the late nineteenth century, the depression in fact encouraged the process. In 1937 three companies produced 80 per cent of the country's automobiles; and another three produced 60 per cent of the steel, a trend that has persisted to the present.

While the Roosevelt administration sought to deal with the Great Depression, the maintenance of the international order was threatened by Japanese aggression against China in the Far East and in Africa and Europe by Adolf Hitler's rearmed Germany and Benito Mussolini's imperialistic Italy. The underlying causes of the First World War—alliance systems, militarism, imperialism, etc.—had persisted unsolved into the 1930's. After the failure of the League of Nations to assert the rule of law in the Ethopian crisis, it became completely ineffective; and Europe divided into two hostile camps. The Rome-Berlin-Tokyo Axis took shape, and the question that remained to be settled was one of whether Great Britain, France, and Russia could coalesce to maintain the balance of power and prevent war. But the communism of Russia proved an insuperable barrier in diplomatic negotiations between the West and Russia, and in 1939 the latter country signed a nonaggression pact with Germany that flashed on the green light for the Second World War. In the early stages of the war France was defeated, and much of the country overrun; but though Great Britain stood alone temporarily against Nazi Germany, the balance of power was restored when the United States, after Pearl Harbor (December 7, 1941), entered the war on the side of Great Britain and six months later Germany invaded Russia.

Though the Second World War ended in the defeat of the Axis powers, the rise of the Cold War by 1948 indicated that war sacrifices had brought no enduring peace. Despite the establishment of the United Nations, the world has divided, once more into hostile camps; the West centering upon the democratic, capitalistic United States, and the East on totalitarian, communistic Russia. Armament races have become the order of the day, and the danger of a terrible war has been brought close to every household in an age of nuclear and hydrogen bombs and great technological advance in airpower. Another problem with which man must cope is the steep rise in population pressing against the world's resources. The United States by 1960 attained, for example, a population of 179,323,175 (Census of April 1, 1960); and in the first six months of the administration of President John F. Kennedy another 1,446,443 were added.

It will be seen in the course of this chapter that the fortunes of physical education since 1918 have been affected by war and depression. In the 1920's the Battle of the Systems ended in the triumph of the new physical education as formal gymnastics were pushed decisively into the background. In this decade health education and intramural sports gained stature in the school and college curriculums. The prosperous course of the new physical education, which can now be called simply physical education, was interrupted by the onset of the depression, which led to cutbacks in financial outlays for school programs generally. On the other hand, the depression gave a decided impetus to the growth of recreation as an allied professional field to physical education while the recreational sports and games of physical education found new outlets in the manifold activities undertaken by a paternalistic federal government. Interruption in the normal course of events came once more with the outbreak of the Second World War. Its effect was to solidify the place of physical education in the training and recreational programs of the armed forces and reveal the potentialities of physical education in relation to rehabilitation, thus opening up the field of adaptive physical education. Since 1948 the Cold War has produced an entirely new set of conditions in peacetime, within which physical education has evolved, and these conditions will be described in Chapter 4, discussing recent developments in physical education. Looking at the period as a whole from 1918 to 1961, one can see that in these years physical education became a profession based upon scientific research in the many aspects of the field. These were the decades of the shaping of a profession.

Prosperity and Leisure

After 1918 support for physical education came from a cross-section of American society as the United States entered an era of unprecedented prosperity. In the wake of the Industrial Revolution came leisure and increased income for the working classes, and they responded by purchasing automobiles, sports-and-games equipment, and other luxuries to brighten their individual lives. Business and industry quickly grasped the significance of their new pattern of recreation and capitalized on the mass market for leisure-time activities. Radio sportscasts and sports pages in newspapers and magazines, extolling sports and games, lured the working man into becoming both a participant and a spectator in the widely varying recreational pursuits that existed for the mass of people. Even the "Blue Laws" were modified as church organizations yielded to the recreational interests of the masses.

The End of the Battle of the Systems

All across the country there came a marked increased in the building of stadiums, gymnasiums, and other recreational facilities to accommodate the surging sports-and-games movement as formal gymnastics lay dying in the apparatus rooms. The sports-and-games program was posed on the threshold of a rewarding future in schools, colleges, and communities. As the school enrollments soared, physical-education programs comprising the popular sports and games were welcomed as an extracurricular activity, if not always as a part of the academic curriculum. The statistics of the First World War, showing a disgracefully low state of health and physical fitness among the prime youth of the country, had changed the collective mind of reluctant school boards. Though there were, as usual, numerous hostile forces opposing all types of physical education, none proved capable of halting the march to victory of the new physical education.

As was to be expected, most leaders of formal gymnastics resisted the sports and games, which were rapidly undermining the earlier favored programs of formal gymnastics. Dr. Dudley A. Sargent, one of the formative thinkers in physical education, stated his views of the displacement of formal gymnastics by the new physical education when he told the National Convention in 1920: "Read into physical education everything you can of the slightest value but don't read out of it the most fundamental thing of all—that is, all-round muscular exercise." Two years later William A. Stecher of the Philadelphia Public School System openly took issue with the criticism of formal gymnastics made by Dr. Jesse Feiring Williams when he stated at the Springfield Convention: "In fact, I am not afraid to say that in the hands of a skillful teacher a lesson composed mostly of formal work can be made enjoyable." But their defense of formal gymnastics availed little. (*See Document 21.*) The "Battle of the Systems" was now over, and sports and games had been declared the winner.

Molding a Twentieth-Century Program

The new physical education, developed principally by Dr. Thomas D. Wood and Clark W. Hetherington at the turn of the century, bore fruit in the 1920's under the able leadership of their successors: Dr. Jesse Feiring Williams and Dr. Jay B. Nash. In retrospect one can see from the vantage point of the 1920's that the modern program, firmly rooted in the fertile soil of the first decade of the twentieth century, ripened more rapidly into maturity because of the catalytic effect of the First World War.

Dr. Jesse Feiring Williams, trained in formal gymnastics at Oberlin College, was involved in the "Battle of the Systems" prior to his appointment at Teachers College, Columbia University, under Dr. Thomas D. Wood. Becoming convinced of the superiority of the new physical education, championed by Dr. Wood as the natural program, Dr. Williams developed a personal philosophy of physical education from which he never wavered, and as teacher, lecturer, and writer set forth the dimensions of modern twentieth-century physical education. So effectively did his program meet the needs of a restless, ever-changing society that his teachings continue to the present to dominate the profession, meeting successfully the challenges posed by depression and wars.

Education Through the Physical

The leaders of the new physical-education movement, who were versed in the findings of the new psychology, were instrumental in developing a program that centered on the complete human being, not just physical fitness or sports and games, as the first responsibility of the physical-education teacher. (*See Documents 22, 23, 24, 25.*) They believed, like their forerunners at the turn of the century, that physical fitness and sports and games acquired significance only as the mind, emotions, and human body formed a complete action. They considered that the program of physical education should be academically sound and meet the age, needs, and interests of those involved. The individual as a complete person was, in their estimation, essential to any and all human activity.

This approach to physical education placed emphasis on the actions of the human body as the physical manifestations of the mind, emotions, thoughts, and feelings. Its exponents, notably Dr. Jesse Feiring Williams and his disciples, maintained that it was the physical self, primarily, that a person presents to those whom he encounters. Through physical movements he expresses the thinking and actions which make him unique, and the very act of movement modifies and affects his thinking. (*See Document 26.*) An integral part of the new educational approach was to teach physiologically sound movement patterns and build them into avenues of expression essential in performing activities in the home, in the professions and vocations, and in leisure-time pursuits.

Thus, after a century of experimentation with essentially foreign programs of physical education and with programs incorporating foreign elements, a program indigenous to the American people became a reality. It was based upon the social, economic, and political conditions of the United States. The philosophy, principles, objectives, and activities of the new program differed greatly from those of earlier programs and were firmly based upon the latest advances in biology and medicine, sociology and psychology, and education. Of primary concern to its exponents were the age, the needs and interests, and the abilities of the students.

Physical activities were the medium through which the values of physical education were to be communicated. They emphasized that the physical-education program should be composed of sports and games, rhythmic activities, self-testing activities, and selected gymnastic progressions based upon educational objectives. Selected from the formal gymnastic program were progressions on the horse, parallel and horizontal bars, flying rings, and tumbling. Sports and games were, however, the most popular part of the program. In 1922 a report on physical education in 341 cities showed the following sports and games to be the most popular in the physical-education program for boys: football, basketball, baseball, volleyball, track, soccer, tennis, and hockey. The girls preferred basketball, dodgeball, tennis, track, and baseball. By 1930 the new physical-education program had replaced nearly all the formal gymnastics programs.

Progress in physical education was interrupted after a prosperous decade by the Great Depression, which began in 1929 and was followed a decade later by the Second World War. Physical education, though placed on the defensive by the two crises so close together, weathered the storm of some fifteen years' duration and, in fact, made important contributions to the national welfare in this highly critical period. The postwar era was marked by a resurgence of physical education that has carried it to the highest point of scientific development in its history. Contributing to an important degree to this advancement and sustaining its momentum was the state legislation, reflecting the nation's concern for improved health and physical fitness, that had been passed after the First World War.

A National Concern for State Legislation

The passage of state legislation owed much to the National Physical Education Service, which was founded under the auspices of the Playground and Recreation Association of America. The first step in this direction had been taken when the United States Commissioner of Education called a special meeting in February, 1918, in Atlantic City to make arrangements for a nation-wide program of physical education.

At this meeting a National Committee on Physical Education was appointed under the chairmanship of Dr. Thomas D. Wood. This group in turn established the National Physical Education Service in November, 1918, to promote state legislation and assist state departments of education with implementation of health and physical-education programs.

Dr. James E. Rogers, a member of the national staff of the Playground and Recreation Association of America, was appointed Director of the National Physical Education Service. His assignment was to travel annually throughout the United States and help secure the passage of laws favorable to physical education by furnishing specific information about physical education, sample laws and material for publicity and by arranging for the special planning sometimes needed to insure passage of a given law. After the passage of legislation Dr. Rogers was active in formulating the physical-education program for which the law provided. He also wrote in support of physical education. (*See Document 27.*)

The harvest was abundant; in the years from 1919 to 1921 seventeen states enacted physical-education legislation, and by 1930 the total was thirty-nine. Increased emphasis on state legislation brought specific requirements in time allotment, type of program, graduation requirements in physical education, and a change in terminology to "health and physical education." Generally a state law would provide for healthful environment, medical inspection, instruction in physiology and hygiene, effective motor control, supervised play, and motor activities which might include sports and games, athletics, gymnastics, dancing, and marching. State legislation made school administrators more deeply aware of health and physical education; and the subject, consequently, secured a more important role in the school curriculum.

The State Director

The most rapid advance in the development of the state directorship, an office that had been established during the First World War, was made after World War II. In January, 1947, the United States Office of Education published the results of a study concerning the duties and responsibilities of a state director of physical education, which were evaluated in the ensuing months by the Board of Directors of the American Association for Health, Physical Education, and Recreation. They incorporated the major duties and responsibilities that had been compiled in this study into a sample state law for physical education. The opportunity for the state directors as a group to voice their opinion came at the national conference of the Society of State Directors of Health and Physical Education, which met in Kansas City, Missouri, in 1948. They approved the duties and responsibilities of a state director, as prepared in the manner just described by the United States Office of Education and the American Association for Health, Physical Education and Recreation. In the final result it was concluded that the duties and responsibilities of state directors fall into six broad categories: development of curriculums and the formulation of courses of study, the development of program standards, the development of standards for facilities and equipment, teacher preparation and certification, in-service teacher education, and professional and public relations.

By the early 1960's almost all states had a state director of physical education or a comparable person to whom the responsibility is assigned. Increasingly he has been burdened, however, with responsibilities arising from additional programs in health education, recreation, safety, and driver education. Outstanding among state directors was Carl L. Schrader, who was active in Massachusetts in the 1930's. In a paper entitled "Physical Education Becomes a Fundamental," he sought to clarify the meaning and purpose of physical education, one of the constant tasks in physical education facing the state director. (*See Document 28.*)

Supply and Demand in Physical Education

The complexity of the new physical-education program, combined with the desire on the part of those involved in the program to have physical education accepted as part of the academic curriculum, meant that a more academic program of teacher education was needed. But the shortage of teachers in physical education slowed the raising of standards. The shortage materialized in the 1920's because of the rapid increase in state legislation immediately following the First World War, which made physical education a requirement in elementary and secondary schools. Teachers of physical education were needed, in addition, in colleges and universities, recreation centers, youth organizations, camps, and military services.

Institutions with teacher-preparation programs attempted to meet the growing demand for physical-education teachers by formulating more courses leading to the bachelor's degree and making them available not only during the academic year but also in summer schools and through extension courses. The supply-and-demand equation was balanced just as the Great Depression arrived. A new situation then arose. As physical-education programs were reduced, a surplus of physical-education teachers was soon in evidence; and this situation persisted until the United States entered the Second World War in 1941. Another shortage then developed because of the manpower requirements of the military services. Since that time the demand has continued for well-qualified teachers of health, physical education, and recreation, especially for women.

Teacher Preparation Strengthened

A perennial problem in the professional preparation of physical-education teachers has been the lack of standardization of the professional curriculum in teacher-education institutions. Even though state departments of education formulated certification requirements for public school teachers, which increased the number of four-year undergraduate programs for the bachelor's degree in physical education, the institutions with teacher-education programs were left sufficient latitude so that there were still great variations in courses for a degree. Courses became so varied as, in some cases, to have almost meaningless descriptions.

The abuses produced a reaction. A shocking report reached the public in 1930 when the California State Department of Education made public a study of 28 college catalogues showing that courses listed for teacher preparation in physical education were found under 671 different course titles. A major attempt to resolve this problem came on July 1, 1931, when the Department of School Health and Physical Education of the National Education Association authorized the President of the Department, Dr. Jay B. Nash, to organize a National Committee to develop standards to be used in evaluating teacher-education curriculums in physical education.

Events moved rapidly. Dr. Jay B. Nash selected Dr. Neils P. Neilson, state director of health and physical education in California, as Chairman of the National Committee. A plan was drawn up to have all state directors of health and physical education as members of the National Committee. Six national organizations were asked to work with the National Committee for two years. They were the American Physical Education Association, Society of State Directors of Health and Physical Education, City Administrators of Health and Physical Education, Women Directors of Physical Education in Colleges and Universities, College Physical Education Association, and the Department of School Health and Physical Education of the National Education Association.

The National Committee organized a subcommittee in every state to assist with the evaluation of teacher-education curriculums. The combined professional evaluation was known as The National Study of Professional Education in Health and Physical Education. In the form of an evaluation with recommendations for changes, an annual report, every year through 1937, was made at the national convention.

One of the most important reports made by the National Committee was in 1935 when it presented a code of standards that became a professional yardstick for physical education. Standards were included for the preparation of secondary school teachers, selection of students for

teacher education, and for courses, staff, and facilities in physical education. Several later committees, which were outgrowths of the National
Committee, continued to make recommendations for teacher education,
state supervision, and certification standards required by state departments of education.

Two Important National Conferences

Teacher education received strong support from the Athletic Institute,
an organization founded in 1934 by manufacturers of sporting goods
equipment, to promote physical education and recreation. One of its
most memorable contributions was the financing of two exceedingly
important national conferences. On the undergraduate level the Athletic
Institute sponsored the National Conference on Undergraduate Professional Preparation in Health Education, Physical Education, and Recreation, which was held in 1948 at Jackson's Mill, West Virginia. It studied
and set forth recommendations for principles, standards, and programs
in teacher preparation. A comparable conference, this time on the graduate level, was the National Conference of Graduate Study in Health
Education, Physical Education, and Recreation, which was held at Pere
Marquette State Park, Illinois, in 1950, also under the sponsorship of the
Athletic Institute. These two conferences were invaluable in shaping the
present structure of teacher education in physical education.

Accreditation

An important decision affecting teacher education in health, physical
education, and recreation was made by the American Association for
Health, Physical Education, and Recreation in 1960 at the national convention in Miami, Florida. It was to accept the National Council for Accreditation of Teacher Education (NCATE) as the official accrediting
organization for teacher education in health, physical education, and
recreation. The National Council for Accreditation of Teacher Education
accredits teacher-education programs for elementary and secondary
teaching on both the undergraduate and graduate levels. The complete
program of teacher education within an institution is accredited; and
policies, procedures, and standards for accreditation are formulated. An
annual list of accredited institutions is published; the latest list, effective
July 1, 1960, to June 30, 1961, included 343 accredited colleges and
universities.

The American Association for Health, Physical Education, and Recreation has requested state departments of education not to certify teachers
in health, physical education, and recreation after June 1, 1964, unless
they are graduates of institutions accredited by the National Council
for Accreditation of Teacher Education. New professional memberships

in the American Association for Health, Physical Education, and Recreation will require the applicant, after June 1, 1964, to have earned at least one degree in an institution accredited by the National Council for Accreditation of Teacher Education. The new requirements are expected to have a far-reaching effect upon raising academic standards in the profession.

Within the physical-education profession a concerted attempt is being made to raise the academic standards of courses in teacher education. Increased academic emphasis has led to a marked increase in the number who hold advanced degrees. For professional advancement in health, physical education, and recreation it is now very important for the public school teacher to have earned the master's degree and for the college teacher to have earned the Doctor of Philosophy degree (Ph.D.) or the Doctor of Education degree (Ed.D.). With improved academic preparation in physical education there has been a rapid increase in research, tests and measurements, and professional publications.

Scientific Progress in Research and Tests and Measurements

In the 1920's the word "objectives" became part of the vocabulary of the physical-education profession. Used to mean an aim or goal, it was carried into education from the military experiences of the First World War. Among the objectives of physical education that were commonly mentioned were physical fitness, personal health, social and moral values, and the acquisition of leisure-time skills. To determine whether objectives were being attained, the profession turned to tests and measurements. (*See Documents 29 and 30.*)

Since the physical-education programs comprised sports and games, it followed that a multitude of athletic achievement tests would be constructed. These tests attempted to check such physical requisites as fitness, capacity, ability, and development. Numerous classification tests were constructed that used achievement scales derived by statistical methods. Some of these tests that enjoyed considerable reputation were Dr. Charles H. McCloy's Classification Index (1920), which used a formula based upon age, height, and weight; Dr. Dudley A. Sargent's Jump Test (1921), which tried to isolate factors involved in power and efficiency of performance; Dr. David K. Brace's Motor Ability Test (1927), which was based upon the physical performance of twenty athletic stunts; and Dr. Frederick W. Cozen's test in 1929 for measuring general athletic ability. By the end of this decade approximately twenty-five per cent of the schools had a testing and measuring program in physical education. The highly skilled teacher of physical education was utilizing the scientific testing program as a motivating force in the basic instruction program as well as to determine the physical status of the student.

During the early years of the Great Depression there was a marked trend in the direction of measuring intangible values that a student might have gained from physical education, such as sportsmanship, and social and moral values. For this purpose rating scales were constructed that reflected the latest advances in psychology. One of the earliest of these tests was a character-rating scale developed by Dr. Charles H. McCloy in 1930. An article by Dr. Jay B. Nash in 1951, entitled "Character Education as an Objective," expressed the need to recognize the direct relationship between behavioral patterns and physical education. (*See Document 31.*)

Graduate programs of teacher education in physical education also expanded rapidly, and research studies became a major part of academic preparation for many students earning advanced degrees. The need was felt for a professional journal that would publish research articles and the results of research studies. The American Physical Education Association responded in 1930 with the publication of the *Research Quarterly* under the editorship of Dr. Elmer D. Mitchell of the University of Michigan.

Physical Education and Military Fitness

The Second World War created an urgent need for a military fitness program; and again physical education responded to the challenge, but not without serious opposition. At the War Fitness Conference in 1943 the chief of athletics and recreation for the United States Army dealt physical education a serious blow with the statement: "Our physical programs in high schools have been a miserable failure. Physical education through play must be discarded and a more rugged program substituted." But Secretary of War Henry L. Stimson came to the rescue of physical education when he advised the U.S. Commissioner of Education, Dr. John W. Studebaker, that military drill could be given to the men in a very short period of time after assignment to a military base. But he recommended retention of the physical-education programs, saying "The War Department . . . does not recommend that military drill take the place of physical education in the schools and colleges during the war period."

Physical-education programs played a very important role in schools, colleges, communities, and military services throughout the War. As might be expected, research and tests and measurements made rapid strides in the area of physical fitness. All branches of the military services experimented with physical-fitness programs in an effort to formulate a program that would give participants a high level of physical fitness in a very short time. Notable among these programs were the physical-fitness programs of the Navy, especially the Navy V-5 and the Navy V-12 programs. The special emphasis on physical fitness continued after the

War with state and national organizations sponsoring physical-fitness programs.

Advances in Research and Testing

In the last fifteen years research and tests and measurements in physical education have attained a high point of scientific development so that it is possible to measure, with considerable accuracy, motor ability, fitness, skills, and physical development. It is also possible to rate physical performance and to measure acquired knowledge in physical education. The profession is on the threshold of developing tests that will measure, with validity, behavioral patterns that involve motivation, muscular and nervous tension, visual patterns, rhythmic movement patterns, and social and moral values related to physical activity programs. To facilitate this complex research the American Association for Health, Physical Education, and Recreation compiled in 1949 *Research Methods Applied to Health, Physical Education, and Recreation.*

Valuable research studies are being carried out through co-operative research programs with specialists in biology, physiology, medicine, public health, psychology, sociology, and anthropology. Recently, strong support has come to physical education from the American Medical Association. This group has become active in research programs concerning the value of physical education in preventive medicine, postoperative cases, rehabilitation, and psychiatry.

The construction of research laboratories in physical education in colleges and universities has shown a marked increase, especially in graduate schools. In many cases staff members are designated as research professors with time made available for research studies. Noteworthy examples include Dr. Charles H. McCloy at the University of Iowa, Dr. Arthur Steinhaus at George Williams College, and Dr. Thomas K. Cureton at the University of Illinois.

The physical-education profession is moving closer to a foundation based upon scientific research, as it follows the lines long urged by Dr. Charles H. McCloy who was known as "the research professor of physical education." He always maintained that physical education must rest firmly upon the results of scientific research carried out in every segment of the field. (*See Document 32.*)

Professional Literature, Organizations, and Honor Awards

With the proliferation of graduate instruction in physical education came an abundance of professional articles, pamphlets, and books. Mounting school enrollments, with physical education generally a required subject, heightened the demand for the latest professional materials. Since the Second World War, in particular, physical-education films on sports and special subjects have been prepared by commercial and educational organizations. A valuable service to the profession has also been rendered by the production of microfilm and microcards, which make readily available unpublished graduate theses and invaluable physical-education materials that are either out of print or otherwise inaccessible. The University of Oregon is well known for this service. The principal source for keeping members of the physical-education profession informed, however, are the publications of the American Association for Health, Physical Education, and Recreation and the meetings held under its auspices on state, district, and national levels.

The AAHPER

The American Physical Education Association and the Department of School Health and Physical Education of the National Education Association merged on June 28, 1937, to become the American Association for Health and Physical Education, a department of the National Education Association. (*See Document 33.*) A year later, in recognition of the stature gained by the play and recreation movement, the title was changed once more, this time to read The American Association for Health, Physical Education, and Recreation (AAHPER). The increasing complexity of the organization resulted in the creation of six districts: Eastern, Central, Southern, Middle West, Southwest, and Northwest. The Association publishes two official journals: *Journal of Health, Physical Education, and Recreation,* and the *Research Quarterly.* Affiliated at the present time with the Association are some eighteen national organizations such as the American College of Sports Medicine, American Youth Hostels, Inc., and Boys' Clubs of America.

The Academy of Physical Education

The present American Academy of Physical Education (which is the outgrowth of an earlier Academy organized in 1904 by the ubiquitous Dr. Luther Halsey Gulick) was founded in 1926 for the purpose of providing a private forum where major professional issues could be discussed in a serene, intellectual atmosphere. The founding fathers were Clark W. Hetherington, R. Tait McKenzie, Thomas A. Story, William H. Burdick, and Jay B. Nash; and since then the most distinguished leaders in the profession have usually been chosen.

Association Awards

The Luther H. Gulick Award is the highest honor presented by the American Association for Health, Physical Education, and Recreation. It was established in 1923 in memory of Dr. Luther Halsey Gulick, who was one of the most distinguished members of the profession from the viewpoint not only of length of service but also from the surprisingly rich variety of his contributions. Only a hint can be given here of the multiplicity of activities to which he gave time and energy, but a listing of a few of them indicates that in his person he gathered together and symbolized many of the strands of modern physical education and the groups and organizations informally affiliated with it. Briefly, he helped work out the philosophy of modern physical education, he was one of the founders of physical education in the YMCA, he was instrumental in launching the Playground Association of America, he presided over the founding of the Camp Fire Girls and was a founder of the Boy Scouts of America; the list can be extended almost infinitely. The famed Gulick Award depicts a young man in the prime of life wearing a victory wreath and holding an olive branch in one hand.

The William G. Anderson Merit Award was established in 1948 in memory of Dr. William G. Anderson, who was the founder of the modern physical-education profession. His activity was prodigious. He founded and actively served in key positions in the Brooklyn Normal School of Physical Education, the Chautauqua Summer School of Physical Education, the American Association for the Advancement of Physical Education, which became later the AAHPER, and the College Gymnasium Directors' Society. In addition he influenced physical education for almost forty years at Yale University and wrote a number of the early books and articles in the field. (*See Document 3.*) The Anderson Merit Award, given for outstanding service to the profession, has been given since 1955 to persons outside the profession who make a lasting and creative contribution to health, physical education, and recreation.

The American Association for Health, Physical Education, and Recreation undertook the presentation of fellowship awards in 1931. These awards were established to honor outstanding members of the profession while they are still alive, and the recipients are known as Honor Award Fellows. The first member of the Association to receive the honor was Amy Morris Homans, one of the early, very famous women in the field whose career began in the later nineteenth century and who was a close associate of Mrs. Mary Hemenway.

The National Interest in Sports and Games

The American people, keenly interested in sports and games and generously endowed with leisure, spending money, and the means of rapid transportation and communication, have engaged avidly since the Second World War in a great variety of sports and games. Opportunities in these activities have been plentiful for both the participant and spectator in such recreational pursuits as bowling, golf, tennis, softball, swimming and boating activities, and fishing and hunting. Amateur competitive-sports programs have attained new heights of popularity in schools and colleges, attracting thousands to the arenas and fascinating millions through television. The expansion of professional sports across the United States, as nation-wide franchises have multiplied, provides a career in sports for gifted athletes and enjoyment for millions of fans.

International sports contests are creating a greater interest than ever before in sports as television brings the exploits of foreign athletes into American living rooms. A prime example may be seen in the nationally televised Winter Olympic Games from Squaw Valley, California, in 1960. The perfection of color television and international television reception, in the near future, can be expected to enhance interest in sports hitherto little known in the United States as American viewers see the Olympic Games, Pan-American Games, British Empire Games, and All-European Sports Festivals. Having a somewhat similar effect are the activities of amateur and professional organizations in the field of sports and games, such as the Amateur Athletic Union and the National Collegiate Athletic Association, who are co-operating with the State Department of the United States in sending athletes on good-will missions to foreign countries. All in all, sports for the American people seem to have an unparalleled opportunity for growth even though some aspects of the programs of interscholastic and intercollegiate athletics have raised disturbing questions.

Competitive Sports

In the 1920's athletics and physical education merged in schools and colleges for two very important reasons. First, the medium of physical education became the popular sports and games as they replaced formal gymnastics. Secondly, the student-sponsored athletic programs of the nineteenth century, which became the highly competitive interscholastic and intercollegiate athletic programs of the twentieth, were placed under faculty control, usually as a division of the physical-education department. To this merger each group brought its own staff, facilities, equipment, and a rich heritage of physical activity. Leaders in each group possessed definite ideas about the proper organization of a sports-and-games program in an academic institution. Frequently their views clashed on the issue of the proper emphasis to be placed on competitive sports.

Social, economic, and political pressures shaped the programs. When interscholastic and intercollegiate athletics are developed to satisfy a sports-conscious community, questions inevitably arise as to whether the resulting programs are consistent with educational objectives. If athletic policies are allowed to circumvent stated educational objectives, the program becomes more like a business enterprise with ultimate success rest-ing upon the securing of gifted athletes and capable coaching staffs. According to leaders in physical education, educational objectives are best obtained through a basic instruction program in physical education for all students, an intramural sports program, and a varsity athletic program whereby the gifted athlete may engage in wholesome competition strictly as an extracurricular activity without the aspects of a business enterprise. (*See Document 34.*) The program of physical education, directed by Thomas E. McDonough, at Emory University is considered to be one of the best examples, among the colleges and universities, of a program devoted to educational objectives.

Recruitment and subsidization of intercollegiate athletics is an increasingly troublesome problem, and this is especially true in the area of football and basketball. Interest in winning teams spreads in a spectacular fashion, especially when, after winning conference titles and state and national championships, they receive opportunities to play in post season "classics." The exalted position of the gifted athlete sometimes results in a callow youth engaging in unethical practices and coping with pressures which he does not understand.

The college basketball scandal of 1961 is a recent example of gambling interests preying upon nondiscerning youth as the pressures of society envelop sports programs of intense interest. The seriousness of the situation was underlined in an article in the *New York Times* of July 16, 1961, in which Asa Bushnell of the Eastern College Athletic Association was quoted as saying: "Basketball's sorry mess demands a searching reappraisal of the intercollegiate athletic program in all its fundamentals." But the question remains of how the abuses can be eliminated from highly competitive programs of athletics. In the same article Walter Byers, executive director of the National Collegiate Athletic Association is quoted as saying: "We know that eventually the NCAA must take leadership and make positive recommendations." College administrators, as a whole, feel that the first step to correct the situation must be the enactment of legislation that will make bribery of athletes a federal crime.

Regulation by the NCAA

The National Collegiate Athletic Association has moved from an advisory position to acting as the principal regulatory and enforcement body in the attempt to enforce faculty control of intercollegiate athletics in member institutions. Control is exercised through eight geographic districts which work with conferences and individual institutions. Athletic conferences were formed to promote and regulate athletics by grouping institutions according to size, similarity of background, academic interests and standards, and by geographic region. A new era opened in the enforcement of standards when the National Collegiate Athletic Association placed on probation certain academic institutions that possessed some of the most powerful athletic teams in the nation.

Regulation of Competitive Athletics in the Schools

Highly competitive sports programs are becoming more common in elementary, junior, and senior high schools, though the situation is not new. The interscholastic athletic program reached such proportions in the Middle West in 1920 that the Midwest Federation of State High School Athletic Associations was formed to regulate competition, its jurisdiction covering rules of eligibility, schedules, and tournaments. Two years later the Federation evolved into the National Federation of State High School Athletic Associations so as to control both the policies and procedures of member schools. To help raise athletic standards the Federation adopted a code of "Recommended Minimum Eligibility Requirements" in 1929. Since these beginnings there has been an attempt in all states to exercise a proper measure of control. The values of school athletics, in a properly regulated program, have been thoughtfully discussed by William L. Hughes in his article "The Place of Athletics in the School Physical-Education Program." (*See Document 35.*)

Competitive Sports for Children

The rise of competitive sports, especially football, in elementary schools created deep consternation among such professional groups as physicians, psychologists, and health and physical-education teachers. The American Association for Health, Physical Education, and Recreation adopted a resolution in 1947 that interschool competition be abolished in elementary schools. The American Medical Association and allied groups have given public support to this resolution because of potential physiological and psychological harm to participants.

Competitive sports programs for children are fostered outside the schools by such organizations as Little League, Church Leagues, and Dads' Clubs. The Little League, for example, began baseball in 1939 and now has some one million children playing baseball throughout the country with state and regional tournaments leading to a Little World Series, held annually in Williamsport, Pennsylvania.

Competitive Athletics for Girls

Sports and games have also won a following among the girls in schools and colleges. There were serious attempts, especially in the 1920's, to organize highly competitive interscholastic and intercollegiate athletic programs for girls. The sports were usually coached and officiated by men, who, emphasizing the importance of winning, converted the program into competitive athletics. The exploitation of feminine athletes through sensational advertising and degrading exhibitions produced a reaction. Leaders in physical education for women vigorously protested the trend and started a crusade for a safe and educationally sound program of physical education. A vigorous protest against unsound practices in athletics for high school girls was made by Agnes R. Wayman. (*See Document 36.*)

Since the girls' competitive athletic program often centered on basketball, it was in this area that one of the first organizations to control competition for girls appeared. The National Women's Basketball Committee, organized in 1905, expanded into the National Committee on Women's Sports in 1917. Subsequently it went through a series of structural changes before finally becoming in 1957 the Division of Girls' and Women's Sports (DGWS) of the American Association for Health, Physical Education, and Recreation. This organization, which has in large measure guided the programs of sports and games for girls and women in schools and colleges, has proved invaluable in eliminating the abuses that frequently creep into programs for men.

The Play Day

During the 1920's, a critical decade for girls' sports, a new type of program became popular. The Play Day proved to be a transition program between athletics and the present intramural sports and games that are found in nearly all schools and colleges. Started in 1925 at the University of Washington High School by Mary Gross Hutchinson to provide a wholesome activity program for girls, the Play Day spread quickly through the high schools and entered the colleges in 1928 by way of the University of Cincinnati. It required several schools, in close proximity, to meet for a general field day of sports and games; and the urge to win over a rival institution was eliminated by selecting girls from different schools to make up the competing teams.

The need for Play Day, which explains the rapidity of its rise, was less pressing after the development of a more complex academic and social rountine in the schools and colleges and particularly after the appearance of the intramural sports program. The intramural program has enabled girls interested in competitive sports to play safely on a team that competes with another within the institution and to profit under optimum conditions from the values intrinsic in an educationally sound program of physical education. Reasons for and against intercollegiate athletics for girls were compiled in a noteworthy study by Mabel Lee. (*See Document 37.*)

The Intramural Sports Program

Intramural sports competition developed to fill a need for a competitive program of sports and games for all students. The accepted name of the program came to be "intramural," a term constructed from the Latin words *intra,* meaning within, and *muralis,* meaning wall. In schools and colleges intramurals consist of competive sports and games played voluntarily by students within an institution who meet stated requirements such as class year and status, medical certification, and residential location.

The rise of the intramural movement paralleled the inclusion of sports and games into the physical-education programs of the early twentieth century. The educational values inherent in intramurals were recognized when Ohio State University and the University of Michigan appointed intramural directors in 1913. That the program spread rapidly can be seen from a survey in 1916 that listed some 140 institutions with intramural programs.

The appointment of Dr. Elmer D. Mitchell, pioneer in the intramural movement, as director of intramural sports at the University of Michigan in 1919 ushered in a new era in the field of physical education. Dr. Mitchell was instrumental in developing a program of competitive sports and games that provided students who were not members of varsity teams with an opportunity for sports competition tailored to meet their needs and interests. Through promotion of intramural sports he translated the philosophy of play and recreation into tangible assets for physical education. (*See Document 38.*) In 1925 intramurals were started in high schools, and soon the program was national in scope. The physical activities in the early programs generally included basketball, swimming, handball, tennis, football, and baseball.

The intramural program provides students with a wide selection of recreational activities, sports for leisure-time pursuits, social and individual physical activities, and a competitive program of sports and games. Intramurals are a logical outgrowth of a basic physical-education program in which all students learn fundamental playing skills in individual, dual, and team sports. Those students who desire the next level of competition in sports may engage in the voluntary intramural program. Students who develop into gifted athletes generally prefer to engage in interscholastic or intercollegiate athletics. Since 1930 the recreational values of intramurals have been widely recognized. Co-educational activities were added, especially after the Second World War, when returning servicemen wanted to engage in recreational sports with their wives. Nearly all high schools and colleges have intramural programs, and some fifty per cent of elementary schools conduct selected intramural activities.

In addition, intramurals have become an integral part of industrial athletics, church recreation, physical activities in youth organizations, and municipal recreation. Intramurals symbolize the spirit of play and recreation in physical education.

Play and Recreation

Play and recreation, viewed at the turn of the century primarily as an outlet for surplus energy, became in the 1920's, to leaders in physical education, a means of self-expression, an opportunity for growth and personal satisfaction, and a training ground for citizenship in group behavior. Back of the change loomed the Industrial Revolution with its somewhat contradictory results. Although the factory system encouraged the movement of the population from the country to the city—a process which has gone so far by the 1960's that the distinction between the two has been virtually obliterated—with the misery that attends the relocation of people and though it increased the monotony of work, the Industrial Revolution also promoted a higher standard of living and increased the leisure of great numbers of people. For the first time worthy use of leisure time became a source of major concern to the leaders of physical education. They would have agreed with the statement made by President James A. Garfield when he declared in 1881: "We may divide the whole struggle of the human race into two chapters: first the fight to get leisure and then the second fight of civilization, what shall we do with our leisure?" So consequential was the problem considered by the National Education Association that in 1918 it listed the worthy use of leisure time as one of the seven cardinal principles of education.

The problems created by increased leisure caught national attention when President Coolidge called the "Conference on Outdoor Recreation" in 1924 to place a special emphasis on recreation and to encourage government support for recreation programs. His action, combined with the work of the Playground and Recreation Association, helped to bring about the passage of legislation for recreation in some twenty states. This legislation usually provided communities with legal power to establish public recreation programs under the jurisdiction of a municipal park board, a school board, or a separate recreation commission. A special tax was generally authorized to raise money for the support of public recreation.

The Playground and Recreation Association, rapidly expanding in response to the need to supply leisure-time activities for as many groups as possible, adopted in 1930 the name National Recreation Association (NRA). Among its manifold services were these: an advisory service on recreation research involving business, industry, and government; consulting services with regard to recreation facilities and equipment; a research service for special recreation problems; the publication of an official journal titled *Recreation;* and zealous support for play and recreational activities in physical education and youth organizations.

The impact of the Great Depression led, at first, to the slashing of recreation budgets, laying off of personnel, and a serious decline in the building of facilities and equipment in recreation. A novel and terrible situation faced the nation as unemployment became a problem of national dimensions. The federal government, deeply alarmed at the prospect of a breakdown in national morale, attempted a number of solutions, one of which was the provision of public funds to finance public recreation. The result was the establishment of the Works Progress Administration (WPA), which was the single most potent force in the expansion of public recreation facilities and equipment. For public recreation facilities alone the federal government spent in excess of one and a half billion dollars in the five years from 1933 to 1938, a sum unheard of for such a purpose in American history.

Recreation during the Great Depression

The Works Progress Administration constructed recreation facilities and equipment in every state except Maine. In establishing its operational procedure it was able to draw upon recreation personnel to supply a nucleus of skilled leaders for directing the vast enterprise. The public recreation programs that materialized included five divisions: physical recreation such as sports and games; social recreation such as dance activities; cultural recreation such as arts and crafts; therapeutic recreation such as special activities for the handicapped; and children's play centers. Recreational facilities and equipment built under government auspices included picnic areas, camping sites, and hiking trails in state and national parks; playing areas for softball, handball, tennis, archery, and badminton; shuffleboard and horseshoe areas; swimming pools; and golf courses.

Twelve departments of the federal government were promoting recreation by 1937 in an effort to ease the problems of unemployment. In the public housing program the government required the construction of indoor and outdoor recreation areas. It also encouraged recreation programs among private groups such as camps, youth hostels, settlement houses, Boy Scouts, YMCA's, church groups, and industries.

The example set by the government was pervasive. As soon as it was fully realized that public recreation programs could be invaluable in helping to ease the crisis of unemployment, many private organizations gave their support to recreation. The Congress of Industrial Organizations

(CIO) established a recreation department in 1937, directed by a physical educator who held the title of International Representative to the Union. The American Federation of Labor (AF of L) went on record as favoring recreation as a means of raising morale among the unemployed. This early activity in providing recreation for the workers evolved into the present industrial recreation programs in business and industry.

The philosophy of American recreation was largely shaped by the changing social, economic, and industrial conditions during the Great Depression as recreation, like physical education, was molded into a program indigenous to the American people. The popular play and recreation activities changed the program content in allied organizations. Recreation activities and sports and games with carry-over values to the community recreation programs were introduced into physical-education instruction programs and intramurals. The acceptance of play and recreation as a constructive force in society by the American people is reflected in the programs of youth organizations, church groups, and the industrial recreation movement.

During the Second World War recreation personnel organized and promoted recreation programs for servicemen at home and in foreign countries. A new recreation development, the United Service Organizations (USO), provided comprehensive recreational services through a co-ordinated plan that made maximum use of recreational personnel, staff, facilities, and equipment. Military recreation programs, seasoned in two World Wars, are now considered indispensable by military leaders in maintaining morale among the servicemen.

Following the Second World War municipal recreation programs were built upon the solid foundation laid in the depression years. Promoting the modern concept of recreation is the National Recreation Association, which promotes recreation for all age groups, including recent programs for the aged. The programs are usually operated under local government control and financed mainly through taxation. Recreation programs now receive widespread support in schools and colleges and from numerous private organizations.

Professional preparation of recreation leaders has been expanded to provide training for a much larger and more varied group. The memorable Jackson's Mill Conference of 1948 and the Pere Marquette State Park Conference two years later, centering upon professional preparation in health, physical education, and recreation, outlined standards that have improved both undergraduate and graduate programs of professional preparation in colleges and universities.

The age-old dream of widespread leisure for great numbers of people has come true in twentieth-century America with the startling technological advance that began after the Civil War. With leisure has come the paradox that men do not always know how to use it worthily. The prob-

lem has been well stated by Dr. Jay B. Nash, a thoughtful and distinguished leader in the field of recreation, who has recognized the need for
a healthy balance between work and leisure. (*See Document 39.*)

Recent Developments in Camping

Since World War II organized camping—a century old in 1961—has
moved from the recreational sports-and-games program, which almost
exclusively dominated the movement through most of its history, to the
special content programs that may be drawn from drama, music, science,
religious training, language instruction, or sports and games. A popular
new approach to camping was the day camp, inaugurated in 1921 by
the Girl Scouts. It allows families to give their children some camping
experience in a less expensive way. The day camp provides interest
programs and has proved to be a valuable service to mothers who wish
to have children safely cared for during the day and returned home for
the night. The camping movement gained stature during the depression
with the organization of the American Camping Association and the
publication of a national magazine titled *Camping*. The educational objectives of the modern camp movement have allied it with physical education, recreation, and the dance.

The Dance in Education

Several forms of the dance have had a measure of success in schools
and colleges since the First World War, especially the square, clog, and
tap dance and also the several styles of modern dance. A product of the
social, economic, and cultural conditions of a specific period, some of
the dances gained stature for only a few years and then disappeared;
others evolved into new types of dance, while a few continued to the
present as they had begun, fundamentally unaltered by the changing
patterns of society.

The square dance, its popularity rising very slowly, indeed, in the early
years of the century, gained in public favor in the 1920's. Henry Ford
helped finance a revival of the New England style of square dance. The
rise of interest in the East encouraged enthusiasm once more in the
Southwest and South for the cowboy and mountain style of square dance.
The square dance, symbolizing the frontier culture, remains today a very
popular form of dance in education and in the community.

The clog dance, although it appealed little to the general public, had
a devoted following for a few years in the schools and colleges. Its success in education was due largely to the unremitting efforts and tireless
zeal of Mary Wood Hinman, Helen Frost, and Marjorie Hillas. The clog
step, based upon a shuffle and intricate tapping of the feet to ballad and

folk song music, had some success in recreation and physical education; but never a favorite with the public, it evolved into the more acceptable tap dance. Prominent as a leader in the tap dance movement was Marjorie Hillas, who received capable support from Dr. Anne Schley Duggan. Dr. Duggan's forte lay in analyzing movement patterns, creating dance routines, and explaining how specific forms of the dance contributed to educational objectives. (*See Document 40.*)

In the dance movement in education the natural dance, which was the link between the earlier aesthetic dance and modern dance, went through a complex transition in the 1920's before emerging at the end of the decade as the present modern dance, its final form owing much to the formative influence of the more advanced dance movement in Germany.

From Germany Mary Wigman, a student of the famous dance teacher, Rudolf Leban, brought to the United States the German version of the modern dance, which had been molded in Germany during a period of deep social and political unrest. In 1925 Mary Wigman toured the United States demonstrating her modern dance routines. Dancing without musical accompaniment, she employed, not a specific style of physical movement, but rather a rhythmical routine that expressed emotional and intellectual feelings through physical movements. Subsequently she modified her dance technique to include flutes, percussion instruments, and the piano.

Although to many leaders in American dance it appeared that Mary Wigman's style of dance was one more physical activity transplanted to the United States, in fact this was a mistaken viewpoint since the German style of modern dance was only an ingredient, though an important one, which blended into the ever-changing natural dance to become ultimately the modern dance. The German style was not adopted in its entirety, but exercised, nevertheless, a great influence upon the interpretations of Martha Graham, Doris Humphrey, and Charles Weidman, who borrowed from Mary Wigman her dance movements and techniques in teaching.

Meanwhile, a young dance enthusiast, Margaret H'Doubler, journeyed to New York where she studied with the noted Russian ballet teacher, Louis Chalif, and two leaders of the natural dance, Gertrude Colby and Bird Larson. Amalgamating their teachings with her own creative ideas, she produced her own style of dance, denominated both "the dance" and "interpretive dance." Her dance philosophy flowed from a deep appreciation of physical and spiritual beauty, which left its impress upon her dance rountines.

By 1926 Margaret H'Doubler had established at the University of Wisconsin the first major program in the dance found anywhere in the United States, a milestone in the history of the dance in education. Making use of insights gained from modern psychology, she dramatized the need for creativity in social and intellectual activity while urging the evolving modern dance as an appropriate medium of expression for attaining this creativity. To her the modern dance was not an end in itself; it was an aesthetic expression essential to life. In her thinking, the human body became a unified whole through the creative expression of a complex of ideas, moods, emotions, and feelings, these being expressed by means of movement. Rhythmic movement, according to Margaret H'Doubler, is "a constant law of all muscular movement." (*See Document 41.*)

Special contributions to the dance in education were also forthcoming from Mary Patricia O'Donnell and Martha Hill. To the former belongs much of the credit for the action taken by the American Association for Health, Physical Education, and Recreation in adding a Dance Section in 1932. Martha Hill established the School of Dance at Bennington College in Vermont, which operated during the summer as a national teaching and research center for modern dance teachers and students. Another outstanding center was the Summer School of Dance, founded in 1948 at Connecticut College. Martha Hill's work received recognition when she became director of a dance department, established in 1951 at the famed Juilliard School of Music in New York City.

The Golden Age of Health Education

The most significant gains in school health education were achieved in the years following the First World War. These were stimulated by the revelations of the shocking state of poor physical development of American youth, in the age group from eighteen to thirty-one, which alarmed professional groups, especially those in education and medicine. Physicians had discovered that one-third of the men called by the selective service were unfit, by the standards of the day, for military service, while another one-third were troubled with pathological deficiencies. The response of leaders in education and medicine was to demand the passage of state legislation that compelled the teaching of health education and physical education in the public schools. "Health" became a magic word, spurring medical men into action, imparting energy to state legislatures who passed laws in health and physical education, and raising the sums of money required to improve health-education and physical-education programs in the schools.

Student health and physical fitness became of primary concern in education, and health moved into the number one position among the Seven Cardinal Principles of Education. A student health service began to be a vital part of the school curriculum as its personnel co-ordinated health activities such as medical examinations, follow-up procedures, and plans for corrective measures. For a time health became the dominent objective in physical education; and many a department of physical education, responsive to the trend, was transformed into a department of health and physical education.

State legislation in health education was also sought by the American Child Health Association, which was formed in 1923 as the result of a merger between the American Child Hygiene Association and the Child Health Organization. The new Association conducted health demonstrations, surveyed child health activities, and promoted teacher-education programs in school health education.

A White House Conference on Child Health and Protection, called by President Herbert Hoover in 1930, served the cause of health education in several meaningful ways. It made an evaluation of the developments in school health education since the First World War. It attempted to reach a synthesis of sound philosophy and principles in health education on the basis of which the profession could move ahead. And perhaps most important of all, the conference, by the mere fact of its meeting, dramatized the national concern for health and physical fitness. From this National Conference came specific recommendations for student health services and school health instruction programs.

Since 1930 a special emphasis has been placed on environmental conditions within the school area. State departments of education have adopted building codes and architectural plans which facilitate markedly the construction of safe and sanitary school buildings, usually more pleasing from an aesthetic viewpoint than the buildings of the past.

The Second World War, like all wars, introduced changes. School health education programs became more comprehensive as they evolved into three main divisions; namely, school health services, school health environment, and school health instruction. Medical examinations were more far-reaching for the students, and the more advanced communities began to include periodic medical examinations for faculty and other school personnel. The services of medical doctors and nurses increased to the limits permitted by school budgets.

Advancing medical research, which has made it possible for human life to be sustained beyond limits that earlier generations had conceived as possible, has raised the question in some minds of whether modern medicine has rendered health education obsolete. Yet leaders in medicine are, themselves, quick to point out that the present life span of some seventy years is the result not only of medical research but also of preventive medicine. School health education *is* preventive medicine, leading to the quality of health which leaders in medicine consider their primary goal.

Adaptive Health and Physical Education

Scientific research in both health education and physical education led to an adaptive program of health and physical education for the children and youth who deviate from the normal. The aim of adaptive health and physical education is to provide the opportunity for social recreation by means of a modified program for exceptional children, interesting to them and enabling them to understand their limitations and to learn to make maximum use of their capacities. Such activities as swimming, shuffle-board, horseshoes, archery, wheelchair basketball, and seated games such as darts form the nucleus of the adaptive program. Interest in such a program was heightened by the reconditioning and rehabilitation work of physical educators, who were assigned to military convalescent hospitals during the Second World War; and since then the American Association for Health, Physical Education, and Recreation and the American Medical Association and the National Education Association through committees have studied a set of principles for such a program, which is available for use in schools and colleges.

Chapter 5

RECENT DEVELOPMENTS
IN PHYSICAL EDUCATION

The AAHPER: Spokesman for the Profession

The advances made in health, physical education, and recreation won public acceptance and support for the relatively young profession with the help of the American Association for Health, Physical Education, and Recreation (AAHPER). Since the Second World War the Association, spokesman for the profession of physical education in the United States, has moved forward with resolution and confidence. It has rapidly expanded its services to become the guiding and directing force in the promotion of physical education. Two of the serious problems faced in physical education in the immediate postwar era were the building of facilities and the establishing of desirable standards in teacher education. The Association took the lead in solving both by holding three national conferences that are now landmarks in the history of American physical education.

In the area of facilities the Association was responsible for organizing and directing a national conference on facilities, held at Jackson's Mill, West Virginia, in 1946. The recommendations of the conference were subsequently published as *A Guide on Planning Facilities for Athletics, Recreation, Physical and Health Education,* which served as a guideline for gymnasium construction and planning recreational areas. Its popularity and widespread influence were evident from its having sold 25,000 copies and going through eight printings. The *Guide* was revised ten years later by a second conference, this one meeting at Michigan State University.

In the area of establishing desirable standards in teacher education, the Association was almost equally prompt. As was stated earlier in this chapter, two extremely important and influential conferences were held for this purpose. The first, a National Conference on Undergraduate Preparation in Health Education, Physical Education, and Recreation was held at Jackson's Mill in 1948; the other, for graduate study at Pere Marquette State Park, Illinois, in 1950.

The most rapid strides made by the Association in professional activities were in the 1950's as it made use of conferences, consultant services, and publications. Some twenty-five national conferences were sponsored in this period that focused attention upon national problems in health, physical education, recreation, and athletics. Consulting services have become part and parcel of the work of the Association. The national staff in Washington, D.C., includes consultants in the following professional areas: recreation and outdoor education; physical education and women's athletics; physical education and boys' and men's athletics; health education; sports and industrial relations; national membership and student major clubs; and special projects such as the Outdoor Education Project and Operation Fitness—USA.

An invaluable service performed by the Association is the publication of the *Journal of Health, Physical Education, and Recreation,* the *Research Quarterly,* sports guides, research materials, specialized textbooks and yearbooks, and pamphlets concerning special problems such as physical fitness and athletics. As its functions have expanded, so has its membership. The Association has grown to some 25,000 members, largely through the efforts of the leaders in physical education who have directed its affairs, encouraged and motivated its members and lay groups as well, and sponsored the complex professional services for which the demand seems insatiable.

In these years physical education has become international in scope. The United States was one of the founders of the United Nations, which has its headquarters in New York City, and since the Second World War has taken on a whole series of international commitments that extend American interests around the world. The gain in internationalism in the country after 1945 was reflected in physical education. At the Second Pan-American Congress of Physical Education, held in Mexico City in 1946, the Pan-American Institute was formed to promote research in physical education in the member countries. The first president was Dr. Charles H. McCloy, well known for intensive research in physical education. International physical education gained stature with the formation of the International Council on Health, Physical Education, and Recreation in 1959. The Council, of which Dorothy S. Ainsworth was the first president, is a division of the World Confederation of Organizations of the Teaching Profession.

A new element was injected into the history of physical education when the Soviet Union, in October of 1957, launched into space the first Sputnik (a satellite placed in orbit by rocket thrust) and raised a whole series of fundamental questions about the nature of the curriculum in American schools. To many it appeared that the United States, if it were to match Russia in a space race, must abandon the so-called less necessary courses in the school curriculum in favor of greater amounts of technology and science; and physical education came under attack from critics as one of what they called the less "solid" subjects that were expendable during the Cold War. But a counter current was set in motion when national attention turned to the findings of the now famous Kraus-Weber tests, which contrasted the physical fitness of American children unfavorably with that of European children. Physical fitness is, of course, a by-product of physical education.

The Kraus-Weber Tests

The report that "shocked the President" (Dwight D. Eisenhower) was first published by Dr. Hans Kraus and Ruth Hirschland in the *Journal of Health, Physical Education, and Recreation* in December of 1953, four years before the Sputnik was launched. Entitled "Muscular Fitness and Health," the Kraus-Weber tests were given to 4264 American children and 2870 European children of comparable environmental conditions. The test included six basic maneuvers measuring strength and flexibility of trunk and leg muscles. Among the American children 57.9 percent failed while only 8.7 percent of the European children failed. Dr. Hans Kraus, a medical doctor, stated that the passing mark represented only minimum muscular fitness, and to fail this test could mean possible orthopedic and emotional difficulties.

The results of the Kraus-Weber tests were publicized in the ensuing months on all sides, by newspapers, magazines, radio, and television. The *U.S. News and World Report* of March 19, 1954, carried, for example, a feature article describing the test results and evaluating the implications for American youth. Its author, noting the apparent softness of American youth disclosed by the study, stated: "In terms of muscle and ability to do jobs requiring physical strength, the average American youth appears to be growing soft. His counterpart in some nations of Europe, enjoying fewer of the advantages of modern civilization, is stronger." As if to underscore the results of the tests, Dr. Kraus stated in May of 1954 that "children coming into the first grades of the school system are already seriously deficient. . . . They leave elementary school in very much the same condition as when they entered it—if anything a little worse."

The startling implications of the Kraus-Weber tests were brought to the attention of President Eisenhower by John B. Kelley, Sr. and Senator James Duff of Pennsylvania. Kelley, a personal friend of Dr. Kraus, had served as Director of the Division of Physical Fitness during World War II and feared another crisis in the physical fitness of American youth.

President Eisenhower Calls a National Fitness Conference

A National Conference on Physical Fitness of American Youth was called by President Eisenhower for September 27–28, 1955, in Denver, Colorado. Arrangements for the conference were made by Vice-President

Richard M. Nixon, who met to make plans with Dr. Ray O. Duncan, President-elect of the American Association for Health, Physical Education, and Recreation, and Dr. Carl A. Troester, Jr., executive-secretary. The decision was made to focus attention upon a comprehensive activity program for all children and youth. Before the Conference met, President Eisenhower suffered a heart attack, and the Conference was postponed indefinitely.

The Conference was postponed, but not the issue of physical fitness, as an anxious nation awaited every medical bulletin on the physical condition of President Eisenhower. It could scarcely overlook the fact that during the months of recovery Dr. Paul Dudley White, an internationally famous cardiologist serving the President as one of his chief medical specialists, prescribed a carefully regulated program of exercise during the convalescence. Later, in response to a question about the advisability of prescribing exercise for those who had suffered a heart attack, Dr. White declared: "It is well to establish a regular habit in some form of exercise and to maintain it through thick and thin. One should regard exercise just as essential to good health as eating, sleeping, and walking." (*See Document 42.*)

The President's Conference on the Physical Fitness of American Youth was finally held on June 18–19, 1956, at the United States Naval Academy —the first national conference on physical fitness ever held in peacetime under the auspices of the White House. The purpose of the Conference, called by President Eisenhower, was to stimulate interest in preparing American youth for carrying out their tasks in a highly complex society and to discover the action that the federal government might take to promote effective programs for children and youth in the age group from five to seventeen.

The words of government spokesmen revealed the seriousness with which the White House viewed the problem of heightening physical fitness in the country at large. Vice-President Nixon, as Director of the Conference, gave the keynote address. He considered, so he said, that the objective of an adequate physical fitness program could be realized in the participation of all American boys and girls in some form of physical activity. These were his words: "The objective of an adequate physical fitness program can be summed up in one word—participation—participation on the part of every boy and girl in America in some form of healthy, recreational, and physical activity." Less than fifty per cent of high school students, he pointed out, actually participate in physical-education programs; and he noted that there were no gymnasiums at all in over ninety per cent of the nation's 150,000 elementary schools. Marion B. Folsom, Secretary of the Department of Health, Education, and Welfare, after asking the delegates to consider the meaning of the phrase "total fitness," stated his own definition, which suggested that he had been in consultation with leaders in the field of physical education, when he said: "There is a third dimension to fitness, and that is the capacity to function in every way at one's own best—physically, mentally, and spiritually."

The statements presented by both Vice-President Nixon and Secretary Folsom suggested strongly that they had been influenced by the American Association for Health, Physical Education, and Recreation, the spokesman for the overwhelming majority in the profession. In this connection, however, the comment of a rather pointed critic of the language and philosophy of the Association is worth quoting. George Munger, Professor and Director of Physical Education at the University of Pennsylvania, writing in *Sports Illustrated* (July 31, 1961) declared: "We are plagued today with a . . . grandiose and tasteless term: Total Fitness. Fitness totalitarians surrounded and captured the previous administration. Under President Eisenhower, their nebulous program called for the attainment not only of physical fitness, but social fitness, spiritual fitness, and any other kind of fitness that came to mind. . . ."

Following the Conference, which had demonstrated the interest of the federal government in physical fitness, President Eisenhower took further action by appointing a National Council on Youth Fitness with Vice-President Nixon as chairman and Dr. Shane MacCarthy as executive director. A liaison group, called a Citizens Advisory Committee on the Fitness of American Youth, was appointed to work with local and state problems. It is too early to evaluate the results of the actions in the area of physical education taken by the Eisenhower administration, but it may safely be said that no president before him had gone so far publicly in support of it.

The AAHPER Fitness Conference

Encouraged by presidential action on physical fitness, the American Association for Health, Physical Education, and Recreation (AAHPER) called a Conference on Youth Fitness in Washington, D.C., on September 12–15, 1956. The 116 leaders of the profession who assembled were asked to help plan and implement a program to improve the fitness of youth in schools and colleges. Dr. Shane MacCarthy, executive director of the Council on Youth Fitness, represented the federal government. The report "Fitness for Youth," outlining the proper physical education requirements for children and youth, emerged from this Conference.

The NCAA Promotes Physical Fitness

Other groups now became active. The National Collegiate Athletic Association (NCAA) at its 51st annual meeting, which was held in St.

Louis in January of 1957, adopted a sixteen-point program on youth fitness. Among the recommendations, which member institutions were asked to promote, were these: increase intramural programs both in number of participants and sports offered; increase the number of teams in intercollegiate sports; require a four-year program of physical education for all students with credit given toward graduation; provide a physical-fitness program for girls; and establish a youth-fitness council in each state.

The First Governors' Conference on Fitness

The signal from the White House alerted the state capitals; and Illinois, one of the largest states, proceeded to become a pacesetter in establishing the pattern of activity that was soon followed by other states. Governor Stratton of Illinois called the first Governors' Conference on Youth Fitness on May 5–7, 1957, in Allerton Park, Monticello, Illinois. This Conference was sponsored by the Illinois State Department of Education, the University of Illinois, and the Illinois Association for Health, Physical Education, and Recreation. The purpose of the Conference was to support the national program of youth fitness, as outlined by President Eisenhower, and to center attention upon the physical-fitness needs of Illinois youth. At the conclusion of the Conference Governor Stratton appointed an Illinois Council on Youth Fitness, with a state executive director, and an Illinois Youth Fitness Advisory Committee. The *Proceedings* of the Governor's Conference were published and served as a guide for other states, which adopted the Illinois pattern.

Operation Fitness—USA

The American Association for Health, Physical Education, and Recreation threw its great weight dramatically behind the drive for physical fitness as it announced, on January 21, 1959, its sponsorship of a nationwide fitness program called Operation Fitness—USA. In carrying out the program, which has gained in strength each succeeding year, the Association serves mainly as an organization to motivate and encourage the implementation of fitness programs among all interested groups in the nation. Providing the spark for others, it has given direction to professional leaders, solicited financial support, and prepared fitness materials and projects. A National Youth Fitness Test with a manual providing national norms and recording forms is used in physical education and other fitness programs. As an incentive to participation, awards of all types are used such as certificates, emblems, and sports clothing symbolizing the fitness project. The Association has encouraged the holding of some thirty-five state fitness conferences and approximately thirty college and university fitness institutes. In short, Operation Fitness—USA was justly characterized by *Sports Illustrated* as "a truly ambitious national program which may yet put the fitness show on the road." (*See Document 43.*)

The American Medical Association Supports Physical Education

Some of the most important support for physical education forthcoming since the Second World War emanated from the American Medical Association when the House of Delegates, meeting in Miami, Florida, in June of 1960, approved a series of resolutions invaluable to the advance of both health and physical education. The resolution of greatest moment to physical education was "that the American Medical Association through its various divisions and departments and . . . medical societies do everything feasible to encourage effective instruction in physical education for all students in our schools and colleges." The American Medical Association went on record as supporting programs of sports and games as imparting leisure-time skills that would relieve tensions and help alleviate the effects of a sedentary life resulting from automation and labor-saving devices. Health was described in the resolutions as a key factor in enabling a person to contribute to the best of his ability to community and natural welfare. Dr. Paul Dudley White voiced the position on personal health taken by the American Medical Association when he asserted: "Simply the absence of disease is not enough. What we should aim for in our programs is postive health. Let us, therefore, while working for the fitness of our minds and souls, not neglect the fitness of our bodies."

Support for Physical Fitness from President Kennedy

In going beyond the support for physical fitness given by President Eisenhower, President John F. Kennedy has reminded observers of the vigorous President Theodore Roosevelt because of their mutual interest in sports and games and physical fitness. Even before taking office in January of 1961, President-Elect Kennedy was the author of an article in *Sports Illustrated* (December 26, 1960), titled "The Soft American." Stating that a growing lack of physical fitness among the American people was a threat to national security, President-Elect Kennedy cited the Kraus-Weber tests as demonstrating that physical fitness of American children had fallen far below that of their European counterparts. To facilitate physical fitness in the United States, he presented a blueprint for Governor Abraham Ribicoff, who was to become the Secretary of Health, Education, and Welfare in the forthcoming Kennedy administration. President-Elect Kennedy's four recommendations, which had significant implications for physical education, were to establish a White House Council on Health and Fitness; to place the Department of Health, Education, and Welfare in charge of youth fitness; to invite all the governors of the states to attend an annual National Youth Fitness Congress; and to advise all departments of the federal government that the promotion of sports and physical fitness is a fundamental policy of the United States.

After President Kennedy took office, numerous signs indicated that his interest remained unflagging in physical fitness as essential to the national welfare. A "Special Message on Education" (February 20, 1961) was issued a month after his inauguration in which he outlined to Congress a plan for amending and explanding the National Defense Education Act. It contained a recommendation that health and physical education be included under the terms of the Act. Another example of support for health and physical education was provided when the President created the Peace Corps. In a public statement concerning it, he underlined the importance of health and physical fitness in the training program by noting that participants would be traveling to underdeveloped countries where environmental conditions would tax their stamina.

President Kennedy summoned a National Conference on Physical Fitness of Youth on February 21, 1961, in Washington, D.C., during which he asked the delegates to work out answers to two major questions. First, how should the federal government proceed in order to give firm support to youth-fitness programs? Secondly, how could the federal government work most effectively with state and local groups to promote youth fitness? His next act was to appoint, on March 23, 1961, Charles B. Wilkinson, Athletic Director and Head Coach of Football at the University of Oklahoma, as a personal consultant to the President with the task of formulating a youth-fitness program at the national level.

A Presidential Proclamation on Fitness

At the President's News Conference, on July 19, 1961, President Kennedy issued to the American people a statement concerning physical fitness that had far-reaching implications for physical education. The strength of the country, he said, is no greater than the well-being of its citizens; and he urged that physical fitness become a major concern of the American people. Schools were asked to adopt three recommendations, made by the National Council on Youth Fitness, to strengthen the health and physical development of all children and youth. The recommendations, as given officially in the *New York Times* on July 20, 1961, were "First, to identify the physically under-developed pupil and work with him to improve his physical capacity. . . . Two, provide a minimum of fifteen minutes of vigorous activity everyday for all our school students, boys and girls alike. Three, use valid fitness tests to determine pupil physical ability and to evaluate their progress."

Following the policy statement by President Kennedy, Attorney General Robert F. Kennedy addressed a Conference of State Directors of Physical Education and offered a further explanation of the viewpoint of the White House. He stated that specific action on physical education, which had been too long in the talking stage, should be taken throughout the country. Further details were supplied by Charles B. Wilkinson, who stated that the astronauts, the men being trained for space exploration, would be used as a first step to promote physical fitness. He added that they were the favorite heroes of children above the second grade and that they would make recordings on the need for physical fitness that will be used on radio and television.

The picture in physical education on the threshold of the 1960's is comingled of light and dark shadows. It darkened when the Russian Sputnik shot into an October sky in 1957 and raised in some minds the question of the place of physical education in the schools, whether it should be retained at all or, if retained, whether it should be minimized. The light entered when the American people were rendered more keenly conscious of the importance of physical education than ever before in their history. The necessity of exercise, systematically maintained, came to the forefront during the illness of President Eisenhower; and the American people were instructed as well as disturbed by the results of the Kraus-Weber tests, which brought action from both President Eisenhower and President Kennedy. The urgency of this action was heightened by the Cold War. After his illness President Eisenhower gave the public support of the White House to physical education by summoning the delayed Conference on Physical Fitness of American Youth in 1956. The most dramatic and repeated support was forthcoming, however, from John F. Kennedy before and after he took office as President of the United States. If the first six months of his administration should prove the index to its future course, with regard to physical fitness, the American Association for Health, Physical Education, and Recreation, which has for so long carried the burden almost alone of making the American people aware of the value and importance of physical education, will have help of an unprecedented quality from the highest and most influential office in the land.

DOCUMENTS

1

The First Academic Program of
Physical Education in American Education *

EDWARD HITCHCOCK, M.D.

The earliest pioneer in the modern American physical-education profession was Dr. Edward Hitchcock, who spent fifty years working to establish a scientific foundation for the profession. Born in 1828, he attended Amherst College, where his father was the third president, and Harvard University Medical School, where he received the M.D. degree in 1853. The next seven years were spent teaching natural science at Williston Academy, after which he decided to devote his life to the study of comparative anatomy. This decision took him to London in 1860 to work under Sir Richard Owen, curator of the British Museum. But in 1861 his career changed again when he accepted the position as Director of the new Department of Physical Education and Hygiene at Amherst College; here he established the field of anthropometric measurement in physical education. In 1885 Dr. Hitchcock was chosen chairman of the meeting at Adelphi Academy which resulted in the founding of the American physical-education profession, known then as the Association for the Advancement of Physical Education; he served as its first president. He also served as President of the College Physical Education Association. The following documentary account describes the first academic program of physical education, based on scientific materials and on anthropometric measurements, to be found in an American college. It is in the form of a report, made by Dr. Hitchcock to the board of Trustees of Amherst College, on the program that he carried on there for two decades.

In presenting a report of the history of the first twenty years of the Department of Physical Education and Hygiene in Amherst College to its Trustees, the first and most natural mention should be made of the men who have been the most active in its inception and support.

To the Trustees of the College this department is chiefly indebted not only for its life, but for its success and growth. They have invariably

* Edward Hitchcock, A Report of Twenty Years Experience in the Department of Physical Education and Hygiene in Amherst College to the Board of Trustees (Amherst, Massachusetts, Press of C. A. Bangs and Co., 1881), pp. 3–14.
107

given it their best counsels and wise supervision, and never has a dollar been asked for necessary work or supplies, but that it has been readily appropriated. And while it was at first with them considered an experiment in the College course, they have not ceased to watch it with interest and give their best efforts for its success.

To the wise and patient efforts of President Stearns, this department owes its beginning. We know of no thoughts farther back than those lying in his mind which demanded that an education and care of the body could and should be maintained in Amherst College at least. And up to the latest days of his life, it ever enjoyed his cordial support. . . .

There are a few members of your board who may remember some performances preliminary to the establishment of this branch of the College Curriculum about twenty-one years ago, when in Village Church, upon an elevated platform, before a large and interested audience, Dr. Winship exhibited himself as able to lift with his hands and shoulders immense weights. The hardware stores in town were levied upon to loan their casks of nails and spikes, the old iron of the College cellar was brought out, and all to enable Dr. Winship to show how much he could lift. And these feats, remarkable as they surely were, were then considered as indications of health, and held up to the students as the means for the true hygiene of college life. Soon the gymnasium was equipped with apparatus, not the lightest of which were one hundred pound dumbbells, and apparatus by which a young man could be induced to try and lift a ton; and the dumbbells for class exercises weighed ten pounds each. But at this time it was the prediction of Dr. Dio Lewis that we soon should adopt the lighter dumbbells for exercise and discard the immense in muscular effort, which has proved true, for now we use bells that weigh two pounds to the pair, and the original lifting machines are in the pile of scrap iron.

The idea of physical culture has too often been that great muscular development is the only essential element in it, and the fact is indeed true that the really well man is muscularly strong. And for valetudinarians, for those who are able to give very much of their time, means, and thought for their own health, who can give a large share of their energy and thought to self-culture and preservation, without doubt the muscular system is the principal one to be attended to. But the problem to be solved by us has been what arrangement of required muscular exercise and recreation combined is the best for our students as a whole. In what way can we best help them to keep body and mind working harmoniously and effectually together? How shall the man physically be made efficient so that the intellectual, moral, and spiritual may at the same time secure its full development?

In order that our students be in the best condition for work it seems demanded that the muscles be not trained to their highest powers. For the most healthful and intellectual men are not those who have the most muscular power. They are often well-developed men, it is true, and of excellent physical inheritance, but they are not muscle men.

Physical culture as expressed to Amherst College Students by the experience of the past twenty years means something besides, something in addition to muscular exercise. It includes cleanliness of skin, attention to stomach and bowels, relaxation from daily mental work, freedom from certain kinds of petty discipline, but with so much requirement and restraint as will give coherence, respect, and stability to the methods of maintaining health and the men enjoying them.

The way in which students here are called upon to secure health, and its correct and normal maintenance for college requirements, is to be sure of some active, lively, and vigorous muscular exercise at stated periods; not requiring a rigid military or hardening drill of certain portions of the body, but offering them such exercises as shall while regularly obtained be vigorous, pleasant, recreative, and at the same time, even without a manifest consciousness of it, be calling into exercise their powers in active, vigorous, easy, and graceful movements. Light wooden dumbbells, weighing about one pound each, are placed in the hand, and then a series of movements are directed and timed by music, occupying in all from 20 to 30 minutes each day, which are simultaneously performed by a whole class under the lead of the Captain.

Believers in heavy gymnastics are apt to regard our exercises as perhaps well enough for girls and children, because they are only the swinging of one pound dumbbells for less than half an hour. And they would reflect upon the exercise and call it calisthenics, and not dignify it by the term gymnastics. To this we would only say, "what's in a name?" If calisthenics only accomplishes what we need, our wants are satisfied. And we doubt if some of those who "pooh, pooh" light dumbbell exercises are conscious of their utterances, or ever have swung even those wooden dumbells with the vigor and energy of a College class, to a polka or any lively music, with the metronome at 90° for a continuous exercise. For certain it is that the young men at the close of one of these exercises, with the temperature at 60°, have ordinarily secured moisture on the skin, are breathing full and deeply, the blood circulates, the abdominal viscera are sufficiently stimulated, and their muscles are limber and elastic; they have gained good exercise, and the whole man has the feeling that he has worked in a physical way, and yet is not exhausted. The whole body in the loose and easy uniform, unconstrained by a rigid piece of apparatus, is given a freedom of action which cannot be acquired by the stolid march, or the constraint of either fixed or many kinds of movable gymnastic apparatus; and lastly, the students generally feel, with all, that they have had a good time. And the mental and social freedom allowed and encouraged in these exercises conduces to the rapid and healthful evaporation of superfluous animal spirits generated by the physical and mental confinement of study.

And while our methods are not so perfect as might be devised with more complete apparatus and better men to direct it, if health of College is the only thing to be considered, they do seem to be good as far as they go; enough for the large majority, and of some service to all. And though there are some in every 40 or 50 young men among us who would be undoubtedly better for more stern and rigid discipline, yet College seems, with the present appliances and the time which can be taken for physical care and guidance, to be doing the best thing it can for the bulk of the students, in the matter of required exercises. And the rapid, easy, vigorous, and rhythmical movements of a class, guided and timed by music, with a light bell in each hand, heavy enough to require an appreciable muscular resistance, is what has been proven in Amherst College for twenty years a means of greatly promoting the health of the students.

During the first few years of our work, the simpler and easier forms of heavy gymnastic work were required of all the class; every man was expected to practice heavy gymnastics under direction of the leader, one of the class. This became very tedious work, irksome and impossible for some men to do except with such effort, moral and physical, as was injurious to be put on a large part of every class. Not all the men could, with advantage to themselves, make a vault, turn handsprings, take "dips," "walk grasshopper," or perform many other gymnastic feats, any more than every man could dance gracefully or lift enormously. But it was found out that the men who were sound in all four of their limbs and eyesight could go through movements enough with wooden dumb-bells to secure the necessary muscular waste and development for health-ful study, and hence no requirement for heavy gymnastic work has been made of any student for the past fifteen years. At the same time there are a few who take as naturally to heavy gymnastics, and as profitably too, as ducks to water, and these are allowed and encouraged to reasona-ble efforts in this direction. These at first are guided and watched, but they are at length allowed and expected to go on with their exercise in this direction at their own discretion, save with the aid of one of the older classes who has shown himself the best gymnast in College.

At once during each year a prize exhibition is held, when the indi-vidual students may compete with each other in heavy gymnastics, and the classes may show their proficiency in light exercises with dumbbells and marching. For the first few years, the morning hour was secured as the best time for the physical exercises of the College. And while in theory, and perhaps fact, this is the best time for exercise, yet the hour of early evening, between daylight and darkness, has come to be the time which we have of late most largely employed for gymnastics. At this hour the mind is weary from study, and if this work has been faithfully attended to, both the body and the mind demand physical exercise. Besides this, the relief to the eyes at this hour of the twenty-four is no inconsiderable reason why the twilight hour is considered by us as the appropriate and valuable one for gymnastic exercise. . . .

One of the first duties I felt called upon to perform after your appointment to this Professorship, was to prepare blanks for several anthropometric observations of the students of college. This I did partly to enable the students to learn by yearly comparison of themselves how they were getting on as regards the physical man. The ulterior object, however, was to help ascertain what are the data or constants of the typical man, and especially the college man. I have conceived no theory on the subject, and have instituted but very few generalizations; but my desire has been to carefully compile and put on record as many of these observations as possible for comparison and verification of statistical work in this same direction by many other persons in America and Europe.

In many of the final results of these twenty-years' data it is interesting to find a general correspondence to the established data of more numerous measurements of the human body, and in the variation from authorities of large experience we find the differences as a whole in favor of the student. These results seem to show that we must expect different physical characteristics in those who pursue the scholarly life, from others whose occupations are unlike them in so many ways; and when properly understood and carried out we believe that the advantages will be found on the side of the scholarly life.

In the fall of 1861, I took measurement of all the college students in seven particulars, and have faithfully made these examinations of almost every sound man since connected with the college up to the present date. The measurements are made of the Freshmen soon after entering, and are repeated upon them near the end of each year of the course. Thus every man who goes through college has been observed five times. These observations during the first year were the Age, Weight, Height, Chest Girth, Arm Girth, Forearm Girth, and Body Lift. The second year the Capacity of the Lungs was added, and for the last five years, the Finger Reach, and the Chest Expansion, and for the last two years the Comparative Strength of the two hands. . . .

In athletic sports, rowing, baseball and football, and college games generally, this Department has ever given encouraging though not inciting words. We have encouraged home sports and games, and not stimulated the young men to enter into the hot and violent contests with professional gamesters. With the example of the oldest and largest colleges, and with the comity, rivalry, and good fellowship so largely existing, it is but natural that our college should desire to compare its muscle and wind with those in similar positions. We have had several trials and been as successful as we ought to expect with smaller numbers to select from, and some disadvantages incident to our geographical location.

In our home athletic sports we have taken a deeper interest. The annual and semiannual field days have always been well attended, both by contestants and spectators, and we have a good record. And the preparation and participation in these contests, this Department has ever regarded as a full equivalent for the required Gymnasium exercises, as they are always undertaken under leaders or directors, who have carried them through with systematic and thorough drill. And for the training of all the students, it seems clear that there are a certain number who must have these hard and severe tests in developing and maintaining their powers up to their best possibilities.

Besides the regular class exercises, as required, and the heavy work as encouraged and allowed, there are always a few who need special exercise and advice. These are attended to as well as our limited apparatus will allow. But in the coming near future when we can see an enlarged and well-equipped health building, we may then hope for advanced hygienic development in the few who require special training to secure the normal and healthful development.

All of which is respectfully submitted,
EDWARD HITCHCOCK
Amherst College, Amherst, Mass.
Barrett Gymnasium, June 27, 1881

2

The Sargent System of Physical Education *

DUDLEY ALLEN SARGENT, M.D.

Dr. Dudley Allen Sargent, one of the most influential of the early leaders in physical education, was instrumental in merging the early systems of physical education into an American program of physical education. Born in Belfast, Maine, in 1849, Dr. Sargent acquired an early interest in gymnastics and became a gymnast and trapeze artist with a circus; his special act was to swing on a trapeze while seated in a rocking chair balanced delicately on a trapeze bar. At the age of twenty he became Director of the Gymnasium at Bowdoin College while completing his undergraduate education. Later he founded the Department of Physical Training at Yale University and completed the M.D. degree there in 1878. In 1879 he was appointed the Director and Assistant Professor of Physical Training at the Harvard University Hemenway Gymnasium. He organized the Sanatory Gymnasium in Cambridge, Massachusetts, in 1881, which later became the Sargent School of Physical Education. Dr. Sargent was a founder and president for five years of the American Association for the Advancement of Physical Education, now the AAHPER. In addition he was president of the College Physical Education Association. At the Boston Conference of 1889 Dr. Sargent was one of the principal speakers; he discussed his program of physical education at Harvard University and closed by stating that an American program of physical education should comprise "the strength-giving qualities of the German gymnasium, the active and energetic properties of the English sports, the grace and suppleness acquired from the French calisthenics, and the beautiful poise and mechanical precision of the Swedish free movements, all regulated, systematized, and adapted to our peculiar needs and institutions." Excerpts from this paper are printed below.

. . . In the fall of 1869 I accepted a position as Director of the Gymnasium at Bowdoin College, Brunswick, Me. At that time I began to make measurements of students, and to observe the differences in size,

* D. A. Sargent, "The System of Physical Training at the Hemenway Gymnasium," *Physical Training: A Full Report of the Papers and Discussion of the Conference Held in Boston in November, 1889* (Boston, Press of George H. Ellis, 141 Franklin Street, 1890), pp. 62–76.

strength, and development that characterized different habits and conditions of life. . . .

The conclusion that I reached was this: If actual labor will produce such good physical results in certain directions, why will not a system of exercises in the gymnasium, resembling actual labor, accomplish the same result in opposite directions, and in this way be made to supplement the deficiencies of one's occupation, and to develop him where he is weak. With this idea predominating, I began to work for its attainment in 1871. . . .

After the completion of my medical studies, in 1878, I elaborated my old system of measurements, and had the first patterns of my long-contemplated developing appliances constructed.

These consist of what are familiarly known as chest-weights, chest-expanders and developers, quarter-circles, leg-machines, finger-machines, etc., to the number of forty different pieces.

These appliances were first used in my private institution in New York City in 1878, and were placed in the Hemenway Gymnasium in 1879. It would seem that this style of apparatus met a long-felt want, for it immediately sprang into popular favor.

As it has been publicly announced that these appliances were not patented, but were given to the public for educational purposes, they were soon copied in one form or another by various manufacturers, and have since been generally introduced into the school, college, athletic club, and Young Men's Christian Association gymnasia throughout this country, and in different parts of Europe.

To what extent this style of apparatus is now used in the United States may be inferred from the fact that some of it has been put into three hundred and fifty or more institutions, representing a total membership of over one hundred thousand.

Thus it will be seen that the system to which I invite your attention is not a thing of recent growth, but one that has been undergoing a process of slow development for the past twenty years.

That you may understand what it is in its present form, as carried out at Harvard University, let me ask you to follow me through one of the physical examinations of a student, and see what we do for him. Every student who enters the University is entitled to an examination, and eighty-seven per cent of the whole number avail themselves of this privilege.

As soon as the student presents himself at the director's office (which is done by application and appointment), he is given a history blank, which he fills out, giving his birthplace, nativity of parents, occupation of father, resemblance to parents, natural heritage, general state of health, and a list of the diseases he has had, all of which information is absolutely necessary in order for the examiner to put a correct interpretation upon the observations to follow. The student is then asked to make certain tests of the muscular strength of the different parts of his body, and to try the capacity of his lungs.

He then passes into the measuring room, and has his weight, height, chest-girth, and fifty other items taken. His heart and lungs are then examined before and after exercise, and a careful record made of the condition of the skin, muscles, spine, etc., which the tape measures fail to give.

All the items taken are then plotted on a chart, made from several thousand measurements, and the examiner is then able to know the relative standing of this individual as compared with others for every dimension taken, also his deviation from symmetry and the parts which are in special need of development.

To confirm the plotting of the chart, and to awaken in the young man a genuine interest in his physique a photograph of each student desiring it is taken in three positions, and preserved for comparison with those to be taken of him later.

From the data thus procured a special order of appropriate exercises is made out for this student with specifications as to the movements and apparatus he may best use. At the present time this special order consists for most students of an illustrated handbook, in which the apparatus, the weights for it, and the times to use it are carefully prescribed, together with such suggestions as to exercise, diet, sleep, bathing, clothing, etc., as will best meet the needs of the individual under consideration.

Now I think it will be admitted by all thoughtful persons that one-half the battle for mental education has been won when you arouse in a boy a genuine love for learning. So one-half the struggle for physical training has been won when he can be induced to take a genuine interest in his bodily condition—to want to remedy his defects, and to pride himself on the purity of his skin, the firmness of his muscles, and the uprightness of his figure.

Whether the young man chooses afterwards to use the gymnasium, to run, to row, to play ball, or saw wood for the purpose of improving his physical condition matters little, provided he accomplishes that object.

The modern gymnasium, however, offers facilities for building up the body that are not excelled by any other system of exercise. The introduction of the new developing appliances has opened up the possibility of the gymnasium to thousands to whom it was formerly an institution of doubtful value. The student is no longer compelled to compete with others in the performance of feats that are distasteful to him. He can now compete with himself,—that is, with his own physical condition from week to week, and from month to month. If he is not strong enough to lift his own weight, the apparatus can be adjusted to a weight he can lift. If he is weak in the chest or the back, he can spend his time and energy in strengthening those parts without fear of strain or injury.

In fact, he can work for an hour, going from one piece of apparatus to another, keeping always within the circuit of his capacity, and adding slowly and surely to his general strength and powers of endurance. If the heart is weak, the lung capacity small, the liver sluggish, the circulation feeble, or the nervous system impaired, etc., special forms of exercise can be prescribed to meet these conditions.

Gentle running is usually advised as a constitutional exercise for all of those who can take it. This is usually severe enough to start the perspiration, and make a bath of some kind desirable. A tepid sponge or shower bath is generally advised; and in my opinion, the bath which regularly follows the exercise at the gymnasium, and the habit of bathing established thereby, is almost as valuable as the exercise itself.

After a period of six months or more, the student returns again to the Director's office and has another examination, in order to ascertain what improvement he has made and to receive any new suggestions.

This, in brief, is the educational part of the system of physical training carried on at the Hemenway Gymnasium.

The system of athletics and heavy gymnastics carried on at the college during term time the authorities are in no way responsible for. These are managed by the students themselves through their different athletic organizations. The faculty exercise a conservative influence, in requiring every man to be examined and get a certificate from the Director of the Gymnasium before he can enter as a competitor in athletic contests. By taking this precaution, many a student, whose zeal for athletics was in excess of his ability, has been undoubtedly saved from injury, and the character of the sport has been maintained. The authorities believe that athletic sports, kept within bounds and carefully regulated, are a valuable adjunct to our system of physical training, and they are constantly making endeavors to increase Harvard facilities in this direction.

Some of us believe it is more to the credit of a university to have one hundred men who can do a creditable performance in running, rowing, ball playing, etc., than to have one man who can break a record, or a team that can always win the championship.

The great aim of the gymnasium is to improve the physical condition of the mass of our students, and to give them as much health, strength, and stamina as possible, to enable them to perform the duties that await them after leaving college. . . .

Perhaps the most important work the University is doing in the way of physical training is at its Summer School for Teachers.

This has only been established three years, but within that time we have had one hundred and sixty-one pupils. The most of them were teachers in physical exercises at colleges and secondary schools in different parts of the country. Among the list were several physicians, thirty-two college graduates, army officers, school superintendents and principals, and many teachers and professors in other branches, who attended for their own improvement or in the interest of the institution which they represented.

The list of instructors last summer comprised seven physicians, six specialists, and seven student assistants. The theoretical work of the course comprised lectures and recitations in the Elements of Applied Anatomy and Physiology and in Personal Hygiene, also lectures and practical talks on Anthropology, Anthropometry, Physical Diagnosis, Methods of Prescribing Exercise for the Individual, Physical Exercise in the Treatment of Spinal Curvature, Testing for Normal Vision and Hearing, and Massage and its applications.

The practical work of the course consisted in Free Movements, Calisthenics, Light Gymnastics, Marching, Methods of Conducting Squad, Class, and Division Exercises, Gymnastic Games, Heavy Gymnastics, Track and Field Athletics, Physical Examinations, Practice in Measuring and the Use of Testing and Developing Appliances, Boxing, Fencing, Swimming, and Voice Training. . . .

Knowing what is desired [from physical exercise], it is an easy matter to prescribe the appropriate training. . . . There should be a better understanding of the physiology of exercise, a recognition of the supreme value of unity in development, and more information as to what constitutes the normal man for different races, ages, and conditions of life.

Until these questions are settled there will continue to be the widest difference of opinion as to the kind, amount, and place of physical training in a scheme of education. The present aspect of the subject in Europe and in this country furnishes illustrations to the point.

Germany, tired of the dull, stereotyped exercises of the Turnverein, is making a plea for sports and games; old England and our New England, perplexed with athletics run wild, are attempting to substitute a rational system of exercise for competitive sports; while France and Sweden are beginning to realize that calisthenics and free movements, though beneficial to the graces, afford little or no exercise as such. Yet these are the nations that gave us our first ideas on the subject.

What America most needs is the happy combination which the European nations are trying to effect: the strength-giving qualities of the German gymnasium, the active and energetic properties of the English sports, the grace and suppleness acquired from French calisthenics, and the beautiful poise and mechanical precision of the Swedish free movements, all regulated, systematized, and adapted to our peculiar needs and institutions. . . .

3

The Founding of the
American Physical-Education Profession *

WILLIAM GILBERT ANDERSON, M.D.

There are some men whose minds are always ahead of their time and who translate their vision into action; Dr. William Gilbert Anderson was this type of person in physical education. Born in St. Joseph, Michigan, in 1860, he attended the Boston Latin School, University of Wisconsin, and Western Reserve, where he received the M.D. degree in 1883. An astonishing facility as a tumbler and horizontal-bar performer brought him an offer to become a gymnast with the P. T. Barnum Circus; but he declined the offer to enter the teaching profession. In 1885 Dr. Anderson became Director of Physical Training at Adelphi Academy in Brooklyn and several months later founded The Brooklyn Normal School of Physical Training and The Chautauqua Summer School of Physical Education. At this time there was great controversy over the merits of the several "systems" of physical training; and he called a meeting on November 27, 1885, at Adelphi Academy to discuss the "systems" with the leading physical-education teachers of the period. At this meeting The American Society for the Advancement of Physical Education was founded, which evolved into the AAHPER. From this meeting, then, can be dated the beginnings of the present physical-education profession in America. Dr. Anderson's excellent account of the founding of the profession is printed below.

It will answer several questions, if in a brief forward I tell why the Association was formed and under what conditions it came into existence. . . . In 1883, when I was twenty-three years of age, I was called to "teach gymnastics" in a large and exclusive school in Brooklyn, N.Y. . . . I was a finished gymnast, for in those long ago days this ability was considered necessary in any teacher of "physical culture." I knew little or nothing about teaching children or young men and women. . . .

* This document comes from the following two articles: William G. Anderson, "The Early History of the American Association for Health, Physical Education and Recreation," *The Journal of Health and Physical Education*, Vol. 12 (January, 1941), pp. 3–4 and 61–62; and William G. Anderson, "The Early History of the American Association for Health, Physical Education and Recreation," *The Journal of Health and Physical Education*, Vol. 12 (March, 1941), pp. 151–153 and 200–201.

My initial shock came when the first class appeared before me in the spacious "Calisthenium." Nearly one hundred little folks. It did not take them long to find out that I was only a neophyte and needed praying for. They had a good time if the teacher did not, for the teaching and discipline were wretched. . . .

My pupils liked me and the kindergarten children often pulled me to the floor in their enthusiasm, while the boys were won over by clever apparatus work, especially on the bars and in tumbling. They wanted that kind of work and not "baby wooden dumbbell stuff." Well aware that I had much to learn, I first went to Mr. James Douglas Andrews, the teacher in the local YWCA gymnasium, for help. "What system do you teach?" I asked. "My own which I got in Scotland and England and I have no other." I visited every gymnasium near New York and Brooklyn, always watching the classes and asking the same question. The answers were identical. "I use my own system, I have no other, I'm satisfied." This criticism did not apply to the German Turners for they had a splendid system in which I had been trained in the Turnverein in Quincy, Illinois, when a boy. Feeling that I got little from these visits and interviews and strongly impressed that every man was for himself, the Turners excepted, and that there was neither agreement nor co-operation among the so-called "Americans," I wondered if we could not come together and discuss carefully the situation. . . .

I thought out a scheme that might be worthwhile so went at once to Mr. Charles Pratt, the head of the Standard Oil Company and the President of the Adelphi Academy Board of Directors. He said, "Good, go ahead." Mr. Pratt founded the Pratt Institute while I was teaching in Brooklyn at which time I was of some help to him in arranging the physical education program. . . .

One evening I was asked to act as a judge at the Athletic Meet of the members of the twenty-third regiment in Brooklyn. On the printed program of events was the name of Mr. Buermeyer. I had never met this gentleman, so went to Mr. George Goldie, the famous Scotch Athlete and gymnast, who was also a judge, and said, "Mr. Goldie, who is Mr. Buermeyer?" The canny, candid Scott eyed me severely and said, "Young man, not to know is not to be known." I learned a needed lesson even if the caustic remark of the Scott cut deep. George Goldie was then at the New York Athletic Club. Later he went to Princeton as head of the Department of Physical Education. He was one of the best friends I ever had.

In planning the call to the meeting for organization, I remembered what was said to me at the armory, so gathered about me men and women who were known and whose names carried great weight.

In 1883 Cornell University organized its Department of Physical Education and sought a Director. I was requested to meet the special committee and did. I was the guest of President Andrew D. White, and was with him in his home. I was "too young" and so was informed that Dr. Edward Hitchcock, Jr., of Amherst had been appointed. Their decision was a wise one for I was too inexperienced for such an important post.

The friendship between Dr. White and me lasted as long as he lived. When I went to Germany the first time to study the methods used in that country, Dr. White opened the doors to me, for he was the United States Ambassador to that country.

When I asked him in 1884 if he would aid me in my efforts to bring together leading physical educators in the Eastern States in order to form an Association, he replied as follows:

Ithaca, N.Y., Jan. 14th, 1884

My dear Doctor:

We shall always remember your visit here with pleasure. Hope to see you from time to time; shall always, also, be glad to co-operate with you in any efforts you may make for the spread of rational physical culture.

Very truly yours,
Andrew D. White

President White was also a member of the Board of Directors of the Brooklyn Normal School of Physical Education and of the Chautauqua Normal School of Physical Education. . . .

Returning from New York City one afternoon I sat by the Rev. Henry Ward Beecher, the eminent Divine, and with the nerve of verdant youth told him of the plan and remarked that I was acquainted with his sister Catharine's book on calisthenics for women and had a copy. In reply to my question, "Do you think the idea is worthy of your sympathy?" he said, "Surely." I had with us the best-known minister in the country.

In referring to the list of ministers and to Charles Pratt of the Standard Oil Company, a witty gentleman said, "This ought to have succeeded for it is the first time there had been such a happy blending of religion and oil."

With these influential names I wrote to Dr. Edward Hitchcock of Amherst College. He was most enthusiastic and at once joined us.

Now I felt that I could go to Dr. Dudley A. Sargent of Harvard who was the most influential or powerful man in physical education in the country. The Doctor was not overardent, but said he would give the matter consideration. He attended the gathering and put back of it his strength and ability. He should receive the credit due him for he was a tower of strength. . . . So the little craft was launched. . . .

(This begins the second article by Anderson)

In response to invitations from William G. Anderson, M.D. of the Adelphi Academy, about sixty representatives of various educational institutions and friends of Physical Culture assembled at Adelphi Academy, Brooklyn, N.Y., November 27, 1885, at 10:00 o'clock.

Albert C. Perkins, Ph.D., the Principal, called the meeting to order, and cordially welcomed his guests as colaborers in a department of service of the highest importance. Physical Education, he said, was vitally related to the intellectual and moral well-being of society. He congratulated them on the progress made since he entered college thirty years ago, and expressed the belief that this gathering would give a wide impulse to a cause which was now commanding the attention and enlisting the sympathies of all intelligent men.

Professor Edward Hitchcock, M.D., of Amherst College, was then introduced as chairman. He simply remarked that the work before us was that of fraternal conference, and that perhaps a permanent organization might be the outcome of it. He suggested the choice of a temporary secretary, and Mr. Henry S. Anderson was chosen. The roll was then read and completed.

A motion was offered that a committee on Permanent Organization be appointed to consider the advisability of forming an Association, and if such be regarded feasible, to report a plan of operations. Carried. The chair appointed the following: William G. Anderson, M.D., Adelphi Academy; Rev. E. P. Thwing, Ph.D., President New York Academy of Anthropology; J. W. Seaver, M.D., Yale College, New Haven, Connecticut; Miss C. C. Ladd, Bryn Mawr College, Pa.; and C. M. McIntire, Jr., M.D., Easton, Pa.

The report was made the first business of the afternoon session. The list of topics was read by the Secretary: (1) Methods of Teaching; (2) What is the best system of Measurement?; (3) German, English, and American systems compared; (4) Normal Classes; (5) Manufacture of Apparatus; and (6) A Permanent Organization. The first theme was taken up, and voluntary remarks were requested.

Rev. Dr. Thwing said: Physical Education has a literature. Its history is an engaging feature. This study is related to Pulpit and Forensic Oratory, the Plastic Anatomy, to Music, to Histrionic and Mimetic Art; to Sanitary Science, Anthropology; and so to Ethics. For these reasons it deserves a thorough, scholarly consideration. The Greeks saw in one's gait a key to character. His "walk and conversation," or life, had more than an accidental connection. I was reading Plato this morning. He says that a good soul improves the body, and that he is but a polished clown who takes no interest in gymnastics. . . . We may approach the study of Physical Education from many points; that of the drill master, the artist, actor, the athlete, the musician, the physician, or the psychologist. The utterances of representative men here today deserve a permanent record for the perusal of those who are not present. Many years of experience in college and seminary instruction have deepened my conviction of the vital importance of the themes we are now to discuss.

Dr. J. W. Seaver of Yale College, said, in substance: My method is both didactic and practical. The lectures are informal and illustrative; the drill is made prominent. Attendance three evenings a week is required. Scientific and academic departments are represented. Personal defects in gait, posture, and motion are pointed out. From club swinging and other simple exercises the pupil is judiciously advanced to more laborious work. No serious accidents have ever occurred. The relation of physical to mental development is continuously insisted upon.

The Chairman [Dr. Edward Hitchcock] as a Nester among us, was called upon. He remarked, that he had no pet plan, no ideal method. However, during the twenty-five years he had been at Amherst, he had diligently tabulated statistics. He advised a medical examination of each student on entrance, as to his physical condition, his defects or aptitudes, and a strict systematic training. Yet military precision cannot be insisted on. . . .

William Blaikie, Esq. of the New York bar followed. He extolled this method of individual supervision as a vital coefficient, whether in the college or primary school. The time is come for a broad basis to be laid for the study, which shall continue all elements of demonstrated success. How shall we make it less a drudgery? . . . Any judicious system is valuable. I am not a champion of any one method. He closed with reference to Gladstone's well-preserved health.

Prof. Chas. L. Bristol of Poughkeepsie referred to his recent observation of English students on the cricket field. England appears to me, he said, to be monumental. The people are proud of their country and proud of us. Politically they seem rapidly tending to a strong centralized government. Educationally, they are, I think, ahead of us.

Dr. Sargent of Harvard College asked, whom are we to teach? where are we to teach? what are we to teach? A college is not a YMCA. Local conditions must modify. Economy of time is to be sought in each case. Medical examination is desirable. Generous pecuniary support should be guaranteed to this department.

Dr. W. L. Savage of St. Peter's Hospital, Brooklyn, spoke of ill-ventilated school houses and weary children, and of the relief which open windows and physical exercise even for sixty seconds would bring the pupils.

Prof. H. C. Barrett of Philadelphia urged that the same personal supervision of students be had that physicians have of their patients.

Mr. T. J. Turner of Princeton, N.J., spoke of the adaption of weights to varying muscular strength.

Dr. Anderson gave an account of the Adelphi daily drill with music. Fifty per cent of my success is due to the pianist. Wands, bar bells and sword exercises with wooden rods are used. Reports to parents are given. Our anthropometric tables are printed in the September *Adelphian*. We stimulate a noble ambition and point, for example, to the conspicious beauty of well-developed biceps when one is seen in a bathing suit.

Prof. Koehler of West Point said that his method was a modified Swiss method. The drill master takes the applicants after the physician's examination. The men are then put into the gymnasium. Exercises are taken with military precision. . . . *Afternoon Session:* Rev. Mr. Thwing reported in behalf of the Committee that a Permanent Organization seemed desirable, and suggested the following:

PLAN OF ORGANIZATION

Name and Object: This body shall be called The Association for the Advancement of Physical Education.

Membership: The payment of one dollar shall secure membership.

Meetings: An annual meeting shall be held on the day following our National Thanksgiving unless otherwise ordered by the Council.

Officers: There shall be a President, three Vice-Presidents, a Secretary, and a Treasurer chosen annually. These six with three other members shall constitute the Council, to whom the general affairs of the Association shall be intrusted. The Council shall have authority to fill vacancies in their number, which may occur between the annual sessions of the Association. They may draft a Constitution and By-Laws, if such be needed, and report the same at the next meeting.

Officers proposed: Dr. E. Hitchcock, President; Vice-Presidents, Prof. E. L. Richards, D. A. Sargent, M.D., and Miss H. C. Putnam; Secretary, W. G. Anderson, M.D.; Treasurer, Prof. J. D. Andrews; Additional members of the Council, Prof. Koehler, Charles McIntire, Jr., M.D., and William Blaikie, Esq.

The report was unanimously adopted, and the Board of Officers declared elected. . . . The Association adjourned at 3:15 P.M. to meet in the same place on the last Friday in November, 1886.

4

A Nineteenth-Century View of
Physical Education *

EDWARD MUSSEY HARTWELL, Ph.D., M.D.

An outstanding leader of the physical-education profession in the late
nineteenth century was Dr. Edward Mussey Hartwell, biologist and
physician. His philosophy of physical education and scholarly contributions to the literature of the field had a profound influence on the making
of American physical education. Following his undergraduate career at
Amherst College, where he was captain of his class in the gymnasium and
a member of the crew, he completed the Ph.D. degree in biology at Johns
Hopkins University in 1881 and the M.D. degree at Miami Medical College in Cincinnati in 1892. An interest in physical training led to a position
as Associate in Physical Training and Director of the Gymnasium at Johns
Hopkins University. He combined the position with extensive travel in
Europe to study German and Swedish gymnastics. In 1890, at a time
when interest in Swedish gymnastics was at its height in the Boston area,
Dr. Hartwell was appointed Director of Physical Training for the Boston
Public School System. The year before, his unique educational background resulted in his selection as the keynote speaker at the now famous
Boston Conference in November of 1889. His address, printed below with
some deletions, helped to set the tone of discussion and evaluation in
physical education at this critical period in the history of American physical education. Dr. Hartwell contended that a system of physical training
to be worthwhile must provide first of all and continuously for training
and exercising the central or fundamental muscles of the body. For this
purpose he preferred German and Swedish gymnastics to the athletic
sports favored in England.

In ordinary speech it is convenient to speak of moral, mental, and
physical training as if they had little or nothing in common; though,
strictly speaking, the principles which underlie each are practically the
same. My main contention in regard to the nature of physical training
is, that bodily exercise constitutes so considerable and necessary an element in all human training that physical training is entitled to be recog-

* Edward Mussey Hartwell, "The Nature of Physical Training, and the Best Means
of Securing Its Ends," *Physical Training*, pp. 5–22.

nized and provided for as an integral and indispensable factor in the education of all children and youth.

The aim of any and all human training is to induce faculty, to develop power. As the means of developing power, certain actions are selected, taught, and practiced as exercises; and power when developed takes the form of some action or exercise due to muscular contractions. Viewed thus, muscular exercise is at once a means and an end of mental and moral, as well as of physical training; since without bodily actions we have no means of giving expression to mental power, artistic feeling, or spiritual insight. Without muscular tissue we cannot live or move. . . .

The arm of the blacksmith has been brought into play so often, by writers and talkers upon exercise, that every school boy credits the statement that muscles grow larger, harder, and stronger when duly exercised, and become weak, flabby, and wasted if they are suffered or forced to remain inactive. It is less obvious, though it can hardly be doubted, that use and disuse work similar effects in the case of nerve cells and fibers, both sensory and motor. There is abundant evidence, though much of it is of the negative sort, to show that the exercise of the muscles not only reacts upon the nerves and centers with which they are connected, in such wise as to enhance the power and ease with which they originate and transmit stimuli, but that it also leads to an increase in the size, number, and elaboraion of their parts. . . .

We have seen that the effects of exercise upon a single muscle are chiefly two. On the one hand, there results a general condition which may be termed the heightened health of the neuromuscular machine, which state of health involves the attainment and maintenance of a normal degree of size, strength, and working power in its structural parts; and on the other hand, a more complex and special effect, viz., the acquisition or organization by its neural parts, of proper habits as regards the origination, transmission, and regulation of stimuli. The ends of exercise may then be characterized as the promotion of health and the acquisition of correct habits of action. The first is a hygienic end, while the second is a distinctly educational end. It matters not whether we consider a single muscle, which admits of only a single limited motion, or a group of muscles, or the communal structure we call the human body, or a class of school children, or a regiment of soldiers; the ends of exercise in each case are the same and can only be attained by a combination of hygienic and educational measures.

The main field of education is, then, the nervous system, and the especial province of physical training is found in its accessory portions. The principles of all forms of physical training, however various and divergent their special ends may be, are based upon the power of the nervous system to receive impressions and register them or their effects —in other words, upon its ability to memorize the part it has played in acquired movements, and on occasions to recall and revive such movements.

It is coming to be clearly recognized that the function of our public and preparatory schools and colleges is not to fit their scholars to engage as specialists in either intellectual, commercial, or industrial pursuits. The same rule holds good as to the kind, or, rather, degree of physical training which should be aimed at in our schools and colleges. It is not their business to train up ball players, carpenters, clerks, or professionals of any kind. General bodily training is the kind demanded; but training so general that it is vaguely, or spasmodically, or halfheartedly carried out, or worse still, that is left to run itself in accordance with the whim or frenzy of the persons to be trained, will surely and deservedly fall short of success. Intelligence, system, organization, funds, and patience are just as imperatively required in physical training as in the training of engineers, musicians, or philologians.

The law of the evolution of the nervous system seems to me to furnish a sufficient criterion by which to estimate the worth or success of any scheme or system of physical training. Any system that does not provide first of all and continuously for the training and exercise of the central or fundamental groups of muscles will fail utterly in securing either the hygienic or the educational end of exercise; and any system which substitutes training of the accessory neuromuscular mechanisms for that of the fundamental ones, or which exacts undue work of undeveloped accessory centers, or attempts their training out of the proper order of their ripening, is bound to contribute more toward the promotion of brain forcing than towards its prevention.

The most fundamental mechanisms of the trunk are those which are concerned in the movements of respiration and of circulation. They are quite fully organized at birth; but the need for their exercise ceases only with the life of the organism. The centers which represent the muscles by means of which the trunk is kept erect and balanced upon the pelvis are accessory, if compared with those mentioned above, but are fundamental as compared with those which represent the muscles of locomotion. The muscles of the trunk are called into fuller and more frequent play as soon as the child ceases to go on all fours, and it must then learn, after a fashion, which may exigently demand correction or further training later on, to co-ordinate the movements of its limbs with those of its trunk. The child learns to flex its thigh upon the body, the leg upon the thigh, and to elevate the heel from the ground considerable earlier than it can raise its toes, so that the foot shall swing clear of the ground and it be enabled to begin another step. What folly it would be to try to teach a toddling infant to run, or jump, or dance.

Similarly the training of the hand and fingers should not only be preceded, but accompanied by the exercise of the muscles of the forearm, arm, shoulder, and trunk. You shall not gather ripe manual cunning from a limb whose trunk attachments are undersized, untrained, or deformed. This fact points to the danger of exacting genuine manual training from young pupils, especially if it be divorced from its proper adjuvant and corrective general gymnastics. It is simply impossible to make any technical drill, such as wood turning, penmanship, singing, piano exercises, or even the manual of arms, meet the proper ends of bodily education either for children, adolescents, or adults. Technical training, appealing as it does to the most accessory mechanisms, should be grounded on general hygienic and educational training, should not be pushed at too early a stage, and should be left, where it belongs, in the hands of special trainers.

Pastimes, out-of-door sports, and systematic gymnastics are the forms of exercise which yield the best results in the physical training of school children and college students. The plays of the kindergarten, the athletic sports to which British and American youth are so devoted, and the systematic gymnastics of the Swedes and Germans have all developed from one germ, from healthful play, that is; the vital energy of this germ is found in the universal and ineradicable impulse of all healthy children to play. The children of every generation, no matter how prim, or sour, or ascetic their parents may be, are always playing animals. That it is so is a most fortunate thing for the race; were it not so, the victims of war, pestilence, and education, and of that voracious monster that men call business, would be vastly more numerous than they are.

In the athletic sports of young men we see the highest and fullest expression of the play instinct. The essential difference between athletics and gymnastics is one of aim. The aim of athletics, unless of the illegitimate professional sort, is pleasurable activity for the sake of recreation; that of gymnastics is discipline or training for pleasure, health, and skill. We have but to compare the aims, methods, and results of each, and to call to mind the characteristics of the nations which have affected athletics on the one hand and gymnastics on the other, to perceive that gymnastics are more highly developed and present more features of educational value. Gymnastics, as compared with athletics are more comprehensive in their aims, more formal, elaborate, and systematic in their methods, and are productive of more solid and considerable results.

I have no disposition to disparage athletic sports. I would that they were more general and better regulated than they are in our country. I believe that they are valuable as a means of recreation, that they conduce to bodily growth and improvement, and that their moral effects are of value, since they call for self-subordination, public spirit, and co-operative effort, and serve to reveal the dominant characteristics and tendencies, as regards the temper, disposition, and force of will of those engaged in them. But they bear so indelibly the marks of their childish origin; they are so crude and unspecialized as to their methods as to render them inadequate for the purposes of a thorough-going and broad system of bodily education. It is well to promote them, and it is becoming increasingly necessary to regulate them; but it is unwise and short-sighted to consider them as constituting anything more than a single stage in the best bodily training.

Gymnastics have been most popular and general among the most highly trained nations, such as the Greeks of old and the Germans of today. The most athletic, and, at the same time, one of the most ill-trained of modern nations, is the British. I mean simply this, that an Englishman believes, and acts upon the belief, that you come to do a thing right by doing it, and not by first learning to do it right and then doing it; whereas, the Germans leave little or nothing to the rule of thumb, not even in bodily education. German gymnastics embrace three well-marked fields or departments: viz., popular gymnastics, school gymnastics, and military gymnastics. The organization of the last two departments is maintained and controlled by the government for strictly educational purposes; while the Turnvereine, as the popular gymnastic societies are called, are voluntary associations of a social and semieducational but wholly popular and patriotic character. The fondness of the German people for gymnastics is as marked a national trait as is the liking of the British for athletic sports. The German system of gymnastics has been most highly developed in Prussia, where not far from a fifth of the population is undergoing systematic physical training at the present time, under the combined agencies of the schools, the army, and the Turnverein. In Switzerland and in Norway and Sweden, you will find school and military gymnastics, especially in Sweden, quite as fully developed as in Germany, and popular gymnastics not so much so. . . .

My plea is, that inasmuch as physical training enters of necessity into the training of every school child, every apprentice, every recruit, those who undertake to train scholars or craftsmen, artists, or authors, should see to it that mental training should not be pursued to the neglect or detriment of bodily training, that each kind of training should be given its proper place in the compulsory curriculum of our public schools, and that bodily training should be given in appropriately fitted places, by specially trained and well-qualified teachers in a systematic, well-ordered, and rational way.

It is not within the scope of this paper to set forth the lessons to be learned from the best European systems of physical training, or to show how fragmentary and defective our so-called American systems have been and are; but I may remark, in passing, that a careful study of the German and Swedish systems of school gymnastics will be found an indispensible preliminary step for those who propose to organize a natural, rational, safe, and effective system of American physical education.

The price of wisdom may be beyond that of rubies; but the price of health, which Plato conceived to be the natural order and governance of one another, in the parts of the body, its price is above that of either gems or wisdom.

The German System of Gymnastics *

HENRICH METZNER

Mr. Henrich Metzner of the New York German Turnverein prepared this paper for the Boston Conference of 1889, which was held at the Massachusetts Institute of Technology. In Mr. Metzner's absence the paper was read by Carl Eberhard, who was Superintendent of the Boston Athletic Club Gymnasium. In 1890 Dr. Edward M. Hartwell stated that the Boston Conference of 1889 was "the most important conference ever held in physical education" in America. It proved to be, he said, the climax of the Battle of the Systems. At the time of this Conference German gymnastics were the most widespread program of physical education in the United States. The German turners were proclaiming the need to introduce German gymnastics into all American public schools and colleges. The program, they said, was the best system of physical education yet devised for it was "based upon the knowledge of the human body, its diverse organs, their relative functions, and of the laws of anatomy and physiology." The paper prepared by Mr. Metzner, which is printed below, discussed the values and techniques of the German system of gymnastics and outlined its distinctive features.

The desire to improve or to attain a higher standard in culture and civilization, natural to almost every human being, is the cause of all education; its aim is the perfection of mankind, and its means are the gradual development of all faculties mental and physical, by instruction, example, and exercise. Education should therefore strive to avoid a partial or one-sided development by preferring either body or mind at the expense of the other, or to strain any one faculty to great proficiency and thus destroy and disturb the harmonious activity and cooperation of both mind and body.

This maxim, however old and often demonstrated, has not yet gained that public recognition which is necessary to secure its practical application in the schools of this country.

As gymnastic exercises, we denote all bodily exercises and movements produced by the controllable muscles with consciousness and intention,

* Henrich Metzner, "The German System of Gymnastics," *Physical Training*, pp. 23–28.

for the purpose of developing all bodily faculties in an agreeable manner, and at the same time of bringing out all those qualities which are the natural result of health and strength: namely, courage, self-reliance, and joyfulness. A gymnastic system we may call the scientific combination of the gymnastic exercises, based on physiological laws, their classification, and the instruction of their practical application. A method is the application suiting the different wants as to sex, age, bodily condition, and health. The system is based upon the knowledge of the human body, its diverse organs, their relative functions, and of the laws of anatomy and physiology. The method is the result of practical experience.

The German system of gymnastics ranks high among all the different systems known. It is not an experience of late years, like so many others which have been put forward with great promises and pretensions by their inventors, in order to meet the want of bodily training in our present school education, which, however, have been laid aside again after a short trial on account of their insufficiency. The German system has been diligently built up during almost a century by men of science, especially physicians, physiologists, and pedagogues of high reputation. It is in practical use since that time, and is today in vogue in many European countries, in a more or less modified form: in the army, as military gymnastics; in the education of the youth, as school gymnastics; in the halls of the German turners, as popular gymnastics. It is practised in classes by hundreds at the same time, as well as by single individuals as home exercises.

The German system embraces all the different branches of gymnastics: exercises with apparatus, light gymnastics or calisthenics, and also all those exercises known as outdoor sports, as running, leaping, jumping, throwing the stone and the use of all hand apparatus, as wands, dumbbells, and clubs. The German system has three marked features which no other system can claim in so predominant a manner.

It aims at general physical culture, and not at the culture of one special branch. Therefore it declines the development of a certain organ or faculty at the expense of others. In regard to this we may call attention to the fact that all who have gone through a regular course of exercises in accord with this system have been thoroughly developed, and rank as high in proficiency as any person educated by another system. The contests among the turners are thus arranged that exercises in all the different branches must be performed. This is also the case when testing scholars in regard to their proficiency. The numbers gained, added together, decide the grade of development. The strife for specialties is even not permitted, and a partial or one-sided development is therefore unknown. Yet this does not prevent individual skill and inclination from bringing about a greater result in a certain branch; this result, however, is not gained by a loss or lack in any other branch.

It allows, or rather, induces the exercises in classes. The classes are selected by a careful investigation as to strength, ability, age, etc., and for that reason it suits as well those who practise merely for physical development as those who aim at a proficiency of a higher grade. The exercises in classes are a source of endless pleasure, refreshment of mind, and joyfulness not only to children, but even to adults. They are furthermore an inducement for promotion and the ambitious desire to keep step with other scholars. They act as a stimulant for greater exertion. It is an undeniable truth that all those who have continually practised in a German gymnasium, or in a school in which the German system of gymnastics had been introduced, acknowledge that the hours spent there count among the happiest of their childhood or manhood. The variety and great number of exercises of the German system and their scientific arrangement allow new and indefinite combinations. The teacher can always select a certain number of exercises suitable for his class which are as agreeable as instructive and interesting to everyone of the classmates. Not only the body, but also the mind is kept in a wholesome and refreshing activity which will keep away all weariness and tediousness which are so often found in other systems. The class exercises of the German system allow also the instruction of a large number at the same time, providing sufficient room is at hand.

The instruction begins with the most simple and easy movements and proceeds gradually to a higher degree. All fear of danger or harm to the body is a priori excluded. The apparatus used in school practice is not at all complicated or expensive. A number of climbing poles, ladders, and some light apparatus for the high and long leap are sufficient. They may even be omitted altogether if the necessary room for such could not be provided for. In this case, however, we cannot call the training a complete one, as the aim of training is not only the achievement of a development of muscles, limbs, and organs, but also the achievement of courage and self-reliance. It is a fact that many a man or woman could have avoided danger or saved their lives had they been courageous or resolute enough to risk a leap or to take hold of a ladder in a moment of need.

The great variety of useful exercises that may be made with the above-named apparatus, together with the utilization of the almost endless variety of simple and complicated free exercises, with or without the common hand apparatus, as wands, dumbbells, clubs, etc., which may be executed in the schoolroom, bring about as satisfactory results as any other system. In addition to this we may proudly assert that its scientific and educational value has met with approval wherever it was allowed a fair trial. And we also may assert that no other system has so large a variety of exercises and combinations as this. . . . it is more qualified for introduction wherever gymnastic exercises are wanted. . . .

The German system is not in vogue only in the halls of the turners and in their schools. It has already gained its ground in some of the colleges and athletic clubs, in private and in public schools, where teachers educated in the seminary of the North American Turnerbund act as instructors.

The German system does not claim to have any special exercise of its own, or to be the sole proprietor of any that no other system may also produce. But it may properly claim that it has correctly and practically arranged the gymnastic material for the use of anyone who seeks health, strength, or refreshment of mind and body.

In the German gymnasia and schools the lessons begin regularly with a series of free and order exercises. Every scholar has to participate in them. The rhythmical order in which they are produced calls forth absolute attention, and allows no backwardness. They impress on each a feeling of responsibility toward his associates. The mistakes or errors, or an insufficient execution of any one, injures the good impression of the whole, and thus tends to greater carefulness and prevents negligence on the part of the scholar.

Class exercises on apparatus follow the free exercises. A change of apparatus takes place, and then the lesson ends with some exercises left to individual inclination. The latter, however, are limited to a short time according to the ability of the scholars, or may be prohibited altogether to beginners. Thus under the eye and control of the teacher a scene of activity and liveliness is exhibited, which the educator will look upon with satisfaction and delight.

In consideration of the above-stated facts a careful examination and a fair trial of the German system of gymnastics, free of all prejudice, may properly be demanded when the question is practically to be decided which of the different systems is best apt to be adopted in the programme of our public schools. The German system has not been influenced by any other. Since the days of Guts-Muths, Jahn, and Eiselen [Ernst Eiselen, Jahn's disciple and aid], the founders of German gymnastics, and Adolph Spiess, the founder of the elaborate structure of school gymnastics, it has had material enough to give freely from its wealth to other systems, and many of the latter boast features of German origin. May the decision of the question be based on a fair and close examination. Neither this paper, which states but a few points of merit of the German system, nor a short exhibition of exercises by scholars is sufficient to show the educational value of it.

But whatever the result of this agitation may be, let us hope that wise and cautious observation and study, uninfluenced by prejudgment or prejudice, will bring about the decision. . . .

6

The Chief Characteristics
of the Swedish System of Gymnastics *

BARON NILS POSSE, M.G.

The first important interest displayed in Swedish gymnastics in America was in Boston in 1888 when Baron Nils Posse, Mrs. Mary Hemenway (Boston philanthropist) and Miss Amy Morris Homans developed a program of Swedish gymnastics for the Boston Public School System. Baron Nils Posse was born of Swedish nobility in 1862 and attended the Royal Military School and the Central Institute of Gymnastics. His fondness for physical activity led him to join the Stockholm Gymnastic and Fencing Club, the Rowing Club, and the Skating Club, where he won the fancy skating championship of Sweden. In 1885 he came to the United States and settled in Boston, where he hoped to interest physicians in Swedish medical gymnastics. Mrs. Hemenway learned of his program and invited him to give a series of lessons in Swedish gymnastics to selected Boston teachers, which resulted in a physical-training program of Swedish gymnastics for the Boston Public School System in 1890. He founded the Posse Normal School of Gymnastics in Boston and the *Posse Gymnastics Journal*. A prolific writer, he was the author of many articles and books including his very well-known treatise, *The Swedish System of Educational Gymnastics*. When the Boston Conference, which was sponsored by Mrs. Hemenway, met in November of 1889, Baron Posse made one of his most important professional contributions with the address "The Chief Characteristics of the Swedish System of Gymnastics" which is printed below.

. . . The Swedish system of gymnastics, devised by P. H. Ling in the beginning of this century, was already at its birth founded upon the laws of nature and upon the laws of the human organism. Since the days of Ling the system has been much perfected and improved by Ling's followers, who have made it keep even pace with the progress in those sciences upon which it is based. For that reason the system is not altogether as antiquated as some of its antagonists would fain have the uninitiated think; and the fact that it has survived in a country where

---

* Baron Nils Posse, "The Chief Characteristics of the Swedish System of Gymnastics," *Physical Training*, pp. 42–51.

nothing is done in a superficial and irrational way ought to be a guarantee for its efficiency.

First let us consider how the exercises are selected. The exercises are chosen according to their gymnastic value, which quality depends on how the movement combines the utmost effect on the body with simplicity and beauty of performance. Only such exercises are used where local and general effects are fairly well known and proved to be needed by the body. Not only the needs of the individual, but his abilities as well are to be taken into consideration; and for that reason the teacher must know how to vary the execises according to the degree of physical culture possessed by the pupil. The movement should have its developing effects in a short time; it should be simple so that every pupil can do it fairly well; and it should have beauty of execution according to each one's ability.

In order to supply the needs of the organism and to develop the body harmoniously, the exercises have to overcome a great many tendencies to faulty growth or bad posture; and the greater or less value of a movement depends on its power to counteract or correct these tendencies. It naturally follows that the system uses no exercises which would encourage such faults (for instance, using chest-weights for beginners, etc.). If an exercise gives rise to faulty posture, it is discarded, or at least postponed till some future day when it can be correctly executed.

In accordance with the physiological truth that the first, greatest, and most extensive effect of exercise is on the respiratory organs, and that hence, during exercise, these organs must be allowed perfect freedom of motion, the Swedish method disapproves of and discards all movements which compress the chest (such as Indian club swinging), or which in any way interfere with free respiration; and the greatest attention is given to the proper development of the chest. In recognition of the fact that, to be truly strong, a man must know how to breathe well, much prominence has been given to "respiratory" exercises. "Breathe!" "Don't hold your breath!" are common exhortations in gymnasiums where this method is used.

In judging of the effects of an exercise, we think the least of the muscular development produced; for, the effect of all general exercise is to develop muscle, and this aim is reached without especially working for it. But we think all the more of the effects produced on nerves, vessels, etc., for the results in this direction can be vastly changed by varying the movements (as demonstrated in medical gymnastics); in other words, the exercises have been made to harmonize with the laws of physiology. How this is done will be understood from the description of the exercises which are contained in each lesson (to which I shall soon refer).

Measuring a man's strength, we compare the man to himself; we do not say that a man is strong because he can hold so much air, or because he can lift so many pounds, or because he can jump so high. But when he possesses a healthy, well-balanced, and well-proportioned body which his will has under good control, then he possesses physical culture, even though in the eyes of some he may seem weak as compared to others. It is this health, symmetry, and harmony we aim at in selecting the exercises; and that the Swedish method accomplishes its purpose has been too well demonstrated to leave room for doubt.

Movements are never chosen "because they look so pretty," for educational gymnastics do not aim at beauty of performance. When gymnastics do have such an aim they are called "aesthetical," and these have but little effect toward physical development. And yet we claim that when a movement is well done it is graceful as well. Some persons mistake a languid manner of motion for grace, and hence claim that the Swedish exercises "are too jerky to be graceful." It is to be remembered that all gymnastic movements are not slow, nor do they have an even velocity; there are some that can and always should be done with great and accelerating speed, and you can move quickly and yet do it gracefully. By making the component motions of movements like the arm-extensions merge into each other in a "graceful" manner, the effect of the movements is completely lost. On the other hand, if exercises like leg-elevations, backward-flexions of the trunk, etc., are done in a "jerky" manner, these movements are incorrectly executed and have lost their best effects.

Our second point for consideration is the regularity of method. In order that gymnastics be systematic there must be progression. In the Swedish method this is adhered to very strictly, so that the exercises, beginning by the very simplest, gradually become stronger and more complicated. So closely has the effect of movements on the human organism been studied, that the slightest change of position—even the turning of a hand—has its recognized influence in the progression; and it is here that the system demands the most from the teacher; without a good knowledge in this direction he becomes worse than useless. No movement is attempted unless the previous ones of the same kind have been thoroughly practised; and no exercise is used whose commencing position has not already been practised sufficiently to guarantee its correctness; for, if the commencing position is faulty, the movement cannot be rightly executed.

The Swedish method does not disapprove of chest-weights, dumbbells, and allied forms of apparatus; but through years of constant practice it leads up to them, claiming that before increasing the weight by external means, you should make a progression by prolonging the lever of the weight already present. So, for instance, a backward-flexion of the trunk with the arms extended upward and the hands holding weights must necessarily be preceded by the same movement without the weights, and that by a flexion with the hands fixed behind the neck, and still earlier with the hands on the hips, etc.

In a like manner the method prepares the way for aesthetical gymnastics, for fencing, military drill, and other forms of applied gymnastics, yet insisting that educational gymnastics form the basis of all these. This is reasonable, for unless you have learned to control the involuntary co-ordination of motion, which is the cause of "faults" in gymnastics, you will hardly be able to produce the great voluntary co-ordination required in all forms of advanced gymnastics.

Now, when you are to put this progression into practise, you will not feel as if groping in the dark; for, in this method, the movements have been thoroughly systematized and included under distinctive headings, where there is no more a jumble, but where the rules of progression can be well carried through by a teacher familiar with the theory of gymnastics. After years of practical investigation it was found that if, in every lesson, the exercises followed each other in a certain, comparatively unchanging order, the movements could be made stronger; they could be given more duration; ill results could be completely prevented; and hence the good effects became all the more pronounced. For that reason all movements were divided into classes, and this order was made the basis for the classification. . . .

In addition to the free-standing movements, each class contains numberless exercises on apparatus, and supplies a sufficient number to form a progression from early infancy to well-developed manhood—through all the grades in school and college, and in afterlife as well.

The third point in which the Swedish system differs from the majority of others is in the method of applying the exercises.

The movements are applied to words of command, this being the only method enabling the pupil to concentrate his mind on one thing at a time, that thing being his own movement. This is in accordance with the definition of gymnastic movement, which tells us that, unless a movement is done with full volition, it ceases to be gymnastic. In those methods which use imitation, memorizing, etc., the movements become mechanical, the pupil dividing his attention between himself and something outside him, *i.e.* they cease to be gymnastic. Objections have been raised to using words of command, because "it is too tiresome," "too soldier-like," etc. To this we can answer, that to get the full recreation and rest out of exercise we should put our whole mind into it, this being much less tiresome than to exercise while we think of something else. On the one hand we have the theory of a small minority of antagonists, that gymnastics without music do not give enough recreation, especially to children, because there is not enough exhilaration in such exercises; on the other hand we have the statement of a large majority of children and others who have tried gymnastics to music as well as to words of command, the children saying that there is "much more fun" in the latter, and the adults that there is "much more to them." As for the second objection, we claim that discipline is necessary not only for a soldier but for everybody, if we are to have any control whatsoever over ourselves; and hence discipline should form a part of everybody's education. Words of command have other advantages. They teach the pupil to think quickly, to act as quickly, and to do a thing in the shortest possible time. This is no little gain in the present age of hurry and competition. Besides, the use of commands enables the teacher always to keep his class "in hand"; it becomes easier for him not only to teach but to correct as well.

The Swedish method disapproves utterly of the use of music, for the very simple reason that but few gymnastic movements are rhythmical, and cannot be made to be so without sacrificing the movement. On the other hand, every gymnastic movement has a rhythm of its own, which, however, distinctly differs from the rhythm of music. If music were to be used, its rhythm would have to change at every motion. . . . Besides when exercising to music, the pupil will be found to pay more attention to the rhythm of the music than to the form of the movement (if we presume that the latter could be made rhythmical), and we get the same result as in all cases where work is done with divided attention—one of the things has to be sacrificed for the other.

From the above it will be seen that the system is rational, since it seeks a reason for everything that it uses or adopts: it makes theory and practice harmonize. But it is practical as well; for it does not rely on elaborate apparatus for existence, since the exercises, not the apparatus, constitute the system. The movements can be taken anywhere where there is sufficient floor-space to stand on and sufficient oxygen in the air. On the other hand, though the system prefers its own apparatus, the exercises can be most easily adapted to apparatus belonging to other systems, or to such simple means as ordinary chairs and desks, or other furniture. Though apparatus is desirable, it is not absolutely necessary for good physical development, especially in gymnastics for children.

Whatever its deficiencies, the system has not only survived on its own merits, in spite of the close scrutiny to which it has been subjected by gymnastically learned men all over the world, but it has finally been adopted in every country where its principles have been thoroughly tested, even conservative England having at last yielded.

Before closing, I take occasion to warn you against confounding Swedish Educational Gymnastics with Medical Gymnastics, commonly known as "Swedish Movement Cure"; . . . the two are entirely different, not only as to their purposes, but in the exercises used as well.

Should Physical Education Be a
Required Subject? *

DUDLEY ALLEN SARGENT, M.D.

(For a biographical sketch of Dr. Dudley Allen Sargent, including his professional contributions to physical education, scc Document 2.) The reasons why a physical-education program should be required in schools and colleges, as seen by Dr. Sargent, are printed below.

. . . Is it not time that more constructive work should be done in the way of increasing our mental and physical vigor, quickening the senses, sharpening the intellect, and augmenting as far as possible vitality and the natural powers of resistance? In other words, in the terms of the subject assigned to me, "Does not physical training in view of its effect on the intellectual and will as well as on the body, deserve to become a compulsory subject in school and college and to receive corresponding credit in the system of marking?" . . .

Our organic functions are molding our bodies and determining our constitutions and our temperaments and working on our wills and characters. Through the influence of the blood, muscles, and nerves the complex mechanism which we term the body is unified. This absolute unity of the body, this condition in which the part everywhere works in the whole and the whole in every part, is becoming more and more apparent to the educational psychologist.

. . . According to the biologist the brain has been evolved for the purpose of guiding and controlling the movements of the body through the actions of the muscles. How is this guiding and controlling power developed? The earliest movements of the child are the reflex, instinctive, and impulsive. It does not will to move its arms and legs—it simply moves them in response to the stimuli playing upon its senses from without. Later, if you place your finger in the child's hand the hand will grasp it; put a glass stopper in its mouth and the child will suck it; exert a little upward pressure on its feet and it will extend its legs.

---

* Dr. Dudley A. Sargent, "Physical Training as a Compulsory Subject," *The School Review*, Vol. 16 (January, 1908), pp. 42–55.

The eyes will follow a light, the head turns in the direction of a sound, and every sensation will be followed by a motor impulse. When the infant become a child, toss a rubber ball to it to catch. The ball will go through its hand and strike its body or face. The child cannot will to catch the ball because it cannot act purposely or intelligently. It has no idea of what it must do to catch the ball. Here again, to quote Professor James "Before the idea can be generated, the movement must have occurred in a blind, unexpected way and left its idea behind. Reflex, instinctive or random execution of a movement must, in other words, precede its voluntary execution."

Put it still another way, we cannot do an act voluntarily unless we know what we are going to do, and we cannot know exactly what we are going to do until we have taught ourselves to do it. In more senses than one we learn by doing. The simplest movement brings about a change in the organic structure of the brain, and this change leads to more complex movements and further improvement of brain structure. Most skilled movements give more exercise to the central nervous systems than to the muscles. Movements calling for a high degree of skill, correlation of the different senses, sense discrimination, fine co-ordinations, and a rapid and responsible exercise of judgment all tend through action of the association fibers to a high degree of brain development. . . .

But how are the vigorous body and brain attained? No one familiar with the growth and development of the human body, especially with its bones, muscles, brain, nerves, and tissues, can doubt for a moment that useful activity has played the most prominent part in its upbuilding. The natural history of the muscular system alone makes clear to us that there is not a single movement capable of being performed by man which has not been performed thousands and thousands of times before by his near or remote ancestors. In the history of the bones, muscles, nerves, and other tissues of the body we read the records of his primitive acts and struggles through the ages. Who can doubt the part that walking, running, jumping, swimming, climbing, throwing, pushing, pulling, lugging, tugging, kicking, wrestling, and fighting have played in the development of the human organism? Who can question the developing influence of the great industrial epochs through which man has passed such as hunting, fishing, pastoral, and agricultural stages of his existence, and the age of metals, travel, trade, and transportage when men acted as a beast of burden? Consider the probable influence of the house industries from time immemorial and the period of the handicrafts lasting from the tenth century until the beginning of modern times. Need I say that these manifold activities have stamped their imprint upon every bone, muscle, nerve, and brain cell of the human organism, and if we would maintain it in its present integrity must we not from necessity repeat in some form or other the sensory and motor activities to which the present development is due?

Did time permit, it would be possible to show by further illustrations that even reason, judgment, and the so-called higher faculties are rooted in the mechanism. We have spoken of the influence of the bodily organs upon mental states, but mental states also influence the bodily organs. All mental states are followed by bodily changes. As the psychologists tell us "all consciousness leads to action." The action of the body upon the mind, and the reactions of mind upon body go to make up the sum of human experiences. These experiences postulate a succession of functions that have been capitalized in structure as faculty. All that we are able to do today is the result of our previous physical education given us through heredity or through our experiences in former years. It is only when we consider how helpless we would be but for such physical training as we have received through our past efforts at work or play, or when we consider that there could have been no language, no art, no music, no agriculture, manufactories, or commerce —in fact no history, without physical activity and muscle training— only then is it that we begin to realize the dignity and importance of the subject.

. . . Montesquieu said: "We receive three different kinds of education, one from our parents, another from our teachers, and another from the world." The education which we would naturally receive from our parents and home surroundings is now to a considerable extent wanting in consequence of the absence of home chores and industries, the large numbers living in city tenements and apartments, and other great changes that have taken place in the family life. The education that the world gives to most of us is, in consequence of the division of labor, narrowed to the smallest fraction of a trade or vocation, where the physical and mental efforts required, though often intense, are not varied enough to keep body and mind from deteriorating. Hence the cry of shattered nerves, heart failure, and broken constitutions.

. . . No nation has ever attained intellectual greatness that has not first laid the foundation in the physical training of their youth. If a requirement of physical fitness and efficiency is not introduced and maintained in our preparatory schools and colleges we shall have a continuance of the conditions that prevail today where one class of pupils carries bodily training in athletics to excess, a few exhaust their vitality through excessive mental application, while the largest class does not get enough bodily training to keep in good physical condition, or to permit the realization of half their mental and physical possibilities. This is the inevitable result where body and mind are thought to have separate interest and are made to antagonize each other. This course would seem to put a premium upon the student neglecting his body in hopes of advancing his mental and moral efficiency, as did the monks and philosophers of old. We now know that such a course in the long run is suicidal, and the institution that encourages it by failing to recognize the just claims of the body assumes a responsibility for which it should be held accountable. What we need to foster among our youth is not the spirit of competition as so many think, but the spirit of emulation that makes the highest mental and moral attainments the goal to be won, recognizing the necessity of physical efficiency to this end.

. . . From an economic point of view plays, games, free exercises, and light gymnastics would be the most serviceable in the public schools, but a wider range of exercises should be arranged for preparatory schools and colleges. With such a variety of exercises we would expect to bring about not only a harmonious development of the muscles, invigorate the heart, lungs, and other vital organs, as Huxley says, but to train the body as to make it the ready servant of the intellect and will, and enable it to do with ease and pleasure all the work that as a mechanism it is capable of. Some of the specific mental and physical qualities which would be developed by such a course would be increased powers of attention, will, concentration, accuracy, alertness, quickness of perception, perseverance, reason, judgment, forbearance, patience, obedience, self-control, loyalty to leaders, self-denial, submergence of self, grace, poise, suppleness, courage, strength, and endurance. All these mental and moral qualities may be trained and developed through the physical activities. Moreover, if much of the so-called intellectual training obtained through books was correlated with these physical activities at the same time in life when they dominate the interest of youth, much greater progress than is now realized would be made in the attainment of intellectual results. Here is a new field of research and scientific investigation. If, however, the teacher should be so unfortunate as to tell a boy that a baseball could not be curved by a pitcher, that the speed of a boat could not be hastened or retarded by the movements of a person within it, or that the human body is always lighter than the same volume of water, I am afraid that the boy's respect for science might be shattered for his daily experiences would have taught him to the contrary. I say daily experiences, but when we consider that there are boys today at Harvard who have never driven a nail, sawed or split a stick of wood, or built a fire, perhaps this assertion needs qualifying. The only field today where the mental and physical activities are correlated to any considerable extent, is in the field of athletic sports. I think I may say without fear of contradiction that these physical activities have furnished a greater opportunity for mental training through the expression of terse, vigorous English than any other subjects—primarily because the boy is interested in these matters and knows more nearly what he is talking about.

The weakness of this great athletic movement today from an educational point of view is the failure of young men to apply the teachings of the classroom to the problems that arise in connection with their sports, games, and physical exercises. Not only do they ignore the teachings of the chemical, physical, and physiological laboratories, but even the teachings of morality, ethics, and the principles of brotherly love. What has the teaching of the classroom to do with the practice on the ball field? To use an illustration which I have used before: If a student attends a course of lectures on hygiene and repeats to the professor "parrot-like" what the professor has told him, about the care of his health, the importance of physical training, etc., he receives a mark to his credit toward a diploma. If on the other hand the student is moved by the lecturer to take a systematic course of physical training which is applied hygiene, he gets no credit for it in terms by which his other school and college efforts are judged. In one case he has sat in a stuffy lecture room and improved his memory in hearing what he ought to do; in the other case he has formed correct habits of living—increased his physical and mental vigor, improved conduct and character, and made himself a better man for anything a man may be called upon to do. Does anyone question for a moment which of these two men is best prepared for life—or which one is most likely to render service to his fellow-man? Does not the same principle apply to the teaching of ethics in the classroom and the practice of ethics on the ball field? Can we reasonably expect a student to be unmindful of the importance of applied hygiene, and not become equally obtuse to the importance of applied ethics? Is not this indifference to the practice of hygiene and ethics the legitimate outcome of our faulty methods of teaching—thinking without acting, words without deeds—precepts without examples? Can anything in education be more pernicious? I do not know of any better way of correcting this evil, and unifying the aims and purposes of education, than by giving a scholastic value to every effort toward self-improvement in physical training, just as always has been done for purely mental efforts. At the present time, in many schools and colleges, it is customary to forbid students to take honors in athletics, unless they have a creditable standing in their studies. In order to be consistent this requirement should be coupled with another, i.e., that no student should be given honors in his studies unless he attained a certain grade in his gymnastics or athletics. This last requirement would insure the conscientious student against sacrificing his health in view of raising his standing in scholarship, which at the present time he is likely to do on account of his keen competition to which he is subjected.

Judging from my experience at Yale some years ago, if physical training were made a part of the school curriculum, the class that stood the highest in scholarship would invariably stand the highest in physical exercises. In order that such a requirement be fair to all classes, the grading should be based upon three factors, namely, the effort, the achievement, and the mental and physical results. In conclusion I will say that I believe such a scheme as I have described to be essentially practical, and when adopted will not only add to the physical vigor of our youth but also to their mental power and efficiency. Is not such a "consummation devoutly to be wished?"

⋈⫤⫤⋈

A New Profession? *

LUTHER HALSEY GULICK, M.D.

Of Dr. Luther Halsey Gulick, one of the foremost leaders in physical
education in the late nineteenth and early twentieth centuries, Dr. Dudley
A. Sargent once wrote: "In power of concentration, in intellectual discern-
ment, and in ability to sum up a complex situation and state it in clear
and concise terms, he had no equal among the physical educators" of his
period. Born in Honolulu of missionary parents, Luther Halsey Gulick
had travelled widely in Europe and the Orient before attending Oberlin
College, where he came under the influence of Dr. Delphine Hanna. He
began the study of physical training at the Sargent Normal School of
Physical Training in Cambridge in 1884, and five years later he completed the M.D. degree at the University of New York. Important positions followed, such as Superintendent of Physical Education at the
YMCA Training School in Springfield, Director of Physical Training for
the Public Schools of Greater New York, Director of the Department of
Child Hygiene under the Russell Sage Foundation, and Director as well
as President of the Camp Fire Girls of America. He was also President of
the American Association for the Advancement of Physical Education
(now the AAHPER), President of the Playground Association of America,
and President of the American School Hygiene Association. Commemorat-
ing his achievements are the Gulick Award, the Roberts-Gulick Award,
and the Gulick Medal. In the field of research and publications he was
editor of *Physical Training, Physical Education, American Physical Education Review,* and the *Triangle,* for which he created the "Triangle
Emblem" of the YMCA symbolizing the trinity of mind, body, and spirit.
Among the most memorable of his articles was "Physical Education: A
New Profession," in which he pointed out that physical education was a
profession in its own right, which would increasingly be recognized as a
broad, scientific, philosophic field as well as a part of education.

There seems to be a very general misapprehension, even among intelligent men, as to the nature of the work in which we are engaged. By
many it is regarded simply as a speciality in medicine; others think it

* Luther Gulick, "Physical Education: A New Profession," *Proceedings of the
American Association for the Advancement of Physical Education* (Ithaca, American
Association for the Advancement of Physical Education, 1890), pp. 59–66.

145

merely a department in athletics; others still, with more gross ideas, regard us as men who devote our time and energy to the building up of muscular tissue.

Perhaps I can best define the profession by stating its objects. It is difficult to formulate any classification that is at once logical and complete. The following, therefore, is presented, not without feelings of diffidence, as in some respects at least, it differs from any that have been hitherto presented.

I will make three grand divisions of exercises, according to their purpose: namely, Educative, Curative, and Recreative gymnastics. Hard and fast lines cannot be drawn, assigning each exercise to a particular one of these classes, as frequently it will be found that one exercise belongs to two or more classes at once, as in medicine, opium is a hypnotic, cardiac stimulent, antispasmodic, cerebral stimulant, anodyne, etc. This is a division of the objects of exercise, and not of exercises themselves. I will now take up the divisions somewhat in detail.

1. Educative Exercises, or Physical Education. We adopt the following definition for the object of educative exercises: "To lead out and train the physical powers; to prepare and fit the body for any calling or business, or for activity and usefulness in life." This may be divided as follows:

a. Muscular Strength. This includes strength of the heart and respiratory muscles, as well as the arms, legs, and body.

b. Endurance, a matter of the heart, lungs, and nervous system as well as of the extrinsic muscles.

c. Agility or quickness of action, being largely an affair of the central nervous system.

d. Muscular Control. Excellence in almost any art or trade involves accurate control or discipline of certain parts of the body. In playing the violin, a great deal is demanded in this direction; first as to the co-ordination of the fingers of the left hand, being able to place them rapidly, independently, and with absolute precision, both as to time and locality, upon the finger board of the violin, in a position that is naturally awkward; second, to be able to use the right and left arms with entire independence, the muscles of the wrist being used principally in one case, and of the fingers in the other. In piano playing there is similar training. The hands have to learn to work independently, and even the fingers independently of each other. They have to learn to act with extreme rapidity, with absolute certainty, with automatic regularity. And so on with all the musical instruments, there is a large amount of work to be done which is primarily, fundamentally, and essentially physical training.

In the trades there is a similar state of affairs. Perfect control is fundamental and is usually secured only by years of practice on the thing to be done. . . .

There are numerous departments in the trades, the arts, and daily life where the excellence of work depends largely upon physical training in some branch. Today these are manned by specialists,—specialists, not in physical training, but in the end for which the training exists. To make my meaning plainer, let me refer to the violin player again. The music teacher teaches the violin, and gives finger exercises, and a large portion of the time of the music teacher is spent, not in teaching music, but in physical training. Now, the music teacher, unless exceptionally qualified, as music teachers are not orinarily in this direction, is not as competent in physical training as a man of equal abilities would be who gave his whole time to the subject. Thus the physical-training part of learning to play the violin or piano could be done better by a man who made a speciality of physical training than by a man who was primarily a very fine musician, and who took up this physical training as an incidental matter. Flexibility of the wrist, perfect control and co-ordination of the muscles, independent action of the hands, action and quickness of the fingers, can all be gained better by other means than by mere finger exercises on the violin or piano; but in general it is not the teacher of music who is best qualified to take up this work, for the questions are primarily those of physiology rather than of music. Let each do what he can do best: physical trainer, physical training—music teacher, music and not physical training.

e. Physical Judgment. This may be called a correlative of muscular control, this the intelligence telling when and where. "It is a sort of psychic trigonometry by which the trained mind calculates the distance, position, and motion of objects." None of the important points already considered can take the place of this, nor can we get along without it. A man wishes to jump a ditch; he has no time to measure it and calculates how much muscular effort will be required to clear it, but physical judgment enables him to do all this at once. There seems to be confusion as to the difference between muscular control and physical judgment. Take a catcher behind a baseball bat; physical judgment tells him where to put his hands and the exact instant that the ball will reach them; muscular control enables him to put his hand where he chooses. One might be able to put his hand where he chose, but not know where; or he might know where without being able to place his hands there.

f. Self-Control. This may be described as the power of the mind over itself. It is the power which gives self-possession, allowing a man to act naturally in time of excitement and danger.

g. Physical Courage, that which renders a person willing to undertake, that quality which comes to one naturally, from a knowledge of his ability, gained through experience. "There is sometimes a constitutional timidity, or lack of what we may call physical faith, that has to be overcome." A presumptuous daring is not physical courage, being born usually of ignorance of the real dangers rather than a calm meeting of them.

h. Symmetry, harmonious, or all-round development of the body. The strength of a chain is represented by the weakest link, and this is not untrue of the body.

i. Grace, which is fundamentally economy of action. It differs from muscular strength and from muscular control. A man may have both these and not be graceful. Comparing grace and symmetry, grace is beauty of action, while symmetry is beauty of form.

j. Expression. In this country we do not know very much about these special exercises. The Delsarte gymnastics, perhaps, are the best example of this type, their aim being primarily to enable the body to express the thoughts, ideas, emotions of the mind in the most intelligible way to other minds through their eyes and ears, thus including much of gesture, elocution, etc.

2. We now come to the second division, Curative Exercises. It is not designed to trench upon the field of the medical profession; but it is well known that some disturbances of the system can be cured, and many prevented, by the correct use of exercise. The same is true in relation to some bodily deformities. Certain cardiac, spinal, and nervous diseases and disorders of the nutritive system are peculiarly susceptible to gymnastic treatment. I will not speak further of this branch, as its importance is already coming to be understood.

3. Recreative Exercises. There is a real and fundamental difference between recreative or play exercises and educative gymnastics. It consists primarily in the attitude of the will, and it matters little so far as this is concerned whether it has to exercise itself in confining the mind to a difficult task in arithmetic, or to keeping a fixed and sustained attention on the leader of a calisthenic drill. . . .

I wish next to speak of the opportunities that are offered for scientific work in the profession. It is hardly possible at the present day for a man to look forward to adding materially to the sum total of knowledge in any one of the older professions. A man who goes into physical education with fair abilities and preparation expects in the course of a few years to have acquired all that has been known up to his time (the scientific side of the subject is as yet young) and to add materially to the sum total of knowledge on this subject. In this respect, then, does this profession differ from others, in that it is new, and every man may expect to do that scientific work which will be not merely original with him, but original to the world. In fact, each man will have to depend to a considerable extent on the results of his own investigations, for he has not as in medicine, reliable and elaborate treatises on which to rely. The science is as yet too young to have developed them. He must expect to assist in the development of such works for the use of those who come afterward. An oak tree during the first year of its existence is susceptible to slight influences which would be entirely unfelt a few years later, even if multiplied a thousandfold. This profession has still to be defined, it has not yet crystallized, and thus it is possible to stamp it with one's own character as it will never be possible again.

. . . There are few scientific fields today which offer opportunities for the study of problems of greater value to the human race, or more fundamental in regard to its ultimate sucess, than does that of physical education. It is a factor in modern life, that is as yet unappreciated. It deals with life on a broad side, is in line with the most thorough modern physiological psychology in its appreciation of the intimate relations of body and mind, is in line with our modern conception of evolution, as it works to develop a superior race. This profession offers to its students a large and broad field for intellectual activity, involving for its fullest appreciation a profound knowledge of man through psychology, anatomy, physiology, history, and philosophy. To sum up this part of the argument, I would say that physical education offers a greater field for original work than almost any other. Second, on account of its youth and plasticity, it offers the possibility of a permanent influence that is never offered except in the youth of such profession. Third, this work is intrinsically of great value. Fourth, it offers a great field for intellectual activity.

This profession, then, differs from any that now exists. It is readily seen that it is not merely a department of medicine, which relates primarily to the prevention and cure of disease. The mere fact that a man is an excellent medical practitioner will not qualify him to take hold of educative gymnastics, although it would qualify him to understand curative gymnastics. On the other hand, the study of psychology and pedagogy will not qualify a man to take hold of curative gymnastics, although it might qualify him to understand educative exercises.

I take it that there is no other factor which is as prominent in the development of any profession as the kind of men who take upon themselves the functions of that profession. The advance of physical education will depend more upon the kind of men who take up this work as their profession, than upon any other one factor. If it is largely taken up by men of little education and small abilities, the work will never become of the greatest value, nor will it be favorably known to the general public. If however, on the contrary, men of collegiate training, philosophic minds, of broad purposes and earnest hearts, are induced to enter this field, the profession will show that it is intrinsically a broad, scientific, philosophic field, and it will be recognized by thinking men as one of the departments in education, fundamental in the upbuilding of the nation.

I have endeavored in this paper to show: First, that this is a profession, and in the rough to define its aims. Second, to show that opportunities for valuable work are abundant. Third, that great importance is to be attached to the kind of men who enter this profession.

9

The Scientific Approach in Physical Education *

THOMAS D. WOOD, M.D.

Dr. Thomas D. Wood established for the American physical-education profession the first graduate work in health and physical education, the first professorship in health education, and the first school-health program. Born in Sycamore, Illinois, in 1865, he was graduated from Oberlin College in 1888 and then completed an M.D. degree at Columbia University. His first professional position took him to Stanford University in 1891 as Director of Physical Education and College Physician. At Stanford University he established the "natural program of physical education," based upon sports and games and outdoor living, in opposition to the European and American gymnastic systems, which he considered an autocratic-response type of activity program rather than an experience in democratic behavior. From 1901–1932 Dr. Wood continued his professional career at Columbia University, first as Director and Professor of Hygiene and Physical Education and College Physician and later as Professor of Health Education. Among his many professional honors and accomplishments were these: committee chairman at the White House Conference of 1930, called by President Hoover, on the School and the Child; organizer, and chairman for some 25 years, of the Joint Committee on Health Problems in Education of the American Medical Association and the National Education Association; a fellow of the American Academy of Physical Education and of the American Association for the Advancement of Science of the New York Academy of medicine; and the recipient of the Gulick Award. In the following documentary account Dr. Wood presents his philosophy of physical education as it had been formulated by July, 1893. Of this account Dean William Russell of Teachers College, Columbia University (later President), said in 1932: Dr. Wood "advanced a program for physical education leading to health education, which was so far in advance of its time that it hardly has been realized today. He had the vision, he charted the course, and he sailed the ship in accord."

The great need in physical education today is the scientific spirit—the spirit which inspires the student to seek for truth and for its useful appli-

* Thomas D. Wood, "Some Unsolved Problems in Physical Education," *Selections from the Addresses of Thomas D. Wood* (New York, Teachers College, Columbia University, 1932), pp. 1–4.

cation; the spirit of generosity toward all, and of mutual helpfulness among those engaged in the same or similar lines of work; the spirit which precludes petty personal competition or jealous rivalry among those who are working for other than selfish ambition or mercenary ends.

There is today, in an embryonic and crude form, a science of physical education; and for the sake of the honorable future, the idea of the science should exist first in the minds of the profession, and then in the minds of laity. The science of physical education should take the place of the so-called systems of physical training. We can conceive of a system or series of definite exercises, arranged to produce a desired effect upon a given person, or upon a class of persons; but the only adequate name for a department of human knowledge and of research is that of a science.

Science is classified knowledge; but for the most part the words "unclassified ignorance" represent the present condition of our new science —physical education. Now, the intelligent understanding of the problems which need solution is the first step in the opening out of any new field of study. Here is a field of study as broad as human thought, involving questions important, far-reaching, and impossible of immediate settlement.

The term physical education is so misleading, and even misrepresented, that we look for a name which shall represent fairly the real idea of the science. What is physical education? This is one of the unsolved problems. Many people answer: "The training and development of the physical"; and they consider that the aim and end may be found in anthropometric apparatus, physical measurements, athletic contests and exhibitions, with graphic representations of measurements and of averages.

Now these things are very well in their places, but if our science is to be worthy of the best efforts of men and women, and of the respect and recognition of the educational world, physical education must have an aim as broad as education itself, and as noble and inspiring as human life. The great thought in physical education is not the education of the physical nature, but the relation of physical training to complete education, and then the effort to make the physical contribute its full share to the life of the individual, in environment, training, and culture.

The aim must not be primarily utilitarian, simply physical betterment, strength, skill, and fine proportions. It must be high and comprehensive. The ethical teacher tells us that the human ideal, the first and chief end of life, should be self-realization, the attainment of the best that there is in the possibilities, powers, and faculties of the individual. This guiding thought, this one ultimate end, brings into harmony all departments of human training. The ideal gives us the basis of our science, and suggests many questions of fundamental importance.

For example, what is the relation, more exactly than we know yet, of voluntary muscular activity to the activity and training of motor brain centers, and through these to general development? Again, what are the laws which indicate the order and method of growth and development in all the tissues, organs, and activities in man? In such study as this, thousands of individuals must be carefully observed and accurately tested with the various methods of statistical study, which has come to be a distinct specialty. Then types are to be brought out in strong relief, not to mislead but to assist us. Independently of all personal bias or prejudice these questions must be settled through the scientific study of man himself. Here are the fields for the biologist, the physiologist, the psychologist, the physical and the general educator. These fields have been too much separated. They should overlap with generous margins, so that each may verify the results of the others, and that there may be unanimity among all. At present our exact knowledge with reference to these most important problems is very meager, especially in the field of physiological research.

Dr. George W. Fitz has well brought out this thought in his excellent paper in the September number of *Harvard Graduates' Magazine:* "In the absence of exact physiological knowledge, various more or less reasonable and far-reaching hypotheses have been assumed, and elaborate theories and systems of training based thereon. The advent of new systems, and discussions provoked by them, have made clear to physiologists the ignorance in relation to some essential facts."

The rational study of the science of physical education will stimulate the efforts of investigators in many fields, and make plain the vital connection between facts hitherto unrelated even in the scientific mind. The work of the physical educator lies much in the field of the physical, but always from the standpoint of the ideal man, in whom the physical is the essential condition of his existence and activity. "It is seen," says Dr. G. Stanley Hall, "that the most perfect physical development involves the choicest knowledge, the best morals and religion." Here "best physical development" is related not to the material brute body, but to the possible admirable man or woman.

What forms of exercise will best develop, or assist in development of, strength, speed, skill, self-control, accuracy, grace, endurance, automatism, courage, moral fiber, mental power, will power, character? The question of movement and the precise effect of each movement upon the human organism is to be determined by exact laboratory method.

We are glad to know of the investigators who are working upon these problems. We rejoice at the establishment of such workshops as the laboratory in the Lawrence Scientific School of Harvard University, designed for the experimental study of the physiology of exercise. Several new and important pieces of apparatus testify to the early success in this special laboratory. May such institutions be multiplied!

The field of deformity, abnormality, and disease is of great importance for the physical educator, because the conditions named exist in slighter form although complicating the problem of many lives with which the teacher has to deal.

What I have given you will serve to suggest the scientific basis of physical education. Here we must have definite knowledge. Whatever individual investigators have contributed to our scanty fund of knowledge we recognize with gratitude. The history of physical education among the different nations offers us much of great value.

These two thoughts, then, let me emphasize: first, that there is a science of physical education, based, with the other human sciences, upon a philosophy of human life. This science presents problems which are at once most interesting, important, and difficult, whose answers must form part of the foundation of all education. Second, that the ever-present, interesting, important, and difficult problem in physical, as in all education, is the individual living human being.

10

The New Physical Education [*]

THOMAS D. WOOD, M.D.

(For a biographical sketch of Dr. Thomas D. Wood, including his professional contributions to physical education, see Document 9.) In the excerpts from the article printed below, Dr. Thomas Wood, writing under the influence of John Dewey and the new psychology, explained that the aim of physical education continued to be health, but that it was attained as a by-product of guiding students into doing things that resulted in the acquirement of mental, moral, and social benefits. The subject matter of physical education, he continued, was to be found in activities such as play, games, outdoor sports, and gymnastics, although the last-named were to be reconstructed to satisfy educational needs. Much of Dr. Wood's article was devoted to detailing the conditions for exercise in physical education if the best results were to be obtained. It is particularly valuable because of its exposition of the new physical education.

. . . There is at present . . . throughout this cosmopolitan country great diversity of opinion with reference to controlling ideas in physical education and complete lack of agreement regarding material and methods of instruction. This is inevitable and probably salutary, as opportunity is thus given for free experimentation and for local adoption of ways and means for recognized aims.

It is apparent to many, however, that physical education, more particularly in the public-school system of this country, has on the whole lacked the support of a well-organized body of thought which is in harmony with the best current educational theory. To many, again, it is evident further that the principles of physical education, even as formulated, have not kept pace with general educational progress.

Several reasons may help to explain this condition of affairs. Not until the last few years has there been a practical recognition of the broader social scope of education with the implied obligations to the physical and social, as well as the intellectual and moral needs of the pupil. Beyond this, it is but recently that modern psychology and physiology have pro-

[*] Thomas D. Wood, "Physical Education," (Part I, Health and Education), *The Ninth Yearbook of the National Society for the Study of Education* (Chicago, The University of Chicago Press, 1910), pp. 75–104.

claimed the scientific facts which have shown the more vital and intimate interdependence between the different aspects of life, which are called physical, intellectual, and moral. . . .

It is the business of physical educators, in co-operation with the agencies which should provide for hygienic care, to secure for the pupil, through a rational distribution of motor activities, certain health values represented by favorable posture, organic vigor, and other desirable biologic qualities. If necessary, these health qualities must constitute the main goal in this field, but it is most desirable that physical education should occupy itself with a programme of activities for the young which would secure these physical aspects of health without fail, as by-products, as it were, while the pupil is being guided in the doing of things which will result in the acquirement of mental, moral, and social benefits. Health, then, in the narrower sense, becomes an essential means or condition in physical education to the accomplishment of certain exceedingly valuable results in the general education of the child. . . .

Physical education has not yet an integral place in the educational theory and programme of the country. It has been given certain space and time, and often grudging recognition in response to the hygienic demands (usually the protests of the physicians) in the effort to counteract, or to compensate for, the unhealthful influences of school life.

Physical education has had, however, not nominally perhaps, and not always adequately, but in effect, a very logical place in the kindergarten. Its position in the curriculum of the school above the kindergarten has been more uncertain. The petition of the physical educator is very commonly for more time in the curriculum. There is suspicion in the minds of some that the preferred material of physical education has frequently not been of the character to rationally compel the recognition asked. When physical education presents a programme which is psychologically and physiologically sound, and therefore, pedagogically acceptable, it will find itself in organic relationship with education as a whole and to the other subjects or departments represented.

Physical education should provide, in instruction and supervision, for the desirable margin of motor activity which is not otherwise supplied in the school curriculum or in the life of the pupil outside of the school.

The main function of education, perhaps, is to train the human mechanism toward efficiency as an instrument of self-expression, with reference to the various opportunities and responsibilities of life, at the time and later. The child learns far more of permanent value through what he does—and this always means neuromuscular action of some sort—than through what he sees or hears or perceives in any way directly with the five senses. In fact, perception of sensation depends on some degree of activity. Motor sensation is the great cornerstone in the foundation of human education. The experience of Helen Keller demonstrates how much can be accomplished in education without sight and hearing if the main avenues of sensation from movement are left open. . . .

The subject matter of physical education is found in play, games, dancing, swimming, outdoor sports, athletics, and gymnastics (reconstructed to satisfy educational needs). These headings are not mutually exclusive but are used to cover the range of activities. . . .

Cerain conditions seem necessary for rational exercise in physical education if the best results are to be obtained.

I. The activities of physical education should be carried on out of doors, whenever this may be made possible. The gymnasium should be considered an emergency-space, valuable to be sure, when required by inclement weather and under other circumstances; but it should never interfere with possible use of nature's infinitely better playroom out of doors.

II. The exercises should be natural in type, satisfying by their execution the play instinct and the fundamental powers and faculties as they develop, with due regard to the ancestral habits of activity and to the future practical needs of the individual. . . .

Education . . . should secure to the pupil, beyond mere bread-and-butter needs, the ability to meet the wider opportunities and the possible emergencies in life. . . . There are many "fancy stunts," as well as exact and intricate performances in various branches of education which lack rational sanction from modern educational theory. In the past they have been considered extremely valuable, not only because they were showy, but for drill and discipline. They are dropping very rapidly out of use in relation to reading, spelling, writing, manual training, and most of the departments of teaching.

Formal gymnastics, free-hand movements, for the most part, and much of the apparatus work of the gymnasium, belong to the category of artificial "stunts," mechanical movements lacking the purpose, mental content, and objective which are essential to sensible educational performances. Most of the free-hand exercises, particularly, are mechanically rigid, jerky, and awkward, as compared with natural useful movements of the body. They are uninteresting and distasteful to most boys and girls except in the early elementary grades, when they are considered by the physical educator even relatively less important.

Formal gymnastics in physical education correspond to drugs in medical practice. The movement in medical treatment even is away from the use of drugs. In a similar way progress in physical education must be away from all formal, artificial kinds of movement.

It is important that a reasonable amount of physical education should be required of every pupil and student in school and college. It is correlatively important that this training should enlist the interest and enthusiasm of each pupil, not primarily in keeping healthy, but in the doing of things having intrinsic objective interest, whose performance will insure good health. Much of the required physical education at present cultivates a dislike for healthful exercise. This is inexpressibly unfortunate, and forms an indictment against such instruction in as much as one of the most important purposes of physical education should be to cultivate the liking for rational, pleasurable, healthful exercise.

III. In physical education . . . the pupils in practice should either (a) express an idea, feeling, or emotion, which seems worth expressing, e.g., in dancing, pantomine, or other form of dramatic representation, or (b) there should be some definite objective aim or effect to be attained as the result of the muscular effort performed, as in maintenance of squad formation in marching, hitting a ball, throwing a ball into a basket, swimming to a given point, outrunning a competitor, or any one of the indefinite number of things to do in games. . . .

IV. The activities in physical education should be correlated whenever feasible with the subjects and activities with which the child is occupied elsewhere in the school or outside. Games vary with the season of the year, with climate and weather changes. There are many opportunities in connection with study of literature, history, nature-study, art, industry, and other subjects, to employ dances and games which have definite relation to the subjects in hand and give the child a most valuable opportunity to express himself more completely in relation to the interest which occupies his attention. . . .

Folk dances may be correlated with seasonal interests and festivals, e.g., Harvest time, Christmas celebration, patriotic anniversaries, May Day, etc. . . .

V. Gymnastic technique (as distinguished from marching, dancing, games, athletics) . . . should consist in the practice of movements involved in actual and natural kinds of performance . . . for the purpose of acquiring greater strength and skill, so that the complete action or original performance may be more effectively executed. . . .

VI. The pupil, while intent upon some external result in individual or co-operative effort, should be unconscious of his own body or of the purpose of exercise to benefit his body or health. . . .

VII. Mechanical uniformity and precision of movement, in a group or class of children, can logically be demanded . . . only when the situation, expressed as an external problem, requires it. Evolutions in marching, and sometimes dancing, necessitate precise uniformity in movement among smaller or larger numbers of actors, and these evolutions must be changed by word of command of teacher, officer, or leader. In general, however, it is most desirable that mechanical uniformity should not be demanded, but that, with the observance of certain general principles of action, the pupil should be left free to express individuality in action. . . .

VIII. Physical education should be supervised and directed with reference to the beneficial social and moral results which may be gained by the right performance, in play, games, and athletics, of the large fundamental types of human action. . . .

Very little profitable instruction in theoretical ethics can be given in the elementary or even in the high school. Children and youth get most of their moral instruction in relation to action, and many important ethical principles may be instilled in connection with the large primitive types of conduct involved in personal health problems and in games and sports. The playground, gymnasium, and athletic field afford the best opportunities for the learning of moral lessons, sometimes even by college students. The president of a great university said a few years ago, "The instructor of physical education has a more powerful influence upon the morale of students than the teacher of any other subject." It is most important then that this teacher should (1) have an adequate appreciation of the moral influence that should be exerted, and (2) have personality, character, and tact to exert such influence wisely and effectively.

IX. In the fifth or sixth elementary (or the first or second grammar) grades when some of the girls enter the preadolescent period of greatly accelerated bodily growth, boys and girls should have the more vigorous games and exercises in separate classes, and from that time onward in their physical education the forms of exercise should be adapted to sex differences as well as to advancing age and personal needs.

X. While in physical education certain psychic, social, and ethical results should be directly sought, the forms of exercise should always be arranged and controlled so that favorable physiologic values may be obtained. In other words, physical education should always be hygienic in the highest degree. More than this, physical education must . . . be safe and hygienic for each individual pupil. This can only be accomplished on the basis of knowledge of the health condition of each pupil. Many students . . . have been injured . . . by participation in games and exercises which are too severe for them, with their individual health weaknesses and limitations. The health inspection . . . provides an intelligent basis for the individual adjustment of exercise. . . .

11

Fundamental Education *

CLARK W. HETHERINGTON

Known as "The Modern Philosopher of Physical Education," Clark W. Hetherington spent a lifetime analyzing the fundamentals of education and physical education. According to Dr. Charles H. McCloy, Hetherington's "thinking laid the base . . . for the philosophy of physical education" in the United States. Born in Lanesborough, Minnesota, in 1870, he moved to California at the age of four and began acquiring valuable experience as he observed mining operations, mule teams, and prairie schooners. As a young man, he tried his hand as a cowboy, dentist's assistant, warehouse clerk, businessman, and architect apprentice. Fond of athletics, he became a highly skilled gymnast and acrobat by a successful imitation of circus performers, which led to his own show in a home-made gymnasium. At the age of twenty-one, he enrolled at Stanford University and began an association with Dr. Thomas D. Wood, who soon made him a gymnasium instructor while studying for his degree. His professional teaching career started in the prisons and reformatories of California where he proved that wholesome play and recreation are essential in the development of healthy men and women. This experience led Hetherington to Clark University to study individual differences and character training under Dr. G. Stanley Hall. In 1911 he became Director of Physical Education at the University of Missouri, where he had the opportunity to put his "Theory of Play" into operation as he pioneered in curriculum development to enable all students to have the opportunity for recreation and mass play. In later years he continued to put these principles into practice while on the faculty at the University of Wisconsin, Columbia University, Wellesley College, New York University, Stanford University, and as Supervisor of Physical Education for the State of California. Hetherington was a founder of the American Academy of Physical Education and of the Pacific Coast Physical Education Association; a founder and President of the Midwest Physical Education Association and of the Athletic Research Society, in which he was a vital factor in raising the standards of amateurism in the United States; and the recipient of the Gulick Award and the Posse Medal. A gifted writer, he is especially well known for his treatise on "Fundamental Education," which is printed below. It contains an exposition of the philosophy of the new physical education.

* Clark W. Hetherington, "Fundamental Education," *American Physical Education Review*, Vol. 15 (December, 1910), pp. 629–635.

Education is a process in which the infant is conducted from birth through the period of growth and development to maturity, and in which his powers are developed and adjusted to a social order for complete living.

This paper aims to describe the function and place of general neuro-muscular activities, primarily general play activities, in the educational process. We use the term *general play* to include plays, games, athletics, dancing, the play side of gymnastics, and all play activities in which large muscles are used more or less vigorously.

The interpretation given might be called the new physical education, with the emphasis on education, and the understanding that it is "physical" only in the sense that the activity of the whole organism is the educational agent and not the mind alone. The key to our interpretation lies largely in that suggestive formula concerning the order of growth and development: from fundamental to accessory. With this warning there will scarcely be any confusion between the use of the formula and the title of the paper, "Fundamental Education."

Back of the thesis maintained is the general idea that education is neither for body nor for mind alone, but for all human powers that depend on educational activities for development.

To present the thesis four phases of the educational process will be considered: organic education, psychomotor education, character education, and intellectual education.

Organic education is the process that develops vital vigor, *i.e.*, high nutrition, perfect elimination, a large capacity for activity with relative immunity from fatigue and the common ills of life. This means a development of power in the organs of vegetative life.

All are familiar with the influence of vigorous exercise on the development of the skeletal muscles. Few are so familiar with the indirect influence of this exercise—the influence with which organic education is chiefly concerned.

When a group of muscles is exercised vigorously, the influence spreads through the whole body, due to the call of the working muscles for oxygen and the elimination of waste products. All the organs involved in nutrition and elimination are heightened in activity as indicated by the throbbing heart, increased respiration, heat, perspiration, etc. Coincidently, through the increased circulation, all the organs and tissues of the body are saturated and bathed in a fresh supply of blood, while subjected to a natural massage of joltings, pressures, tensions, and strains resulting from the movements, positions, bendings, and torsions of the body. This profoundly increases the influence on the active organs and extends it to the passive tissues.

Thus while we have practically no direct volitional control over the organs of vegetative life, we can control and exercise these organs indirectly through making them function in service on the voluntary skeletal muscles. This is the method of organic education. We can control the amount of work done by the character, amount, and duration of the work of the skeletal muscles. The familiar and extreme example of this process is the development of the heart of a distance runner—as truly an educational process as the development of language power.

Organic power must be gained by organic education during the period of growth and development. It cannot be gained in full after maturity because the nascent periods of the various organs have passed. It cannot be gained in full until after established adolescence because the development of the latent inherited resources of the various organs must wait on growth. This principle makes organic exercise an essential element in the educational process during the entire period of growth and development.

Adult organic efficiency rests on organic development gained during the period of growth and development. If this organic development has not been gained in full the program of maintaining organic efficiency for strenuous living is proportionately difficult. Given organic development, the maintenance of efficiency becomes for the adult simply sane living and proper recreation.

Organic education has no other concern than the development of power. It is concerned with the power of which health is a by-product. Of the factors controlling growth and development, i.e., activity, proper food and fresh air, sleep and rest, sunshine, cleanliness, temperature, wholesome mental moods, and freedom from the inhibiting influences of disease, activity is the only factor that is educational. The other factors give the conditions for growth and development, activity alone constructs power.

The first function of education, then, is to develop the inherited resources of the vegetative organism. The place of general or vigorous neuromuscular activities, naturally play activities, in this phase of the educational process, is that of the stimulant to activities that develop functional power. Like all educational activities, they are effective in proportion as they have an effective hygienic background.

Psychomotor education is the process that develops power and skill in neuromuscular activities.

It is a simple matter to trace the order of development of psychomotor activities from infancy onward—the first on the side of locomotion, from crude kickings and squirmings through creeping and standing, to running, jumping, dancing, etc.; second, on the side of handling objects, from crude fumblings to the skill of the gymnast, juggler, artisan, craftsman and pianist; and third, on the side of speech, from crude gurglings to oratory and singing.

In this progress in neuromuscular powers, there are two sides: the development of muscular tissues and the development of nervous centers controlling the muscular tissues. It is in the development of the nervous centers rather than in the development of the muscular tissues that we must look for the differences in power and skill between the infant and the adult.

The development of power and skill in a neuromuscular center depends on the exercise of that center by muscular activity. It is purely an educational process. Psychomotor education is the education of the whole complex mass of the reflex arcs of the nervous system with the crude neuromuscular reflexes at one end of the system and volitional life at the other. By exercise each level is developed and looped up with higher and lower levels until the mind becomes master of all the complicated activities and special skills of life. The intellectual and character elements in this process are given separate treatment; here attention is confined to neuromuscular power in action.

It is the function of education by general neuromuscular activities, naturally general play activities, to develop the fundamental neuromuscular centers. To manual, industrial, and art education is left the development of the accessory centers and powers.

In the natural order of development of psychomotor powers the activities of the fundamental centers predominate until approximately ten years of age; then the activities of the accessory centers naturally begin to predominate until approaching maturity, when they may be exclusively accessory. The most important principle in this shifting of predominance of activity, from fundamental in childhood to accessory in youth, is that the fundamental neuromuscular centers are not completed in their development when the striking development of the accessory begins. The development of the fundamental cannot be stopped with children. The latent inherited resources of the fundamental centers cannot be developed until after growth nears completion. These powers must be developed before maturity or the nascent periods of the various centers pass. This principle fixes the place of vigorous exercise in youth as well as in childhood. Fourteen to twenty is the age for the development of functional power as distinct from growth.

Violation of this principle of education has had serious consequences. The rise of modern nervousness has paralleled the emphasis of civilization on accessory activities without a corresponding development of the fundamental. Power in the fundamental centers is necessary to give nervous stability in sustained effort and capacity to resist the wear and tear of excessive activity in the accessory. There will be no writer's cramp where powerfully developed shoulder neuromuscular centers carry the burden of excessive writing.

The second function of education then is to develop a nervous system. The function of general or vigorous neuromuscular activities, naturally general play activities, in this phase of the educational process, is to develop primarily the fundamental nervous centers by exercising the fundamental muscles until the nervous system can carry the burden of civilization. To manual, industrial, and art education is left the development of the accessory nervous centers.

Character education is the process that develops the moral, social and spiritual powers.

Character education during childhood and youth takes place in the home, in the schoolroom (including the Sunday school), and at play. These cover practically the life of the young. Industrial work may take the place of the school, but this is a special problem not considered here. Ideally, the home, the school, and the playground should co-operate in moral education, but as educators have no control over the home, educational effort must be confined to the school room and play life. If the home influence is of the best, all else will follow, but most homes do not present this ideal condition, and even the best need supplementing by outside effort. The Sunday school does not include all youth, and there is mighty little of it. The public school has yet developed no generally effective or practical method of moral training and the possibilities of instruction in the classroom are limited because the activities are limited. The outside play life is the only agent that touches all children and youth, which lasts through the entire period of growth and development, which is naturally character forming, good or bad, and which is peculiarly sensitive to leadership, good or bad.

The most conspicuous thing about play is its character-forming power. Vices are learned in play, not in the classroom. In the anxiety of earnest parents concerning championship is seen the moral power of leadership. Criticisms of intercollegiate athletics are eloquent testimonials of the moral power of athletics and the quality of the leadership. In 1898, after studying for two years the careers of 480 inmates of a juvenile reformatory, personal data indicated that 75 to 80 per cent might have been saved an institutional career had they had a normal play experience. Social workers agree that the "bad boy" is largely the product of restricted or misdirected play energies. Juvenile delinquency diminishes in districts where playgrounds are established. A moral toning-up is the universal testimony of experts on the results of directed play.

The character forming power of play lies in its nature. It is the child's soul life. Play may be defined as human nature growing up. The immature organism expresses every mental and nervous tendency and every developing instinct and reacts upon every experience according to its growing capacities. In the supervision of these play tendencies we have the foundation for all moral training. Character education by doing precedes moral education by precept. All higher moral education must be built on these habit-forming activities. They are basic. This is fundamental character education. Several natural stages of character development are clear. The first years are spent in gaining elemental adjustments to nature and society. This is followed by the age of aggressive self-preservation, Lee's "Big Injun" age. Then follows the "gang" age, with its co-operation, loyalties, self-subordination, and leadership, and finally comes the age of moral and religious interest. Character power is gained naturally in this order. Failure to gain development during the nascent period leaves limitation for life.

This fundamental character education through the guidance of conduct in play is not completed in childhood. It continues through youth and long after moral education by intellectual inspiration may be well begun. The athletic field of the late adolescent years is as truly a laboratory of conduct as is the playground of the child. This is the last chance age for intensive moral training by direct personal guidance and discipline. Fourteen to twenty is the critical period in which all the larger fundamental social character traits and moral habits are formed, and they are formed in large measure on the play side of life. These facts indicate the necessity of supervised play in youth as well as in childhood.

During infancy nature cares for this functional moral education. Every child's mother is his first play director. By instinct she is a playmate and a play leader, guiding her infant's developing activities to material and social adaptation. Later this leadership is withdrawn or neglected as the child gains the elemental powers of self-preservation, but the character-forming activities go on and accumulate in intensity and influence as age advances. All the bad habits known to youth are the result.

The third function of education is the development of a character, morally and socially sound. This must be done primarily in youths' natural laboratory of experience-play. All higher methods of moral education must be based on the habits of conduct gained largely by play. These habits are the vital, the fundamental things in moral education.

Intellectual education is the process that develops intellectual skill and gives information and culture.

On the side of training for intellectual skill, the discipline of perception, attention, memory, judgment, etc., in general, neuromuscular activities, is well recognized. This is however only mental discipline in psychomotor activities. While this discipline is not completed until the mind is master of the accessory activities in industrial or professional occupations, the power gained is only slightly if at all transferred to power in the study of science, art, or literature, and vice versa. The athlete may be a fool in the classroom, and conversely the theoretical scholar may be for all practical purposes a motor idiot. Each gains power by thinking in terms of his own activity. Thus while intellectual discipline by general neuromuscular activities is only a part of psychomotor discipline, and this in turn only a part of all intellectual discipline, it is discipline on the level of the fundamental.

On the side of information, the child learns by doing—primarily through play. The early years are spent in learning, testing out, the material environment in action. This hunger for experience continues through and is strikingly characteristic of youth. Social workers have learned its meaning and are using it in organized hikes, excursions, outings, collecting and hunting trips, experience with animals, gardening, and what not. This is reading nature from the sources. In the same way social life is learned. In imitative and dramatic plays of adult activities, for example, the child plays himself into an understanding of human ways of living and doing. The process is continued among companions in plays, games, sports, and in later social experience. A great store of insights, sympathies, understandings, habitual reactions are built up, which become the foundation for all social thinking. The ideas thus gained soon sink to the level of the automatic. This is knowledge in the backbone. It controls doing, feeling, thinking, and is only another way of saying that all social sympathy, good or bad, has its roots in play.

In the hunger for experience and the hunger for expression, we have the natural incentives to intellectual education. If not organized in wisdom for educational ends they will be organized in ignorance for less wholesome ends. By feeding these hungers in an organized play experience education should give a virile contribution to intellectual education along with character education, psychomotor education, and organic education.

The fourth function of education, then, is to develop a skillful intellect, well stocked with insights and information. Education by general neuromuscular activities or general play gives the fundamental intellectual discipline in action and the fundamental knowledge on which higher modes of discipline and the higher information may be built. . . .

12

ⅩⅭ══ⅩⅭ

Physical Training in the Modern City [*]

LUTHER HALSEY GULICK, M.D.

(For a biographical sketch of Dr. Luther Halsey Gulick, including his professional contributions to physical education, see Document 8.) A special contribution to the making of physical education was Dr. Gulick's address "The Problem of Physical Training in the Modern City." In it he pointed out that machines were eliminating or reducing the muscular work that formerly had maintained muscular health even as the city by its nature opened new avenues of nervous expenditure. These conditions must be faced, he said, by administering the period of childhood and youth so as to develop maximum power and health, and he laid down the lines to be followed in solving "this problem in biological engineering."

. . . Our generation for the first time meets the city problem on a large scale. The answer which we give to the problems propounded to us by the conditions of the city are to be measurably the answers which shall determine the character of our civilization. If the United States is the most significant country, and in the United States our New York City is the most significant city, then the privilege of here and now working out a fundamental problem is a privilege of the ages.

Gerald Stanley Lee has called our attention to the significance of making the city beautiful that it may adequately express the superb life of the day. It is my privilege tonight to call your attention to the potentiality of the city with reference to the maintenance of superb health, to the development of a higher type of manhood and woman-hood—a type having greater power, a type having a more intense and powerful personality. If it is true that Man's personality has ever corre-sponded to the increasing complexity of his environment, then the type of personality which will ultimately be developed by the city will be largely more complex, more powerful, and more healthy than any per-sonality which has been produced in the world so far. Our faces are toward the future, not the past. The past was good; the future is better. The evil of the city is temporary; the good is permanent. The evil of the city is a problem for solution; the good of the city is a power for mastery.

[*] Luther Halsey Gulick, "The Problem of Physical Training in the Modern City," *American Physical Education Review*, Vol. 8 (1903), pp. 29–34.

The city represents opportunity, such opportunity as is new in the world's history. The consciousness of the world, the moving spirit of the Zeitgeist, seems to be focused and epitomized by this great, ugly, beautiful, patient, irritable, majestic, magnificent city.

It is our function to help answer the question as to whether human kind can permanently maintain the higher, faster, psychic level and pace of city life. Those of us who are working at this problem may be divided into three groups.

1. Those who are concerned directly with the cure of disease,—our body of physicians, a strong, able, numerous, well-equipped class,—they are doing noble work. To cure disease is dramatic. It always has and always will command the immediate attention of the world. But it is, on the whole, a mending process, a patching process, by which existing machines and boilers may be induced to go on somewhat longer and work.

2. The second class is composed of those who are concerned with the prevention of disease. These persons, these boards, are concerned with the purity of our water supply, the prevention of the spread of contagious diseases, the exclusion from our city of foreign sources of disease, the securing of pure food supplies and the like. Their work is great. It has already in civilized lands largely prevented the disease scourges which have decimated whole peoples in former times. Even such tragedies as those now occurring at Cornell are trivial as compared to those which have swept Europe during previous ages. This work of preventing disease is less dramatic than that of curing disease, but is more fundamental, more profound. We all of us know, nevertheless, of people for whom these two classes of agents have done all that is possible. They have no specific disease to be cured; they are surrounded by the wall of protection with sufficient care and thoroughness, so that they are not exposed to the ordinary sources of disease, still they lack power and vitality. The fundamental conditions of life are somehow not adequately met. Their lives are dominated by the necessity of caring for themselves; they have but little energy for work; they are unable to rear strong offspring, or in many cases any; they are liable to be upset by any and every irregularity in their course of life; they lack power; they lack vitality; they lack the power to live full, rich, effective lives.

3. The third class of persons to which I refer are those who are engaged not in the cure of disease, directly, but whose work consists in developing within the individual to the maximum the power of life, treating each individual, so that his may be the conditions under which the greatest power of living shall be developed. Theirs is a work of biological engineering. The city has presented new problems to this class of engineers. The sewage system, the elevated railroad, the tunnels, the buildings of the city, have all presented fresh problems to our mechanical

and civil engineers and architects. New conditions have had to be met. And so with those of us who are concerned with the foundation of human life itself, the city presents new conditions. These conditions have taken away the world's muscular work and are doing it by machinery. In the United States there are ten and a half horse power, steam power, for every man of us, and yet it is through muscular work largely that the muscular strength of the men of the world has been in previous ages developed. How long will that muscular health and power which has been developed in connection with muscular labor be maintained without such labor? How many generations can we live without doing this muscular labor? The records of older cities, of Paris, London, and Berlin, seem to show that three generations of city life are sufficient to exhaust the strongest stock.

Coincident with this taking away of the world's muscular work, we have increased many avenues for nervous expenditure. The news of the world is brought to our doors daily, almost hourly, by the daily press, steam and electricity. Our hearts throb with the passions of the whole world; action is immediate and necessary; consciousness is intense. These conditions we who are concerned with the maintenance of health must face in a new way. Individuals must come into the world's work with strong, enduring natures. That is, the period of childhood and youth must be administered that the maximum power and health shall be developed. As Superintendent Maxwell so well remarked at the dedication of the Wadleigh High School, "It is not sufficient that the boys and girls of our high schools shall graduate without breaking down; they must graduate with a maximum of health and power for the world's work." There is no other subject in the whole curriculum so basal as this. In fact it is not difficult to show that all of education is worth but little if it is won at the sacrifice of health. The primary condition for success in business, in the professions, or in life itself, is not the knowledge which comes from books. The primary element is capacity for intense, prolonged work, and this is related primarily to health. It is not a question of how time may be found in the curriculum for physical training, but a question of what time is really necessary to be taken for physical training, and the adjustment of the rest of the curriculum to this end.

It has been demonstrated beyond peradventure of cavil that muscular exercise adequate in kind and suitable in quantity is one of the fundamental conditions to physical health and power. During the past ages of the world children have secured muscular labor by play and by co-operating in the work of their parents. It is no longer possible for boys and girls to get adequate exercise in the original way, doing chores about the country farm, co-operating with the father as a laborer, and in work about the home. That no longer suffices. The chores of the world can no longer be used as muscular exercise for the boy; and assisting in the domestic work of the house is no longer an adequate source of muscular exercise for the girl. The conditions under which the great traditional plays and games of the world have been developed have also changed. Hide and seek, tag, ball games, swimming, running, and the like, all demand ample space for their adequate development, and the city lacks space. Everywhere there is no time, our city children are not in possession of plays and games which are adequate for physical development under said conditions. The city brings large numbers of children together. This in itself produces social friction and expenditure of power.

We have seen thus far that with the development of the city we need a higher type of man, keener and tougher,—a man who constantly lives at his best, who is able to fix all the powers of his being on intense effort, a man who lives finely and well. We have seen that this power must be developed during the growing period of life. We have seen that the city conditions have taken away the chief elements which have been of service in the history of the world in developing this vital power in the young. It is now our problem as biological engineers to face the situation, to show what needs to be done and to carry it out that our children shall, under the conditions of city life, not only maintain the average health of the past, but become stronger and finer children than the world has ever seen before, children who as men and women will be adequate to the superb opportunities of the city of the future. This is not the occasion for any complete discussion as to the details in the treatment of this problem in biological engineering. Its five main lines may be briefly referred to.

Our first proposition is that children of the city are without much necessary muscular exertion and without opportunity or incentive toward much voluntary muscular exercise through adequate plays and games. The first necessity, then, for us as physical trainers is to provide for the development and fashioning of out of school play and games that shall engage large numbers of children, which shall be as interesting as the traditional games of the past have been, which are as adequate for the development of the body as the old games were, and which shall be feasible under the conditions of city life. Our primary dependence upon general muscular exercise can never be in enforced gymnastics. A careful watching of a day's average play of a boy or girl under normal conditions indicates that two, three, or even four hours per day of active exercise alone is adequate, and to have this amount of exercise in formal gymnastics is wholly out of the question. Gymnastics can never take the place of play, and upon play we must depend in the future, as we have in the past, for the fundamental conditions for the development of organic life and power.

Second, children sit at the school desks approximately five hours per day. Sitting, and particularly writing and reading, is biologically abnormal and tends to the induction of positions of the body which restrict circulation, respiration, and assimilation, the three fundamental biological processes. The school desk seems to be necessary. It must be met by frequent breaks throughout the school day, when the individual will rise, will vigorously exercise the muscles which counteract the desk attitude and which will at the same time increase the circulation and respiration.

Third, in order to develop conscious control of the body, the maintenance of good position of the trunk, a large part of the time for exercise during the school day must be given to these forms of formal gymnastics which are distinctly educational in their character, which shall progress from year to year, in their educational demands, which shall secure that prompt response of body to mind, that immediate control of all parts of the body as well as that organic vigor which we have seen to be connected with such gymnastics.

Fourth, there must be throughout the day one or more brief periods given completely to mental relaxation. Gymnastics involve as keen if not keener conscious attention than any other form of education, and to substitute gymnastics for recreation is to make a fundamental mistake. The old-fashioned recess no longer gives the old-fashioned recreation. The large numbers of children engaged at a time, the limited space available for their play, their lack of games suited to their conditions, make the recess of doubtful value under present conditions. Accordingly, a definite part of the program of the future will be to provide such plays and games as are suitable under the conditions of the city school which shall be genuinely play, but the traditions of which shall be carried out by the teachers. In suitable communities there always arises a group of play traditions adapted to the environment of that community, and these traditions are passed from generation to generation of child life. But the conditions of cosmopolitanism in New York, of newness in environment, have not yet permitted the development of these games, and where some have been partially solved the size of the city prevents their rapid spread throughout the city by the personal contact of the players. Hence, it is imperative that there be some more adequate means of social tradition for these plays and games than is afforded by the children themselves. Organized plays and games for mental relaxation available under the conditions of school life, both temporal and special, seem to be an essential part of our necessity.

And lastly, there are no average children. Children, like adults, are all individuals, and excel or are weak in specific qualities. But within certain well-defined lines, children between certain ages work together readily. They keep step in physical, mental, and moral progress in the main. But there are always individuals who depart so far from this normal and ordinary rate of progress that it is prejudicial to them, and also to the others from whom they differ, to make the attempt to keep step. Some with exceptional speed and power can outstrip their fellows. Others, because of congenital peculiarity, or because of the tragic condition of their early lives, are deficient. These need segregation and that emphasis upon physical health and physical education which Seguin, Wey, and others have so amply demonstrated to be a primary condition to the most wholesome development of these individuals. To cooperate in the segregation and training of these individuals that they may, so far as possible, ultimately come into condition for self-support must be a definite and important part of the work of this department.

What is the chance of success with reference to this which seems to us so important and fundamental a part of the educational curriculum?

I would mention the great interest which there is all over our land to aid in matters of physical training. This interest, while it has its waves and its superficial indications like that of the eruption of correspondence schools of physical training whose wane we are already beginning to see, is appreciated most profoundly by the large men of our times. There is a present conception of the fundamental importance of physical health and power among the thinking men of our land, and this has penetrated pretty well into popular consciousness. This affords a background of public opinion upon which our work may adequately rest. . . .

13

Health and Motor Activity *

FRED E. LEONARD, M.D.

Fred Eugene Leonard (1866–1922), historian of physical education and physician, was born in Darlington, Wisconsin. After graduation from Oberlin College in 1889 he received three years later the M.D. degree from the College of Physicians and Surgeons, Columbia University, and at that time entered his life work as Professor of Hygiene and Physical Education at Oberlin College. While he is undoubtedly best known for his scholarly and unhurriedly systematic *History of Physical Education* (1922), now in its third edition, his continuous interest in medicine was manifested in his serving as President of the Town and College Hospital in Oberlin. His professional accomplishments were recognized by election as President of the College Physical Education Association and as President of the Society of Directors of Physical Education in Colleges. In the article from which excerpts are printed below, medical knowledge has interacted with his observance of European systems of physical education and his strong historical background to produce a balanced analysis of the kind of physical-education program needed to correct the difficulties in the physical development of children posed by the transition of the United States from a rural to an urban society.

Two contradictory views of the human body have at various times profoundly influenced the attitude of educators towards its care and training. One, which we may term the *ascetic,* reflects the dualistic philosophy of Oriental religions. Men believed that evil inheres in matter, of whatever sort, while mind or spirit is essentially divine and pure; and it followed as an inevitable corollary that soul and body must wage perpetual warfare on each other. . . .

According to the second view, the *biologic* or *physiologic,* the body is a machine with which man does his work in the world. Care and training are necessary that it may be perfect in all its parts at maturity, and handled skillfully and economically. Huxley stated the idea in a nutshell in an address . . . in 1868, when he began his definition of a liberally educated man by saying that he must have been "so trained

* Fred E. Leonard, "The Relation of Motor Activity to Health and Education," *American Physical Education Review,* Vol. 20 (November, 1915), pp. 513–522.

in youth that his body is the ready servant of his will, and does with ease and pleasure all the work that, as a mechanism, it is capable of." . . .

I doubt whether biology can furnish a stronger argument for physical training than that which is yielded by a study of the part played by motor activity in the evolution of higher forms of animal life, and of the way in which it has led to the type of body which man now possesses. . . .

The muscular system . . . as Professor Tyler says [in *Growth and Education*, from which Leonard had quoted liberally in his description of the evolution of the human body], "must be of far greater importance and have far larger latent capacities than we have usually supposed. It is the strategic center from and through which we can reach, exercise, and strengthen all the organs essential to life, but which are beyond the direct control of the will." It is also "the key to the development of the brain. . . . Nervous development followed the increase of locomotion and increased use of the sense-organs, especially of the eyes. Arboreal life and the use of the hand were exceedingly important factors in the development of the cortex." In the case of man himself, physical education has been an almost universal condition of existence, down to recent times, and to it we largely owe our present type of body. As Dr. Gulick puts it,

A biologist, having brought to him a human body and being asked for a statement of its functions from an examination of the structure, would say that both in form and function the organism must have been adapted to a life of considerable muscular exertion; that the lungs as well as the heart indicated far more capacity than would be needed for a life exclusively or even largely sedentary; and finally, that the nervous system was designed predominantly for the initiation or control of muscular movements. . . . No argument is necessary to the evolutionist to show that the necessity for muscular exercise has been constant and predominant throughout the whole history of the life of the species; that it has been so constant and so large a factor in adjustment to the total environment as to have had a chief share in determining the character of the organism itself; and that those conditions which have been decisive in determining the form and functions of the organism are the conditions in which it functionates the best.

This biologic view of the body as a servant of the mind, and the recognition of motor activity as fundamental in education, have led to the general introduction of courses in hygiene and the rudiments of human physiology into the curriculum of our schools and colleges, and to widespread attempts to supply facilities for bodily exercise, with more or less provision of expert oversight and systematic instruction. Such steps mark a noteworthy advance in the right direction, and yet they indicate only a partial grasp of the real significance and purpose of physical education. For there is still a third view of the relation of the body and mind, the psychophysic, which finds increasingly clear and forceful expression in the recent home and foreign literature of physical training. . . . Montaigne foreshadowed it . . . when he says: "Our very exercises and recreations, running, wrestling, music, dancing, hunting, riding, and fencing, will prove to be a good part of our study. . . . It is not a soul, it is not a body, that we are training up; it is a man, and we ought not to divide him into two parts." In a word, the whole man is reached through his motor activities, and is involved in them. Mind and body are interdependent, and what we have been calling physical training may, if properly applied, make direct and most important contributions to the intellectual, social, and moral progress of the child and youth.

It is time that we adopted a new definition of physical education. The term has been used, as, in Spencer's "Education," to include the entire personal hygiene of childhood and youth. Others have understood by it the systematic exercise of the neuromuscular mechanism for the correction of defects or deformities, for the restoration or preservation of health, and to secure ready control of the human machine and right motor habits—a view which makes the physical results the chief or only ones. A better usage, and one more in conformity with the present conception of man's nature as a unit, is that which regards his motor activities as a means of influencing for good the entire individual—in mind and character as well as in body; it employs the word *physical* to denote the means, and not the end.

From the time of the Athenian philosophers down to the present day men have always realized, more or less consciously, the truth embodied in such a definition. The Greek gymnastics—contests in wrestling, running, jumping, throwing the spear and the discus—were intended to develop the body and the will. At the Olympic and other pan-Hellenic games spectators witnessed striking exhibitions of human strength, skill, speed, and endurance; but also of concentrated and intense effort, resoluteness, alertness, presence of mind, resourcefulness, steadfastness, and perseverance. For the Roman youth, at least during the years of the Republic, when every citizen except those of the lowest class was liable to military service for thirty years after his entrance into man's estate, the life of the camp, the march, and the battlefield promoted not only physical hardihood and skill in personal combat, but self-mastery, subordination, physical and moral courage, and a spirit of loyalty and cooperation. The ascetic conception of the relation of body and mind or soul . . . recognized the effects of intemperate yielding to bodily promptings upon the life of the spirit. . . . But the hermit of early Catholic legends was gradually displaced as a popular hero by the

knight, and . . . the training of the knight stood in sharp contrast to
the education imparted in the monastery schools, and the practices of
chivalry were a schooling in knightly *virtues,* as well as in horsemanship
and the adroit use of weapons.

The popular gymnastic societies (*Turnvereine*) of Germany . . . are
a direct result of the work of Friedrich Ludwig Jahn . . . and reflect
his spirit and aims. Such a thing as a formal training in gymnastics was
foreign to his purpose. The essential feature was the active, wholesome,
common life in the open air, and the opportunity to promote harmony
and to kindle public spirit. . . . Ling, who opened in 1814 the Royal
Central Institute of Gymnastics in Stockholm, . . . was also elected to a
seat in the Swedish Academy as a tribute to his literary works . . .
whether teaching or writing he sought to revive in his countrymen the
old Norse vigor of body and character. . . .

In an oration delivered before the Phi Beta Kappa society of Harvard
University in 1893, President Francis A. Walker called attention to the
fact that

the favorite athletics of today are, in great measure, such as call for more than
mere strength and swiftness. They demand also courage, coolness, steadiness of
nerve, quickness of apprehension, resourcefulness, self-knowledge, self-reliance.
Further still, they often demand of the contestants the ability to work with
others, power of combination, readiness to subordinate selfish impulses, personal
desires, and even individual credit to a common end. These are all qualities
useful in any profession . . . and it cannot be gainsaid that it is the normal
effect of certain kinds of athletic sports to develop these qualities among the
contestants, as well as to afford impressive examples to the minds of the
spectators. . . . It is unquestionably the opinion of most educated Englishmen
that the cultivation of [football] in the public schools of that country has had
not a little to do with the courage, address, and energy with which the graduates
of Rugby, Eton, and Harrow have made their way through dangers and over
difficulties in all quarters of the globe. . . .

Discarding, then, the ascetic view as no longer tenable, and accepting
both the biologic and psychophysic as together supplying the foundation on which our argument is to be built up, let us next remind ourselves that phenomenal changes . . . have largely robbed the home and
daily occupations of their power to furnish physical activity, and have
made it necessary for the community to meet the need through the
agency of the school and the playground. As late as the middle of the
last century it was still true that the farm, and in the town the home,
with its "chores" about house, barn, yard, and garden provided for a
large majority of the young a motor training that was in many respects
ideal. But now, with an abruptness of transition that is fairly startling,

the massing of population in cities and the substitution of machinery for human muscle have practically banished these factors in education from the lives of all but a few. . . .

The community is thus confronted with a new problem, one which hitherto the family has for the most part been left to solve for itself. It must not only safeguard the bodily welfare of the child, under the changed conditions and in a variety of ways undreamed of by our fathers; it must also take over the task of providing the growing boy and girl and the adolescent with an amount and kind of motor training which will be sufficient for his needs at every stage of growth and development. The gymnasium and the playground have become a necessary part of the educational plant, and the school is called upon to extend its curriculum and enlarge its powers in order to incorporate and control these educational agencies. Its tasks is a fourfold one: first, to conserve the health of the individual pupil and the group; second, to give instruction in the essentials of personal, domestic, and public hygiene; third, to provide systematic and progressive physical training throughout all but the earlier years; and fourth, to organize and supervise the activities of the playground and the athletic field.

The first and second of these duties need not enter into our present discussion. As to the reasons for systematic and progressive physical training throughout the greater part of the school course, and regarding the manner of carrying out such a comprehensive plan, there is still a surprising confusion of ideas, even among men who have made a professional study of the subject and who occupy conspicuous positions of leadership. Play, games, and athletic sports, although their value can hardly be exaggerated, are no more able to take the place of formal gymnastics than are the popular magazine, the picture show, and the public library to serve as substitutes for the orderly discipline of the school and college. There are drooping heads and shoulders, bowed backs, and flat chests which must be made to yield to carefully chosen corrective exercises. The rudiments of neuromuscular control must be acquired through frequent practice of varied forms of movement graded according to difficulty and advancing from the simple to the complex. The confinement of the classroom must be offset by vigorous use of the large, fundamental groups of muscles, those of the shoulders, trunk, and legs, whose contractions stimulate the activity of heart, lungs, and skin. The foundations of self-reliance, courage, and decision of character must be laid by means of exercises that call for the overcoming of some difficulty, or that present the element of danger involved in hanging and swinging by the arms and in jumping and vaulting over obstacles.

The almost endless number and variety of such exercises make it possible to meet the needs of the most backward and to progress by easy gradations to any desired degree of proficiency. Character and will-training, no less than the purely physical effects, should be sought from the start. Hanging and climbing exercises have played an important part in bringing the human thorax to its present shape and they are indispensable factors in promoting its due development in every individual, giving him at the same time valuable training in self-confidence and steadiness of nerve. Exercises in jumping and vaulting are a veritable school of courage. It follows, then, that a fully equipped gymnasium, indoors and out, is needed for all but the most rudimentary and meager physical training. Every pupil must be reached by this orderly discipline, and economy of time and space requires that the system and method be most carefully elaborated. Late fall, winter, and early spring, when the playground is usually deserted, are seasons when the need for regular exercise is greatest.

But the hour or so a day devoted to formal physical training is far from supplying all the motor activity required for the normal development of the child and youth. It is desirable that a still longer time be spent on the playground and athletic field. Here organization and supervision are again demanded, but only with the object of giving each individual a chance to play and of preventing the few from usurping facilities that all should enjoy. Freedom for self-expression and self-control, subject only to the rules of the game and the dictates of true sportsmanship, are the very essence of play. Social and moral training are chief among its benefits, and the teacher's business is to suggest and lead, not to dictate or compel. . . .

Thus reason and experience both lead to the conclusion that neither the gymnasium nor the playground is alone sufficient, but that each is an essential part in a complete scheme of physical education.

A Plea for More Theoretical Instruction in
Our Normal Schools of Gymnastics *

JAY W. SEAVER, M.D.

Dr. Jay W. Seaver was one of the first leaders in American physical education to place a heavy emphasis on a sound educational background for
all physical-education teachers; this view is clearly illustrated in this
document. Born in Craftsbury, Vermont, in 1855, Dr. Seaver attended
Williston Seminary and then Yale University, where he received the M.D.
degree in 1885. After several years of teaching in Scranton, Pennsylvania,
and Williston Seminary, he accepted a position at Yale University as Physical Director and Lecturer in Physiology. Along with this assignment he
served as Lecturer in Anatomy and Physiology at the New Haven School
of Gymnastics. A strong interest in teacher preparation in physical education led Dr. Seaver to become a founder and later President of the
Chautauqua Summer School of Physical Education. He was a founder
and early President of the American Association for the Advancement of
Physical Education (now the AAHPER), and President of the College
Physical Education Association. His interest in anthropometric measurement led to the publication of several articles and a book on anthropometry and physical examinations.

The problem of physical education today is vastly different from that
in the past. The work has not yet grown into a science, but it is moving
toward scientific accuracy by constantly improving methods. The great
purpose of gymnastics fifty years ago was to serve as a safety valve for
the exuberant vitality of the few; today, let me try to indicate its leading
object as to the upbuilding of the vitality of the masses, with special
regard for the weak, and only casual consideration for the strong.

In a certain sense, physical training was formerly destructive in scope;
today it is constructive. When surplus energy was to be used up, the
method employed was one of bruising, and the "bruiser" was employed
to do the work. When impaired vitality is to be restored, the method

* J. W. Seaver, "A Plea for More Theoretical Instruction in Our Normal Schools
of Gymnastics," *American Physical Education Review*, Vol. 6 (September, 1901),
pp. 217–221.

of the physician must be employed and so the doctor has been called in to take charge of physical training in many of our important schools and colleges. As professional skill has been sought, technical schools, laboratories, and accessory institutions have been called into life, until today the Normal School of Gymnastics stands forth as the highest product of the evolution of the modern idea of physical education.

Just what the normal school shall be in the future will be determined by the needs of the people. Today, it is the professional training school of the teachers who are to do for the next decade the best that they can do for the physical uplifting of our people. What do we want these people to teach? Or in other words, what kind of a product do we want them to put forth? For the public is only interested in the teacher and not in the method of producing that teacher.

We are here to study the methods of training teachers for the great public. We are the manufacturers who are trying to improve methods and processes and products, and to educate the public to demand the best that can be turned out. There are about seven normal schools of physical education which are trying to meet the demand for teachers, and at least half of these are located in Massachusetts, which is rightly entitled to a leadership in any educational movement. A glance at the circulars issued by these schools and a comparison with those issued ten years ago impresses one with the fact that there is a distinct movement toward the enlargement of the curriculum in the direction of the so-called theoretical branches of study, and this enlargement shows not only a broadening, but a decided deepening of the work, until the amount of mental application required in these schools is vastly in access of the physical.

This I believe to be a healthy indication, but I beg you to notice that the popular appreciation of gymnastics has grown faster than the curricula of the schools, until today the best positions are filled by physicians who have had ample preparation along certain theoretical lines, but whose training is decidedly uneven and constitutes a bold landscape made up of sturdy hills seamed by yawning chasms of ignorance that indicate an earthquake or cataclysm somewhere in their preparatory course of training. This should not be the case. The physician does not leave his office to fill the pulpit, although this might temporarily help the somewhat diseased condition of theology today; nor does he step from the clinic to the school room, for he has had no training as a teacher. Why should he crowd the teacher of gymnastics from the best positions? The answer will give strength to my plea for more theoretical instruction in our normal schools.

Every graduate goes forth with a sufficient complement of movements that if properly employed would move the world, but unfortunately, the knowledge of when to employ certain exercises and when to use others, rests on so narrow and empirical a basis that it topples over and crushes the teacher very frequently, and it ought to obliterate him oftener than it does. The remedy for this must be found in giving the pupil who is preparing for teaching gymnastics, as thorough and complete instruction as is furnished in the medical schools of the country. This is not an impossibility, although it looks toward the endowment of such schools by friends of physical education or by the state. Until such conditions can be obtained, I beg to suggest that an alliance should be formed by each of these schools with some medical school, so that the instruction should be made as thorough and inexpensive as possible.

As a fundamental requirement, all pupils should be required to have a high school education before beginning their technical training, and this high school course should be, if possible, along the lines of natural sciences, rather than in the classics, as a familiarity with the conditions of everyday life seems essential in this line of work. A few high schools give more than a slight theoretical knowledge of chemistry, and since chemistry is destined to play a constantly increasing role in the interpretation of physiological facts, and even in domestic life, it is absolutely essential that each pupil at the beginning of the course should have a practical knowledge of fundamental reactions as evidenced in chemistry. This course should cover at least twenty weeks of the first year, of eight hours per week, and should precede any instruction in pure physiology.

Coincident with the course in chemistry, instruction in the use of the microscope in the study of low forms of life, both animal and vegetable, should be given; and this may be considered the preliminary step in the study of biology, which should be continued for at least twelve weeks of six hours a week and should lead to the further use of the microscope in the study of microscopic anatomy, or, as it is termed, histology. I would be willing, if necessary, to sacrifice all instruction in human physiology during the first year of the course if thorough instruction could be given in the subjects indicated. However, I believe it is wise to begin the study of elementary physiology by the opening of the second half of the junior year.

The work in anatomy, already given, should be extended by work in dissection, for in no other way can anatomical information be dissociated from the textbook and made applicable to the human body. This dissection should properly come in the second half of the junior year; and the work should aim more at a thorough comprehension of the mechanical conditions displayed by the muscles and bones rather than a study of them separately. Attention must be paid to the position and relationship of the nerves and great blood vessels, for a knowledge of them will be essential in determining the actual value of exercises as applied to various individuals. (Note the discussion of Swedish Physiology in our Review last year.)

This work in anatomy should be continued during the first half of the senior year by practical applications of its principles to the problems of physical training, thus supplementing a course in the physiology of exercise.

The course in physiology should begin with the second half of the junior year, and be continued for at least three exercises per week during the remainder of the course.

Instruction in anthropometry should be given during the first three weeks of the senior year, by lecture or recitation, and I believe that not over ten hours should be devoted to this topic in a theoretical way; and I am not inclined to believe that much time can be profitably spent on the history of the subject, certainly not more than two hours.

A course in medicine pays no attention to the history of the art as practiced by the fathers of the profession except in casual references; so in this course time is too short to be spent on matters of general information, however interesting they may be in themselves. I would much prefer that time should be spent in the practice of anthropometry, that alone will give accuracy and confidence in the work, rather than that it should be spent in extending the information that may be gathered from books at any time when it is desirable.

I beg to suggest that the only way that this subject can be taught is by requiring the pupil to actually measure and test the same person repeatedly and then to compare the records. This will show their tendency to error and permit corrections in method to be made. It also seems advisable that each pupil should understand some independent study, like the variations in the size of different parts of the body produced by exercise, etc.

The subject of strength tests is, I believe, a fruitful one for any person to investigate; but the pupil should not be encouraged to investigate too many points. In fact, the same may be said regarding any other department of anthropometry, for we take many more records than we study and use.

The theory of gymnastic movements should properly be extended through the whole course, and I am fully convinced that much time is spent on the mastery of elaborate movements that might be more profitably spent on a discussion of the physiology involved in the exercise and the relation of one movement to another.

The acrobatic ideas cannot be eliminated from the minds of some of the older directors of gymnasia and we must look to you younger teachers for a new standard and a keener appreciation of our true mission in life.

It must be admitted that in this country we have not developed any standard theory of gymnastics; and there are comparatively few points on which the so-called "leaders in gymnastics" are agreed. This unfortunate fact will explain the delay that has occurred in adopting some form of gymnastic exercise as a part of the school curriculum in many cities where both superintendents and school boards are agreed that some form of physical education is desirable if not absolutely essential. The lack of thorough training in the lines of our professional work, and the consequent necessity of each teacher occupying the position of a pioneer in the work, explains this lack of agreement and has notably delayed scientific investigation as to the best methods of physical training. We have a surfeit of personal opinions, personal methods, personal systems, and patented machines. We can be taught that the gymnastic earth is round or that it is flat according to the price we are willing to pay for the instruction. It will only be when we study the human body with respect to its actual needs and its response to various exercises and conditions that we shall ever work in harmony and thus make every effort tend to the advancement of the cause in which we believe, and to which our life's work is given, independent of personality.

15

⊃⊂⊐⊏

Preparing the Physical-Education Teacher *

DUDLEY ALLEN SARGENT, M.D.

(For a biographical sketch of Dr. Dudley Allen Sargent, including his professional contributions to physical education, see Document 2.) In the following account Dr. Sargent explains the reasons why a teacher of physical education should have a broad and liberal background.

. . . The chief province of the physical director should be to make the weak strong, the crooked straight, the timid courageous. He should strive by every means within his power to develop harmoniously all parts of the body. He should improve as much as possible the functional capacity of the vital organs and internal mechanism—including heart, lungs, stomach, brain, and nervous system. He should increase the power of the neuromuscular system for self-preservation, skilled labor, and for educability in the arts and sciences. Finally he should endeavor to increase the constitutional vigor of his pupils, and augment their power to withstand fatigue and resist disease. In order to accomplish these manifold results, some of them appearing to be almost antagonistic, the physical director should have a broad and liberal education. He should be well grounded in English and have a reading knowledge of French and German. He should be familiar with elementary physics, chemistry, zoology, and botany. For professional studies he should have taken courses in anatomy, physiology, histology, personal and school hygiene, and the hygiene of occupation, anthropometry, physical diagnosis, applied anatomy, remedial and corrective gymnastics, and massage. He should know how to meet emergencies and have had some practice in bandaging. He should know the theory and practice of physical education and the principles underlying the different systems. He should also be familiar with the theory and practice of athletic training for different sports and events. He should be a student of psychology, know the history of general education as well as physical education, and be well ac-

* Dudley Allen Sargent, "Should the Teacher of Physical Education in Public Schools have the Training of a Physical Director and Instructor in Hygiene or That of a Physician?" *National Education Association Journal of Proceedings and Addresses* (Winona, Minnesota, The National Education Association, 1908), pp. 1006–1011.

quainted with the principles and practice of teaching. He should have made a study of children, know the nature and philosophy of play, and recognize its importance as a great social and educational factor in our civilization. He should also be a student of environment, be familiar with the social problems, and know the evils that beset the young in the country as well as in the slums of the great cities. In order to round out his theoretical knowledge he must also know something of the organization, construction, equipment, and practical management of gymnasiums, playgrounds, running tracks, athletic fields, etc. Finally, all of this knowledge will be of little avail to the physical director unless it is grafted on to a previous training and practical experience in some of the many forms of calisthenics, light and heavy gymnastics, plays, games, and athletic sports.

The want of this practical all-round training has brought many an educated physical director to grief, while the possession of this practical knowledge, supplemented by a little tact and a pleasing personality, have often made the athletic trainer without much theoretical knowledge a great success. The man who comes the nearest to the boy in his physical life, aids him in his sports, and sympathizes with him in his ambition to excel in them has a greater power for good or evil over that boy than any other member of the school board or teaching staff. When we consider that the natural desire of boys to run, jump, play, and compete with one another in all sorts of active exercises is fundamental and to be encouraged if we wish to develop them into men—that it is only the abuses, excesses, and injudicious practice of otherwise healthful exercises that bring about the evils so much deplored—it would seem that in the intelligent direction and supervision of these youthful activities there is a field for the establishment of a new profession. Many physical directors have met the qualifications I have enumerated and have already entered upon the practice of this new profession in many of the schools and colleges of the country. Educators are already recognizing the social, moral, and educational value of the services of well-trained physical directors, and the demand for such men at high salaries is much greater than the supply. In order to meet this practical difficulty in obtaining well-trained men, school authorities are forced to look to athletic trainers, professional gymnasts, book hygienists, or young physicians, because they are most available, as the men who are most likely to render the most desirable service. Each of these specialists may be capable of doing good work in his chosen field but none of them measure up to the qualifications of the instructor of physical education for the public schools. The athletic trainer is expected to enable the school team to win prizes or victories. He cannot sustain his position unless he does— for the one thing impetuous youth can never realize is the possibility of the rival school having better men. The trainer has learned this fact,

and his chief function now is to discover and exploit the superior qualities of the few, rather than to improve the physical condition of the
many. The gymnast bases his reputation upon the "stunts" or "feats"
which, on account of long years of practice and highly specialized development, he has been able to accomplish. He must therefore necessarily have a small following. The tact and ability to make elementary
work attractive, which is the only way to hold the masses, are arts
which the professional or star gymnast never seems able to acquire.
The book hygienist teaches his lessons—as some persons teach ethics
and the Bible—by words rather than through deeds, conduct, and behavior. The teaching of hygiene without the practice of hygiene is worse
than useless. If preceded by the study of anatomy, as it should be, it
often leads to a morbid curiosity and habit of introspection which in
young people had better be allayed. The best way to teach hygiene is
through the physical activities.

Physical training under proper instruction is applied hygiene pure
and simple in which the ambitious boy learns what to eat, drink, and
wear, how to bathe, sleep, and exercise—in other words, he learns the
correct habits of living. Let it never be forgotten that the grandest people physically and intellectually the world has ever known were nur-
tured and developed by the practical observation of these simple hygienic
measures. The weakness of most of the teachers in book hygiene is that
they try to read into their lessons what they have never known, lived,
or experienced in their daily lives, and the pupils are bright enough
to see the hollowness and insincerity of this method of instruction.

The physical directors who are now holding the prominent positions
in the country have for the most part been college-bred men, who have
supplemented their college education and fine all-round gymnastic and
athletic training with a three or four year course in medicine. The medical degree being the last one usually obtained before accepting a prominent position, the impression has gotten abroad that it is the medical
education that has qualified the physical director for his job. I regret
to state that in all my experience in the physical work, dating back over
a period of thirty-five years and embracing a personal knowledge of
several thousand students and teachers, I have not known of a single
instance where a medical man or physician has made a success of teaching physical education without a previous or subsequent technical training in gymnastics and athletics. Many have tried to acquire the technical
training late in life or when they were too old for it, and have given it
up, and returned to the practice of medicine. Many physicians have
assumed the position of medical examiner or school physician, medical
inspector, or medical visitor, and physician and surgeon for the sick
and injured on the various athletic teams, and many have given courses
of lectures in schools and colleges on physiology and hygiene, first aid

to the injured, and social purity. In all of these positions physicians have rendered valuable service to the school, the family, and the community. This is the kind of work which physicians as a class from the very nature of their medical education are best prepared to do. But where is the medical school that gives its students the technical and special training needed by the director of physical education? The training in the fundamental studies—anatomy, physiology, and histology—is essentially the same for both classes of students; so is the training in physical diagnosis and hygiene; but how different are the applications of the principles involved. The physician from necessity has been obliged to treat sickness and disease. He sees only the morbid and pathological side of human nature. Patients rarely consult a physician unless they are sick, or think they are. If he is called to see the healthy and athletic, it is usually to set a fractured bone, bind up a wound, or to treat some other form of injury. In order to keep up to date and be able to help the sick and afflicted in time of need the physician must spend his days and nights in the practice of his profession. This he is often obliged to do from economic reasons. The advice that he is able to give in the way of prevention of disease is often worth more than the treatment—but the treatment is the only part of the consultation that the average patient is ready and willing to pay for. For the traditions of the people in regard to the treatment of disease, the medical profession of the past is largely responsible. To the honor of many of the present-day medical practitioners be it said that their chief efforts are in the direction of the health education of the people which often tends to render their medical services unnecessary. It is just here that the work of the physical director anticipates that of the physician. The vast majority of those whom the director sees are in good health, or in conditions varying slightly from the normal standard. His aim is not only to keep them well and prevent disease, but to lift them to a higher plane of living, morally and intellectually, as well as physically. To do this he must use all the agents of health available, and by improving the functional activities of the individual, build up, broaden out, and reconstruct him generally. The teacher of physical education who would accomplish this work in the public schools or colleges must have all the vigor, energy, and technical ability of the physical director, most of the book knowledge of the hygienist, some of the scientific attainments of the physician, combined with a great deal of the moral earnestness and devotion of the Christian minister. This is the kind of man the world of education is waiting for. This is the type of man needed in the new profession.

16

The Early Teacher-Preparation Programs
in Physical Education *

DELPHINE HANNA, M.D.

As one of the first pioneer women in American physical education, Dr. Delphine Hanna's deeds, thoughts, and vision did much to advance the profession in scientific research and teacher preparation. Born in Markeson, Wisconsin, in 1845, she spread her formal education over many years. Dr. Hanna was graduated from the Brockport State Normal School of New York in 1874, the University of Michigan with an M.D. degree in 1890, and Cornell University with a Bachelor of Arts degree in 1901. As a teacher in the public schools of New York and Kansas, she became deeply concerned over the lack of stamina in both students and teachers. She enrolled in a Dio Lewis summer-school course to study physical culture, but became disillusioned with this person and transferred to Sargent Normal School of Physical Training in Cambridge and graduated in 1885. While in Boston, Dr. Hanna studied under Dr. Bradford to learn the skills needed to diagnose and treat lateral spinal curvature, which led to her special interest in orthopedic work; and she attended the Currie School of Expression in Boston to learn the principles of poise, balance, and posture. She then accepted a position as Instructor of Physical Culture at Oberlin College and became known as an inspirational teacher with marked managerial ability. Among her students at this time were Luther Halsey Gulick, Thomas D. Wood, and Fred E. Leonard. As a result of a productive thirty-five years career at Oberlin College, she was selected for the University of Michigan Hall of Fame, the first woman in America to become a Professor of Physical Education, and the first woman in physical education to receive a Carnegie pension. Dr. Hanna had a special interest in teacher preparation, and in 1903 she published a status report which presents in historical perspective the early teacher preparation in physical education.

* Delphine Hanna, "Present Status of Physical Training in Normal Schools," *American Physical Education Review*, Vol. 8 (1903), pp. 293–297.

LOCATION.	NAME OF INSTITUTION.	WHEN ESTABLISHED.	LENGTH OF COURSE.
Milwaukee, Wis.	Normal School of the North American Gymnastic Union.	New York City, 1886–9. Chicago, 1871. New York City, 1872–3. Milwaukee, 1875–88. Indianapolis, 1889–91. Milwaukee, 1891.	10 months.
Cambridge, Mass.	The Sargent Normal School of Physical Training.	1881.	1881–1902, 2 years. 1902, 3 years.
New Haven, Conn.	The New Haven Normal School of Gymnastics.	1885–92, Brooklyn Normal School of Physical Education. 1892–1900, The Anderson Normal School of Gymnastics. 1901, The New Haven Normal School of Gymnastics.	2 years. Graduate Courses in Massage and Medical Gymnastics.
Springfield, Mass.	The International Y.M.C.A. Training School.	1886.	3 years.
Oberlin, Ohio.	Oberlin College, Normal Course in Physical Training for Women.	1886.	1886–92, 1 year. 1892–1900, 2 years. 1900, 4 years.
Boston, Mass.	Boston Normal School of Gymnastic..	1889.	2 years
Boston, Mass.	The Posse Gymnasium.	1890.	1890–2, 1 year. 1892–7, 1 and 2 years. 1897, 2 years.
Chicago, Ill.	The Secretarial Institute and Training School of Y.M.C.A.	1890.	2 years.
New Orleans, La.	Department of Normal Physical Education, Newcomb College.	1892.	2 years.
Philadelphia, Penn.	Philadelphia Normal School of Physical Training.	1895.	2 years.
Milwaukee, Wis.	The Burnham Normal School of Physical Training.	1895.	2 years.
New York City, N.Y.	New York Normal School of Physical Education.	1898.	2 years.
Berkeley, Cal.	University of California.	1898.	4 years.
Lincoln, Neb.	University of Nebraska.	1899.	4 years.
Bloomsburg, Penn.	State Normal School.	1902.	2 years.
New York City, N.Y.	Columbia University, Teachers College, Department of Physical Education.	1903.	2 years.

Name of Director.	Literary Requirements for Entrance.	No. of Teachers Employed.	No. of Students Enrolled 1902–3.		No. of Graduates.		No. of Graduates Teaching.		Certificate, Diploma or Degree.
			Male.	Female.	Male.	Female.	Male.	Female.	
Geo. Wittich.	High School Diploma.	7	8	9	216	4	159	...	Diploma.
D. A. Sargent, A.M., M.D.	Diploma. High School	20	...	74	....	215	...	172	Diploma.
E. H. Arnold, M.D.	High School Diploma or Equivalent.	12	2	36	6	208	6	156	Diploma.
J. H. McCurdy, M.D.	High School Diploma or Equivalent.	15	45	...	83	...	64	...	Diploma.
Delphine Hanna, A.M., M.D.	College Entrance Requirements.	4 Special 27 from College Faculty.	...	29	1-yr. Course. 2-" " 4-" "	10 35 1	...	25	A. B. Degree and Diploma of Normal Course.
Miss A. M. Homans.	High School Diploma or Equivalent. Probation, 1 month.	18	2	66	7	255	7	155	Diploma.
Baroness Posse.	High School Diploma or Equivalent.	18	2	38	11	200	11	140	Diploma.
H. F. Kallenberg, M.D.	High School Diploma or Equivalent.	5	8	...	27	...	23	...	Diploma.
Miss C. G. Baer.	Graduate Academic Courses.	4	...	9	....	24	...	10	Certificate.
H. S. Wingert, M.D.	High School Diploma or Equivalent.	12	14	12	14	39	12	20	....
Miss S. M. Burnham.	High School Diploma or Equivalent.	3	...	12	....	12	...	10	Certificate.
W. L. Savage, M.D.	High School Diploma or Equivalent.	13	...	38	....	27	...	27	Diploma.
W. E. Magee.	College Entrance Requirements.	8	2	9	15	21	12	17	Bachelor Degree and Certificate.
Raymond G. Clapp, M.D.	College Entrance Requirements.	.. ...	4	16	....	...	...	...	Bachelor Degree and Certificate.
A. K. Aldinger, M.D.	High School Diploma or Equivalent.	7	8	...	....	...	...	...	Diploma.
T. D. Wood, A.M., M.D.					....	...	...	...	Bachelors' Diploma in Physical Education (as work develops courses for graduate degrees will be developed).

189

Location.	Name of School.	When Established.	Length of Course in Weeks.	Name of Director.
Chautauqua, N.Y.	Chautauqua School of Physical Education.	1886	6	J. W. Seaver, M.D. W. G. Anderson, M.D.
Cambridge, Mass.	Harvard Summer School of Physical Education.	1887	5	D. A. Sargent, A.M., M.D.
Bay View, Mich.	Bay View Summer University.	1887	5	....
Cottage City, Mass.	Martha's Vineyard Summer Institute.	......	5	Miss Charlotte Carne.
Lake Geneva, Wis.	Secretarial Institute and Training School of Y.M.C.A.	1890	4	H. F. Kallenberg, M.D.
Boston, Mass.	Posse Gymnasium Summer School.	1890	4	Baroness Posse.
New Haven, Conn.	New Haven Normal School of Gymnastics.	1885	5 med. 1 Play. 4 Gym.	E. H. Arnold, M.D.
Monteagle, Tenn.	Monteagle Summer School of Physical Education.	1898	5	C. G. Baer. A. K. Jones.
New York, N.Y.	Summer Session Columbia University.	1899	6	J. C. Egbert. W. L. Savage, M.D.
Ypsilanti, Mich.	State Normal College.	1895	6	Mrs. Fannie Cheever Burton.
Berkeley, Cal.	University of California.	1900	6	W. E. Magee.
Ann Arbor, Mich.	University of Michigan.	1900	......	C. T. Teetzel.
Madison, Wis.	University of Wisconsin.	1898	6	J. C. Elsom, M.D.
Peru, Neb.	State Normal School.	......	......	Mrs. E. Graham.
Terre Haute, Ind.	Indiana State Normal School.	......	......	J. P. Kemmell. Miss. E. M. Love.

Literary Requirements for Entrance.	No. of Theoretical Courses.	No. of Practical Courses.	No. of Teachers Employed.	No. of Students Enrolled 1902.	
				Male.	Female.
High School Diploma or Equivalent.	8	15	10 Faculty. 16 Instructors.	23	55
High School Diploma or Equivalent.	4	4	44	40	90
None.	Mixed (Theory and Practice in same lesson).		2	40	35
. . . .	. . . .	1	1	. . . .	50
High School Diploma or Equivalent.	9	9	8	83	. . . . .
Good General Education.	5	6	2	. . . .	8
Normal School Graduates.	1 1 4	1 1 4	1 1 3	. . . .	11
High School Diploma or Equivalent.	9	10	4	1	10
None.	Mixed (Theory and Practice in same lesson).		5	20	68
High School Diploma or Equivalent.	4	4	1	. . . .	150
None.	. . . .	2	2	25	80
. . . .	. . . .	. . . . .	. . . .	. . . .	. . . . .
High School Diploma or Equivalent.	3	3	3	15	10
. . . .	. . . .		. . . .	. . . . .	
. . . .	. . . .		. . . .	. . . . .	

The Foundation of Amateurism *

CLARK W. HETHERINGTON

Clark W. Hetherington, known as "the modern philosopher of physical education," worked through the Athletic Research Society to raise standards of amateurism in the United States. For an account of his professional contributions to the field of physical education see Document 11.

The amateur problem is one of those discussions that is always with us. It began with the dawn of athletic rivalry between groups. It existed among those people we are wont to think ideal in sports as in art. It arose with the rise of sports in England. It has grown in prominence with the development of American athletics.

Our present situation is the result of social conditions. With the rapid rise of American athletics without traditions to guide us we have gone on many by-paths of athletic adventure. Neglect in proper leadership brought on corruption which authorities met with drastic legislation. Those hit, countered with a voluble attack on the traditional ideals of amateur sport. Having no deeply rooted public opinion on athletics as an educational and social force, there has developed through lack of information and insight a widespread doubt of the wisdom of amateurism. In the attack, Anglophobia has taken its part. Even intellectual leaders have been heard to say that the amateur law came from England, from entirely different social conditions, that it had no place in American democratic life, etc., without once pausing to consider whether the law had any foundation in human needs or any necessary significance in human relationships. . . .

The social impulses, with perhaps some sexual elements, add their force. The desire to be noticed leads to showing off, especially by boys. A desire for social applause and approbation leads often to self-exhibition and a display of skill and courage. Especially keen is the pleasure of achievement in competition under social conditions, perhaps the highest stimulus and satisfaction in youth to the egoistic impulses and emo-

* Clark W. Hetherington, "The Foundation of Amateurism," *American Physical Education Review* (November, 1909), pp. 566–578.

tions. Cravings for self-testing, self-evaluation, the determination of one's social status, superiority or inferiority, become prominent. Where these impulses come in contact with developed or traditional play activities as in athletics, there arises spontaneously a craving to gain one's place in the social system, to become a member of the team, to represent one's fellows, to support the honor of the institution and to win the satisfaction and applause of achievement. Public interest intensifies these expressions. To be in the swim is the most general of social motives.

In this brief summary of the impulses, pleasures, interests, and motives that create play and playful athletics, we see revealed all the meaning and significance of play and athletics. They are Nature's means of securing organic, motor, mental, and social education, which comes from strong motor social activities. The motives and the normal results are purely educational. The boy's aim is pleasure; Nature's aim is education. Educators and social workers are interested in the motives and the activities because of their educational and moral meaning. In the activities boys have inherent rights; parents have rights in the boy's rights, and in protecting these rights educators and social workers have rights. The boy who takes part in athletic contests purely in obedience to these impulses and for the pleasure derived is an amateur. His interest in the satisfaction of the impulses and in the pleasure derived reveal the content of those motives we commonly call "sport for sport's sake"; this is amateurism. It is the attitude of mind that determines the root of amateurism. Whoever exhibits this attitude in all his play is psychologically an amateur, no matter what the man-made law or definition of amateurism for social control may be. Here we make a sharp distinction between the principle of amateurism and the law formulated for its administration in practice. Like all human law the principle may be sound, the law enacted may be defective. The principle of amateurism is the concept of the natural mental attitude in play; the law is an enactment for social control. This analysis shows further that Nature's aim in play, the boy's pleasure, amateurism as a principle, and educational athletics as an administrative endeavor, have at the root one and the same purpose. Usually the professional interest in athletics is contrasted with the amateur. The amateur motive, however, is the flower of a primary human need and interest; the professional interest is not. This is a secondary interest derived from the spectator's interest which is primary.

Glance for a moment at the spectator's interest and see how deeply rooted it is in human nature. Human interest in contests is as broad as the struggle of nature and man. A storm, ants at work, men blasting rock or launching a lifeboat excites interest. Especially strong is the interest in fighting contest. Human nature loves to see a fight. A dog fight excites even the refined. The emotional extremes to which the indulgence of this impulse will lead is best illustrated by the world's great fighting spectacles: the gladiatorial contest, the chariot race, and the bull fight of earlier times; the horse race, the prize fight, and the professional baseball contest of modern times. From out of this primal interest in any struggle comes the spectator. As indicated in the social elements of the players' motives, the spectator's interest in witnessing contests has had a profound influence on the higher development of contests. He supplies the social setting, the approbation, and the applause which stimulates development. He has also supplied most of the money for the support of highly organized contests. This fact has given him his power in the development of contests. Still, to make his status clear, it should be understood that the spectator is not essential to highly organized athletics and the educational ideal that all should participate.

Our interest in the spectator, however, centers in his influence in creating the professional and professional motive. It is impossible to conceive of a professional athlete without the spectator. There would be no reason for his existence. The professional is created by the spectator's interest acting as an economic demand on those who have interesting feats to exhibit. The economic needs of those having personal skill and physical prowess impel some to supply this social demand resulting from the general human interest in feats and contests. The interest is satisfied for a consideration. Interesting stunts and contests are held at a price. Often the large rewards and the social applause or notoriety are intense stimuli for effort. Historically this is the origin of all professional performers in sporting spectacles. The spectator's influence does not stop with the creation of the pure professional. He creates in athletics the petty money motive which is expressed in irregular and intermittent demands for reward. The process is simple. The spectator becomes a partisan. He wishes one side or the other to win. Where one special group is organized for contests with another social group the rivalry become intense. It is play war. Group pride enters into the contest. The group partisan's craving to win exerts pressure on contestants for skilled performance. The effort to supply the skill makes training severe, the time consumed the maximum. Fun is often replaced by work. As a natural result there develops in some athletes the question, What is there in it? This the spectator tends to meet by extra encouragement and rewards. The play motive is replaced by the petty-money motive. The motive is perpetuated by custom.

The concept of professionalism complements that of amateurism. The athlete who caters to the spectator's interest and holds his participation in contest at a value, or who desires a reward for such participation, is a professional. It is the attitude of mind that determines the root and motive of professionalism. Whoever exhibits this attitude is psychologically and in social motives a professional, no matter what the man-made law of professionalism may be. The professional may have all the interests of a pure amateur but he adds something to the amateur motive which has no direct or indirect connection with the biological, psychological, sociological, or educational purpose of play. Producing this attitude of mind was the point emphasized by educators a few years ago in their bitter denunciation of our "commercialized and professionalized" college athletics.

To make our discussion unbiased the social status of the professional should be clearly stated. It has been said many times that there is no objection from the standpoint of play or the amateur propaganda to professional athletics or the professional athlete. There is no objection to earning money or to making a living by the use or exhibition of one's skill in any physical feat. Accepting money for playing baseball or teaching boxing or coaching a basketball team are not acts that in themselves are immoral. These are economically legitimate methods of making money or one's entire living. These acts become immoral when and only when the individual commits them while pretending to be something that he is not, or when he violates a social or educational law enacted on the theory that it protects the natural rights of the many in play. . . .

Educators dealing with play must realize the folly of leaving children and youth to their own devices in play. They must have proper opportunities, stimuli, examples, sympathy, and guidance. Each child must be taken where he is in the process of development and led on to a higher realization of his powers. This means organization based on a classification of children by age, sex, height, weight, strength, vitality, experience, habits, etc. . . .

In contests between individuals or teams that are supposed to be equals the law of competition has full sway. The law is emphasized by the rivalry of partisan backers. The desire for fairness in an equal opportunity becomes insistent. The sharper the rivalry, the more closely are the lines drawn. Nowhere in life does the demand for a square deal so promptly assert itself. Unfairness ruins the contest.

Here we come to the core of the problem. We are concerned chiefly with the upper end of play, the contest, in the later adolescent years, when rivalry is most keen. This is the contesting age. It is here that the law of competition becomes peculiarly important in determining and classification for participation.

This brings us naturally to the last division of our analysis and the ultimate question in the amateur discussion. What place and influence has the professional motive among the factors controlling participation? To put it another way: What effect has the professional motive on participation when brought in contact with the playful or amateur motive?

The effect of the pure or regular adult professional is seen at a glance, is recognized by all, and gives no cause for discussion. He eliminates the amateur under the law of competition. Given partisans with money and no amateur regulation and he would eliminate the amateur from all highly organized contests representing a group. The extent of this elimination, if allowed, down the years into boy life, is limited only to the living wage and the financial capacity of partisans. If we are to have highly organized contests to satisfy the amateur motive, it is clear that pure professional activities must be kept separated from the amateur by an effective law of classification. Over this there is no dispute.

Our difficulty is not with the pure professional but with the petty professional who has irregular or intermittent professional experience. The money motive in the petty professional is linked with desires for a little extra spending money, a trip, a pleasant summer outing, or a means of making expenses in school, etc. Our first interest in these experiences is not in the moral nature of the acts themselves but in the results which they have on participation in contests when the actor is brought in contact with the pure play motive.

It is clear that professional experience makes more expert performers. Practice gives skill; practice among the devotees of an art gives superior knowledge. No one denies this; it is one of the stock arguments used by those opposing the amateur law. Other things being equal the boy with professional experience will always have greater chances of making a place on the team of his group than the boy who has no professional experience. This means that among the typical mass of boys the professionally experienced is a special or exceptional case. Against him in the contest the typical boy is handicapped. He is defeated; the professionally experienced wins. The two parties are not equally matched; the contest is unfair. By the law of competition the typical boy is deprived of competition. This undemocratic influence alone establishes the place of the money motive as represented by the petty professional among the influences controlling the participation of the many and explains the necessity of a law fixing a classification, separating the money motive from the amateur.

But the results do not stop with the elimination of the majority. This is only the first step. A little experience in athletics, and contact with the petty professional, teaches the typical boy interested in athletics why he is handicapped. He is outclassed because of his competitor's superior experience. If his athletic impulse is strong and he craves to make the highest team of his group the incentives to gain skill by the methods of his competitors will be strong. He is denied the pleasure of participation until he gains superior skill either by a large expenditure of time or by professional experience. He must accept defeat, or do as the Romans do.

In this connection there are two points to be noted. First, the time element controls those with the higher ambitions even if they have no scruples against professional experience. To the ambitious, time is valuable; a disproportionate amount of time cannot be spent on things purely physical and recreative. Among college men the influences here are striking. College athletes, even under present conditions, have little time free from routine studies and athletics. They must forego other recreative and culture activities. Ambitious men refuse to make the sacrifice. They tend to withdraw from athletic participation in proportion as the administration disregards their higher interests. They not only lose the benefits of athletics but athletics lose the influence of them. What these boys want is not money but their athletic rights. They have a right to the education of athletics without a loss of culture life. They have a right to enter an athletic organization that gives the hope of achieving athletic honors without sacrificing their higher ambitions. A custom that either discourages general culture or the education contained in athletics must be condemned. In so far as the petty professional tends to create a situation requiring an excessive expenditure of time in sports, he must be legislated out of existence. . . .

In closing we might call attention to the fact that amateurism as a principle and as a law in the administration of athletics is democratic. It aims to conserve the natural rights of the many against the privileges of the few. The selfish seekers after personal profit in addition to social applause through pleasant and exciting activities, will always oppose it. Thoughtless and short-sighted partisans who gain a cheap pleasure from the selfish privilege seeker will also oppose the law. The amateur law and the administration of the law must seek to eliminate the few seekers after special privilege for the benefit of the many. Administrators must teach the public that professional athletics are for the pleasure of the spectator and that amateur athletics are for the pleasure and benefit of the participant.

Physical Education and Military Fitness [*]

JAMES H. McCURDY, M.D.

The professional career of Dr. James H. McCurdy centered upon Spring-field College (1895–1935), where he carried on the Springfield tradition of sound academic, spiritual, and physical preparation for all students and physical-education teachers. Born in 1866, he completed his education at Clark University, Springfield College, and New York University, where he received the M.D. degree. During World War I Dr. McCurdy served as Director of Physical Activities for the YMCA with the American and Allied troops and as a member of the Training Camp Activities Commission. Professional honors and contributions include the following: President of the College Physical Education Association; a charter member of the American Academy of Physical Education, executive-secretary of the American Physical Education Association, and editor of the *American Physical Education Review* for twenty-four years. Among his many publications is the book *Physiology of Exercise* (1924), which was the first of its kind in America. The poor physical condition of young men during World War I led Dr. McCurdy to stress even more heavily sound programs of physical education. The following documentary account represents the American and Allied thinking on physical proficiency as presented by Dr. McCurdy, Sir George Newman of England, Monsieur Henri Pate of France, and the Honorable Newton D. Baker of the United States.

The Army rejected 35 per cent of the men called to the colors. In 1917 the rejections of the local board were 29 per cent plus. The camp surgeons added 5.80 per cent. In 1918 the rejections of the local board were 29.59 per cent. The camp surgeons added 8.70 per cent.

Shortly after arrival in France training battalions were formed to care for a considerable number of men unfit as fighting men. I had personally, on the invitation of General Summerall, an opportunity to arrange for testing the physical efficiency of a full brigade of soldiers. Figures from one regiment tested illustrate what I believe to be average conditions. Twenty-eight per cent of the regiment failed to jump over a trench six feet wide in a standing broad jump. Seventeen per cent of

[*] James H. McCurdy, "Physical Efficiency as A National Asset," *American Physical Education Review*, Vol. 25 (1920), pp. 101–111.

the regiment failed to qualify in running the 220-yard dash in thirty seconds. . . . In aviation, according to the latest figures published in the June number of *American Medicine,* 2 per cent of the fatalities in American aviation were due to the Huns; 8 per cent were due to faulty aeroplanes; 90 per cent were due to faulty human mechanism.

No man could have observed the Army as I did for over sixteen months without having a deep impression of, and an overwhelming pride in, the deeds of valor of the American soldier. No careful student of health and physical education could but be deeply disappointed at the initial rejections and eliminations all along the line because of physical disabilities. The knowledge of these rejections and eliminations has brought about a very large popular demand for a larger health and physical-education program in this country. I am not critical of the Army. It did a marvelous piece of work. I am critical of public sentiment which allows young men to reach eighteen years of age with such deficiencies. . . .

It is evident from a study of public school children, of soldiers, and those engaged in industry, that our physical efficiency is considerably below what it might be. It also seems evident that this physical inefficiency lessens health, decreases production, and interferes with the joy of living. I object strenuously to any plan that does not improve the health and vigor of the children. We are in danger of substituting military drill and close-order marching for the real things that make for vigor: namely, camp life, regulated regimen, and large bulk of big muscle work. The introduction of military drill into the public schools has been a serious blunder. It will not serve the health of the high school pupils but will hinder the introduction of an adequate health program. . . .

England, during the war, has reorganized her whole educational plan. The experiences of the war have led them to place great emphasis upon the health and physical education of children and adolescents.

Sir George Newman, in his report to the British Ministry of Health for August, 1919, says: "The health and physique of the people is the principal asset of a nation" (page 7). In his annual report for 1917 to the English Board of Education (page 21), this statement appears:

The fundamental purpose of the new Act is "the progressive development and comprehensive organization of education" available for all persons capable of profiting thereby. It is indisputable that the primary factor in such an organization must be the physical factor. A system of education, however perfect, must fail if the physical and mental condition of the person to be educated be not healthy, responsive, and alert. Indeed, the association between physique and education is even closer, for the education and development of the young child is largely a question of bodily nature and nurture. Not only must the body be sound and unimpaired by defect or deformity, but its training and development is an integral, essential, and vital part of all true education. . . .

In conclusion he says:

The war has compelled us to realize more clearly the value to the state of healthy, well-grown children and adolescents, and of all educational and social measures conducive to this end, a practical and comprehensive scheme of physical training stands in the foremost place.

France—Monsieur Henri Pate, Deputy for Paris, in the Chamber of Deputies, Session of 1919, introduced a compulsory physical-education bill for all persons of either sex up to the age of twenty years. In his address in introducing the bill he states:

Physical Education is not merely a means for making future soldiers; its purport is higher and more general; and whichever way the conflicts arising between nations may be settled in the future, it possesses a primordial interest which is to give each man that physical and mental balance no man can dispense with, if he wants to discharge his duties in society. Moreover, would not this ideal, if it were realized, constitute the best military preparation? In fact the great war has just shown us that a number of able-bodied, high-spirited men, well grouped and making use of improved scientific methods and industrial products, is sufficient to make up an unconquerable Army.

It is now forty years since it was deemed necessary to enforce primary instruction on every French boy and girl, in order to insure the intellectual development of every citizen. Is it not today quite as useful and necessary to develop the body, and I may add the character as well, for we shall see further on that those methods set forth in physical education at the same time constitute the best training school for characters.

The best means to develop our children into "men" capable of defending (should that so happen) their property, their freedom, and honor is not to have them play at being soldiers, but to compel them to practice such physical exercises as may develop their muscles and strengthen their courage. So, no scholar battalions, but fresh air, hygiene, athletics, and exercises that harden the body.

The bill presented before the Chamber of Deputies applies not only to all of France but to Algeria and the colonies. Both France and England, as a result of their war experience, have reorganized their whole physical efficiency plan. America is in the process of doing the same thing through state compulsory physical-education laws. . . .

AT THIS CONFERENCE THE HONORABLE NEWTON D. BAKER, SECRETARY OF WAR FOR THE UNITED STATES, COMMENTED ON PHYSICAL EDUCATION AS FOLLOWS:

We have had a clinical opportunity to study the matter of physical training, such as our country has never had before, and we have been able to gather from the observation of the mass training of practically the entire youth of the country some lessons both as to its fundamentals and as to the best methods, of which some of you experts are now taking proper account. It goes without saying that the strength of a nation in the last analysis depends upon the physical vigor, the mental vigor, and the morale of its young men. We proceed on idealistic lines and with high morale, perhaps, in our relations with other people; and when we are met in the same spirit, a disposition of difficulties is always easy; but when we are not met in that spirit, the time may come when the hope of our own moral purpose is in the measure of our capacity for defense, and we must resort to the physical vigor and the manhood of the race as the last test of our right to endure. We have just passed through such a period as that, and it was a matter of great surprise, I am sure, and of great delight to everybody to see how swiftly the youth of America accepted the democratic method of selection for military service, and to observe the springing to arms and the extraordinary readiness with which the youth of the country lent itself to adaptation for military preparation.

I think it must have been a great surprise to you, who have had the best opportunity to measure the physical strength of the men of the country, to find what the training camps did, the original officers' training camps. Of course it was the product of your training that came to these camps. The young men from the colleges crowded into them. They quietly took on as much military training as was necessary; but it was what they had learned in the classroom of the colleges that made their minds subtle and flexible. What they learned in the gymnasium and on the college athletic field gave their bodies a certain capacity for endurance and resistance that made this training exceedingly easy, and speedily filled the Army of the United States with an enormous number of highly trained, invaluable, usable leaders of men.

If it had not been for the college gymnasium and the athletic field, I venture to say that the American Army could not have been officered in any such small space of time, for we needed not only the trained mind and trained muscles of the American youth, but we needed the spirit of fair play. We needed the spirit of teamwork, the spirit of organized games, which has come to be the characteristic of college athletics. We needed all of that, and it was a contribution of inestimable value, and one which in any future emergency that confronts this country we must look to you again to supply. . . .

We substituted for the brothel, for the saloon, and the horse play which leads to violence among men through losses of temper, the wholesome recreation of the athletic field, the highly organized games, well-conducted boxing bouts, and wrestling matches. We carried with us, when we went to France, American recreational ideals, and we played ball from Paris to the Rhine; we played baseball, football, polo, every game that we play at home. Boys who came from the mountain tops of Tennessee learned to play tennis, a game of which they had never heard; and now, all over America, we have come to realize that these wholesome and attractive substitutes for the ordinary things that get young men into trouble are all that are necessary to keep them moral and upright, as well as to make them strong and valuable.

The Army, therefore, has a very deep interest in what you gentlemen are doing. Of course, we all live in the hope that no such collection of our strength, no such mobilization of our manhood for a similar purpose, will ever again be necessary, and I say it with all sincerity. We had the same hope before we went into this war, and I trust our hopes now are better founded; but we must remember that the unexpected always happens, and if the War Department is ever called upon again to mobilize the manhood of America, we want to find them better prepared physically, and we ought to eliminate a very large part of the 35 per cent of the men who are questioned as to their physical vigor.

If we are to have an era of peace, if we are not to take up arms and form ourselves into fighting mediums and make that great and terrible sacrifice for the preservation of our institutions, still the conflicts of peace require strong bodies in order that there may be strong minds; and it is justly suggested by the morale section of the General Staff of the Army that if 35 per cent of the young men of America have some physical defect which is enough to raise a question as to their capacity for military use, then 35 per cent of the young men of this country are living their lives in peaceful occupation under a serious handicap as compared with the other 65 per cent of the young men of the country.

What we are engaged in is not merely making men stronger for military purposes, but for the present and pressing demands which peace makes upon every one of us. It is from that particular aspect that I am anxious now that you go forward in this movement, and wish to lend all the encouragement I can to the plan you are formulating on this subject, and to say that the Army itself is trying to learn and apply the lessons of this war. . . .

War-Time Revelations in Physical Education *

THOMAS A. STORY, M.D.

Dr. Thomas A. Story brought an unusually fine educational background to the field of physical education. Born in Burden, Kansas, in 1875, he completed the Ph.D. degree at Stanford University and later the M.D. degree at Harvard University in 1905. During his professional career he was Professor of Hygiene and Physical Education at Stanford University, Director of Physical Eduction in the Hygiene Department at New York University, General-Director of the School of Hygiene and Physical Education at Stanford University, and Field Representative of the American Social Hygiene Association and U.S. Public Health Service. Among his many professional honors were the following: member of the Academy of Medicine, President of the American Student Health Association, executive-secretary of the Interdepartmental Social Hygiene Board, and recipient of the Gulick Award and the Medal of Honor from the American Physical Education Association. Dr. Story's account of the "War-Time Revelations in Physical Education" is a perceptive picture of physical education just before and during World War I. It gives an insight into the deplorable state of physical fitness among the young men at the time; and it shows how the United States was psychologically ready to embark on a greatly expanded program of physical education, especially in the health-education and personal-hygiene divisions of the field, in the period immediately following the first World War.

The perilous emergencies that have confronted America and her Allies during the last few years have revealed the qualities of our peacetime procedures, heartlessly and with calculating accuracy. Our deficiencies, our failures, and our liabilities have been exposed, to our consternation, often to our chagrin, and sometimes to our shame. Our utilities and our resources have been made over into wartime applications at high pressure and on a wholesale basis wherever and whenever they seemed likely to help defeat a brutish enemy.

The horror, the cruelty, and the inhuman passion of that enemy, the fear of his lust, the knowledge of his plans, and the abject misery of his

* Thomas A. Story, "War-Time Revelations in Physical Education," *American Physical Education Review*, Vol. 25 (February, 1920), pp. 47–51.

victims, were compelling reasons for our assembling every resource for his defeat.

Among all these wartime revelations those that disclosed the status of peacetime physical education were the most disappointing. We of the allied world should hang our heads in shame because of the facts of prewar physical education that have been made public through this great war peril. When one thinks of the army of young men who were found physically unable to support the supreme obligations of citizenship when the very existence of this country was dependent upon its manpower, when one remembers the physical unpreparedness of the recruits and the necessity for their careful intensive physical training, when one recalls their lack of informational hygiene, when one learns the large percentage of illiteracy in the national army, and when one realizes the generally poor habits of constructive hygiene found in our soldiers—when one faces all these evidences of neglect and of careless waste of the most precious assets of a nation, there is no escape from the conclusion that we, the people of the United States of America, have failed to meet our obligations to our children and to our citizens-in-the-training. Under our stewardship 70 per cent of our children never reach the high school and only a little over 10 per cent of our boys and girls pass through our elementary and secondary schools to graduation from the high school. More than one-half of our future citizens are taught by teachers who are immature, short-lived in the work of teaching, inadequately educated, and possessed of a deplorably meager professional equipment. If hardly 11 per cent of our boys and our girls go through our elementary and second-ary schools and if more than one-half of those boys and girls are taught by immature poorly trained, poorly educated and inexperienced teachers, it is obvious that less than 5 per cent of our young men and our young women received any physical education at all while at school under pre-war conditions. It is obvious, too, that the physical education received by the majority of these must have been inadequate and ineffective. Under these circumstances it was inevitable that our young men should fail in large numbers to qualify physically at the draft. We did not give them a sporting chance!

Before the war there were a few among the hundred million people that live in this country who were discussing the shortcomings of physical education: there were a few who understood its larger scope, and there were a few who were vigorously concerned with its more complete development. We knew that evidences of physical deterioration and pre-mature organic decay were appearing earlier in each age period in Amer-ica than in France or England or Norway. These diseases of degeneracy were, we were told, due to our unsatisfactory physical education in childhood and youth.

We were told that at least 50 per cent of our population were in need of some form or other of reparative or corrective hygiene. We knew that for want of protective and preventive hygiene our death rates from avoidable disease amounted to something like 1700 cases a day. Our Army records indicated that sometimes as high as 85 per cent of the men applying for admission were rejected because of physical defects, a large proportion of which could have been avoided, remedied, or corrected. Those of us who would listen, those of us who would read, those of us who would observe, were well aware of the fact that America needed a great deal more of the information and a great deal more of the practice of hygiene. Various agencies were at work patiently, persistently, and unselfishly for the better care of our boys and girls and for the better care of our men and women. But it may be very truthfully said that as a nation we were extraordinarily ignorant of the inadequacy of our physical education—how few people it reached and how little of it was given to most of the people that it did reach. Furthermore, not many of us had awakened to the wide scope of physical education and to the necessity for carrying on all of the essential activities of its larger program in order to accomplish its more important results.

Then the war came on with its fearful possibilities and its acute demands, and we learned with dismay that a third of our boys were found at the draft physically unfit for the supreme duty and obligations of citizenship. We, a nation of a hundred million people, found at a period of extreme peril, when our very existence seemed dependent on our resource in manpower, that we were to blame for a staggering loss of precious human resource, scrapped because of avoidable and remediable physical and health defects. We learned that our productive citizenship was penalized because of our careless indifference to the physical needs of the infancy, childhood, and youth in the years before the war, and there was dangerous possibility that our neglect would be paid for in blood and tears.

The war revealed this 30 per cent of our young men of military age physically unfitted for military service; it demonstrated an extraordinary lack of information on the part of a great majority of our young men concerning protective and preventive hygiene. It discovered to us a growing, untrained army made up of our own flesh and blood, demanding for its better security and for its greater fighting efficiency protection from the agents that injure health and from the carriers of disease, and calling for the organization and operation of programs of constructive hygiene, particularly along the lines of recreation, play, athletics, and entertainment. Rapid and more or less unconsciously our various military, naval, and civilian agencies developed policies in relation to the preparation and conditioning of the army which were built up out of our peacetime procedures. The broad program of physical education, or hygiene, was finally covered by a composite organization in the Army and in the

Navy, and in the civilian population in its relationship to the Army and the Navy with an emphasis that brought out every important factor of the larger program of physical education. As the war neared its close we were informing our boys concerning important facts of hygiene. We were giving them careful health examinations and advising them as to the proper care of their lives. We were instituting for them a policy of protective hygiene that freed them from infectious diseases, except in relation to those infections that we do not understand, and we were providing them with a program of constructive hygiene that gave them the nourishment, the work, the exercise, the entertainment, and the rest that are essential to vigorous, effective health. The war revealed the utility of physical education to the army and to an enormous number of people that had never known it before. It revealed the scope and content of physical education to many of us who have not clearly seen its structure in detail.

Today there are twelve of our states that have laws requiring more or less physical education in their public schools. We have a national committee on physical education that is concerned with stimulating other states to enact even more effective laws in physical education. That committee is further concerned with the stimulation of Federal legislation for the assistance of the states in developing physical education for the children of the nation. Last December five national organizations adopted resolutions, pledging themselves to support actively all reputable agencies in the field engaged in plans for state and national legislation for physical education, and to make every reasonable effort to influence state educational authorities to make general physical education a preliminary requirement for every teacher of every subject in every grade, elementary or secondary. . . .

Physical education involves a program that begins at the cradle and ends with the grave. It is a program that is concerned with the acquisition and the conservation of a quality of health that is not satisfied with merely being well, or with a degree of strength that merely enables the individual to keep out of bed and eat three meals a day, or with a mere absence of abnormal temperature. It is rather concerned with a quality of health that means vigor, energy, endurance—a health that produces normal growth, normal development, normal co-ordinations, and normal physiological integrations. The standard of physical education is a health made up of the perfect function of each and every organ of the human body, so that the individual may meet his physiological obligations to himself, to his family, and to his country. Physical education involves a program of informational and applied hygiene, the effective operation of which would satisfy the patriotic obligations of every citizen—man or woman—to be vigorously, enduringly, and usefully healthy for service in peace or in war. . . .

And now we have won. The battle appears to be over and our boys are coming home. Are they any less important now than they were then? Do you cease to make provisions for their efficiency and their usefulness?

We know that the citizen of tomorrow is being trained today. We know that the training which we have given the citizen-in-preparation in the past has been incomplete and inadequate. We know that the great majority of our boys and girls get no organized training at all in their earlier years, and we cannot be surprised that their young manhood and young womanhood finds them possessed of avoidable health deficiencies and remediable physical defects. The revelations of the war have stressed these inadequacies of our program of physical education so that they ought to be perfectly clear to all of us.

But the war, at the same time, has shown with dramatic brilliancy the gains that may be secured through an intelligent and adequate application of physical education. Military training has become largely physical education. There will never again be an army trained wholly or even largely along the lines of military drill. Modern military training must be made up of patriotism, physical education in its broadest sense, and vocational training. The physical education that begins in infancy and continues through life will be the necessary preparation for citizenship, whether that citizenship serves in peace or in war. If America can pay for such a preparation for war, it cannot afford not to provide even more carefully for peace. Our government has revealed the shortcomings of our prewar physical education and has made the knowledge of those failures the common property of the nation. We have never before possessed a clearer or more accurate information concerning the inadequacy of our program for the conservation of man power. Our government has made the most brilliant demonstration of the values of applied hygiene that the world has ever seen. It has operated this applied program of physical education under the pressure of a great war need, but in so doing it has demonstrated the practicability of that program for the greater needs of peace.

It follows that the American Physical Education Association faces today an opportunity that is unique in history. There has never been a time when so many agencies and individuals were awake to the importance of health. In my judgment this Association should concern itself with establishing and perpetuating in every state in this nation the comprehensive and important program of physical education which was so brilliantly justified and so dramatically emphasized by America in this great war.

An Evaluation of the First Twenty-Five Years
of the Profession *

GEORGE L. MEYLAN, M.D.

Dr. George L. Meylan, born in Le Brassus, Switzerland, in 1874, moved
to America and became one of the leaders in physical education during
the first quarter of the twentieth century. He attended Harvard University,
Columbia University, and New York University, where he received the
M.D. degree. His professional career started at Columbia University in
1903 when he became Chairman of the Department of Physical Education and Medical Advisor. He made swimming a requirement for graduation at Columbia University—the first college in America to have such
a requirement. During World War I he served as Director of Recreation
for the French Army; and, as one part of his program, he established
some two hundred rest camps for the soldiers near the trenches. Upon
his return to America he combined his position at Columbia University
with a new career in camping. In 1920 he established Camp Arcadia for
Girls in Casco, Maine—the town which became his new home when he
retired from Columbia University in 1929. In Casco, Maine, Dr. Meylan
operated a model dairy farm, and one of his thoroughbred cows took
first prize at the World's Fair in 1939. Honors bestowed upon Dr.
Meylan are the following: President of the American Physical Education
Association, President of the College Physical Education Association, a
founder of the American Academy of Physical Education, and the first
President of the United Camping Association. In 1911, in his Presidential
Address delivered before the American Physical Education Association,
Dr. Meylan evaluated the developments of the first twenty-five years of
the American physical-education profession; this address is printed below.

This city is a fitting place to hold our convention because Boston and
Harvard University have played a conspicuous part in the development
of physical education in America. More teachers of physical education
have obtained their professional training in the normal schools of Boston
and vicinity than in all other normal schools in the United States.

This convention marks the beginning of a new epoch in the history of

* George L. Meylan, "Presidential Address," *American Physical Education Review,*
Vol. 16 (June, 1911), pp. 353–359.

the American Physical Education Association. Organized in November, 1885, under the name of American Association for the Advancement of Physical Education, the Association has grown steadily from the beginning. In 1897, the *American Physical Education Review*, a quarterly magazine, was founded as the official organ of the Association. In 1903, the name of the Association was changed to American Physical Education Association and in 1908 the *Review* was changed from a quarterly to a monthly published during nine months of the year.

The growth of the Association in twenty-five years, from 1886 to 1911, is shown by the increase in members from 49 to 929; the annual income from $34. to $5532. and the publication from an eight-page pamphlet to a monthly magazine of 725 pages in 1910.

The growth in members, income, and amount of published material is an index of the activity and importance of the Association, but the success obtained in accomplishing the ends for which the Association was organized is of far greater importance. Through the papers presented, the discussions, and the intercourse between members at conventions, and through its publications, the Association has exerted a potent influence in bringing about the remarkable development in physical education which has taken place in the United States during the last 25 years.

In 1885 physical education was not generally recognized as an essential part of the educational curriculum. The emphasis in formal education was placed on mental training to such a degree that the psychomotor training needed by the individual for the conscious control of his body was almost entirely neglected and little effort was made to counteract the evil tendencies of the school itself upon the health and normal physical development of the youth. The fundamental principle that "education secured at the expense of health is too costly" was not given due consideration in the general scheme of elementary, secondary, and higher education.

The influence of the American Physical Education Association and the activities of its leading members during the period from 1885 to 1895 were directed to the introduction of physical education in educational institutions, the Young Men's Christian Associations, and various other philanthropic institutions. The meetings of the Association provided a forum for the discussion of principles and methods for the conduct of physical examinations and physical exercises.

A very striking result of the Association's influence during that early period was the clearing up of the bitter controversies that had been raging between the exponents of the various systems of gymnastics. The broad-minded and progressive men and women in the profession, after mature deliberation and experimentation with the various systems, gradually worked out principles and devised methods based on the sciences of anatomy, physiology, education, and hygiene, and adapted to American conditions. The Swedish and German systems contributed much that is valuable in the various schemes devised by leaders in physical education. There are those who deplore the fact that we have thus far failed to secure any considerable degree of uniformity in our plans and methods of teaching, but this lack of uniformity and absence of centralized direction has, on the contrary, stimulated individual thought and research, and resulted in more rapid progress than would have ensued from the early adoption of a uniform system.

The period from 1895 to 1905 was marked by a rapid and widespread extension of physical education in all kinds of educational and philanthropic institutions. Other characteristics of this period are: first, the assigning of physical education to a regular place in the academic curriculum with examinations and credits as in other branches of study; second, the extensive development of athletics, plays, and games in educational institutions and in municipalities; third, the addition of dancing to the forms of exercise used in the physical education of children and girls; and fourth, a very large increase in the number of professional schools for physical-education teachers with an even greater increase in the number of students fitting themselves for the physical-education profession.

The last period, from 1905 to the present, has been characterized by considerable progress in various directions: first, in the raising of standards in the professional schools of physical education. Six years ago, less than 10 per cent of the graduates in physical education received the bachelor's degree at graduation, whereas now over 30 per cent complete courses leading to the first degree, and an increasing number pursue graduate studies for the master's and doctor's degrees; and second, during this period has occurred a phenomenal growth of interest in all matters pertaining to the conservation of life and health, and the normal physical development of children, public and personal hygiene, and all matters pertaining to health and healthful living. All these interests are related more or less closely to physical education in its broadest sense. Of these new interests, those which are most directly related to physical education are the playground and school-hygiene movements. The leaders in these two movements are nearly all members of our Association and much of the practical work in these activities is carried out by physical-education teachers. Two national associations, the American Playground Association and the American School Hygiene Association, were organized and magazines founded to advance these interests.

The suggestion was made by some of our members that these two new associations should be affiliated with the American Physical Education Association in the interests of co-operation and economy, but after careful and deliberate consideration of the matter the project was finally abandoned because it was found to be impracticable. Co-operation has been secured to the mutual benefit of all concerned, but organic affiliation is not feasible, at least for the present.

The growth of interest and activity in playgrounds, hygiene instruction, school hygiene, and all matters pertaining to community and individual health places new and important responsibilities upon all directors and teachers of physical education. It is not feasible nor desirable to dissociate those activities concerned primarily with physical education from those having to do with play, hygiene, and supervision of the student's health. In many colleges and preparatory schools and in some public schools the director of physical education is held directly responsible for all these interests, with the result that in institutions where the director is competent and possessed of high ideals, strong personality, and human sympathy, he exerts a strong and wholesome influence on the whole life of the institution. On several occasions, college presidents and head masters of preparatory schools have told me that the director of physical education in their respective institutions was the most influential and valuable officer on the staff. One college president said that if he were a young man he would fit himself for the vocation of college physical director because it offers larger opportunities for service in molding the lives of young men than is afforded by any other position.

That the value of physical education is now fully recognized in American colleges is shown by some figures obtained last year from 124 of the leading colleges and universities.

Ninety-five per cent offer regular courses in physical education and in 87 per cent these courses are prescribed.

The prescription applies to freshmen only in 27 per cent of the colleges, to freshmen and sophomores in 44 per cent; in the other institutions the courses are prescribed for more than two years or only to students who are below a certain standard of entrance.

In more than half of these colleges the courses in physical education were prescribed later than the year 1900.

The standing of these courses in the college curriculum is shown by the fact that positive credit towards the bachelor's degree is given in 58 per cent of the colleges and the students are marked for proficiency as in other courses in 63 per cent of the institutions.

Ninety-eight per cent of the colleges have gymnasium facilities, 96 per cent have athletic fields, and 37 per cent have swimming pools.

The academic standing of the directors of physical education in colleges is steadily increasing. Seventy-six per cent have seats in the faculty, 25 per cent have the title of professor, and out of 58 per cent who have the title of director of the gymnasium or physical director many have professional rank. . . .

In the public high schools only 8 per cent offer regular instruction in gymnastics, 5 per cent prescribe this work, and only 3 per cent give academic credit for it. . . .

But the growth and extension of physical education have enlarged the horizon of the physical educator and brought forth new and larger problems for solution. On the scientific side, we must ascertain many facts yet unknown concerning the effects of the various forms of exercise upon heart rate, blood pressure, respiration, and metabolism; we need more accurate methods for measuring functional capacity, vitality, and endurance; and we need further light concerning the influence of mental states upon physical conditions. On the educational side, we need a more complete correlation of physical-education procedure with the educational curriculum; and there is still a large work to be done in the organization and correlation of play and athletics with other forms of physical education before we shall realize the full benefits of these most valuable activities as agents for organic and moral training. Finally, the increasing importance and complexity of physical education demand a higher type of teachers and directors. We must continue the raising of standards for admission and graduation in our professional schools of physical education. . . .

21

✕◯✕

The Confessions of a Once Strict Formalist *

ETHEL PERRIN

One of the earliest leaders in public-school physical education, Ethel Perrin made significant contributions to the profession in the areas of dance, games, anthropometry, and public-school administration. Born in Wellesley, Massachusetts, in 1871, she completed the course of instruction at the Boston Normal School of Gymnastics in 1892 and then taught at this school for fourteen years. Later positions included appointments as Director of Physical Education at Smith College and the University of Michigan and teacher and supervisor of physical education in the Detroit public schools from 1909–1923. She then became Associate-Director of the Health Education Division of the American Child Health Association until her retirement in 1936; in this position she worked to establish the value of physical education in health education through lectures, publications, and radio programs. Among her professional honors are the following: President of the Midwest Physical Education Association, and recipient of the Gulick Award and the Honor Award of the American Physical Education Association. At the time she completed the course at the Boston Normal School of Gymnastics she said: "Dr. Claes Enebuske taught me Swedish Gymnastics as a sort of religion. I was an apostle going forth to redeem the world." In the lively description presented below, Ethel Perrin tells how she abandoned her formalist approach to the teaching of physical education for a greater emphasis on the educational needs and interests of her students.

I know it is dangerous to reminisce, give me credit for that much, but I am not going to begin with an apology, for that is even worse—that is poor psychology. I am giving you some personal experiences, which is almost as boring as telling one's dreams at the breakfast table, but it is with the hope that you of my generation who read this will at least find some amusement in hearing experiences laid bare which resemble your own, and that the youth of the Association will see a bit more clearly how to meet some of their difficulties, and will also decide it is wiser in the long run not to take yourself too seriously.

* Ethel Perrin, "The Confessions of A Once Strict Formalist," *The Journal of Health and Physical Education* (Ann Arbor, Michigan: The American Association for Health, Physical Education and Recreation, November, 1938), Vol. 9, pp. 533–536.

In 1892—yes, do your own figuring—I graduated from the Boston Normal School of Gymnastics, and have held some sort of a professional job without a break till 1936. The pathetic part is the downward trend in the mental caliber of my pupils. I began with the highest, the students of the Boston Normal School of Gymnastics, where I taught as soon as I graduated, for fifteen years. From there I descended to the college level, thence to high school, from there to elementary, and now I am in full charge of the day-old chicks on my farm.

Going back to the beginning of things when I was a student forty-six years ago, we find the graduates of the Boston Normal School of Gymnastics firmly believing this school to be the best school of physical education in the world. It was founded and grounded in the Swedish system of gymnastics and no other system or mixture of systems could be mentioned in the same breath. I remember speaking in disparaging terms, after I had attended this school for a few months, of a fine teacher in a nearby high school because she ran in a few dumbbells and clubs with her Swedish work. I claimed that her Swedish gymnastics were not pure —a terrible thing—and got myself greatly disliked by the lady, and no wonder—but I stuck to it. It seems impossible now that we could have been so narrowminded, but on the other hand it was wonderful to be cocksure that we alone were on the right track. It gave us a great sense of responsibility and we felt it was our mission to spread pure Swedish gymnastics from Maine to California. I suppose many of you never heard of the Swedish Days Order, but I assure you, after going through one under the skilled leadership of Dr. Enebuske or Dr. Collin, for sixty minutes, there was a satisfied feeling of exhilaration and well-being. Just so much time for waking-up exercises: right face, one step forward, side step to the right, and about—march. Then just so much exercise for head and chest; for arms, legs, trunk. Then the great climax, the jump and run, followed by the quieting down exercises and the deep, deep breathing to be heard all over the room. It was the perfect example of the "I yell, you jump" method and this I taught for fifteen years and never dreamed I could do anything else.

We all gave our commands as nearly like Dr. Collin as we could. He would stand at one end of the gymnasium and say, "With right hip and left neck firm and trunk twisting to the right, left outward fall—out," while we would stand in line at the other end of the room and in concert imitate his inflection over and over again. We were taught that in order to make our pupils put the right amount of energy into their exercises, we should exaggerate in all of our demonstrations when teaching—work much harder than we expected them to work. We practiced being a split second ahead in response to our own commands in order to get them there on time. When we said "At-tention!" every pair of heels had to click and every head come up at least two inches.

Professional formality surrounded me and this included not only formal and stereotyped teaching but all matters of behavior and of dress. After seventeen years of this I was sent as a substitute for a year as Director of the Women's Gymnasium at the University of Michigan. It was a far cry from Boston and I shall never forget my astonishment when a freshman looked me over and said "What a pretty dress you have on." A personal remark from a student to a member of the faculty was a new one to me, but I liked the friendliness of it. Then a wild idea came into my head. Why not take these girls out for hikes instead of staying in the gymnasium on nice autumn days—my first really original act in my teaching. I had always before done just what I had been taught to do, and there was no place for a walk in the woods in the Swedish Days Order.

A Middle West college group was a wonderful one to try my wings on, and while they were perfectly willing to conform to some of my Boston idiosyncracies, such as no gum chewing in the gymnasium and keeping both feet on the floor in my office, still I learned more from them than they from me. Anyway, we had a happy year even if the senior basketball team and I did have some rough sledding. Their methods and manners were terrible and I was wickedly glad when my freshmen beat them. The colored janitress and I retired to my dressing room and shook hands on it.

Then came the next step in my downward path when I was asked to interview the Superintendent of Schools and the Principal of Central High School regarding the directorship of the work in the first girls' gymnasium in the Detroit public schools. I had never been interviewed in my life and had never even seen, much less spoken to, a Superintendent of Schools. I brushed up my physiology, anatomy, and kinesiology, and read over seventeen-year-old notebooks—anyone knows how discouraging and futile that is—bought a new pair of gloves, the only point I could remember from my training in regard to interviews, and took the train to Detroit in fear and trembling. I had no knowledge of public high schools, having been to a private school only, and no particular interest in them. I went as I had done everything else professionally, because my school asked me to go.

The Superintendent, the Principal, and I sat solemnly looking at each other, my mind a blank, when the Superintendent burst out with "Can you swim?" Aghast, for I had never even heard of a high school with a pool, I said "Yes, I can swim" and thereupon they hired me. If they had asked me to describe my method of teaching swimming, I might not have been hired.

Here was my first opportunity to build something of my own, for my experiences had all been in carrying out work planned by others. I had no educational philosophy—had never heard of one, and doubt if many of us in physical education had heard of one in 1908. I had many strong convictions and prejudices but not methodology. One conviction was that friction and success did not go hand in hand and that I must have the respect and willing co-operation of those high school girls and of the faculty, whether I got my way in all matters or not. This was very daring of me because in the Boston Normal School of Gymnastics there was but one way of doing things and we did as we were told, whether we liked it or not, because someone else knew what was best for us. I had always followed this regime willingly because I believed that the one in authority always was right, but somehow where I had a chance to be the dictator, I wanted to try out other methods. I was not quite so sure that I was always right. . . .

I still clung to much of my formal work that year and I filled the gymnasium with Swedish booms and window ladders and horses and bucks and boxes and all sorts of truck. I did know enough to get plenty of balls and everybody had a chance to play. I gave every girl an examination and wrote to all mothers of narrow chests, round shoulders, and crooked backs for permission to give their children special exercises. Please note the following very important item. In this group fell the favorite daughter of the Superintendent of Schools and as luck would have it, this procedure both astonished and pleased the Superintendent for he thought only the strong received special training in physical education, and instead of being peeved at my saying his daughter was crooked, he was gratified with the attention. The girl liked to take her exercises and she and I got on together famously. I tell you this because I have always felt I never would have been a supervisor in the Detroit public schools if her back had been straight. The Superintendent did not pay me a visit the whole year through but on the day schools opened the next fall he suddenly appeared before me with the following, "The Board of Education will vote tonight for a Supervisor of Physical Culture. We have had two and they were both dead failures. Somebody is going to present the name of another candidate whom I do not want. May I propose your name?" I had never thought of being a supervisor, but that Superintendent had a forceful personality and a steely blue eye. I seemed to feel him saying to himself "Has she got the nerve?" and I said "Yes" but felt terrified. He always had his way with the Board, so of course I was elected. One member said he would have liked to see me, as he voted for my predecessor because of her fine "fizzykew."

I had no knowledge of elementary schools in general or in Detroit. I had never supervised anything nor anybody, nor had I taken a course or read a book on supervision. School principals, teachers, and school children were unknown quantities. I have always felt that it was the confidence of the Superintendent's daughter and his steely blue eye that drove me to it. So I say to you young people, never be afraid to take a chance even if the opportunity comes by chance.

All that the Superintendent asked of me for the first year was to make teachers and children like it, for in 1908 one and all hated it. I made a few trial visits to discover what was left by my predecessor with the fine "fizzykew." I found black looks from teachers and disgust from children when they stood up and clapped their hands eight times on the right and eight times on the left—all they could remember.

There must have been about eighty schools in Detroit at that time and I knew that my success or failure depended upon the principals and the teachers, and I shall add the janitors, for if they reported me "downtown" —as our headquarters were familiarly called—as a nuisance in their building, there was the devil to pay. And so, I laid my plans for friendliness first and foremost. Shall we say then, gain friendliness before you ask for co-operation.

The first thing I did was to open the Central High School pool for free use of principals and teachers every evening. The comradeship we established lasted me during my fourteen years of service in Detroit, and these few teachers formed a nucleus of friendliness. Next I held those bugbears called teachers' meetings to put across my "subject," as this seemed the way of all supervisors, but I never asked a teacher to take an exercise. They sat after a hard day's work, while I, in a gymnasium suit, stood on a table, gave myself commands and did the exercises, much like a monkey on a string. It seems that my predecessor had stood them up in rows and kept them until six o'clock clapping their hands and what not. Anyway, I scored a hit, and shall we say, if you cannot make your co-workers happy, make them happy as you can. . . .

As for games, we had a terrible enemy in the Supervisor of Buildings. We probably did make some of those old school houses rock, for we played hard, so we made compromises and in some of the worst places the children used a sort of shuffling run that did not shake the floor. That Supervisor one day saw the children sitting on their desks to do some exercises and after that every scratch was laid to me. He said it was their buttons, and my assertion that they didn't have buttons where they sat was of no avail. One of the nicest uses for desks came as a surprise in a third-grade room when on command every boy slowly uncurled in his seat and stood on his head on top of his desk and slowly curled up again and sat down. We had chinning bars in the doorways and when children got restless they would work it off on those bars. I have seen boys turning cartwheels on their way up to the teacher's desk, rather than walk. I remember taking visitors to one room where games were a great success and on leaving I foolishly said "We would like to stay and play with you all day but we must go." Up jumped a little girl and leaning toward me hopefully with both hands on her desk, she said "Oh hey—come on." I want you to get the idea that out of my formal gymnastic background came a program enriched by a corps of the finest teachers and children a greenhorn ever met. . . .

Education Through the Physical [*]

JESSE FEIRING WILLIAMS, M.D.

One of the maxims of modern American physical education is that physical education is education through the physical. This felicitous phrase is usually associated with Dr. Jesse Feiring Williams, one of the most articulate spokesmen in the profession during the years of the momentous expansion of physical education following the First World War. Together with Dr. Jay B. Nash, he carried forward the progress in the new physical education initiated by the great trinity of Wood, Hetherington, and Gulick and played a key role in the firm establishment of physical education in the curriculums of American schools and colleges. Born in Kenton, Ohio, in 1886, Jesse Feiring Williams completed his education at the Chautauqua Summer School of Physical Education, Oberlin College, and Columbia University, where he received the M.D. degree in 1915. During the First World War he served in the U. S. Army Medical Corps and in 1919 received a commission as major in the Red Cross, entrusted with the charge of hospitals for the Atlantic Division. In the years from 1919 to 1940, he was Professor of Physical Education at Teachers College, Columbia University. He was accorded many professional honors: he was President of both the American Association for Health, Physical Education and Recreation and the College Physical Education Association, and he was a recipient of the Gulick Award. Among his many publications were *Personal Hygiene Applied* and *Principles of Physical Education*. In the article printed below in its entirety Dr. Williams made the famous distinction between "an education of the physical," the premise on which physical education was earlier based, and "education through the physical," which epitomized the philosophy of the new physical education. According to Dr. Williams, only the latter view saw life as a totality; and he pointed out that modern physical education (as the new physical education was now being called) was based "upon the biologic unity of mind and body."

No one can examine earnestly the implications of physical education without facing two questions. These are: Is physical education an education *of* the physical? Is physical education an education *through* the

[*] Jesse Feiring Williams, "Education Through the Physical," *The Journal of Higher Education*, Vol. I (May, 1930), pp. 279–282.

physical? It is clear that an education of the physical would have some concomitant learnings in addition and also that an education through the physical would produce some distinct physical gains. Nevertheless, there are in these two questions two points of view, two emphases, two ways of looking at physical education.

Education of the physical is a familiar view. Its supporters are those who regard strong muscles and firm ligaments as the main outcomes. Curiously enough this restricted view is not heeded alone by physical educators but also by those who talk about educational values, objectives, and procedures. In effect, such view is a physical culture and has the same validity that all narrow disciplines have had in the world. The cult of muscle is merely another view of the narrowness that fostered the cult of mind or the cult of spirit.

Modern physical education with its emphasis upon education through the physical is based upon the biologic unity of mind and body. This view sees life as a totality. Correct in their appraisement that the cult of muscle is ludicrous, those who worship at the altar of mental development too frequently neglect the implications of unity. "Socrates with a headache" is always preferable to a brainless Hercules, but the modern spirit in physical education seeks the education of man through physical activities as one aspect of the social effort for human enlightenment. It is the plain truth of the matter that no individual, no community, no nation can depend upon one aspect of life for the whole of living. Deification of only the physical, or the mental, or the spiritual leads to disaster.

This recasting of the scene for physical education is no superficial move but a tendency toward deeper growth. It holds that we need to aim higher than health, than victorious teams, than strong muscles, than profuse perspiration. It sees physical education primarily as a way of living, and seeks to conduct its activities so as to set a standard that will surpass the average and the commonplace. There is in such a view something of the loftier virtues of courage, endurance, and strength, the natural attributes of play, imagination, joyousness, and pride, and through it all, the spirit of splendid living—honest, worthy, and competent—so much desired by each individual.

Physical education, however, stands not alone in the dilemma of special disciplines. Education has been, and still is, confronted with the problem. The old scholastic doctrine that separated mind from body, that held the body as essentially evil, has emphasized the contrast today between an education for life and an education for death. A child born in sin, destined to do evil unless transformed by grace, made the chief business of education a salvation of man from the destiny of his own nature. In this view education is a reclamation project, a corrective endeavor. There are few today to espouse such a view openly, but it underlies the practice of many. On the contrary, educational theory today is dedicated to the proposal of education for life here and now. The child is viewed as being of varying possibilities. The psychology of behaviorism has more forcibly established the fact of plasticity and unformed qualities of the young; the function of education as developed stands approved by science and common sense.

Education for life, or modern education, and education through the physical, or modern physical education, have mutual supports and confidencies. On the one hand, education for life can hardly be conceived without generous allowance for this kind of physical education, and physical education pointed to its own culture, its own minor objectives, becomes not an education for life at all. The identity, then, of education for life (modern education) and education through the physical (modern physical education) requires understanding by educators of the aim, scope, and objectives of modern physical education and by physical educators of the objects and concerns of modern education.

From the view of living as it goes on among people, and not as the view of a specialist or expert in physical education, it would appear that education for life requires the development of these skills, attitudes, knowledges, and habits that make for fine living. The part to be played by physical education in the lives of boys and girls, men and women, in this enterprise of fine living must be studied increasingly. Perhaps its greatest value will be in the interests it arouses, in the values it emphasizes, in the attitudes it forms. Whereas at one time, its chief values were supposed to be posture, health, and strength, these may become obscure in the prominence given to motives, purposes, and incentives for life.

There is a drama of civilization enacted in every community. The play is still to be written and yet its dramatis personae are all trained for their parts. The drama, if written, would show the lives of people who lack the ability to use leisure wholesomely, either because of a great ignorance of serviceable skills or because of intense occupations with the industrial or business world—losing the ability to live wholesomely, and neglecting the very objects for which it is worth while to acquire riches in a feverish preoccupation with the means by which riches are acquired.

We are unable to use for human happiness the magical liberation from the bond of labor undreamed of by our ancestors and striven for since the first log was used as material for a wheel and beasts domesticated for man's work. We fail again and again to use this glorious thing, leisure, because of habits, preoccupation with small things, lack of education for leisure, and the mood of strenuosity that sits so heavily upon us.

Doubtless we will make little gain in the use of leisure until we overcome the notion that play must be profitable. In physical education we have been ready to recommend golf or tennis for their health values when they were of value in themselves—precisely as sitting in the sun, or fishing, or walking along the river bank. All of us have been indoctrinated by the school teacher not to let the golden hours slip by when it would have been the part of wisdom to understand that they are only golden when we let them slip.

Education through the physical will be judged, therefore, even as education for life will be judged—by the contribution it makes to fine living. The ability to punt 60 yards is on a par with some of the esoteric emphases in general education. It should therefore be declared that physical education seeks to further the purposes of modern education when it stands for the finest kind of living.

This declaration of allegiance of physical education to the legitimate purposes of general education demands rather than forbids a statement that will interpet its understanding of that relationship. Such statement will need amplification or modification from time to time as new relationships appear.

Physical education in the university, first, is responsible for the organized physical activities of students. This responsibility is primarily an educational one in which the plans and purposes of physical education are to be reviewed in the light of legitimate instructional purposes. It is obvious, therefore, that varsity sports must come under the complete direction of the university.

The university is, also, responsible for the interests, activities, and development of its students. No university today can cut itself off from the large, vital, social aspects of the life of the students by insisting that the purpose of the college is to train the mind. It is obvious, therefore, that a rational program of physical education is required in every university to the end that men and women may acquire not only mental, but also physical skills with which to live an abundant life.

Physical education is responsible for the teaching of skill and the development of interests in types of activity that will serve the students in the college and the graduates after collegiate days are over. Thus, physical education characterized by neglect of minor sports through undue attention to major ones, or with a chief reliance upon gymnastic drills should be recognized for its limitations. It is precisely this principle of thorough going function in young people's lives that tests the quality of physical education.

The university is responsible for providing adequate space, equipment, and time facilities so that the capacities of young people for leisure-time skills may be developed. A state university making plans for a stadium has at present only four tennis courts for all the students. In the past, in many universities, play facilities for all the students have been provided largely out of surpluses of varsity athletics. The partnership of modern education and education through the physical requires recognition of the need for space, equipment, and facilities. Education for life means vigorous life.

Physical education is responsible as well for leadership in combating all purely professional and educationally poor activities in the field. Therefore athletics, games, sports, dancing, gymnastics, et cetera, must be viewed and organized with reference to significant functions in life. The whole program must be examined to determine major emphases and to eliminate undesirable practices.

Again, the university is responsible for the establishment of standards of fine living. Those engaged in teaching sports and games especially should be selected with reference to their ability to influence the daily preferences of young men and young women. A university conscious of the need to promote the physical education of all its students in types of activity that may serve in living more completely will not appoint as director one who is interested only in the teams or gymnastic uniformity.

Jointly with the university, physical education is responsible for leadership in setting up among boys and girls those standards of behavior that represent the best social tradition of the day. The responsibility rests heavily on this special department because its activities present so many situations where the individual is impelled to act selfishly or antisocially. The leadership is vital to favorable growth in desirable social and moral values, in wholesome attitudes toward play and generous reactions to opponents. While the reciprocal relationships have been indicated in the above items, the joint responsibility of the university and physical education is clear at this point.

23

The Physical as Experience *

JESSE FEIRING WILLIAMS, M.D.

In this documentary account Dr. Jesse Feiring Williams presents the modern concept of physical education in education. For a capsule description of Dr. Williams' professional experience in physical education see Document 22.

Every human experience is a magnificent mixture. We may identify one element as more prominent than another, but we misunderstand the nature of experience whenever we regard any act as exclusively composed of the quality with which we attempt to endow it. Experience is an interaction of the whole organism with its environment, and the environment includes other persons as well as traditions, customs, and the local physical surroundings. Indeed, so clear is this fact that medicine, jurisprudence, and education have rewritten their practices in order to take into account the total situation—the individual reacting to and interacting with all the forces of the environment that play upon the materials of man. Because every experience embodies the reaction and interaction of the individual to and with his environment, the experience cannot be purely physical, or purely mental. Only the need for identification breaks experience into categories such as spiritual, mental, social, moral, intellectual, or physical. These are terms of convenience and largely without reality. Although common sense recognizes that one factor may be dominant, it is never wholly exclusive.

In the popular view, these aspects of experience acquire a rank order that places the spiritual and the mental at the top and the physical at the bottom. In this kind of classification, our patterns of speech conform, our ideas perpetuate unaltered views, and prejudices from the past continue into the present long after the facts of the matter have shown the situation to be quite otherwise. When it was believed that the physical stood in the way of the development of spiritual power, it was reasonable to degrade the former in order to elevate the latter. Over the years, a fastidiousness without wisdom has continued to look down its nose at

* Jesse Feiring Williams, "The Physical as Experience," *The Journal of Higher Education,* Vol. 22 (1951), pp. 464–469.

muscles, but it should never be forgotten that a day of high moral purpose may depend more upon one's circulation, as William James suggested, than upon one's logical grounds. . . .

We shall keep the balance even if we remember that the physical experience is physical in its outward manifestation but mental and emotional, social and moral, in its relationships and meanings. Thus we may help education to abandon the tendency toward an exclusive emphasis upon mind and so change itself into a rational procedure for the education of the whole man.

Everyone is aware of the tremendous prestige associated with a high level of mental activity. Mental competence of a high order is essential in all the large undertakings of government, business, industry, medicine, law, and education. And yet, even as the physical alone is not adequate for the whole of life, neither is the mental a sufficient tool. Thinking is an abstract word that stands for the several ways in which an individual reacts to the forces that play upon him. And in his varied responses, he employs physical, emotional, and mental resources conditioned by experience. To regard thinking as the function of the brain alone and to forget the role of endocrine glands, digestive juices, eliminative mechanisms, muscle tone, and other physical and physiological factors is to ignore pertinent scientific evidence. Apparently we limit ourselves when we stand for anything, and the ability to admire scholarly performance without at the same time losing sight of the value of other traits as equally important has evaded us. The whole man goes to school and college and the whole man should be educated—not merely the speaking, seeing, writing, and reciting person, but also the feeling, believing, doing, and behaving person. President Butler writing of the college student in his 1932 Annual Report said then, "Evidence of his character building should come first; and evidence of his good manners and respect and concern for others second; and these lacking, no amount of intellectual performance of any kind should win him advancement and graduation." There are several suggestions that seem appropriate to make.

First, every experience, including the physical, is dependent upon the conditions of life. Man, like every other form of life, persists in accordance with the ability of the vital functions to maintain the processes of living. One may not like the physical but it remains, permanent and abiding, going on from generation to generation. It arises from the same soil that produces the birds and beasts, the flowers and the weeds, the loves and the hates of humankind. Whatever virtue we may assign to a kind of life that we admire, we can never properly ignore the physical, for it represents the breathing, circulating, moving, listening, seeing, and thinking person. Moreover, if it is mind that intrigues us, we must remember that the finest thoughts and highest purposes arise out of an organism that is physical. . . . The physical is as much ours as our poems and philosophies, our religions and our morals. It is truly a part of what we are, and nothing can be done to erase it. . . .

Second, the physical experience, like the moral and intellectual, the emotional, social, and esthetic, is to be judged by the purposes to which it is devoted. The crucial question is not whether we shall employ the physical but how we are going to use it. The choice is fundamentally never between the physical and the mental but how to acquire an intelligent attitude about each. For the sponsors of the place of the physical in education and in the life of man there exists a special handicap, because they have so often devoted their energies to ends that are unworthy and at times unrelated to the pressing problems of American life. We import Danish gymnastics without regard for or consideration of the basic facts that ought to determine any practice in the curriculum. The present policy in our colleges of prominence for the athlete and neglect of the nonathlete contributes nothing but woe to the task of achieving proper purposes. We should never forget that an athletic aristocracy in the college, whether recruited inside or outside the Sanity Code, is rugged individualism in social life and has about the same justification. High statues always cast long shadows, but the shadows reveal nothing of the quality of the statues. We can never safely assume that the number of people in the stadium is a measure of anything but the "gate." And while Bowl games increase in number, the course of action must be viewed in relation to the purposes that prevail. The chaotic sports picture is but one frame in the film of our current society. Although the charters of the American colleges declare that their purposes are educational, neither trustees nor faculties have seriously proposed to use athletics for educational outcomes. The failure at this point can be variously explained. Some would wish to observe that college policy reflected the academic mind as it operated within the philosophy that assumed a dichotomy between body and mind. Others would note that college athletics, in the past, looked to the initiative of students for their origin; and that these students, operating within the culture to which they belonged, used games as business enterprises and not as educational experiences. Whatever the explanation given for the origin of our present difficulties, it is certain that institutional policies in athletics are made in terms of monetary outcomes rather than educational goals. Moreover, the problem is intensified by the failure to accord to the physical a responsible and exalted place in the education of youth, and its consequent assignment to unworthy ends and purposes. Those who are critical of, or merely indifferent to, the place of the physical in education fail to appreciate the nature and intensity of the problem that we face in education; it is to make the physical, as Plato suggested, an effective instrument of the life of ideas, human relationships, enriching recreations, and rewarding enthusiasms. To allow college sport to serve other than socially constructive ends is to ignore the profound educative possibilities in physical experience. Present athletic policies lead to corruption, deny the common good, and breed attitudes in the athletes that later bear their rotten fruit in public life.

Third, the physical in its broadest expressions is one way out of the disillusionments of the present generation. The revolt against our present culture is felt by modern man whenever he encounters the noise, rush, and chaos of city life; and the cure seems to be a new education that will give a proper stress to the place of the senses in the good life. The moralists have been afraid of sense and have condemned it, so that many men and women are without realization of the intrinsic meanings that sense experience can yield.

The cure of disillusionment is not argument or thought but, as Edman suggests, "A renewal of the sources of vitality and interest germane to a healthy human nature." A trip round the links is never merely a game, a hike through the woods is more than a practical hygiene, and a swim in the out-of-doors puts one in touch with the creative forces of nature. There will be those who will call this sort of thing not education but play, and will warn against a waste of time. But the essence of education in the physical is time. A boy will throw a ball thousands of times to learn to throw accurately, and it is this sort of excellence that all but guarantees participation over the years. If time is the essence of the physical experience, space is its correlative. These two items, filled with connotations of infinity, relate in this connection to very finite values. The boundlessness of space that intrigues the philosopher is a mockery for many schools, surrounded by the factories, stores, and homes of an industrialized community. . . .

And, finally, the sponsors of the physical as experience in the development of youth and throughout the life of man ought to be interested in all the agencies, movements, and institutions that give promise of contributing to their purposes. They should be interested in new proposals and yet remember that life in all its exciting forms is too varied to be pressed into a single mold. Any disposition to center attention upon biological objectives leads inevitably to distortion, with weight lifting achieving a prominence quite undeserved. . . . The current movement toward coordination of health education, physical education, and recreation holds great promise for the development of youth and the enrichment of American social life. It is necessary, possible, and desirable to organize these three areas under education, to deal with the problems they involve as a single administrative unit, and to utilize the forces of this unified organization, not for the development of separate and special areas, but for the extension and enrichment of education in which the gains may be more marked for the institution called the school than for the institution called the clinic, the gymnasium, or the playground. . . .

Cultural Aspects of Physical Education *

JESSE FEIRING WILLIAMS, M.D.

(For a biographical sketch of Dr. Jesse Feiring Williams, including professional contributions to physical education, see Document 22.) Dr. Williams, after offering a broad definition of the nature of culture and describing the nature of man, discussed the specific ways in which physical education contributes to American culture.

The culture of a people comprises the entire sweep of life and includes the whole range of activities in which they engage. All their activities contribute to the cultural level. It is therefore a partial view that regards the fine arts only as cultural. "Culture means all the fine arts and the useful ones as well. The painting of the last supper by Leonardo da Vinci is a part of culture; and so is the white washing of farmer Jonathan's corn crib." The library that houses ten thousand titles is a part of culture and so is the football team whose exploits on the gridiron build the library.

There is a disposition, but surely not a growing disposition, to classify the cultural achievements of a people in water-tight compartments. It should be remembered, however, that the man of letters, often a popular synonym for culture, represents in his special interest only a phase of life. For us to think of culture in this limited sense is to ignore the implications of living as it goes on in the life of many people. The classical tradition with its emphasis upon the humanities too frequently remembers the past and forgets the present out of which all past developed. Life is too dynamic for a rigid classification, and yet the effect to pour life into set molds, that continually crack for lack of elastic qualities, goes on. This is an old practice. It is as old as ancient China, or the teaching of Mohammed, or the peripatetic wanderings of the Jesuits. . . .

Any argument for the cultural significance of physical education must rest of course not upon the claims of a physical culture, but upon the urgent requirements of a philosophy of the whole man; not upon the premises of a philosophic dualism, but upon the clear and scientific evidence of unity.

* Jesse Feiring Williams, "Cultural Aspects of Physical Education," *The Journal of Health and Physical Education*, Vol. 3 (November, 1932), pp. 20–23.

. . . The unity of organic functions is so clearly established that biologists and physiologists are saying that thinking is not a function of the brain any more than walking is a function of the legs, but that as we walk with the entire mechanism so also thinking is an expression of the entire organization of man. Thus glands and muscles, as well as neurons, function in thinking. Indeed, mind and body are one.

This emphasis upon unity does not deny of course that certain organs play a major role in certain functions. One needs brains for thinking as surely as one needs legs for walking, but so well established is the notion of an exclusive relationship of one organ to one function that the implications of modern science in these matters have been neglected for years. . . .

These observations regarding the nature of culture and the nature of man lead to an inquiry into the specific ways in which physical education contributes to American culture. It is obvious of course that it is now making a contribution since all the activities of a people express their culture. As teachers, however, trained and set apart to be responsible largely for the transmission of the best in our social inheritance, we are devoted to the social good and purpose therefore that the cultural contribution of physical education shall be as significant for society as possible. . . .

In developing the idea that physical education is a way of living, we shall come in time to emphasize what the last few years have taught many people who are now able to understand. . . .

Ours may well be the professional group to save man from insanity and his nervous system from the wreck that it promises us so surely to become. Gone are the days of physical education as a disciplinary drill in the classroom to keep children in order. Now come the clear demands for positive moods and responses that may make life reasonable, happy, and sane. Physical education will make possible this contribution to our common culture by developing, expanding, and distributing the idea that play is a worthy part of the good life, that fine recreation is not only compatible with but essential to fine living, and that devotion to work and neglect of play are as injurious to a fine life as overproduction of goods is injurious to economic life.

In the second place, physical education in its cultural contribution to society is to be judged by the interests and skills it produces for leisure time. . . . . .

Physical education will enrich American cultural life as it awakens interests and promotes skills that serve people in their leisure hours. The sterilized calisthenics in the classroom of a previous generation, and still found in some pauperized programs today, are responsible for those poor benighted souls who in adult life have to depend upon radio exercises and similar imbecilities. Doubtless we will make little gain in the use of leisure until we overcome the notion that play must be profitable. In physical education we have been ready to recommend golf or tennis for their health values, when we should have insisted that their values may be more mental and spiritual than physical, in this respect greatly like sitting in the garden and listening to music, or just sitting in the garden. All of us have been indoctrinated by the wishes of our school teachers not to let the golden hours slip by when it would have been the part of wisdom to understand that they are only golden when we let them slip. That is what makes them golden—the slipping.

Instead of golden ones, the hours are apt to be rather drab, dragging moments unless we have interests and skills. A physical education that awakens interests and promotes skills for leisure hours is a significant cultural agency.

In the third place, physical education will enrich American culture as it offers opportunity for self-expression in play and art forms. The dance, pantomime, and various dramatic representatives are art more than hygiene, and nothing so impoverishes the cultural significance of dancing as thinking of the dance as a means of exercise. The narrow utility that so often mars sports kills dancing. . . .

Finally, the cultural aspects of physical education are to be assayed in terms of the interrelationships that result from an education of the whole man. L. P. Jacks reports the remark of a speaker at a meeting called to protect the countryside from the invasion of ugliness that everywhere rears its head in commercial enterprises. The speaker said, "You will never keep your beautiful England until you get a beautiful people to live in it," and Jacks himself interprets what he meant by a beautiful people. He says that by "a beautiful people" he meant simply a people whose bodies had been liberally educated to correspond with a liberal education of the mind, and to support it at every point: the eye trained to see beauty and to value it, the ear trained to hear harmony and to resent discord, the hand trained to fine craftsmanship, the whole man, mind and body together, trained to creative activity.

The human neuromuscular mechanism is wonderfully constructed for the performance of skills. It is naturally skill-hungry, and until that hunger is satisfied, there is ill-at-ease, a craving for satisfactions, an inner urge to kinds of living that have been defined. The poet sings of the lark's song, the rose's splendor, the violet's perfume, but these appeals to the senses of hearing, sight, and taste are no more inherent, no more urgent, than that kinesthesia of the joints and muscles which the sculptor, painter, and photographer capture for us. A fastidiousness without wisdom has created absurd prejudices against muscle, but the examples of badly educated athletes or brainless Hercules scarcely justify the snobbery that exists. As we come to appreciate the cultural meanings of physical education, the intellectual respectability of muscular skill will be recognized.

Kinesthesia will come into its own with an education of the whole man.

"Both were faiths and both are gone," said Matthew Arnold of the old Greek Norse divinities. It might be the business of the scholar to ask where they have gone, but it is of more importance to inquire what has taken their place. As the old divinities of fear of and disregard for play disappear, as the insistent demands of leisure for interests and skills sharply increase, as play and art gain a respectful place in the scale of what is of most worth, as the present partial education of man is replaced by thoroughgoing education of the whole man, physical education will gain in the affections and respect of people. These are its cultural opportunities. To these purposes, we stand ready to devote our best energies. We ask those of like minds to accompany us in this significant adventure in American culture. The road is open, the highway of better living ahead.

25

ᗡCᗯ

The Athlete in Sculpture [*]

R. TAIT McKENZIE, M.D.

Considered to be the most gifted, talented, and versatile of all American physical educators, Dr. R. Tait McKenzie achieved fame as a sculptor, writer, scientist, and medical doctor in the field of physical education. Born in Almonte, Ontario, Canada, in 1867 of Scottish parents, he attended McGill University and became a fine athlete and student. Among his athletic interests were football, skating, fencing, swimming, and track, where he won honors in the high jump. Upon completion of the M.D. degree at McGill University he was appointed an instructor in anatomy there and developed an early interest in sculpture as a result of molding anatomical parts. An interest in anthropometric measurement and the need for a balanced athletic life for all students led Dr. McKenzie to study at the Harvard University Summer School of Physical Education and the Springfield YMCA School. He gained valuable experience as Director of Physical Training at McGill University while he carried on, at the same time, a private medical practice. For one year he served as house physician to the Governor General of Canada. In 1904 he became Professor and Director of the new Department of Physical Education at the University of Pennsylvania, where he remained until retirement in 1931. During World War I, as a major in the Royal Army Medical Corps, he did pioneer work in rehabilitation and plastic surgery. But his greatest fame came through the art of sculpture as he molded some 230 figures, medallions, portraits, plaques, and medals. Winners of world-wide recognition were "The Sprinter" in 1902, "The Athlete" in 1903, and "The Competitor" in 1906. For the AAHPER he created the Association seal portraying the profile of the typical American boy and girl. Always interested in the Olympic Games, he worked with Baron Pierre de Coubertin to promote Olympic ideals, and he sculptored "The Olympic Shield" of athletes. Dr. McKenzie served as President of the American Physical Education Association and of the American Academy of Physical Education. Among his many publications are the book *Exercise in Education and Medicine* and an account of "The Athlete in Sculpture," which is printed below.

[*] R. Tait McKenzie, "The Athlete in Sculpture," *The Journal of Health and Physical Education*, Vol. 3 (November, 1932), pp. 41–46 and 54–55.

231

The assembling of this great and cosmopolitan collection of sculpture, architectual plans, paintings, prints, and posters relating to athletic action during this Tenth Modern Olympiad makes a talk on this subject inevitable, if only to direct the attention of art lovers to this phase of our modern life as a potential influence on the art of the future.

Forty years ago, Baron Pierre de Coubertin dreamed a modern Olympic festival; and in 1896 in a marble-lined stadium the games were celebrated at Athens after so many centuries of oblivion.

The last thirty years have witnessed a revival of interest in them and a widening of competition that has made the original games seem like a parochial picnic.

In the last games at Amsterdam in 1928 more than fifty nations were represented. Europe, Asia, Africa, America, North and South, with the Islands of the seas, sent their athletes, white, black, brown, and yellow, in this great international week of athletic competition.

And now in Los Angeles, before eighty to one hundred thousand spectators, comfortably seated in the stadium built for the purpose, the Tenth Modern Olympiad is being celebrated. What a contrast to the hillside on which the ardent Greek crowd stood to see their compatriots compete!

We are now in the era of stadium building. In Europe, France and Germany are replacing the old walls and fortifications about the cities with playing fields and stadiums, and Italy has a grandiose plan for one in Rome to seat 130,000 people. It is to be decorated by ninety-two groups of statuary, each presented by a province and dedicated to Mussolini. The United States are studded by stadiums ranging in capacity from fifty to one hundred thousand people; and the Intercollegiate Track and Field Championships, and the two-day Relay Carnival at the University of Pennsylvania with its three thousand competitors, as well as other such contests, attract nation wide attention.

This is but a tangible indication of the revolution that has taken place during one lifetime in our ideas and habits of life. Games and sports were struggling for a place in the sun at our schools and colleges fifty years ago. Some think that they now take it all and leave the scholastic side too much in the shade. It is only twenty years ago that the school yards and playgrounds were recognized as possible places for organized games and competition, and the growth of summer camps and outdoor life have given us back the cult of physical freedom and the athletic life. The nude or near nude requires no cultivation in America. It is taken for granted at the beaches and camps from Maine to Florida, as a consultation of the weekly magazines will clearly reveal.

Why is it that this great movement has had so little expression from the painter and sculptor? Sculpture is the medium peculiarly suited to portray athletic action. Sculptors have always chosen the human body at rest and in action as the instrument for expressing their ideas, and nothing is more beautiful than the figure in the flower of its youth showing its strength, grace, and agility in the sports and games of the playing field, swimming pool, and gymnasium. The Egyptians of 3000 B.C. recorded the grips and holds of their wrestlers with a completeness that baffles us even yet; and a steady stream of great works with athletics as their motif marks the progress of Greek art from its portrayal of the athletic gods of Homer till it faded into that of Rome. The inspiration of this great movement in art was unquestionably the outdoor life led by the young men and girls of Attica and Sparta, for love of athletics distinguished the Greek from the barbarian. Sculptors had the nude body in action before their eyes continually, but the prestige that attended success in the great festivals at Corinth, Delphi, Nemea, Athens, and Olympia was another great stimulus. There, statues of the heroes of the games studded the grounds, and their praises were sounded in verse and story.

These games attracted the fair, curly headed shepherds from the highlands of Arcadia and the darker skinned landsmen and seamen from the cities and from the islands and colonies of Greece. All competitiors were of pure Greek blood. At their height the Olympic Games drew their competitors from the eastern end of the Mediterranean only, and not more than forty thousand spectators stood on the slopes of Mount Kronos to watch the contests.

We lean heavily on the fifth- and fourth-century Greek ideals for our art in spite of modernistic attempts to substitute the cult of Benin or Easter Island, and never more so than in our interpretation of the youthful figure in action or at rest. But our portrayal of the athletic youth is totally inadequate to express the significance of this great renaissance in which we are unconsciously living.

The modern athlete has already made his own contribution to the possibilities for sculpture that should be celebrated and not overlooked or forgotten. Since the beginning of time, athletes started a race from a standing position with but slight variations, as shown in the vase paintings of 500 B.C. and the photographs in 1880; but in 1888 Charles H. Sherrill, a Yale student, stepped back of the starting line, stooped forward, and put his hands on it, planted his feet six inches apart and 30 inches behind the line, and made the unexpected discovery that the thrust from both feet in this position, apparently unfavorable, gave him a quicker start than the time-honored pose; and so was invented the "crouching start" now universally taken by athletes and giving a beautiful and graceful combination of lines and mass for the sculptor.

The Greeks had little thought that an athlete by the aid of a pole would ever clear an obstacle at the incredible height of fourteen feet, and yet the modern athlete has done this, and is doing it, and has presented to the trained eye of the sculptor a series of graceful and beautiful poses of flight that are a delight to the eye.

The modern high-jumper has exercised an ingenuity of style in the "Reverse," the "Rollover," and the "Scissors" that gave it a thrill the Greeks never had.

The modern athletic program has other events peculiar to itself. Heaving the 56-pound weight for height by a handle is an Irish contribution. Throwing the hammer, first practiced on the village greens of Scotland, and the putting of the "shoulder stone" is now standardized into the 16-pound shot put from a seven-foot circle. This shortening of the approach from one at first limited only by the breadth of Scotland has given rise to a series of evolutions and poses that are peculiarly sculptural from the first stance through the hop and reverse to the final bird-like pose held for an instant after the shot has left the hand. The javelin-throw shows a pose almost identical after the missile has been hurled, although the modern athlete holds it by the shaft and not by the loop or amentum, as shown in the vase paintings of Attica.

But it is with the discus that the greatest diversity of style appears. When the Olympic Games were revived at Athens in 1896, the scholars and archaeologists tried to reconstruct the style in which the discus was thrown by the scattered references from Lucian, Stratius, Philostratus, and others, and from the statues, statuettes, and coins that have come down to us headed by Myron's Discobolos, with its disputed restorations of the head. They made sorry work of it with their Hellenic style, whose restrictions were soon cast aside, and the modern athlete has made use of his imagination to work out the way that seems to him most effective. The misunderstanding of the scholars seems to have been caused by the assumption that the discus was bowled underarm, a mistake founded on the misreading of Myron's statue, which does not by any means require this for its interpretation. It is very probable, that it always was delivered with a circular sweep from a stand, or "scaled"; but it is also improbable that a preliminary turn was used as in the case at present to give additional speed to the final swing, thus increasing the distance by ten to twenty feet.

On analyzing the Discobolos of Myron we find two points hard to explain: (1) the turning backward of the head, and (2) the dragging of the left foot. The head leads in any forward movement and usually anticipates the direction of the throw. This is universal in sports and is why it is so difficult for the golfer to keep his eye on the ball till it is hit. He instinctively anticipates the direction he hopes the ball will take by his glance, and so tops the ball. The gunman who shoots from the hip looks at the object to be hit and not at the weapon. For that reason I like the "improper" restoration of the Discobolos with its head forward, seen in the British Museum copy, better than the more authentic Lanciolotti version in which he looks back at the discus. It is more in keeping with the spirit of the movement. The dragging of the left foot would indicate that it is being brought forward as if to counterbalance the forward swing of the right arm, and after the discus is delivered the right foot again would be advanced.

In the Hellenic style it was ordained that the right foot be kept advanced and the stance unchanged until the discus was bowled, a foolish restriction.

One summer I spent my daily hour on the beach experimenting with the discus. I was accompanied by an accomplished athlete and we tried many variations on the accepted style of throwing with and without the turn. The result was the "Modern Discus Thrower."

I have chosen the same "moment" of the throw as that taken by Myron —the pause between the backward and forward swings. It shows certain radical differences. The body is more crouched, so that the elbow of the left arm is opposite the right knee, whereas in Myron's it is the wrist. The left foot is pushing instead of dragging, and the head is turned sharply forward and to the left, looking in the direction of the throw. The arm is across the back, and the hand in pronation, a position of the hand shown in several Greek drawings and taken by about fifty per cent of the modern experts in the feat. This spiral movement of the body shows better from the back view.

The rotary or spinning action of the throw has its speed increased by the complete turn of the body before the final throw it made. The evolution of the discus throw is still far from complete; and at any time an ingenious modern athlete may discover some new refinement of movement or radical change in mechanical action under the stress of international competition that will revolutionize the technique. . . .

Swimming and diving were part of the daily life of the Greeks; but we have no records of competition in them as part of their athletic program. In the modern Olympic Games, water sports have a section to themselves and bring competitors from all over the world. The flight of the diver, and the flat plunge of the racer each lends itself to the sculptor's interest.

The rhythmic sweep of the oars in a college eight was a sight the men of Attica never saw, although the Athenians had their own regattas and torch or relay races on foot and on horseback.

The winter sports that formed an Olympic festival of its own at Lake Placid this year introduced a whole new series of actions that were withheld from the games of the ancients by climatic conditions; the flight of the ski-jumper, the curving swing of the figure-skater with his bird-like swoop and leap, are charged with grace and beauty; and the flashing, kaleidoscopic dash of the hockey-players on the ice give a new zest to the lover and interpreter of skill and speed.

It would take one too far afield to cover the age-honored sports of boxing, wrestling, and fencing, the more modern golf and tennis, and such purely modern team-games as football, baseball, and basketball, the last a game deliberately invented in 1895 [sic] to fill a definite want on the program of sports and now played all over the civilized world. All are full of inspiration for the sculptor.

Wherever untrammeled youth is found, in camp, field, beach, or gymnasium; on land or in the river, lake, sea, or swimming pool, there should be the sculptor with his appraising eye, his cunning hand, and his will to record his impressions, if an adequate interpretation is to be made of this great renaissance of athletic competition in which we are living for the most part unconsciously and too often with an unseeing eye.

26

The Third Dimension in Physical Education *

ELEANOR METHENY, Ph.D.

Dr. Eleanor Metheny in her treatise "The Third Dimension in Physical Education" illustrates the modern concept of physical education as comprising a program that enables the student in physical education to learn to use all "his potential capacities for movement as a way of expressing, exploring, developing, and interpreting himself and his relationship to the world he lives in." Born in Manhattan, Illinois, in 1908, Dr. Metheny completed her Ph.D. degree at the State University of Iowa, where she gained valuable experience as a research-assistant in Child Welfare and Physical Education. This professional experience was followed by an appointment as Assistant Professor of Hygiene and Physical Education at Wellesley College. Since 1942 she has been Professor of Physical Education at the University of Southern California. She has made important professional contributions through the *Research Quarterly*, *The Foil, American Journal of Physiology, Child Development, Human Biology*, and numerous physical-education periodicals. Among the professional honors received by Dr. Metheny are the Honor Award of the AAHPER, chairman of the Research Section of the AAHPER, and chairman of the University Senate at the University of Southern California. In her treatise on physical movement, which is printed below, she emphasizes that the physical-education teacher must place fundamental importance on the body as an instrument for movement.

Modern education has become a three-dimensional process. From 1-D training of the mind, we moved to 2-D education of a mind-body unity. Now, as the psychiatrists are forcing us to recognize the psychosomatic interrelatedness of mind-body-emotions, we are moving into education in 3-D. This third dimension has special significance to those of us in physical education because of our educationally unique concern for bodies in motion and for the constructive utilization of the great emotional potentials inherent in all movement.

* Eleanor Metheny, "The Third Dimension in Physical Education," *Journal of the American Association for Health, Physical Education and Recreation*, Vol. 25 (March, 1954), pp. 27–28.

EDUCATION THROUGH MOVEMENT

If we may define the totally educated person as one who has fully developed his ability to utilize constructively all of his potential capacities as a person in relation to the world in which he lives, then we may define the physically educated person as one who has fully developed the ability to utilize constructively all of his potential capacities for movement as a way of expressing, exploring, developing, and interpreting himself and his relationship to the world he lives in. This is the part of education we have chosen as our peculiar task. Our job is to help him learn to move his body.

This attempt to educate through movement is no mean task for which we must apologize or make justification. The body is the physical manifestation of the person, his mind, his emotions, his thoughts, his feelings. It is the SELF he presents to the world. Through its movements, he expresses and externalizes the thinking and feeling which make him a unique person. And as he moves, the very act of movement modifies and affects his thinking and feeling and being.

This job of trying to teach a human being how to express through movement the complex which makes up his SELF is not simple. It is complicated from the beginning by the fact that every pupil who comes to us has already had at least six years or more of trial-and-error experience in learning how to move. Somehow he has achieved locomotion, and he is able to maintain himself in some way against the downward pull of gravity most of the time. But his solution of the gravity problem may be woefully inadequate, and he may be thwarted physically, mentally, and emotionally in many of his life's objectives by the hampering results of his inability to move freely and efficiently.

OUR JOB AS TEACHERS

Our first job is to rework these inefficient movement patterns and build them into more efficient ones while, at the same time, we help him expand his ability to move in new ways so that he may find new avenues of expression.

Ideally we begin in the preschool, or at least in the first grade. We provide him with varied opportunities and incentives for experimenting with movement: varied forms and rates of rhythmic locomotion; opportunities to hang and climb and move his body through large and small spaces; opportunities to throw and kick and strike. Our job as teachers is to know when he is ready to accept such opportunities and to provide them in such a way that they are within the range of his capacities for movement and self-expression at that time.

As he becomes kinesthetically aware of his body to the extent that he can consciously repeat movement patterns, we provide him with verbal, visual, and physical cues to direct his movements to more efficient action. We help him relate his movements to other people through partner activities and group formations. We utilize the emotional content of movement and at times we intensify it by providing challanges to his ego, his desire to test his own abilities. We heighten the mental awareness of movement by verbalizing, by letting him sing about the movement and fit the action to the words.

MOVEMENT EXPERIENCE

He creates rhythms and moves to them in his own unique pattern. He stretches his imagination as he moves like the king of the jungle. He learns to control his movements so that he may balance himself in space or so that he may rest quietly. He learns to discipline his body so that it will obey the bidding of his mind and his emotions, and through body movement he finds outlet for the working of his busy mind and his even busier emotions.

Whether he runs and jumps to express his feelings or finds that feelings come from running and jumping, he experiences the dynamics of movement as an interaction of his mind, body, and emotions. As his physical education advances, he makes progress toward the ultimate aim of total education.

Through the elementary school, the secondary school, and into college, he continues to grow in stature and strength and his experience with movement is expanded as new forms are experienced, new equipment is introduced, and new motivations occur. But the psychosomatic process of dynamic interaction of body, mind, and emotions continues.

His early satisfaction in the simple body-naming rhythmic movements of Looby Loo may develop into the abstract expression of an emotion through dance or the social-sexual-rhythmic satisfaction of the samba. His large body movements which resulted in catching a playground ball are refined to provide expression for aggression, competition, co-operation, and extroversion in the playing of basketball. As an adult he uses the artificial motions of golf as an excuse for getting out of doors, for social and business advancement, for ego-satisfaction, or for release of tension through movement. With each new experience in movement, he finds more pathways leading to a better understanding of himself, to establishing his unique relationship to other human beings, and he makes progress toward becoming a better integrated person—mentally, physically, and emotionally healthy.

PSYCHOSOMATIC POTENTIAL

This is the psychosomatic potential which exists in every class in physical education. To realize even 10 per cent of it is to make a vital contribution to the total education of human beings. But, to realize even 1 per cent of it, we must understand much about human beings and we must use that understanding wisely. We must plan carefully and we must build and adapt our curricula to both the immediate and long-term needs of our pupils and to the practical situations within which we must work. We cannot always do all that we would like to do, but we can try, and fail, and yet try again.

Many of our failures occur because, in our enthusiasm for the more complex forms of movements, we neglect the fundamentals. We try to teach dance to girls whose bodies are so poorly aligned that each step puts further stress on joints already on the verge of collapse. We prate about skills, achievements, rules, strategy, and fair play—but we forget that these grow only out of the ability of the body to move freely and without strain. We get so intent on teaching the game that we forget about the bodies with which the game must be played.

BODIES ARE OUR BUSINESS

Bodies, not games, are our real business. The games acquire significance only in terms of the dynamic interaction of the bodies, minds, and emotions that participate in them. And those bodies must be able to move as freely and fully as possible to make that dynamic interaction a constructive rather than a crippling psychosomatic educational experience.

The starting point for the use of movement as a means of education is to make the body free to act. This involves the alignment of the body parts so that efficiency of movement may be hampered as little as possible by the stress imposed by gravity. It involves freeing the joints for action by putting them in their most advantageous position for movement. It involves strengthening weak muscles so that they become able to move powerfully and easily, or so that they are able to balance the pull of an opposing muscle to fixate part of the body as a base over which other powerful movement may take place.

It involves the ability to relax the antagonists while contracting the agonists. It involves stretching tight fascia to make unrestricted movement possible. It involves an understanding of the principles of movement and the ability to apply those principles in action in a wide variety of situations. It involves the awareness of the body and an uninhibited acceptance of it with its capacities and its limitations, both in general and uniquely for each individual. And it involves an emotional drive toward self-expression through free use of body movement.

This is the fundamental part of our job—to start with bodies as instruments for movement and to free them from the restrictions which hamper movement, so that they may become more fully capable of expressing, releasing, or intensifying the thoughts and emotions which are the motivation of movement. This is truly an educational job, and if we can learn to do it well, we shall find that it expands our realization of the educational potential inherent in our more spectacular ventures into dance and sports, into competition and exhibition, into the development of democratic citizenship through group participation.

BACKGROUND FOR MIND AND SPIRIT

The total education of any individual may be likened to the music of a symphony orchestra. It develops from the music of many instruments, each of which makes its own unique sound. In that orchestra, we physical educators play the bass—the solid, rhythmic undercurrent which holds the more delicate tones together. We produce the essential background against which the musical acrobatics of the mental violin and the emotional oboe are displayed.

Without us, the melody is thin. The music lacks depth and resonance. For bodies are the physical unity out of which and through which the human mind and spirit grow. The three-dimensional education of those bodies is our business—a business which we approach with great humility, but with equally great pride.

27

Physical Education a Profession [*]

JAMES E. ROGERS

James E. Rogers was Director of the National Physical Education Service of the National Recreation Association from 1925 to 1942. In this position he was instrumental in bringing about state laws requiring physical-education programs in public schools and the appointing of qualified state directors of physical education. Mr. Rogers was born in San Francisco and completed his educational background at the University of California. His professional experiences also included the following positions: high school teacher, athletic director, founder and director of the San Francisco Public School Athletic League, founder and first secretary of the Pacific Coast Physical Education Association, and Secretary and later President of the Department of Health and Physical Education of the National Education association. From 1930 to 1941, Mr. Rogers wrote a column in the association journal called "Around the Country with J. E. Rogers." This column resulted from extensive travel through approximately 34 states each year visiting school principals and superintendents, state legislators, and officers of Parent Teachers' Associations and American Legion Posts. During World Wars I and II Mr. Rogers assisted communities in mobilizing recreation resources to meet the leisure-time needs of service men and war workers. Among his professional honor awards are the Anderson Award and the Creative Award of the American Academy of Physical Education. Mr. Rogers' valuable and comprehensive experiences in health, physical education, and recreation make him unusually well qualified to write the following account titled "Physical Education A Profession."

. . . I believe that physical education is a teaching profession for the following good and sufficient reasons.

We have a history and a heritage that come to us through the Greeks and the Ancients before them. We need no finer proof of our need and place in life than the statements of Plato and Aristotle. Every profession must have a background and none has a more honorable and ancient one than ours. Through the Hitites, the Egyptians, Spartans, and on up through history, through the modern leaders, youth was, has been, and

[*] James Edward Rogers, "Physical Education A Profession," *American Physical Education Review*, Vol. 32 (September, 1927), pp. 496–499.

is to be educated through motor activity, through gymnastics and sports.

We have a philosophy and a psychology and a science behind our profession that gives us the proofs and basis for our work and status. Unfortunately we have not used these sources. We lack interpreters to give to educators the scientifically sound and psychological proofs of the soundness of the claims we make and the programs we project. We have sometimes unfortunately overstressed the physical and medical side of our profession. This is fine. There is science here. But we have also in psychology wonderful new claims for our profession. If education is the training for behavior, then we are a profession. If the great new field in education is the training of emotions, than we are blessed with a magnificent opportunity.

We have great educational leaders that have given us argument for our claims. Herbart, Rousseau, Pestalozzi, Froebel, Herbert Spencer, J. Stanley Hall, and all the modern educationalists through John Dewey speak of motor education, education through doing is learning, through observation and manipulation, through motor activity as modern education. In the growing child the brain is educated through the hand and the senses. . . . Physiological psychology is our greatest aid. Let us use it.

Our people are being better trained. Lawyers, doctors, all professions, demand two types of education, a rounded general culture and understanding of the needs, the reasons, the aims, the objectives of one's profession and secondly the specific skills, methods, and arts necessary to perform the task. Both types of education are essential. . . . We need to do soon what the other professions have done, standardize these schools and the qualifications of graduates. It means self-protection and will deny the claims made by some. But more of our profession are being trained, better trained, longer trained with a broader and finer outlook on their task. So we are a trained profession. Yet improvement can be made in this direction.

In our program, I believe, we have made professional gains. Our programs are broader and better balanced than ever before. We have enriched the programs, we have graded it and found age aims, we have started to educationally measure our programs through tests. More and more, we are not repeating ourselves, but improving our methods, so that from the first grade through the twelfth, from the age of six to eighteen, from kindergarten through high school, we have worked out a scientifically graded course of physical education, based on the physiological and psychological needs. A graded progressive sequential and hence consequential course of physical education denoting progress, growth, development, and yet there is much to be done along this line. Some things have been done. It will be the one big step toward proving our claim for more time allowance and unit requirement.

Every profession has a common terminology. In law "status quo" means the same thing everywhere, in medicine the streptococcus is the same here as in Bombay, in engineering the hypoteneuse of the right triangle is equal—well, the answer is the same. Clear, concise, exact terminology is essential to any profession. . . .

We have arrived as a profession, but we have not been granted our spurs by educators in other subjects. However, we are rapidly being recognized, as they see we have a better understanding and grip on our tasks, that we are being better trained, that we are teachers not specialists, that we are educators not gymnasts, that we have a well-rounded, well-balanced program that meets the needs of the growing boy and girl, that we are obtaining educational results and filling the sixty minutes with worthy material, that we have a physical quotient that has a higher coefficient correlation than the intelligent quotient. Dr. F. R. Rogers, of New York, has given us one of the best educational bases for our profession.

Yes, we are a profession, but it demands obligations. We must standardize our training schools; we must not have inadequate trained graduates. We all must grow and read and keep abreast of the times. We must not stop reading. We alone can make our profession; we alone can mar it. We all can do our bit to gain for it a proper recognition in the educational field. To live and work at the time when a profession is on the threshold of making good and becoming recognized, is thrilling. Each has a part to play. Play well your part and the profession of physical education is safe in your hands. A man lives by his job, but he lives for his profession.

28

The Deeper Meaning of Physical Education *

CARL L. SCHRADER

The career of Carl L. Schrader was devoted in the main to the building of physical education on the state level while carrying the profession forward on the national level in the years when physical education was making great gains after the First World War. A member of the faculty of the Sargent College of Physical Education from 1905 to 1921, he also worked closely in this period with Dr. Dudley A. Sargent in the Harvard Summer School. During the years from 1922 to 1935 he was the first Director of Physical Education in Massachusetts, working actively to secure the support of state legislation favorable to physical education. Carl L. Schrader won many laurels in the profession. He was President of the American Physical Education Association (1923–1925), founder and first President of the Society for State Directors of Physical Education (1926–1927), and a charter member of the American Academy of Physical Education. And he was the recipient of the Ling Foundation Medal for altruistic service to the children of the country and the Honor Award of the American Association for Health, Physical Education, and Recreation. The address to a department of the National Education Association, printed below with some deletion, was written to enlighten the public on the deeper meaning of physical education and to expose some of the erroneous conceptions and fallacies about physical education current in the 1930's.

The purpose of this address is not so much to plead for recognition of physical education, but rather to clarify on the one hand its meaning and purpose, and on the other, and perhaps mainly, to point out the erroneous conceptions and fallacies under which physical education in many places is still permitted to operate. . . . On the one hand we have the narrow, uneducational, and unsafe concept of excessive interscholastic competition, and on the other an array of high-sounding objectives to which the practice carried on bears no resemblance.

Just as it was not the purpose of forward-looking educators when bringing art and music into the school program to create other Michelangelos, Van Dykes, or Beethovens, so was physical education not in-

* Carl L. Schrader, "Physical Education Becomes a Fundamental," *The Journal of Health and Physical Education,* Vol. 7 (April, 1936), pp. 215–217 and 283–284.

tended to create a lot of Babe Ruths or Tildens. The fact that we may . . . discern genius in any of these mentioned cultural fields does not alter the original underlying purpose, which I believe to be an opportunity for an apprenticeship upon which intelligent choice and habit may be built.

It is safe to say that those who conceive physical education as a way of living more fully and sanely are primarily interested in putting education into play and into athletics rather than putting play and athletics into education. . . .

Physical education is primarily concerned with the building of organic vigor and power, and with the mastering of neuromuscular skills. But it also makes valuable contributions to health, character, and to the worthy use of leisure. The primary objectives, that is, organic power and neuro-muscular skills intelligently accepted, and the teaching and administration intelligently carried on, will make the contributions toward health, char-acter, and the worthy use of leisure an inevitable and accompanying result.

"To think of physical education merely in terms of health would mean to center attention upon a corrective . . . procedure of a bygone age rather than upon the developmental, preventative aspect of modern physical education." One reason often advanced for stressing the health objective and even changing the name of physical education to health education, is that it is easier to obtain funds from the public to maintain such a program.

Expediency, however, should not deter us from enlightening the public on the deeper meaning of physical education. This expediency becomes particularly distressing when health education on the one hand attempts to teach us facts, matters upon which the medical profession is still divided, and then to encourage on the other and tolerate practices which the medical profession as a body recognizes as detrimental to health and proper development.

We, who are engaged in teaching or are administering teaching, are entrusted primarily with helping the child to grow. That is our function. This growth is a many-sided process, but having accepted the oneness of the human being, growth must be stimulated in every one of these direc-tions. Just as we have recognized the mentally retarded and have found . . . means of helping them to grow, so must we recognize the physically and socially retarded and use intelligence to help them to grow. One may think that because the physical lacks are obvious, as compared with the mental shortcomings, that here at least we were doing our best. The fact that we are not is undoubtedly due to this very obviousness, which is misleading. Only when we recognize that physical growth goes on in segments instead of uniformly do we realize that outward appearance is no guide for functional vigor, nor activity achievement a safe device to determine organic power. We are . . . thinking of the growing boy or girl whom we have in our schools. . . .

In the field of competive athletics we still too often mistake bigness for organic power, when in reality the husky looking freshman entering high school may be a far greater risk in competitive sport than the smaller and leaner type. Biology teaches us that frequently in rapid growth in height and breadth the vital organs have not kept pace with this growth, and are therefore less conditioned to stand the great strain which some games and sports demand, particularly in competition. To drive or even encourage boys and girls in this condition to maximum performance is dangerous, and surely a gross violation of any health program so-called. . . . Growing youth needs much of its energy for growing, and while intelligently guided activity, even to the extent of great exertion, stimulates this growth, exhaustion is positively destructive and inhibitive to this growing process. . . .

If we could be but certain that . . . superintendents and principals of schools recognize physical education, of which athletics is a part, as a means of achieving certain educational ends rather than look upon the outcome of a game or competition as the end, we might boast of the greatest youth movement the world has known. The educational ends here referred to are enhanced by the contribution which, rightly conceived and intelligently carried out, physical education makes. The obtaining of these ends in the main is the building habits, either of health or character. . . .

An activity program . . . , full of real life situations, is most promising toward these desired ends. We recognize the advantage of activity in that it can be directed. We can set the one who is wrong, right, and keep the one who is right, right, because we see him do the right or the wrong thing. We do not know what he thinks. We like or dislike each other because of what we do, not because of what we think. Hence we may well define character as a manifestation of deeds. . . .

No other field in education is so rich in variety of activity as is physical education. Classed with music as an art, it shares with music the significance of engaging the whole of man in its practice. The human body is the greatest medium for outward expression and commands the greatest variety of vehicles through which to do it. Who has not been thrilled as spectator by the marvelous and beautiful performance of the skater, dancer, skiier, equestrian, runner, jumper, or player? Even illustrations give us that thrill. But the spectator thrill is as nothing compared with the thrill of the performer—a feeling that cannot be described but must be lived, must be experienced. Here is living, for moments at least, in ecstasy. The whole being throbs in this glow of achievement. This throbbing of life exists in all degrees and levels of efficiency and in a thousand varieties of activities, and may well be termed the conditioning of the inner man. To stimulate ambition toward these experiences is surely worthy of a place in education and surely is helping youth to grow. . . .

These desirable outcomes . . . can only be the result of intelligent leadership. That this leadership must be based upon more than mere techniques should go without saying, yet the fact remains that less care is exercised in the selection of teachers in this field than perhaps in any other. In selecting teachers or supervisors of physical education, the choice too frequently falls upon the man who is an All-American . . . or one who has successfully placed this or that town on the map, but who has no professional qualifications whatsoever and consequently is entirely out of touch with educational objectives. . . .

If it should appear that this dissertation deals solely with junior and senior high schools, may I suggest that the errors in this particular school division are perhaps of greater moment than the omissions in the elementary schools. I refer to practices that are educationally unsound: interscholastic schedules too long, particularly in basketball; unbalanced matching of teams; lack of proper medical supervision; playing of night games; traveling long distances to determine phantom championships; and above all, interference in these supposedly school functions by nonschool authorities. A real representative intraschool mass program cannot thrive where both space and the time of the teacher are monopolized by the few, usually an aristocracy of brawn. . . .

Much as has been achieved in physical education as a whole, the elementary school concept of physical education is still a very vague one, not only in rural districts, but in many city and town systems. The notion of aimless and isolated body movements carried on between desks as physical education, still prevails. Better if need be to curtail the high school program and equipment in order to answer for the needs in our elementary schools than to carry on this present mere skeleton, void of flesh and of life blood. . . .

Tests and Measurements in Physical Education *

DAVID K. BRACE, Ph.D.

Since 1926 Dr. David K. Brace has been in Texas in the key post of leadership in physical education for that state. As a Professor of Physical and Health Education at the University of Texas, he has worked to establish physical education in the curriculum of all Texas schools and colleges. Born in Lincoln, Nebraska, in 1891, he completed his undergraduate work at Reed College and the Ph.D. degree at Columbia University. A very rich professional career includes the following positions: teacher of physical education in Salem, Oregon, Professor of Physical Education in Chihi Provincial Higher Normal College in China, Director of Physical Education in Tsing Hua College in China, Instructor in Physical Education at Columbia University, and Professor and Chairman of the Department of Physical and Health Education at the University of Texas. During World War II Dr. Brace served as Specialist in Physical Fitness at the U. S. Office of Education in Washington, D.C. Professional honors include the Honor Award from the American Physical Education Association, President of the Southern District of the American Physical Education Association, President of the American Academy of Physical Education, and national recognition by developing the Brace Motor Ability Tests. As a research specialist in the field of tests and measurements at a crucial time in the history of American physical education, Dr. Brace presented the following lucid account of the place and value of tests and measurements in physical education.

The educational procedure destined to be followed in this country appears to be that which can be best supported by scientific proof. Subject matter or methods which cannot stand investigation or which cannot be supported by evidence have little ground for support. While it is true that many phases of the physical education program do not easily lend themselves to objective proof, and while it may be some time before we can scientifically measure them, it, nevertheless, seems apparent that the more evidence and the more objective the evidence which can be advanced in their support the greater will be the sanction for their use.

It is logical that this be so. One of the outstanding characteristics of

* David K. Brace, "Possibilities of Tests in Physical Education," *American Physical Education Review*, Vol. 32 (September, 1927), pp. 506–513.

this age is the application of science to human problems. This movement is apparent in the field of education and is reflected in physical education. It is, however, apparent to one who gives the matter much thought that physical and health educators have not as a rule based their selection of curricula upon scientific proof, but rather upon popular practice.

Who can mention an educational survey which has tested and measured the worth of the course of study in physical education, the achievement of pupils in this field, or the efficiency of teaching with the same scientific precision which has been used in testing and measuring other subjects? Yet communities invest large sums of money in equipment and instruction for physical education. The fault does not lie so much with survey committees as with physical educators. We have not provided them with the necessary tools. Those surveys which have considered physical and health education have had to resort to observation, questionnaires, and opinion as means of obtaining data.

A test is a tool. The sort of work to be done determines the kind of tool to be used. No one tool will fit all tasks. Special tools must be made for special jobs. Tests in physical education are tools to measure that for which the test was designed.

It is the purpose of this paper to lead our thinking to consider some of the uses of tests in physical education, *i.e.*, to consider the uses of tools for measuring phases of physical education. . . .

One of the first prerequisites of a good test is that of validity, *i.e.*, is the test a valid test? does it measure that which it is supposed to measure? Proving that a test is a valid test demands scientific procedure. Opinion is of little value for this purpose. If tests in physical education are to be valid tests in the sense that other standardized educational tests are valid tests, statistical proof of validity must be presented. This does not mean that the only tests which can be used are those whose validity has been established, but it does mean that we should prefer to use tests which are valid, that we should endeavor to prove that tests measure what they are supposed to measure, and that we should be cautious in using the results of tests whose validity is not established. . . .

In considering the possibilities of tests in physical education let us return to the three purposes for which tests are usually used, (1) to classify pupils for purposes of instruction, (2) to measure achievement, (3) to aid the learning process. *Tests used for purposes of classifying pupils.* The physical examinations, including anthropometric tests, tests of health and physical fitness, and sometimes tests of physical and sensory capacity are the most common tests used for classifying pupils for purposes of instruction. Such tests are of primary importance. They are intended to show which pupils can safely enter all activities of the program and which students must enter a restricted program. Every school should see that a medical examination is provided for all pupils once a year.

Further research in the development of group tests of physical fitness is needed.

Having determined the physical fitness of students to engage in the activities of the program, at least to the extent of indicating pupils with serious deficiency, many schools are then desirous of classifying pupils into sections in accordance with their ability to profit by instruction offered.

In other school subjects two principal methods are used. The most common method used is to place children in accordance with their educational achievement in the subjects concerned. When a new child enters school he is placed in the grade which he had reached in his previous schooling. It is assumed that the child has mastered the subject matter up to that grade. More advanced schools would submit the new pupil to standardized educational achievement tests and would then place him in accordance with the advancement he had made as revealed by these tests. The latter plan is especially easy of application in a system in which children progress by subjects.

Applying this procedure to physical education, the entering pupil would be given achievement tests which would be intended to show how much progress he had made in the various activities of the program. Such a plan assumes that the program embodies specific objectives so arranged as to insure a progression in the presentation and mastery of subject matter. Few programs of physical education reveal a progression of objectives comparable with that common in most other school subjects. . . .

Other methods of classifying pupils for class work or for competition within classes are used. Some of the bases of classification which may be mentioned are sex, age, height, weight, or combinations of one or more of these and combinations of these with grade. Where several bases are used a system of exponents may be developed to aid in the problem. . . . The use of this type of factors, namely, sex, age, weight, height, and grade, is really a roundabout way of getting at the result which achievement tests and tests of native ability and capacity should produce more accurately. The purpose is to secure groups who can achieve at about the same rate.

Achievement, however, is made up of at least two factors, *i.e.*, natural abilities and capacities, and experience. Pupils may have achieved equal degrees of proficiency and yet may have widely different degrees of natural ability. If all pupils had had the same training and opportunities, those with more natural ability would doubtless make a correspondingly greater achievement if they were given the chance. However, all pupils have not had equal experience nor do all pupils usually have a chance to progress to the best of their ability.

It therefore would be advantageous if we could classify or group pupils in accordance with their ability to achieve. Those pupils with more natural ability could then do more difficult work and could progress more rapidly. Pupils with less motor ability could be grouped in classes where special instruction could be given. The fact that pupils differ as to inherent ability in physical education, as in other school subjects, is well recognized by physical education teachers. . . . The tool needed to meet this problem is standardized tests of native motor ability. . . . *Possibilities in the use of tests measuring achievement.* A survey of tests now used in physical education reveals that a large share of them are directed at one or more of the following purposes: to use in giving grades, to determine promotion, and to guide instruction. Other related purposes are to measure teaching efficiency, to evaluate programs of instruction, and to measure information and attitudes.

Tests to serve such purposes may be grouped under the heading of achievement tests. Their purposes have the common element of the measurement of pupil attainment.

Achievement in physical education, as in any other subject, is the attainment of objectives. Evaluation of the progress of pupils, of the type of activities taught, of the method of teaching them, and of the success of the teacher demands a determination of the extent to which specific objectives have been achieved. In other words, the measurement of achievement is essential to efficient instruction in physical education.

Our programs aim to teach certain skills, information, habits, and attitudes, and thus to help produce healthy, vigorous, and happy individuals. The attainments we expect of elementary school children differ from those we expect of high school pupils. We say that we have different objectives for these different grades.

Heretofore programs of physical education have generally not contained statements of objectives in specific and detailed form. We have stated objectives in such terms as bodily strength, health, sportsmanship, neromuscular co-ordinations, athletic skill, etc. We have failed to state, for example, just what co-ordinations should be developed at just what age, and to just what degree of proficiency this development should be attained by pupils in specific grades.

Perhaps one reason for our inability to state objectives in specific and objective form has been our lack of accurate knowledge of the degree of achievement which we should expect pupils of different ages to reach. This accurate knowledge can hardly come from opinion. It must come from the measurement of pupil attainment in relation to abilities and capacities. . . .

The best sort of achievement test . . . is one which is not practiced as such, but one which is yet a good test of a skill which we have hoped to improve by our methods of instruction. It will be apparent from this that a valid achievement test is one which produces a high correlation with the performance it is intended to measure. The exact achievement tests which should be used in any specific course in physical education will, of course, depend upon the objectives set up for that course. . . . Modern programs are not only interested in teaching skills and in increasing muscular power, but also in teaching information and attitudes. It seems reasonable to expect that students in the regular physical-education classes should be expected to acquire certain information in connection with the activities of the program. . . .

The measurement of achievement, as relates to attitudes, is somewhat difficult of objective measurement. Measurement of knowledge of right attitudes is perhaps of value, but not nearly as valuable as measuring the extent to which these attitudes guide action. Some rather objective observations and records can, however, be kept, especially if the problem is viewed in light of specific objectives to be achieved.

Tests used to aid instruction. The third and last general purpose for which tests are used in physical education, to be treated in this paper, is the use of tests to assist in the teaching process. To be sure, the two previous purposes, namely, to classify pupils for instruction and to measure pupil achievement, aim at indirectly improving the efficiency of instruction. However, many tests are used in order to help children to make improvement in the test itself.

Tests so used may be called practice tests. Their function is to give special practice in specific performances. Often times they are selected to help improve deficiences in performance. Their objective nature gives them a competitive element which increases interest in class work. No effort is made to prevent students working on the tests as much as they like. In fact they are urged to practice the test and keep track of their performance. . . .

In conclusion a word of caution may be in place. Tests are by no means the most important factor in educational procedure. Good tests must be selected and used to perform specific and desirable functions. Caution should be used in basing opinion upon tests not fully established. School programs of physical education should not be evaluated upon the results of three or four tests.

On the other hand, testing and measuring the activities of physical education will not necessarily detract from the joy of play and competition. The keeping of batting and fielding averages in baseball does not take away from the interest of the game. As Thorndike has said, "It is not those mothers who weigh their babies least often who love them most."

30

Intangibles in Physical Education [*]

DUDLEY B. REED

Dudley B. Reed, physician and administrator, after beginning his professional career in Asheville, North Carolina, became associated with the University of Chicago, which he served for over twenty years. He organized and directed its University Health Service. One of the founders of the Midwest District of the American Physical Education Association, he served as its president and later served as the president of the American Physical Education Association (1920–1922). He was also president of the College Physical Education Association. In his "President's Address" to the American Physical Education Association in 1920, from which excerpts are printed below, he discussed the intangible results flowing from physical education which, despite the impossibility of scientific measurement, were, nevertheless, real and important. As he said, "the great things in human experience and the most real are the least tangible."

. . . Ours is a scientific age, an age of efficiency and standardization. We yearn for definite, logical, unwasteful methods of procedure and concrete, laboratory proof of accomplishment. We long for figures which do not lie. This spirit is reflected in our profession. We would have fool proof systems of instruction which prescribe what each teacher shall teach on each day. We would say at the end of a year that group A registers a 25 per cent improvement. We would have standards of efficiency and tests of progress, measurements and proofs. Properly applied these things may be good. Insofar as they aid in attaining our ends they are desirable. If they tend to make us forget the immeasurable elements of human nature, the difficult problems of individuals and the moral factors in accomplishment they are not unmixed good. At best scientific accuracy has proved mutable. What was scientific in the time of Hippocrates is not scientific today. Isaac Newton has recently been dealt a cruel post-mortem buffet. Yet in this world of change, there are things which, as far as our knowledge goes, are immutable. When the first recorded triangle existed in the garden of Eden, a man, a woman and a

[*] Dudley B. Reed, "President's Address," *American Physical Education Review*, Vol. 25 (June, 1920), pp. 225–228.

serpent, fear, hate, greed, joy, sorrow, love, and loyalty were much the same as in 1920. Then as now they were the peculiar heritage of humanity. The great things in human experience and the most real are the least tangible. The weight of a mother's love would not cause your balance beam to quiver. The patriotism of a boy in khaki is not measured in foot-pounds. The calorimeter will not record the beauty of sunset on a mountain lake or a perfectly executed string quartet. Your tape is not long enough to encircle happiness nor your calipers accurate enough to evaluate the grief of a child with a broken toy. But such are the things which make up life. Such are the things which determine personality. And we are dealing with living personalities. To forget individual human nature in lust for figures is to handicap ourselves in the face of opportunity.

. . . Would it not be well for us whose privilege it is to work with individuals on so intimate a footing to take cognizance of man as he is, the imponderable as well as the ponderable? Possibly the specialist in human nature would be the best educator.

In our number we have scientists who are adding in splendid fashion to assets of mankind. I honor them and appreciate their work. We also have men who have not contributed a scintilla to the scientific knowledge of our profession whose accomplishment has been beyond all computation on account of their capacity for sympathetic intelligent judgment and treatment of individuals. Them, too, I honor. Might we not all be better men if we were more scientific, and better scientists if we were more human?

Is it not also true that many of our most important results are difficult of testing by any human standards? Is not one of the reasons for adequate muscle and physical skill the feeling of social adequacy which they give? A perfectly real result of a good game of tennis, a bath, and a rub is the feeling of well-being and fitness to meet all obstacles which follow. If posture is largely psychological may a feeling of fitness not be most important in being fit? And certainly one of the most vital effects of games is their contribution toward the very real but immeasurable things we call manhood and womanhood. . . .

Character Education as an Objective *

JAY B. NASH, Ph.D.

Dr. Jay B. Nash is one of the leaders in American Physical Education in recognizing and perpetuating the recreational values of physical education in education. Born in New Baltimore, Ohio, in 1886, Dr. Nash completed his education at Oberlin College and New York University where he received the Ph.D. degree in 1929. Professional experience includes a position as Director of Physical Education and Superintendent of Recreation in Oakland, California (1915–1925) and then an appointment as Professor of Physical Education at New York University from 1926 to his retirement in 1953. At the present time he is executive-secretary of the New York Association for Health, Physical Education and Recreation. Among his numerous professional honors are the following: a founder and fellow of the American Academy of Physical Education, Fulbright lecturer in India, President of the American Association for Health, Physical Education and Recreation, and recipient of the Gulick Award and the Honor Award of the AAHPER. Among the many articles and books written by Dr. Nash was "Character Education as An Objective," which illustrates one of the fundamental values of physical education.

Character education may be defined as the behavior of an individual upon which the society in which he moves places a stamp of "good." It must always remain a relative term as the qualities which the community pronounces "good" will vary with the community and will develop with the ages. The particular point to be noted in this connection is that character is one of the desirable outcomes of education and hence is one of the desirable outcomes of physical education. In the past few years we have seen the position of health co-ordinator develop. The objective of such co-ordination is to center the attention of every branch or development of instruction upon a particular objective. There is every evidence that the next few years will see character and leisure time co-ordinators as well as vocational and health co-ordinators appearing in the administrative setup of our public schools.

* Jay B. Nash, "Character Education as an Objective," *Mind and Body*, Vol. 38 (May, 1931), pp. 497–499.

Character qualities are the by-products of activities. They are acquired. In other words, they are learned, and when once learned, are definitely habits as fixed as any habit of the individual. How are these character qualities attained? What is their relationship to the whole program as presented in the modern physical-education program? Burnham has forcefully called attention to the fact that a healthy personality is an integrated personality. He also calls attention to the fact that all normal human personalities, or in other words, character in the child or in the adult, represents an integrated personality. Not only is the individual's mind integrated, but the whole organism is integrated. Integration, or any situation in which the whole self is centered, becomes the basis of the interest method, the play way, the project method, the psychological method of teaching—natural education. This integration probably assumes a prepotent drive. It is a heredity urge. It is common knowledge that most of our "wants" are directly or indirectly tied up to hereditary urges—directly, in that they have to do with actual recapitulation of the race—indirectly, in that they have to do with struggling, overcoming, chasing, fleeing, or as Allport would say, "starting and withdrawing." This element of overcoming lies deep in the neurone of the race. It is probably the biological explanation of play. We realize that activity is satisfying and that inactivity is annoying. There appears to be a neural unrest in activity. This is explained very readily in the whole evolutionary process. Wherever organisms have been faced with new conditions, the acting, adjusting, struggling, conquering, overcoming organisms have lived. Thus we have built in the neurons the desire for activity. In entering into these activities the organism is integrated. This concentration of interest lies at the base of health, and especially at the base of mental normality and character.

Standards of conduct are built around "wants." Standards represent so delicate a quality that they cannot be forced. Use force and the spirit flees. You cannot establish a compulsory society for the enforcement of good fellowship. You cannot enforce good behavior. Hence, character traits are built around activities which children want to do. This gives the leaders of these activities tremendous power. We imitate those we admire—we refuse to imitate those we dislike. Leaders who are respected can change conduct.

The application of this to physical education is obvious. We are dealing with activities that children want to do. Thus we think we present them in the right way. Children are interested in activities which conform to the following formula: The activity must challenge the individual—the individual must be within reach of success—social approval must go with success. These elements become the essence of a game—any game. The challenge must be apparent to the child. In too many of our activities the challenge is apparent only to the leader. Hence, a game becomes an activity in which there is a challenge, and in which the outcome waves between success and failure, and can be thrown in favor of success when the individual actually grasps beyond his reach. This will be particularly satisfying if there is a great social approval. Every activity which is taught to children should be judged by this formula. Game elements are dead unless the child connects success in them to success in the game. Nature study, manual training, music, and all other activities are dead, unless the child sees the challenge. We, in physical education, are dealing with activities in which the child can easily see the challenge. Hence, there is a "want." There is integration. There is opportunity for the building of character traits.

We have no evidence today of the existence of elaborate inborn systems of action in man. Attitudes and emotions high on the scale, and prejudices low on the scale are learned. If violent prejudices low on the scale are learned, attitudes high on the scale may be learned. We can become prejudiced in little things—racial, political, or religious.

These qualities that make up character, while they are relative, vary with conditions. For the individual in a particular time, they are specific. Sacrifice, good sportsmanship, and loyalty have particular qualities. Prall, in his book on "Aesthetic Judgment," has called attention to the fact that aesthetic qualities of beauty and loveliness are specific. They must be learned by experiencing them. If this contention is justified, then qualities of character are learned just as we learn qualities of objects—roundness, squareness, smoothness, roughness, lightness, and heaviness, etc. These qualities are transmitted through the sense organs. They must be filed in the associated centers of the mind and comparison makes possible judgments. Hence, qualities of character are learned. The child must sacrifice, and hence learn its qualities. He must do a sportsmanship act to get the feel of it. The feel of these qualities are acquired through leadership. Hence, it is safe to say that activities, under adequate leadership, become a positive part in the development of character, and in the negative sense, they become the moral equivalent of crime. We can displace our racketeer heroes only by our Lindberghs and Ruths. We can replace the challenge of activities which are judged delinquent and crime only by challenging physical education activities which are high on the scale.

Dennison, in his book "The Emotion as a Basis of Civilization" calls attention to the fact that group solidarity can no longer be obtained by means of threats. Fear no longer holds a group together. Democracies must be held together through fraternal bonds of wants, as over against the old paternal bond of fear.

Hence, every activity in which there is a drive offers opportunity for guiding conduct. These specific acts must be analysed. They might be thought of in four parts: *The Situation*. The situation represents a particular act of sportsmanship or unsportsmanship. Most of our character training should be built around sportsmanship acts in which we can commend, but the opportunity is also present in the unsportsmanship acts. *Positive Qualities.* Even in unsportsmanship acts there are positive qualities. In the act there may be courage, initiative, and desire to accomplish. These positive qualities must be preserved. *Negative Qualities.* In unsportsmanship acts there are of course undesirable qualities—violating rules, bullying, selfishness, etc. These qualities must be minimized. *The Solution.* The solution of the problem must strengthen the desirable qualities. It is very easy to destroy good qualities, in other words, to burn down the house to get rid of the rats. Every situation of this type offers opportunities for leadership.

Character may probably be judged as the accumulation of the effects of these various situations upon the individual. Each act in itself is minor—taken together, major. At the Great Divide in the Canadian Rockies drops of water fall from the glacier under the rays of the sun. They flow gently down a little stream. In this stream is placed a very crude partition, the water that goes to the right forms one of the great rivers of the West, the water that goes to the left becomes one of the great rivers of the Mississippi Valley. The drops of water make the stream, the stream makes the river, and the river makes the ocean. In some such manner the accumulation of minor social influences make a character ocean. No phase of education offers so many opportunities for the guiding of this conduct as does physical education.

Professional Progress Through Research *

CHARLES H. McCLOY, Pʜ.D.

Known in physical education as "The Research Professor," Dr. Charles H. McCloy combined the qualities of the physical educator and the college professor that command the respect of the intellectual. Among his academic accomplishments was an ability to speak fluent Chinese and to read French, German, Italian, Chinese, Japanese, and Portuguese. Born in 1886, Dr. McCloy attended Marietta College and Columbia University, where he received the Ph.D. degree. His professional career included the following positions: Director of Physical Education and Acting Head of the Biology Department at Yankton College in South Dakota; Physical Director of the YMCA in Danville, Virginia; physical education work in China from 1913 to 1926, first as Secretary of the Department of Physical Education, National Council of the YMCA, then as Director of the School of Physical Education in National Southeastern University in Nanking; Secretary for Research in Physical Education for the National Council of the YMCA in New York City; and then Research Professor of Physical Education at the State University of Iowa from 1930 until retirement. Dr. McCloy's work during World War II was distinguished. He served as Chairman of the Civilian Advisory Committee for the U. S. Navy Physical Fitness Program, Physical Reconditioning Consultant to the Surgeon-General of the U. S. Army, and Consultant to the joint U. S. Army and Navy Committee on Welfare and Recreation. At the close of the war General MacArthur appointed him a member of an Education Mission to Japan. Dr. McCloy has received numerous professional honors and awards. He has been president of three prominent organizations: the AAHPER, the American Academy of Physical Education, and the Pan-American Institute of Physical Education. Among the awards he has received are the Gulick Award, the Hetherington Award, and the American College of Sports Medicine Award. Dr. McCloy was the author of numerous articles and some 40 books, many of which were also published in foreign countries.

Professional progress in any science leads through at least four stages. The first is that of trial and error. The pioneers, relative inexperts, muddle

* C. H. McCloy, "Professional Progress Through Research," *The Research Quarterly of the American Physical Education Association*, Vol. 1, Part II (May, 1930), pp. 63–73.

along, trying first one thing and then another. By the time-honored process of "try, try again" they slowly progress from a condition of scientific ignorance to a place where some real values begin to accrue.

In the second stage "leaders" of the past are quoted. These are often wrong, almost always have a narrow vision—but state opinions with the assurance and forcefulness of the patent medicine advertiser. These "authorities" frequently hold back scientific progress for decades.

The third stage is that of speculation and argumentation. Authorities are frequently doubted. Solutions of problems of fact are sought through debate. This is the stage of philosophizing.

The fourth stage is that of hypothesis and experimentation. At this point, the leaders of the science seek first to secure the facts, and then to draw their conclusions. This is the stage of research, which may be defined as a careful, extraordinarily earnest, and well-organized effort to ascertain essential facts about something at present unknown. It involves constructive, creative thinking, and scientific analysis based upon experimentation, historical documents, observations, collections of objective data, and careful ratings. It should be as mathematically precise and accurate as possible, as objective as the type of data permits, and should be subject to verification by others. The research worker should be absolutely impartial, unbiased, and intellectually honest. He should set out to ascertain the facts and seek the results with an absolutely open mind. He should not accept the opinion of so-called authorities, of committees, or of a majority as facts. He must not reason from silence or from absence of evidence, but should consider these as historical background until verified.

This fourth, the scientific or research stage of a science, may conceivably be quite inadequate. This is due to the differing temperaments of men, the all-too-frequent contempt of the scientist for the philosopher, and the usual disregard of the "practical thinker" for both.

It is here that I should like to propose for your consideration an outline of an attack upon the problems of physical education. This method seems to me to avoid many of the shortcomings of an approach through research alone. The suggestion is not original with me but is a concept frequently advanced in some form by educational philosophers.

You will agree with me, perhaps, that in all constructive studies of physical education one should first formulate one's own philosophy of a particular field of physical education or of physical education in general. The standard of a philosopher is different from that of a scientist. A scientific study endeavors to ascertain the facts alone. A philosophical study endeavors to present an integrated whole which will most adequately explain all the human facts, and advance the most adequate hypothesis to explain scientifically unknown factors concerning which there is no speculation. Philosophizing upon physical education should illuminate many problems concerning which there is no available scientific knowledge, but which are important to scientific progress. Scientific research should isolate these problems from all complicating factors, make the commonly used phrase, "all other things being equal," an actuality, and ascertain the essential facts. These facts or solutions should then be fitted into their proper places in the philosophy. Some of them may be so revolutionary as to require a complete revision of the philosophy.

To this team of the philosopher and the scientist must be added the technologist—the physical educator who applies the system! He is the door of the job and comprises the vast majority of us physical educators. Such an approach should avoid the not infrequent conflict between the experimental scientist, the philosopher, and the "practical educator." The scientist, the philosopher, and the man in the gymnasium and on the field must be united. They must not be allowed to grow hoary whiskers of inert tradition.

The philosopher, the scientist, and the technologist may be embodied in one person. So complete a balance is rare. I believe, nevertheless, that the research student should start with a well-thought-out philosophy and should not be content to relinquish his scientific research until it has been successfully applied by the technologist and until it has proven an effective solution for the problem. After this introduction to research, let us consider some of the elements involved in it.

Finding the Problem. A research worker necessarily begins with a problem. Probably everyone working in this field has been requested to suggest a problem for someone to study. How are problems born? I hope you will all assist in combating the theory that the doctor brings them. The important ones are legitimate brain children of expert educators. Intellectual stepchildren seldom receive the care one gives one's own. The following methods have proven fruitful in proposing worthwhile problems.

1. Write out your philosophy of physical education. When you come to something you would like to know but do not know and cannot find, write it down on your research hope chest. Analyze the field into separate parts and study these parts.

2. In all reading, discussions, or lectures, and at all other times, write down at once any "hunches" that come to you. Many times reading or philosophizing will reveal gaps in your present field of knowledge. Write these down. Read the best studies made in your own field; think about a problem; and note the questions which arise. Criticize and challenge statements made in current professional periodicals, in books and research studies in your own and allied fields. Literally hundreds of research problems will result.

3. Prepare a paper upon some subject in which you are interested and extend it into unknown realms.

4. When you meet an obstacle in your thinking, analyze it for the problems it suggests.

5. With what are you dissatisfied in your field? What problems does it suggest?

6. Analyze and challenge the popular beliefs in your field. You will be appalled by their unquestioned acceptance.

7. Associate with people in research; confer with faculty members of professional schools; seek the society of the intellectually competent individual who likes to debate the opposite side of any question. He may be wrong, but he will open up useful leads. Especially seek discussion with those who radically differ with your own philosophy.

8. Criticize general educational practices. Again note your "hunches."

9. Observe the problems that grow out of a procedure in which you are interested. For example, if you are interested in the historical method, browse around in the history of physical education for promising problems.

10. Read bibliographies of recent research, of dissertations and the like. These are fertile sources of information.

From these processes of inquiry into all these things many suggestions will come—which of them should one adopt?

Selecting the Problem. In the selection of a research problem there are a number of criteria.

1. Is the problem in the realm of research? Will it add to the store of new knowledge?

2. Does it interest you? It may be a splendid problem but you should wholly pass it by if it does not strike fire.

3. Does it possess unity? That is, does the problem work together into a whole or is it a potpourri of a number of problems which should be attacked separately, or which are only superficially related? I think we should perhaps dwell a moment upon this. Very frequently one selects too large a problem. There are experimental problems, historical problems, and philosophical problems in it, all of which should be separated to clear the way for the main problem.

4. Is it worthwhile? Will it unify knowledge? Has it real content? Will it make a worthwhile contribution?

5. Is it feasible from the standpoint of difficulty, time, expense, and availability of data?

6. Is it timely? That is, are there available measurement tools and is there a demand for its solution? As an illustration, many character-education problems are not timely because there are not adequate tools to measure characters.

7. Is it a problem that you can attack without prejudice? If not, you had better pass it on to someone else.

8. Finally, are you prepared in techniques to attempt the problem? The scientific woods today are full of unprepared statisticians attempting difficult statistical research. . . .

Limitation of the Problem. This step is too often neglected. The amateur research worker almost always chooses too large a problem. One needs to narrow the problem to a single definite field or to break it up into definite elements which are amenable to attack. Special care should be taken to see that the conclusions of the study are not to be based upon unproven assumptions. To illustrate: suppose one began to study health, and used one of the current cardiovascular tests as the sole index of health. It is obvious to the careful student that none of the tests have been sufficiently validated to become a standard upon whch to have a serious research. This stage in the setup of the research problem may necessitate preliminary studies, particularly those which will provide measurement tools. Physical education today urgently needs more research of a pure science nature in the fundamentals of measurement. . . .

Selection of Techniques. At this time one must choose the appropriate type of research technique. The problem may be a descriptive one and require a questionnaire or some variety of interview. It may be an experimental problem requiring the equating of groups. It may be a casual problem necessitating correlation techniques, or it may require the techniques of philosophical research. In any case the selected techniques will frequently need some preliminary experimentation and revision. To illustrate: a questionnaire which seems to be thoroughly adequate may prove obscure, or may lead itself to inadequate classifications. At this stage, one may need to test the technique upon thirty to one hundred cases in order to improve the technique and simplify the study by the early elimination of unnecessary variables. . . .

Finally, begin. There is nothing especially difficult or mysterious in research, nothing that cannot be mastered by any capable mind. There are, however, methods that are good, and techniques that are essential. One must learn them just as one learns to play the violin before giving a concert performance. I believe, however, that there is no reason why a fairly large percentage of physical educators should not do effective research. Furthermore, I am convinced that it is only by the road that I have indicated—that of philosophizing, carrying out scientific research, and making intelligent technological applications that we shall raise the status of physical education in our educational institutions.

33

The American Association for Health and Physical Education Becomes a Department of the NEA *

CHARLES H. McCLOY, Ph.D.

Dr. Charles H. McCloy was President of the American Physical Education Association when this merger occurred; for a description of the professional contributions made by Dr. McCloy to the field of physical education see Document 32.

On the 28th of June [1937] the American Physical Education Association and the Department of School Health and Physical Education of the National Education Association were officially amalgamated to form the American Association for Health and Physical Education—a Department of the National Education Association. This merger marked the consummation of the efforts of many educators within and without the American Physical Education Association to bring this organization within the National Education Association, and to unite the efforts of health educators, physical educators, and leaders in school recreation under one organization.

The final terms of the merger were approved in April by the Legislative Council of the American Physical Education Association, and later by the Executive Committee of the Department of School Health and Physical Education of the NEA by mail vote. The official union of the two organizations was effected at the Annual Meeting of the NEA in Detroit in June. Thus the American Physical Education Association, as a name, goes out of existence, as does that of the Department of School Health and Physical Education of the NEA; and the American Association for Health and Physical Education—A Department of the NEA—arises out of the ashes. . . .

The reorganization carried over the larger part of the organization of the American Physical Education Association, with some changes and additions. The officers elected by the APEA at the New York meeting

* Charles H. McCloy, "The American Association for Health and Physical Education: A Department of the NEA," *The Journal of Health and Physical Education,* Vol. 8 (September, 1937), pp. 416–417.

were continued, as were the Governing Board and the Legislative Council. Three divisions were added, the Division of Health Education, the Division of Physical Education, and the Division of Recreation. . . .

The new Association will continue to publish the *Journal of Health and Physical Education* and the *Research Quarterly,* and will carry on the work in physical education that was done in the past by the APEA. In addition, however, the American Association for Health and Physical Education assumes new and profoundly important tasks. First, the Association, through the Division of Health Education, hopes to give unity and leadership to much of the work in health education as it affects the schools. To this end—just as the APEA did and the new Association will continue to do with physical-education national professional organizations—national organizations in the field of health education that are desirous of co-operating, are invited to become affiliated organizations, to have a voice in the Legislative Council, and to participate as organizations and as individuals in our work, our deliberations, our legislation, and our conventions—state, district, and national. In addition, we are hopeful that the experts in all fields of health education will co-operate with the Association in furthering the service to be rendered by the Association, without in any way lessening or limiting their services as individuals or through other professional organizations through which they have been accustomed to work. We are fortunate in beginning this new enterprise with such excellent leadership in the Health Education Division and Sections.

In the Recreation Division, the organization is not yet as complex nor as complete. This division, however, faces very important issues and opportunities in that field, especially as it affects school systems.

The merging with the National Education Association affects the Association most favorably. No limiting restrictions have been imposed. The same state, district, and national organizations and meetings will be continued and expanded to include health education and recreation in each constituent organization of the Association. In addition, the organized forces of the National Education Association will be at the service of the American Association for Health and Physical Education in every way possible.

Athletics in the College and University *

HARRY A. SCOTT, Ph.D.

One of the most crucial issues facing physical education at the present time is the question of the place of athletics in education and the proper organization of athletic programs to enable all students to benefit from athletic experiences. Since athletics is a division of physical education, according to leaders in physical education, it is imperative that athletics provide sound educational experiences in physical education and education. Dr. Harry A. Scott, who is unusually well qualified to evaluate this issue, has presented, in this document, the educational philosophy of athletics in the college and university. Dr. Scott completed his early education in Parsons, Kansas, and the Kansas State Teachers College in Emporia before enrolling at Columbia University, where he completed his Ph.D. degree. His professional career included positions as Professor and Director of Physical Education at the University of Oregon, Rice University, and Brooklyn College before moving to Teachers College, Columbia University, as Professor of Health and Physical Education in the graduate school. Professional honors include the following: President of the Texas Physical Education Association, President of the Southern District of the AAHPER, President of the College Physical Education Association, and President of the American Academy of Physical Education. Among the many publications by Dr. Scott is the following document, which outlines the role of athletics in education.

In seeking to understand intercollegiate athletics, it is necessary to consider one of the essential characteristics of American institutions of higher learning. Colleges and universities are chartered by the several states primarily to provide for the education of young people and to promote the general welfare of society. It seems apparent, then, that everything that takes place in an institution of higher learning must in some way—through instruction, research, or services—contribute to the educational welfare of the students and of society. It is because colleges and universities promote the general welfare that they, along with religious institutions and charitable organizations, are exempt from public

* Harry A. Scott, "New Directions in Intercollegiate Athletics," *Teachers College Record,* Vol. 58 (October–May, 1957), pp. 29–37. Reprinted with the permission of the Office of Publications, Teachers College, Columbia University.

taxation. Colleges are not (nor were they ever intended to be) commercial institutions. Obviously, then, athletics must exist in institutions of higher learning in order to contribute to the goals of education and to the improvement of the social order. If the program cannot be justified as an integral phase of the educational curriculum, then it is exceedingly difficult, if not impossible, to explain why it belongs in the college at all.

Certainly athletics cannot be justified merely because it provides amusement to the public. Nor can it be defended on the grounds that money derived from athletic contests is essential to the financial structure of the college. In this connection it is true that a few of the more powerful, favorably located colleges and universities, athletically speaking, earn large sums of money through gate receipts, guarantees, sales of television and radio broadcasting rights, participation in bowl games, and similar lucrative commercial enterprises. However, most institutions of higher learning that attempt to bolster their finances through athletics learn by bitter experience that it is easier to force the proverbial camel through the eye of the needle than it is to make money from athletics. Where financial profits from athletics are concerned, the question must also be resolved as to the extent an educational institution, exempt from public taxation, is justified in expecting to profit financially through the toil of nonpaid amateurs, who are supposedly participating in the game because they love it.

Moreover, athletics cannot be justified for its propaganda values to the college, since the proof of a worthwhile institution of higher learning lies not in the championship quality of its athletic teams but in the contribution it makes to the world of scholarship and research, and in the qualitative achievements of its faculty members and students. Obviously, then, if athletics cannot be defended because of its entertainment, money-making, or propaganda values, it must be justified on the basis of its contributions to the educational goals of the college.

Fortunately, as a component of the program of physical education, athletics, if properly conceived, organized, and taught, can be justified as an integral phase of the general education of all students. . . . These programs must in fact, as well as in theory, contribute to the general education of *all* students. This means that athletics, working co-operatively with the traditional academic disciplines, will so conduct its program as to enrich the lives of the students by helping them to engage in experiences designed to produce the maximum development of their total personalities, improve their abilities to live harmoniously and co-operatively with others, attain competences leading to economic efficiency and independence, and enjoy the privileges and discharge the obligations of enlightened democratic citizenship.

. . . If current practice is a criterion, it seems that in some institutions of higher learning there exists a giant conspiracy to bypass established rules and disregard principles of ethical conduct in order to achieve status in athletics. Otherwise it is difficult to explain why students of low academic qualifications are admitted to the college, or how athletics acquire lucrative "scholarships" which have little or nothing to do with scholarly performance, or why special dormitory and dining facilities not available to other students are open to the chosen few in athletics, or why special privileges regarding class attendance are accorded athletes but not other students, and how it is that special curricula are tailor-made for athletes, especially designed to keep them eligible. It is difficult to understand how these things happen when academic faculty members and administrative officers representing a cross section of the entire college are directly responsible for policy and practice in many of the areas involved. . . .

If the crucial issues of athletics have not been resolved by faculty committees on athletics, athletic conferences, the NCAA, the regional and voluntary accrediting agencies, or by others, then who can be relied on to bring about this long overdue and much needed reform? The answer is that reform in intercollegiate athletics is as surely a professional problem as are departmental problems in chemistry, biology, engineering, or mathematics, and must rest squarely on the shoulders of professional personnel in these fields. The colleges must rely for reform upon the teachers of competitive sports (many people call them coaches, but they are teachers) and those in the department of physical education who administer and supervise the program of intercollegiate athletics. Indeed, because of an amazing lack of foresight in the past, and the pursuit of goals that are primarily uneducational, to say the least, these persons must now accept major responsibility for the sorry state of present-day intercollegiate athletics. These are the persons who have intimate knowledge of the malpractices in the field. These are the ones who initiate and nourish the abuses. For these reasons they should be held responsible for bringing them to an end. This is the way it is done in other departments of the college and there is no valid reason why it should not be done in athletics.

This grass-roots approach to the solution of problems in athletics involves some of the basic issues relating to human conduct. One of these issues involves the delineation of responsibilities. The time has come in American education when the program of intercollegiate athletics should be accorded full curricular status. Those in charge should have responsibility for making the program conform to the educational goals of the college and should be held strictly accountable for their actions. The traditional distrust by academicians of anyone connected with athletics has served to deny status to those entrusted with this program. . . .

Before the professional practitioner can cope successfully with the crucial issues of athletics, however, he will need much help from many sources—particularly from the college president and the board of trustees, who are responsible for the over-all policy-making functions of the college. Because of the external pressures engendered by athletics, those in charge of this program find it extremely difficult to count on everyone concerned to hold the line once it has been co-operatively established. It is in strengthening the hand of the professional personnel in charge of athletics that the college president can wield his greatest influence.

From the very beginning of intercollegiate athletics, the college president has been tremendously concerned about his part in the program. In the early days he issued proclamations and posted rules prohibiting the playing of games on the campus, but these were of no avail. When he relied upon the faculty to throttle the athletic giant he met with only limited success. Neither has the athletic conference nor membership in such organizations as the NCAA entirely solved his problems. The college president presently finds himself harassed and sometimes severely castigated for his inability to solve the problems of intercollegiate athletics. Indeed, as most presidents will admit, they are subjected to the same pressures as the football coach. They can be, and sometimes are, summarily discharged for the same reasons the football coach is fired.

At midtwentieth century, however, the college president cannot ignore intercollegiate athletics, even if he did inherit rather than create the problems in this field. Neither can he abolish the program by killing the patient in order to cure his ills. Indeed, if reform is to come in athletics at all, the college president must come to grips with the problems in the field and assume a role of leadership in their solution. To bolster his efforts in this crusade he will need the steadfast support of everyone connected with the college, including the board of trustees. After girding his loins for battle the president can then involve himself in the following matters:

He can be instrumental in crystallizing the philosophy and objectives of his own institution and in delineating the part intercollegiate athletics is to play in achieving these goals.

He can acquaint himself with the crucial issues in athletics and familiarize himself with the recommended principles and practices in the field. He can then set about to discover what is taking place in athletics in his own institution.

Once he has knowledge of what the situation is, he can then set the machinery in motion to make certain that athletics in his institution is controlled through the same channels as all other curricular areas of the college.

As the opportunities arise, he can recommend to the trustees for appointment only professionally qualified educators who are specialists in physical education, including athletics, and who meet the same standards of competence as other members of his faculty. The source of such personnel is likely to be other educational institutions rather than the field of professional sports or business.

Moreover, since they are qualified educators, he can insist that these teachers (coaches) and administrators be accorded faculty rank consistent with their age, education, and experience, receive the same salaries, enjoy all the rights and privileges, and assume the same responsibilities as other members of the faculty.

In addition, he can make the strict adherence to established educational principles a condition of employment, promotion, or retention in his institution.

He can insist that intercollegiate athletics be made an integral phase of the educational curriculum and its benefits extended to all students.

As a phase of the curriculum, he can seek ways of financing the program of athletics in exactly the same manner that other aspects of the curriculum are financed—generally from appropriated funds, tuition, student fees, gifts, and endowments.

He can insist that the teachers (coaches) and other personnel connected with intercollegiate athletics be evaluated in terms of educational goals rather than on such commercial objectives as wins and losses, money taken in at the gate, or the amount of publicity accorded the teams and individuals representing his institution on the field of play.

He can give continuous surveillance to the program of athletics in his institution.

He can make certain that entrance requirements for all students are equal and see that athletes are neither favored nor discriminated against in meeting admission and retention requirements.

He can be instrumental in setting the qualifications and conditions pertaining to financial grants-in-aid and see that these are allocated to athletes, as well as to other students, through regular college channels.

He can make certain that athletes, along with other students, are enrolled in bona fide, educationally justifiable curricula, and in all other respects are treated the same as other students.

He can familiarize himself with the activities of personnel connected with the program of athletics in his institution and dissuade, by force if necessary, those ambitious individuals who believe that, given the opportunity—and the athletes —they can beat "State University" every Saturday afternoon in the year.

And finally, the president can make certain that a competent, full-fledged educator is appointed to administer the program of athletics in his institution.

In making this appointment he can assure this person of the same academic status, confidence, trust, and co-operation accorded heads of departments in other areas of the curriculum. He can then hold him accountable for qualitative adherence to established principles and practices in the field of competitive sports and in education.

In all these matters, the president will find his burdens considerably lightened if his college is a participating member of a conference of institutions attacking these problems co-operatively. Preferably, these conference members should be traditional rivals in the field of sports, hold to similar philosophies and practices, and be somewhat equal in such matters as size, financial worth, and scholarly accomplishments.

35

The Values of Interscholastic Athletics
in Education *

WILLIAM L. HUGHES

In an account of William L. Hughes (1895–1957), written shortly after
his death, he was described in simple words as "an honor to the profession," a description merited by his long and successful career in
physical education. A product of the public schools of Nebraska and a
graduate of Nebraska Wesleyan, he was the Director of Athletics in a
Nebraska high school for four years before entering upon a teaching and
administrative career in the colleges during which he was at Oberlin College, De Pauw University, Teachers College, Columbia University, and
Temple University. At Teachers College he was Acting Chairman of the
Department of Health and Physical Education from 1942–1944, leaving
to assume the Directorship of the Department of Health and Physical
Education at Temple University. Other notable activities included service
during the Second World War as Consultant, United States Division of
Physical Fitness, and member, National Council on Physical Fitness from
1943 to 1945. Honors and professional recognition came to him in abundance. He was President of the College Physical Education Association
in 1934 and of the AAHPER from 1944–1946 as well as a recipient in
1954 of the much coveted Luther Halsey Gulick Award. A prolific writer,
he published some 60 articles and 17 books or monographs, among the
latter being *Athletics in Education* with Jesse Feiring Williams. The
article, printed below with some deletion, contains his mature reflections
on the place of athletics in the physical-education programs of the schools.

"No motivation for the development of good health and rugged physical condition could be found that would approximate that provided by
competitive athletics." So states no less an authority than the eminent
Educational Policies Commission. Probably no reasonable person would
deny that the increasing participation of youth in athletics has been a
remarkably wholesome and constructive influence for them and for the
race. Even a casual observation of the modern boy and girl at their

* William L. Hughes, "The Place of Athletics in the School Physical-Education
Program," *The Journal of the American Association for Health, Physical Education,
and Recreation,* Vol. 21 (December, 1950), pp. 23–27.

work and play substantiates that fact. They ride, swim, and play games as a matter of course.

In this country, our heritage of sports is old. Man has engaged in them for years. Early athletic competition consisted of crude methods of testing skill, speed, and courage. Since those primitive days, the development of athletics has been slow and checkered. Practices have not always been acceptable and the name of sport often has been tarnished by well-known evils; but in spite of all, this sports participation has persisted and has become a vital cultural expression of our people.

Athletics should occupy a prominent place in a school program of physical education because the elements of these games consist of the large-muscle fundamental activities of running, jumping, throwing, striking, climbing, hanging, lifting, and carrying. In spite of profound changes in man's environment, his biological organism throughout the years has remained the same. Individuals born today have the same kind of vital organs and the arrangement of vital systems that has existed in man for thousands of years. It is a fact of real significance that a rapidly changing society has no counterpart in the biological machine.

In the long evolutionary process from the one-celled organism to man, the appearance and the development of the vital organs arose out of the activity of muscles. This same close relationship exists also in physiological functioning. Vigorous activities of the muscles, for example, call for the functioning of the vital organs at a high level. Accelerated breathing, increased circulation, the creation of need for food, the production and elimination of waste, the activity of glands—all these are due to the activity of muscles.

There is no way to avoid the demands of muscles. They are as much the source of man's vitality in today's machine world as they were in the days of the cave man. Biology also teaches us the importance of large muscles, those that involve the trunk, hips, legs, shoulder-girdle, and arms. Because of the way in which the organs of the body arose and developed, we are able most effectively to affect the processes of these organs thru the action of the skeletal muscles of the body.

These facts, then, give us a clue as to the importance of athletics in modern life because of their possible contribution to the development and maintenance of strength in the vital systems. They can be equally important for another reason, *i.e.* the strategic possibilities through sports participation for desirable social and moral education. Man is also, by nature, a gregarious and competitive organism. The desire to excel is almost universal. Play is a natural and spontaneous response to the organic and social needs of the individual. For these reasons, group activity through play in athletics may have very real educational significance.

In the administration of athletics in schools and colleges, there are literally scores of administrative objectives. The outcomes in terms of desirable changes in boys and girls can be described in several kinds of development desired.

(1) Athletics should provide physiological results, indicative of wholesome, functional activity of the organic systems and sufficient for the needs of the growing organism so the individual may live at the highest possible level of efficiency or utility.

The profession needs to know more about the value of many traditional sport activities. When we are able to measure more accurately the effects of vigorous exercise on youth, we doubtless will need to change our whole conception of "major" and "minor" sports. Current practice in awarding major and minor letters usually depends upon the relative importance each sport holds in the minds of students and officials. It is to be hoped that in the near future athletic sports will be rated, not by the public interest in them, but by their value in contributing to the development and education of the participants.

(2) Athletics should have meaning for the participant, they should contribute to the development of a play attitude and provide a carry-over interest that will function during leisure time.

This outcome should be comparatively easy of attainment since young people are endowed by nature with the urge to run, chase, flee, jump, throw, strike, and compete with one another. Yet many participants in athletics, perhaps even a majority of them, tend to backslide after graduation from school or college. In too many cases, the play spirit, the urge to continue to play, is not strong enough to keep them active when the conveniences of gymnasium, athletic field, locker, and shower are removed.

Clearly, this is one of the most important objectives for athletics. If this one is strongly and surely developed in an individual, the other outcomes are almost certain to be realized.

(3) Athletics should provide opportunities for all youth to acquire skills and to experience the satisfaction of performing efficiently in the racially old natural activities. Athletics also should help young people develop an appreciation of skillful performance in others.

There is evidence all about us of the high correlation between skill in an activity and participation in it. The psychologists say we do the things we enjoy doing and we like to do the things we do well. This is so true that it might even be called a law or principle of participation.

Satisfaction in skillful performance is valuable mental hygiene and contributes much to the development of the personality. The obligation of education to develop play skills through athletics is crystal clear when it is pointed out that youth will likely use these skills, rather than undesirable types of amusements, in their leisure time.

Directors of physical education and athletic coaches need, however, to constantly remind themselves that motor skills are highly specific and the athlete who learns the skills of the so-called major sports have only a meager athletic education indeed. In fact, it is quite possible for an All-American football player, or other sport star, to be a "physical illiterate" if he has developed skills at only one position in only one sport. Schools and colleges that permit this are doing a rank injustice to the athlete. On the other hand, if they require a broad athletic education of all youth, including the varsity athletes, the participants will doubtless return later as alumni to bless their coaches and teachers for the requirement.

(4) Athletics should offer opportunity to develop desirable citizenship traits through participating harmoniously and co-operatively in group activities, including those involving intercultural relationships.

Man is gregarious by nature. He seeks the company of others and through his associations he gains experiences which develop . . . understanding, and sportsmanship. Probably the most important objective of all that youth can gain through participation in athletics is the socialization outcome. Athletics, if properly controlled, can provide experiences that insure wholesome expression of the emotions, desirable modification of undesirable instinctive tendencies, and the development of socially acceptable ideals and standards.

Certainly, the ideas and ideals learned through participation in athletics may be more influential in character formation than the sum total of all the lectures in the classroom on ethics and religion.

(5) Athletics should contribute to the relief of emotional strains and tensions.

The tempo of life has been stepped up tremendously in the last decade. Man's physical organism has been catapulted ahead several thousand years overnight. About one-third of all military 4-F rejections were due to "mental diseases, mental deficiencies, and nervous disorders." Youth have been drawn into the whirlpool.

Overcrowded cities, homes, and schools with the resulting noise and confusion; fast eating; artificial and inadequate lighting; the pressure of studies, social affairs, and extracurricular activities; radio, motion pictures, and television, and the resulting reduction in time for active play—these and a thousand other distractions and stimulating influences cause many thoughtful people to wonder if man can survive in the world he has built.

Participation in athletics, if properly controlled, can do much to relieve strains and tensions, or if overemphasized, to increase them. All the more reason why coaches should fight relentlessly against overemphasis unless they would defeat one of the objectives they set out to attain.

(6) Athletic participation should help the participant develop an ap-

preciation of and responsibility for health and fitness, lifelong participation, and such qualities as sportsmanship and fair play.

The athlete who breaks training and deteriorates physically, who backslides on his participation, and who fails to carry over the principles of sportsmanship and fair play into his home and business life has tragically missed the great lessons to be learned in sports, *i.e.*, the application of those principles and practices to everyday living. His failure, too, is a reflection on his coach who probably was so intent on coaching football or basketball he neglected to teach the boy.

In evaluating the place of athletics in education, educators need constantly to remind themselves that athletics exist for the education of youth rather than that youth exist for the performance of athletic games. Educational or developmental objectives in athletics present a difficult problem to the zealous alumnus, with his tribal loyalty and his vanity in belonging to a championship organization, because these objectives are incompatible with the unreasonable demand of always beating the traditional rival and of always winning a majority of games. The courageous coach and administrator, however, will try always to conduct athletics in such a way that the above objectives will be realized in the form of outcomes and thereby contribute most to the welfare of the participants.

. . . To be of maximum effectiveness, the athletic program should be closely co-ordinated with the general instructional program and properly articulated with the other departments of the institution. The program should be designed to reach many rather than a few "stars" and it should be conducted by professionally trained educators.

High-School Competition for Girls *

AGNES R. WAYMAN

Agnes R. Wayman was chairman of the committee that was instrumental in bringing about the affiliation of the American Association for Health and Physical Education and the National Education Association, which was completed on June 28, 1937. Born in Glen Easton, West Virginia, in 1880, she later migrated to the University of Chicago and earned a degree in Greek and Latin in 1903. But an interest in physical education led Miss Wayman to study physical education at Yale University and Columbia University. From 1918 to retirement in 1945 she served as Professor of Physical Education at Barnard College of Columbia University. Professional honors include the following: President of the AAHPER, fellow of the American Academy of Physical Education, and recipient of the Anderson Award and the Honor Award of the AAHPER. Miss Wayman wrote two books—*Education Through Physical Education* and *A Modern Philosophy of Physical Education*—and numerous articles including very timely statements on the need for sound educational policies in physical education and athletics for girls and women.

In order to clear up any misunderstanding or misapprehension as to just what the attitude of the Women's Division is toward the subject of competition, the following is offered.

The Women's Division does not believe whole-heartedly in competition. It believes that competition is the very soul of athletics, of sports, and of games, and without it they could not exist. What it disapproves of is the highly intense specialized competition such as exists when we have programs of interschool competition, intergroup open track meets, or open swimming meets, with important championships at stake. The evil in connection with these events lies not so much in the competition itself as in the emphasis which is placed upon winning and which makes that the paramount issue. The evil further lies, not alone in the competition at the actual time of the game or meet, but in the whole process which produces the few experts who battle for supremacy. The same evils might exist in an intramural program where too much emphasis

* Agnes R. Wayman, "Competition," *American Physical Education Review*, Vol. 34 (October, 1929), pp. 469–471.

was placed upon winning, but it is not so likely to be as the stakes are not so large.

For instance; in a state basketball tournament for girls, let us consider the following, as it applies to just one high school team, we'll say Brown High School.

1. How was the team chosen? Was it the cream which rose to the top as the result of a big intramural program in which each girl had her share of participation, or was it a picked group from the beginning of the season?
2. Were you sure that each girl on the team was physically able to stand the strain?
3. Did she have a thorough physical examination before she started playing and an occasional check up during the season?
4. Was the team coached by a woman and did she foster a high ideal of sportsmanship and friendly spirit of play, or was the team coached by a man or woman who instilled into the team the desire to win at any cost and with bitterness of feeling?
5. Was any check made of the physical condition of each girl at the time of each game? Was she allowed to play regardless of her condition because the championship was at stake?
6. What motivated that team? A desire to *play* basketball or a desire to *win* the championship?
7. Were there desirable educational outcomes in so far as one can judge in the way of friendly social intercourse on the part of participants and spectators, or was there a feeling of bitter rivalry, either between the players or spectators?
8. How was that team financed? By the Board of Education as a part of the physical education program? Or was it financed by the school body, by gate receipts, by the Rotary Club, by the Chamber of Commerce?
9. Did the woman physical director or instructor of that school approve of interschool competition of that type or was she overruled by the man in charge of the boys—or did the man in charge of the boys take charge of this girls' team backed by a principal who saw in it possible prestige for his school, a chance to "get its name on the map?"
10. What about the nervous strain and the time lost from academic work, both because of the excitement before and during the games and the actual time needed for travel, practice, and play?
11. What was the program and opportunity for play for the rest of the girls in that high school? What proportion of time was the "gym" theirs as compared to the time it was being used by the varsity? Was a game of some sort offered to each girl?

These are just a few of the items which make any sensible, intelligent being pause and think. It was this type of situation existing all over the country and which still exists in many places, which brought the Woman's Division into being.

The Woman's Division has two big missions:

First, to encourage the promotion of sports and games for *all* girls and women.

Second, to establish such ideals and principles in connection with sports and games as will make it certain that these sports and games are being wisely chosen, wisely promoted, and wisely supervised.

It wishes to encourage a nation-wide opportunity for girls with the emphasis upon *participation* rather than upon competition. It looks toward the development of play among girls and women on a nation-wide basis. It does not feel that for the school girl or the college girl, or for girls of like age, the intense competitive system is productive of better girls or better women. This does not by any means mean that it disapproves of two schools meeting occasionally in friendly rivalry providing the girls and the activity have been properly safeguarded. But this should be the exception, not the rule, with emphasis upon the social side and not upon the championship.

In furthering its ideals and principles, it offers the "Play Day" as now being worked out and experimented with all over the United States, as the type of event in which several schools or colleges or clubs or organizations living within commuting distance might meet on a friendly basis for play, with emphasis upon play *with* not *against* us. Such an affair might include land and water sports and both less-highly and highly organized sports and games. "A Game for Every Girl and Every Girl in a Game" would place the emphasis where it belongs, not upon *winning* but upon *participation*.

The Case For and Against Intercollegiate Athletics
for Women [*]

MABEL LEE

Mabel Lee was the first woman to become President of the American Association for Health, Physical Education and Recreation and of the American Academy of Physical Education; and she was the recipient of the much-coveted Gulick Award. Her educational background was distinguished. After graduating *magna cum laude* from Coe College, she studied at the Boston Normal School of Gymnastics, Wellesley College, Vestoff-Serova School of Dance, and the California School of Dance. Professional positions included appointments as Director of Physical Education for Women at Coe College, Oregon Agricultural College, Beloit College, and the University of Nebraska. During World War II Mabel Lee was Regional Director of Physical Fitness for the Seventh Army Service Command and Representative for Women's Physical Education on the Chief-of-Staff's National Advisory Committee for the Women's Army Corps, serving under Generals Marshall, Eisenhower, and Bradley. She was a leader in organizing the Women's Division of the National Amateur Athletic Federation and the National Section on Women's Athletics. Mabel Lee is well known for her book *The Conduct of Physical Education* and articles on competition for women that have become guideposts in physical education. A typical contribution was the study described below.

In the spring of 1923 the College Women's Section of the Middle West Society of Physical Education asked the writer of this article to present at its program a study of the situation of intercollegiate athletics for women, including the case both "for" and "against" such activities. At that time 50 colleges located in 23 states replied to the questionnaire sent out all over the country and the information gleaned was presented at this program and subsequently to the public, through the channels of various magazines and pamphlets.

During the summer of 1930 the Women's Division, National Amateur

[*] Mabel Lee, "The Case For and Against Intercollegiate Athletics for Women and the Situation Since 1923," *The Research Quarterly of the American Physical Education Association,* Vol. 2 (May, 1931), pp. 93–127.

Athletic Federation asked that the study be repeated so that it might learn of the tendencies of the past seven years' growth and know the present situation. In response to that request, the following report is submitted. . . .

Questionnaires were sent out to the Directors of Physical Education for Women in 154 leading colleges and universities of the United States. Replies were received from 98 colleges. (Only 50 replies were received in 1923.) Fifty-six directors failed to reply. The 98 directors replying represent 37 different states and the District of Columbia. (Only 23 states were represented in the replies of 1923.)

This study includes agricultural colleges, teachers colleges, state universities, women's colleges, coeducational colleges, junior colleges, and denominational colleges. It includes colleges of all sizes, with the enrollment of women students ranging from 52 to 9709. A study of intramural athletics is not included in this report. It deals only with the problem of intercollegiate athletics or intermurals. . . .

ADVANTAGES TO THOSE WHO PARTICIPATE [1]

1. In keeping necessary training rules they would acquire habits of hygienic living which should be of great value to them.

2. Through contact with strangers as their guests or as their hostesses they would acquire a training in social values and a broadening of experience which cannot be approximated in playing games with none but home teams.

3. Through the greater interest in intercollegiate games they would feel the more keenly defeat and victory so that their instructors would have an opportunity to drive home to them the lessons to be derived from defeat and victory more quickly and more sharply than in the case of intramural or inter-class activities!

4. They would work harder, thereby acquiring better muscular control, coordination, and increased vigor, also increased mental activity in quickened thought reactions!

5. They would acquire alertness, initiative, clear thinking, decisiveness, self-discipline to a much greater degree than they would through lesser interest in home activities.

6. They would have opportunities to make contacts they would not otherwise have.

7. It would give good players a chance to play good games.

[1] The statements in this report under advantages and disadvantages are quotations from those reporting in the questionnaire; quotation marks are omitted.

8. It is a wholesome pleasure.

9. It broadens the vision of the girls.

10. It creates an excellent test of sportsmanship and health training in order to succeed.

11. The varsity type of individual needs opponents worthy of her caliber.

12. It aids women to meet problems of competition in the business and professional world.

13. It gives the girl with exceptional motor skill an opportunity for development and she should have this chance as well as the girl with the exceptional mind.

14. It trains girls for later situations in life, physically and socially.

DISADVANTAGES TO THOSE WHO PARTICIPATE

1. They would be apt to get more physical straining than physical training, showing the most perhaps in nerve fatigue.

2. The emotional strain attendant upon such competition would be injurious.

3. There would be ever present the tendency to take an active part in activities during the menstrual period for the sake of the trip and the honor of having played. Also the members of a team who can be the least spared by their team would be urged to keep secret their condition so the team would suffer no handicap through their absence, the desire to play the best players being so much more intense in intercollegiate games than it would ever be in a series of interclass or intramural games.

4. The intensive training that would come with participation in these activities would lead to the neglect of other school work due to increase of interest in the activity or through physical fatigue from this intensive training, which would make the girl unable to give proper attention to the other work.

5. The one idea to win at any cost would be bound to creep in, bringing in its wake the inevitable qualities of rowdyism, unless the activities and the players themselves are carefully supervised by competent and conscientious instructors.

6. With the usual rush of college life there is no time that might rightly be given up for the intensive training intercollegiate activities demand.

7. An undesirable newspaper notoriety would be sure to come to the girls;

especially undesirable would be the mention of the fact that certain players are to be out of certain games, as is always the case when men players are out for physical disability of any sort.

8. The sense of values of the players would become distorted as now happens in the case of men's athletics.

9. The disadvantages so far outweigh the advantages that we should not even consider them.

10. Girls are too high strung emotionally to participate wisely in such activities.

11. The values, if any, when achieved are not worth the time spent to achieve them.

12. That would make unfavorable contacts through the unfavorable publicity that would come with varsity competition.

13. It is not a wholesome activity for a girl to enter, judging from the experiences college men go through in their varsity competition.

14. Membership on a varsity squad would curtail a woman's freedom to pursue the normal trend of college life just as it now curtails the freedom of a man who is on a varsity squad.

15. A question which should not be ignored is that raised by certain members of the medical profession as to the bad effect of intense athletic participation on childbearing.

DISADVANTAGES TO THOSE WHO DO NOT PARTICIPATE

1. They may not get physical straining but would be quite apt to get little physical training through neglect if the teaching staff had to turn out varsity teams. It seems impossible that the many would not suffer neglect for the few. No school has sufficient staff or equipment to carry out a program for both the many and the few.

2. The many girls neglected are sure to be the very girls who need the most training for their physical welfare.

3. They would not have their legitimate share of athletic and department funds spent upon their training, so high would be the expense of intercollegiate teams. . . .

SUMMARY

Intercollegiate athletic competition for women does not exist in the colleges of the United States except in a very limited number and percentage. Although the number of 12 of the 1930 study as compared to the number of 11 of the 1923 study, seems to show a slight increase, the per cents of the two studies show a decided decrease since the new study covers a much wider area of the collegiate world and we have a 12 per cent participation showing in 1930 as against a 22 per cent participation showing in 1923.

The varsity type of competition was found in 1923 only in one western, one southern, and three eastern states, while in 1930 it is found in the same states, and in addition in one more southern and 3 more eastern states.

The interclass intercollegiate type, although scarcely existing in 1923 with five colleges supporting it, is still less alive in 1930 with only three colleges supporting it.

The telegraphic intercollegiate type has grown considerably since 1923 but it is not even now in especial favor or disfavor. It existed only in certain Middle West colleges in 1923 but now is used in all parts of the country. . . .

While 11 per cent of the colleges of this study are engaged in varsity type of intercollegiate competition this 11 per cent represents only 7 per cent of the women enrolled in these 98 colleges, so that it is indeed only a very small group of our young women that is touched by this problem in any way. Since the average number of sports engaged in for intercollegiate competition is from two to three and 15 players would probably represent a varsity squad for each, it perhaps is not far wrong to surmise that only 495 women are involved in this competition in the 11 colleges. This is 5.7 per cent of the number of women enrolled in these 11 colleges and only 0.41 per cent of the number of women students involved in this study. Therefore we can say that only 0.41 per cent of women college students engage in varsity intercollegiate competition and as this number is so engaged 6.1 per cent of women students (college mates of this 0.41 per cent) may or may not be neglected depending upon the particular athletic organization within each college.

While varsity intercollegiate competition in 1923 called for an average of four sports so used per college, in 1930 the average has dropped to 2.72. There is little interest among people outside the physical-education profession for promotion of intercollegiate competition for women. What little interest there is comes from men rather than women. The Play Day idea seems to have taken our colleges by storm, but the suggestion coming from a few sources that this competition be organized as college vs. college is met with approval by only a minority.

CONCLUSION

It is interesting to note the rising tide of condemnation of men's intercollegiate athletics. It has grown from a mild protest, voiced by a few in the study of 1923, to most emphatic statements of disapproval, voiced by a large number in this present study of 1930. There exists a great fear that once intercollegiate athletics for women gain a foothold, college women might become involved in the same athletic predicament as their brothers. The director who replies in the following strain seems to voice the opinion of the great majority when she says "I would approve of a program of intercollegiate athletics for women if it would actually be conducted as amateur sports should be conducted but not as men's intercollegiate athletics are conducted in this country." There is ever present the alarming thought that women might become involved in something equally undesirable. . . .

In the position of one who is presenting both sides of the question, the writer finds it necessary merely to present and to let the statements of those who are "for" and the statements of those who are "against" speak for themselves, and to let the figures in the statistics tell their own story of the situation as it stands today. Many of the suggestions, especially some concerning Play Days, will most probably sound utterly naive to most men and to some women but they prove how absolutely determined are the women of the physical-education profession and, judging from the report of ACACW for 1930, how determined also are the women college students of today, not to permit women's athletics to follow in the footsteps of men's athletics. They are determined to keep them free of all taint of professionalism and commercialization—to keep them quite informal, entirely sane, and absolutely wholesome.

38

ⅨⅭⅮⅨ

Intramurals: An Integral Part of
Physical Education *

ELMER DAYTON MITCHELL, Ph.D.

Dr. Elmer D. Mitchell, illustrious pioneer in the intramural sports movement, was born in Negaunee, Michigan, in 1889. Academic preparation at the University of Michigan led to an A.B. degree in 1912 and a Ph.D. in 1938; while there he was captain of the baseball team and a member of the band. The professional career of Dr. Mitchell has been at the University of Michigan; after serving as an athletic coach, he became Director of Intramural Athletics in 1919 and later Professor and Chairman of the Department of Physical Education. In 1921 he invented the game of speedball. Among his many publications are *Intramural Athletics* (1925), *Theory of Play* (1934), and *Sports for Recreation* (1936). He was editor of the *Journal of Health and Physical Education* (1930–1943) and founder and editor of the *Research Quarterly* (1930–1943). The numerous professional honors bestowed upon Dr. Mitchell include his being President of the American Academy of Physical Education, President of the College Physical Education Association, and executive-secretary of the American Association for Health and Physical Education (1930–1939). He also received the Luther H. Gulick Award and the Clark W. Hetherington Award. A memorable contribution to physical education was Dr. Mitchell's authoritative Wingate Memorial Lecture on the intramural sports movement in the United States, of which excerpts appear below.

Possibly the first approach that I should make to my subject is to define its meaning and scope. The word *Intramural* is less than twenty years old and is the gift of a professor who once taught Latin in the public schools. Insofar as I can find out, the first use of this name was made by Professor A. S. Whitney, former Dean of the School of Education at the University of Michigan, who was a member of the Faculty Athletic Committee at the time that the first Department of Intramural Athletics was inaugurated in the year 1913. That doesn't mean that intramurals had not been

---

* E. D. Mitchell, "Organization of Intramural Athletics," *School Athletics in Modern Education: Wingate Memorial Lectures, 1930–31*, edited by E. Dana Caulkins (New York: J. J. Little and Ives Company, 1931), pp. 266–283.

tried out here and there before. It means that for the first time a single department was organized with one man primarily responsible for conducing the recreational activities of the students. It may surprise some of you to know that this single word was once two words, and each was capitalized. The next logical step was to hyphenate the two words *Intra* and *Mural;* and then in turn the capitals disappeared and finally the hyphen. By this time the dictionaries were ready to include it—at least the big ones. . . .

A very practical consideration arose at once in connection with this new name. It cost too much money to engrave the long term *Intramural Athletics* on medals or cups at the rate of three or five cents a letter respectively. Illinois tried the dubious experiment of using *I. M. Athletics* but without any marked success. Then out of a clear sky the word *Intramurals* emanated from Ohio State University and the rapid way in which it was taken up demonstrated that it met a real need. This one word now covers quite satisfactorily the previous combinations of *Intramural Athletics, Intramural Activities,* or *Intramural Sports,* as the case may be.

This consideration of the terminology of Intramurals leads naturally into the question of its scope. We usually conceive of two athletic programs, the intramural and the varsity, the one taking place within the school and the other taking place between different schools. . . .

Probably the first trend to be noticed resulted from the insistent demand on the part of the intramural players that the curriculum of sports be greatly enlarged. To make this point more clear, it should be stated that the intramural movement, in its early beginnings, accepted the varsity program as an example to follow, with the result that football, basketball, baseball, track, and tennis were the first intramural sports. This was the meager list of sports for which the varsity "M" at Michigan was awarded even as recently as 1920; and it can be seen that most of the emphasis was on team competition. When, however, the intramural program got under way, there arose an increasing demand for a wider variety of sports, and consequently the department, although greatly hampered by lack of facilities, began introducing the sports of swimming, wrestling, boxing, cross-country, fencing, skating, hockey, handball, golf, soccer, speedball, gymnastics, and playground ball.

As a following grew up for these newer sports, there developed correspondingly in each case a nucleus of the more skilled players, with the inevitable outcome that petitions for varsity recognition and competition were drawn up. That a number of these petitions were successful can be seen by a glance at the present varsity program where, it will be noticed, there are now twelve official varsity sports instead of the five listed in 1920. Here is evidence of one effect of intramurals upon the status of varsity competition.

Out of this situation there developed in turn a most happy outcome for the intramural program. Previously, the facilities for intramural participation had been very limited in the case of many of the more recreative sports, and furthermore, the privileges of instruction had been practically denied. Accordingly, however, as the varsity developed adequate facilities for its newly adopted sports, hours were arranged when intramural competition could take place as well. . . .

The next development is not so apparent on the surface, but it has an indirect effect upon the interest and higher level of ability of the intramural players of today as contrasted with that of the players of even a few years ago. There is no question but that the rapid rise in popularity of the intramural movement has had a decided effect upon the make-up of the required physical education program of exercise. Competitive and recreative sports have made great encroachments upon the older formal gymnastic system. One evidence of this is found in the newer mass methods of teaching athletic skills. This practice has several names. At Columbia it is called *natural gymnastics*. In place of meaningless and uninteresting calisthenic movements, exercises have been devised which permit the teaching of swimming strokes, track techniques, basketball skills, golf form, etc., to large groups of students arranged in class formation. These skills are purposeful and the student submits himself to such instruction with zest. His imagination is captured and the incentive to apply his newly acquired techniques in the voluntary afterschool intramural activities is added. The result is a successful application of the principle that education should relate itself to actual life situations. . . .

This emphasis on teaching the fundamentals of sports and on including competition as part of the work of the required gymnasium classes has had its effect upon the intramural programs of both high schools and universities. Students now become well acquainted with intramurals during their high school years, and on entering college they anticipate this form of participation as a matter of course. It is no longer necessary to use aggressive measures to entice the incoming college freshmen into the activities. It must be admitted, too, that intramurals have by now become so much a tradition of our college life that the new student, even though he were not already acquainted with them would find this topic so prominent among the daily discussions of the students, that he would soon feel the urge to take part. As a consequence of this increased interest from so many new sources, the intramural movement has gained momentum until it has reached a growth which is of practically ideal proportions.

Another trend that should possibly be mentioned is the change in regard to the units used for grouping the students for competition. The experience of "trial and error" has shown which methods are the more compensating in regard to the amount of effort expended upon them. If anything, the tendency is to have fewer units rather than more. This may seem surprising in view of the fact that the program, both in high schools and colleges, has been so greatly enlarged in numbers, but on the other hand the intramural authorities are finding it more profitable to concentrate on the more successful units. More and more the groups are being organized about (1) *residence,* in the form of homerooms, fraternity, or dormitory, and (2) *leaders,* usually obtained from the gymnasium classes or from observation of students in informal play. Except for the earlier grades, the class unit seems to be dwindling in importance, and accordingly as the number of students has mounted, the class spirit has dropped. In the public schools the leader is found tied up with grade, homeroom, gymnasium, or some form of classification according to age, weight, height, etc., either alone or in combination.

This need for group units is one that need only be of concern in the case of sports like basketball or baseball in which a team basis is absolutely essential. The problem of organization for individual sports such as swimming, tennis, archery, squash, golf, etc., seems to become definitely solved with the securing of adequate and attractive facilities. When such facilities are made available it is found that the individuals without a strong group affiliation, such as the "independents" in colleges, will turn out just as numerously as those who are fraternal members.

It is not an impossibility that eventually there will be but two types of competition. These will be the All School meets, leagues, and tournaments for individual sports (as at present) and the All School competition for team events. In such an event, all teams, whether fraternity or independent, would enter together and would play on the same basis. Along with this possibility, there is also the possibility that intramural letters or numerals of the future may be awarded on the attainment of a certain number of points rather than by the present method of being a member of a winning class team. This principle has already been definitely established in the junior high school where there are no varsity teams and a basis is needed for awarding the school letter. The point system as a solution is growing in favor because of the added opportunity it gives to reward merit in the way of leadership, reliability, and sportsmanship, and certainly these attributes should be considered as important as mere physical prowess. . . .

Throughout this discussion the health precautions in regard to exercise have been made apparent. There is no question concerning the fact that exercise needs to be carefully regulated to the needs of each particular individual, and that, to the student not in careful training, too little exercise is better than too much. Moderate exercise is the regimen for the average student. In addition to the health values, however, there are other intramural values of which hints may have been given, but which should possibly be singled out for further mention. School sports certainly give opportunity for wide and democratic social contacts and for the making of valued friendships. The team attachments have their place in training the more sturdy qualities that come from personal self-sacrifice for the common good. All group play requires sociability. It is a pleasure to watch a group of students at our Intramural Building organize informally for a game of basketball or volleyball. Some players leave; others standing on the sidelines are invited in. It does not matter that they are strangers; they are not so for long. In many cases faculty members and students play together on the informally picked teams and the relations are close and sympathetic.

It will be quite readily admitted that the program serves to divert the students' energies to activities that are wholesome in nature. This leisure-time aspect has been a factor in the ruling at Michigan that the Intramural Building shall be opened evenings, Sundays, holidays, and vacation periods, even though no organized play is scheduled. The use of the building does not cease with the warmer weather, because the swimming pool then increases in popularity and the lockers, showers, and dressing rooms prove a boon for those who wield a tennis racket or swing their way around the golf course. During this time of business depression, the building has served as a resource to those students who do not have the usual amount of money to spend on movies, dances, and other luxuries. As a result there has been no depression in the affairs of the Intramural Department, which has been kept busier than ever taking care of the extra demands made upon it.

In retrospect, it would appear that the various changes that have been enumerated have been for progress. No doubt other important changes are destined to evolve with future trends in the special life of the student body. We should keep in mind that leisure should be a means of self-expression and that the recreational hours of students should be kept as free from restriction as is compatible with the best interests of all. The intramural policy should therefore aim to keep close to the current of student interest and to make innovations as a real need arises for them.

Education for Leisure: A Must *

JAY B. NASH, Ph.D.

Recreation can be the salvation of modern man—caught up in a world of stress and strain. Work alone is no longer enough; lesiure alone is not enough to satisfy. Recreation activities provide man with a spiritual, creative outlet of expression and furnish opportunity for challenge and mastery without which life has no meaning. This was the message of concern for the future from an outstanding professional leader who has contributed wisely to our past. For an account of the professional contributions made by Dr. Jay B. Nash to American physical education, see Document 31.

Civilization has completed one of its great cycles—1850–1950—and it must, whether ready or not, start a new one. It was a great century. It saw the rise of the machine, the telephone, the radio, radar, television, the automobile and the airplane, the release of atomic energy, and the conquest of space. The machine has liberated. It has given man mastery of time and space; it has given him the leisure of which he has dreamed. Science has liberated—but for what? . . .

We should ask ourselves: How is man reacting to the undreamed of conquest of nature? Last year we Americans used 45 million aspirin tablets daily, took 20 million sleeping pills, and the next morning chased them with as many million wake-up pills. American doctors are writing 40 million prescriptions for the new antiworry pills called tranquilizers, for those hoping to stave off the anxiety, depression, and fear which grip our modern way of living. . . .

The age-old dream of man has been for leisure—a chance to let down, to do something he has always wanted to do. He has dreamed of a haven where the winds and waves no longer beat on his frail craft. There would be happy days, no more work to do, no schedule to meet, no struggle. It would be a time to realize a vague, lifelong ambition to write, to paint, to sing, even to catch "that big fish."

One of the most characteristic and important aspects of life is the urge to activity. In fact, activity distinguishes the living organism from inani-

* Jay B. Nash, "Education for Leisure: A Must," *Journal of Health, Physical Education and Recreation,* Vol. 31 (January, 1960), pp. 17–18 and 62.

mate matter. The source of the urge to do, the hand on the back, lies in the hereditary background. Because of its strength and universality, the activity drive has important implications in the life and education of each of us.

Life is a going-on process; like a top, when the spinning stops, life stops. We cannot escape the risks and opportunities of living. Life activity never stops. It never stops in anyone. And there is an art of living which in many times and lands has guided or built this essential activity into beauty, power, habitual experience, and collective achievements which appear superhuman and miraculous.

Contrary to much of our thinking, man longs to struggle—he loves to master, to conquer. Even the hope of success keeps him enthusiastic. Neurologists and psychiatrists now say that challenge keeps him normal, if the goal seems significant—but there must be a goal. There must be meaning to the sacrifices one makes for the struggle. . . .

It was through work that men came to have self-respect and dignity and, most of all, to belong, in the family, the community, his time, and for some, to all time. What man wants and needs, if morale is to be built and maintained, is an opportunity to work. Mark you, this is no plea for long hours of repetitive wage work. This is no defense of drudgery for drudgery's sake. This gospel concerns challenging work, for which the individual has sufficient skill to bring himself within the reach of success, so that he may have the expanding joy of achievement—work with security, the only foundation for normality.

Leisure alone is not enough to satisfy; neither is work unless it has significance. Recreation and work together make for fullness. To people who do not work, leisure is meaningless. . . . Leisure and leisure time are all-inclusive words, and the activities implied can range all the way from crime and delinquency through meaningless amusement and entertainment, just a shade above unbearable loneliness, to the creative activities which make life livable.

In contrast to the activities on the lower end of the scale, recreation can be defined as those activities—other than survival—which provide man with satisfactions in their mastery, activities which furnish a spiritual, creative outlet of expression. Recreation activities satisfy the activity drive inherent in man's neural make-up. They meet a pattern for living—a worthwhile goal with self, and possibly group, approval. But in this pattern of challenge and approval there is one thing lacking—hope of success. There must be hope. Hope, like faith and a purpose for life, is medicinal; they are therapeutic. . . . If man is to go on with courage and hope, there must be some chance of arrival, though it be remote. The pattern of life must hold a challenge and a hope of success! This hope of success assumes education for recreation.

No longer, as a rule, does grandfather, or even father or mother, help the child to become skillful. Crowded homes, small yards, busy parents—not one but two (over 20 million of our 66 million workers are women)—form a pattern in which the small child has no contact with older people. In other days there was a "seat for the small child" in the blacksmith shop; near the stone mason, the carpenter, the butcher; by the mother making jelly, hooking rugs, or gardening. To a large extent, these are gone forever, and the schools, recreation departments, and youth agencies must fill the gap. The gap must not, however, be thought of as just sports and games. This misinterpretation, too frequently present in the thinking of physical-education people, is a dangerous disservice to recreation.

Recreation must be a cross section of all human activities and interests. The picture dream could come true. Here they are young and old, with their hobbies: writing poetry, building a cabin, making a piece of pottery, singing a song, playing the guitar, exploring the countryside, sailing a boat, playing tennis. They are taking pictures, calling a square dance, knitting a dress, gardening, redoing old furniture, binding a book, writing a play. They fish, hunt, hike, experiment in science, and collect anything and everything. They go to the ends of the earth to see canyons, climb mountains, chase the caribou, catch a sailfish, visit cathedrals, study pictures, visit youth clubs, follow the migratory birds, record folk songs, or dig dinosaur eggs in the Gobi Desert. On and on they go—in a thousand avocations and vocations. They are in factories, offices, homes, schools, and churches. This is a dream, but it could come true.

We must recognize that stress and strain are killers. If we cannot relieve tensions, we must break the devitalizing chain somewhere. Mere idleness is not enough. Man needs some task or occupation that requires his genius qualities, restores his self-respect, and transforms him from a cog in a machine to a man, proud of his work!

Recreation activities may be the salvation of our professional group in which members are breaking under tension and strains. They will be the salvation of the individual whose work is routinized.

Man must have the thrill of mastery, the "traveling hopefully" concept. There must be another ridge to cross, there must be more bass in the lake, there must be more work for volunteers. These are the thrills that keep people young, that carry young and old into a myriad of indoor contests, to the playgrounds and the tropics and the Arctic. Man endures hardships in long travel and in lonely cabins, devoid of modern accommodations and comforts, he fights heat, cold, flies, and poisonous snakes in order to find thrills. Rob man of this heritage and you take from him one of the great urges to live.

The happy man, the healthy man, the normal man, and the busy man are one, busy but not cramped, active but with sufficient glide for recuperation. The happy man will be the one who has accomplished and

is still advancing. The rung of a ladder was never meant to rest upon;
it is merely a vantage place from which to take the next step.

Who is this happy man? He painted a picture; he sang a song; he modeled
in clay; he studied the stars; he worked on a lathe; he built a cabin. Or perhaps
he sought a rare stamp; he read a good book; he saw a great play; he made
a rock garden. Or again, he romped with his grandchild; he taught youth to
shoot straight; he taught them to tell the truth; he read the Koran; he learned
from Confucius; he practiced the teachings of Jesus. And through all, he
dreamed of northern lights, sagebrush, rushing rivers, and snow-capped peaks.
He was a trooper; he had a hundred things yet to do when the last call came.

40

The Place of Dance in the
School Physical-Education Program *

ANNE SCHLEY DUGGAN, Ph.D.

A specialist in the field of dance, Dr. Anne Schley Duggan has been a key leader in establishing dance as an integral part of physical education. Her educational background in dance was facilitated by graduate work at Columbia University, where she earned the Ph.D. degree, and special study under eminent dance teachers in America and Canada. Dr. Duggan has been a prominent teacher in dance and physical education at Columbia University, the University of Dance in Massachusetts, University of Toronto, the Margaret Eaton School of Dance, and in her present position as Director of Health, Physical Education and Recreation at The Texas State College for Women. Among the many professional honors that have come to Dr. Duggan are the following: President of the AAHPER, Texas President of the National Advisory Council of Youth Hostels, member of the Advisory Committee of Dancing Masters of America, and editor of special issues of *Educational Dance* and *The Southwestern Musician*. Numerous articles and books, published on dance and physical education, have been of special significance in enabling Dr. Duggan to influence favorably the thinking regarding the place of dance in education and in physical education. Her viewpoint is expressed below.

To discuss dance as a general entity is misleading since each individual tends to interpret what he reads in terms of his experience with some specific phase of dance. Viewpoints with respect to the place of dance in the physical education program are predicated, therefore, upon an agreement as to what types of dance comprise this aspect of our field. Over a period of time and as a result of changing philosophies of physical education, the well-rounded, broad program of dance in education has expanded gradually to include the four types which we now designate as folk, tap, ballroom, and modern. . . .

* Anne Schley Duggan, "The Place of Dance in the School Physical Education Program," *The Journal for the American Association for Health, Physical Education and Recreation,* Vol. 22 (March, 1951), pp. 26–29.

An expeditious and graphic way of visualizing the place of dance in the school physical-education program is in terms of its specific objectives like skills to be developed, knowledges to be acquired, and attitudes and appreciations to be fostered. They imply, in turn, values inherent in each type of dance activity and should be examined in terms of their potential contributions to the development of individuals experiencing each type. Inclusion of each phase of dance in the school physical-education program should be based upon the richness of its contributions to the objectives sought.

A primary skill objective of any dance program is the development of a well co-ordinated body. Modern dance contributes more completely to this objective, perhaps, than any other activity in the physical education program. In modern dance, the body experiences the widest range of movement possible; movements must be strong or percussive, smooth or sustained in quality; the body must swing, sway, twist stretch, relax, contract, move through space both quickly and slowly; it must experience the gamut from large, expansive movement to small, delicate movement, from free, abandoned movements to those carefully controlled.

Whereas all forms of dance in the school program contribute to poised, harmonious use of the parts of the body in everyday movement, folk and ballroom dance do so especially through movements of walking and running efficiently in good body alignment. While it promotes general body co-ordination, tap dance makes a unique contribution to co-ordination in the use of the feet; thru the fine co-ordination which tap requires the feet become stronger and lighter as well as more efficient in performance. Often football coaches and tennis teachers require their players to study tap dance because of the carry-over value to good footwork on the playing field and court.

The ability to move rhythmically is an important skill which should grow out of a sound dance program. Tap, folk, and ballroom dance afford a rhythmic discipline in the performance of various steps based upon a given rhythm, which more than likely is one of the fundamental meters, such as 2/4, 3/4, 4/4, or 6/6. Tap dance, perhaps, is the most exacting dance form in this respect because of the intricate rhythms of steps performed in contrapuntal relationship to the meter of the music to which it is performed. Modern dance permits free experimentation with organic rhythms and more unusual rhythmic patterns and meters as well as providing basic training in the established metric system.

Another important objective in this category is the ability to use the body as an instrument of expression. The variety of style found in dances from the different countries of the world makes folk dance a particularly fine medium for the expressive use of the body. The ordered reserve and dignity of the English country dances, the light, precise, refined movement of Scottish dances, the free, vigorous abandon of Scandinavian dance, the change of quality in Slavic dances are illustrative of the scope of expression possible thru folk dance.

Ballroom dance affords variety of quality in movement thru the inherent characteristics of its forms: the lyric, lilting waltz; the smooth, subtle tango; the lively, bouncing samba; the interesting rhythm of the rumba; the abandon of jitterbug dancing. Thru its various types of routine—eccentric, waltz, military, buck, rhythm buck, soft shoe, as well as original compositions based upon these traditional forms—tap dance affords varied expression thru movement.

Modern dance of all types permits the greatest range of expression, using the body as an instrument which becomes a means of communication of emotion, mood, quality, or thought in unlimited possibilities with respect to theme and movement.

The development of strength, endurance, balance, flexibility, and similar components of physical fitness which characterize healthy individuals, is of course, a basic objective for the program of physical education as a whole; dance contributes to this objective as fully as does any other phase of the program. Those familiar with the techniques of modern dance can see readily how it promotes the foregoing qualities as well as the underlying objectives of cardiovascular and respiratory efficiency.

Tap, ballroom, and folk dance contribute to the factors of physical fitness, also—tap especially to agility, ballroom dance especially to balance, and folk dance especially to endurance. Anyone who has danced Morris dances, the Irish Lilt, the Scottish Highland Fling, the Swedish Hambo, the Bavarian Schuhplattlers, and certainly our Western square dances will testify to this contribution of folk dance to endurance.

Important knowledge objectives to be reached through dance include an understanding of the use in dance of space, time, and force—factors inherent in daily experience. Folk and modern dance involve more group and individual movement through space than do tap and ballroom dance. . . . The use of force in dance is reflected in the changing dynamics of modern dance more, perhaps, than in any other forms of dance. Accent is very important in folk dance in stamps and claps and in the changing of phrase and direction. . . .

An understanding of how the body may be used aesthetically, safely, and efficiently in movement is another important knowledge objective. Certain principles of movement, which are stressed especially in dance because of their emphasis upon form, can be carried over readily to all types of activity. These principles include: the proper use of the feet and legs in supporting the body weight in running, jumping, and leaping, as well as in walking; the concept of a tall body with a constant "lift" throughout the entire body to prevent heaviness and sagging of the parts upon each other; and the knowledge of which muscles to use for specific movement for greatest economy and efficiency.

Good posture and carriage, with implications for personal attractiveness as well as for safety and efficiency in movement, continue to be fairly constant goals in physical education. Dance, therefore, remains an irrefutable medium for the achievement of these goals with respect to aesthetic as well as mundane implications.

A final, and very important, knowledge objective for dance is concerned with a concept of the role of dance in the civilization of man. Through a study of the origins of folk dances, students learn that dance is linked inextricably with geographical, sociological, and historical factors in the lives of the peoples of all countries. A study of the history of dance in connection with modern dance reveals dance as a mirror of the history of man. Through ballroom dance, students become acquainted with various social customs which have been handed down from previous cultures and form an important part of a civilized society today. . . .

The fact remains, however, that the essence of dance is movement and that those engaged in the education of youth through physical activities are the best and most logically equipped for their education in the art of movement. Here again teacher-education institutions are at fault when they fail to augment the professional education of their graduates in anatomy, kinesiology, fundamentals of movement, etc., with training in music, drama, stagecraft, costume, design, and other aspects of related creative arts. Only through such a background of training will the potential teacher of dance integrate his instruction with the various arts to the enrichment of all concerned.

In addition to being an art form, modern dance is one of the most valuable activities in the physical-education program for the development of strong, vital, sound bodies. This constitutes one of the primary contributions at elementary, high school, and college levels. Dance is indeed the birthright of a broad program of physical education. . . .

Interpreting Rhythm in Physical Activity *

MARGARET NEWELL H'DOUBLER, M.A.

In the field of the dance Margaret H'Doubler has been described as "scholar, inspirational leader, and author of international recognition." She was born in Beloit, Kansas, in 1889 and completed her education at the University of Wisconsin, receiving a Master of Arts degree in 1924. A milestone in the history of the dance in education was her establishment, at the University of Wisconsin, of the first dance-major program in an American college. Lasting contributions to the dance in education came from such timely publications as *The Dance and Its Place in Education* (1925), and *Rhythmic Form and Analysis* (1932). She was a member of the International Dance Association and the American Academy of Physical Education. Her contributions to the dance internationally included a lecture demonstration in Birmingham, England, and another in Helleran-Luxembourg. An invaluable contribution to physical education is her article "An Interpretation of Rhythm," of which excerpts are printed below. Rhythm, she says, is "a constant law of all muscular movement."

Considering the goal of all education as the building for integrated personality through self-realization, and asked what is the significant contribution physical education has to make, I would mention the making of good motion habitual, helping students to gain mastery of their bodies so that all tasks would be undertaken and executed with an intelligent appreciation for an application of force and effort, and developing them as far as possible within their limits for efficient and enjoyable activity.

The body should be considered as the outer aspect of personality. It is the medium through which we receive impression from the external world and by which we express our meanings. This means that the body should be given as careful study and as high a perfection of technique as the associated processes of thought and feeling. The most completely developed individual is the one who has trained all his powers with equal dignity and consideration that he may be physically, mentally, and

* Margaret N. H'Doubler, "An Interpretation of Rhythm," *The Journal of Health and Physical Education,* Vol. 3 (September, 1932), pp. 16–17 and 54.

emotionally integrated. . . . An attempt is here made to show the important role rhythm may play in such a development. . . .

Rhythm is like electricity—difficult to define but recognizable in terms of what it does. . . . Let us start building from something familiar— take any rhythmic experience, either the swing of a golf club, a tennis serve, a swimming stroke, or dancing. The experience, however, need not be confined to motor experience, for auditory, visual, and tactile stimuli may also give one rhythmical impressions. . . . It is this binding together of related parts into a whole that is the function of rhythm. And further, it is this feeling of the organization of parts into wholes that is the fundamental fact common to rhythm whether experienced in poetry, music, or bodily activity.

To explain the existence of rhythm and to understand it we must go to the laws of our own being and there discover that rhythmic experiencing is a capacity of the human organism. Rhythm is an attribute of man's nature. His physiological and psychological as well as his physical functioning obey the laws of rhythm and out of this involuntary obedience has come the highly conscious appreciation of form.

. . . Therefore, rhythmic experience must be considered subjective and mental. To sense rhythm we must be conscious of it; and to be conscious of it, it must be an experience of the mind. In other words, to be conscious of impressions means the mind is receiving stimuli through the senses. Just as we have special senses of sight and hearing that convey kinds of information to the brain, so do we have a special sense that informs the mind of our movements. This is the kinesthetic sense. Psychologists today quite generally agree as to the importance of kinesthetic sensations in the perception of rhythm. . . . Just as we discriminate sound meanings through the auditory sense in terms of their duration and intensity, so through the kinesthetic sense we may come to know movement in terms of duration and intensity. Kinesthetic sensations then are "those sensations from active movements of muscles and joints by which we judge the force and extent of movement." Through kinesthesia we learn to feel the body in action and in balance, and to adjust to information given by the muscular sensations. But to gain these perceptions there must be attention given to those sensations reported to the brain, and in turn this study must be strengthened by an understanding of the principles of motion. These two phases cannot be separated for one involves the other. . . .

Rhythm is measured energy. It is action and rest—control and release. Therefore, it is a constant law of all muscular movement. Motor rhythm is the form in which muscular experience occurs. It is force manifest in muscular movement. This is saying that any movement, no matter how poorly co-ordinated or executed, has rhythm, but a rhythm that is different from that of the well co-ordinated performance. The difference between the awkward efforts of first attempts and the ease and efficiency of perfected movement is due to the change in the "timing" of the related time and stress values of the movement phases. In other words, "the rhythm" changes.

. . . All the possible rhythms of physical activity and art lie dormant in these two simple factors, time (duration), and intensity. This is because their possible proportionings are infinite. In all experience "rhythm sustains force and gives it orderly sequence." Rhythm thus considered is synonymous with form.

The terms *a rhythm* or the plural *rhythms* and *rhythmic pattern* must not be confused with rhythm. *Rhythm* is the all inclusive term meaning measured energy. It is the feature that all "rhythms" share, while the other terms refer to a particular grouping of time and stress into a definite pattern resulting in a particular form. They embody rhythm. . . .

Rhythmic training has another contribution to offer to the study of motion—its capacity to heighten pleasure in activity. Pleasure in vigorous and stimulating body activity of some kind is universal—probably due to the pleasure in merely obeying the impulse to move. Add to this fundamental pleasure the stimulating and regulating influence of rhythm and the joy in movement becomes intense.

Since rhythm is the law of our living organism, the important role the conscious study and experiencing of rhythm should play in motor learning becomes clear. By "conscious" is meant the developing of a keen discriminating kinesthetic sense, building from an intelligent experiencing of rhythmic values and meanings and their application to as many body skills as possible—including those necessary to daily life as well as to those more finely adjusted skills of sport techniques and dance. . . .

An appreciation of rhythm in its simple beginnings can contribute to the student's realization that rhythm is the universal and controlling force back of all phenomena and that the elements of rhythm exist in all things. It can help him to tune in with the varying rhythms and stresses of life about him. Rhythm in this larger meaning is the form through which all life is experienced and expressed. . . .

42

⊠⊂⊃⊠

Why Exercise? *

ARTHUR H. STEINHAUS, Ph.D.

Dr. Arthur H. Steinhaus is one of the most able and articulate spokesmen on the contributions of physical education to the physiological development of the body. He has spent the last forty years engaged in pure
research in physiology and physiology of exercise. Born in Chicago in
1897, the son of a physician, Dr. Steinhaus completed his education at
George Williams College and the University of Chicago, where he received the Ph.D. degree in physiology in 1928. Since 1920 he has
taught at George Williams College and has held the rank of Professor of
Physiology since 1928. During World War II he was a member of the
Civilian Advisory Committee for the U. S. Navy Physical Fitness Program, Consultant on Rehabilitation to the Secretary of the Navy, and
Chief of the Division of Physical Education and Health Activities for
the U. S. Office of Education (1944). Professional accomplishments and
honors include the following: holder of a Guggenheim Memorial Fellowship in Europe; a fellow of the American Academy for the Advancement
of Science; a member of the Federation Internationale Medico-Sportive;
and a member of the editorial boards of *The Journal of Applied Physiology, Clinical Medicine, Journal of Physical Education,* and *Research
Quarterly.* He has served as President of the Illinois AHPER, of the
Midwest District of AAHPER, and of the American Academy of Physical
Education. Numerous publications include a series of 24 articles on
"Physiology in the Service of Physical Education" which was published
in the *Journal of Health and Physical Education.* The flavor of his work
can be perceived in "Why Exercise?"

The title of my talk, "Why Exercise," might just as well be "Why *Not*
Exercise?" Most Americans are already exercise conscious. Some exercise
because they want to be strong. Some exercise in order to resist colds
and other diseases. Some exercise to lose weight; while others exercise to
gain weight. Some seek through exercise to get more and redder blood;
while others exercise to become more efficient in business. We have been
warned that in exercise lies the danger of sudden death; while others,

* Arthur H. Steinhaus, "Why Exercise," *The Journal of Health and Physical Education,* Vol. 5 (May, 1934), pp. 5–7 and 42–43.

more optimistic, have promised indefinite prolongation of life. Then there are many who exercise just because it is lots of fun.

As physical educators it is our duty to know rather than to guess at the truth about such claims. In our efforts to secure such information we find the science of physiology genuinely in the service of physical education.

Does exercise develop strength? The answer is, yes. The strength of a muscle is directly proportional to the area of its cross section. In other words, a muscle whose cross section is 1 square inch has a pulling power of 140 pounds, while a muscle whose effective cross section measures 2 square inches can life 280 pounds. This pulling power is due to the united contraction of many thousands of discrete cylindrical muscle cells, averaging in length $1\frac{1}{4}$ inches, and in diameter, $\frac{1}{600}$ inch. If all of the four billion muscle cells of the entire body were laid end to end, the tiny strand would encircle the globe four times in the latitude of the Great Lakes. When, owing to muscle, an individual's muscles become larger and therefore stronger, there is no multiplication of muscle cells but rather a thickening of some of the cells which previously had been undersize. This discovery we owe to the painstaking studies of scientists who devised special methods of counting the thousands of fibres in a single muscle. In some cases they observed a virtual doubling of the cross section without any increase in the number of cells. . . .

We return to our main theme with a simple rule: any exercise which is heavy enough to tax a muscle to its limit will stimulate that muscle to grow larger, and with this hypertrophy there comes greater strength. But let us ask ourselves, is strength a desirable goal? Does modern man need large muscles? Let us assume you weigh 160 pounds; 64 pounds, or about 40 per cent of this weight, is in muscle. In other words, you have a 64-pound motor whose function it is to support, move, and transport this total of 160 pounds of the body. Depending on your occupation, this motor must, in addition, do more or less external work, as, for example, shovelling coal, digging a garden, stoking a furnace, or changing an automobile tire. The ideal muscular development is that which has just enough margin of strength or power to maintain posture without effort, to do the day's work easily, and to handle one's body weight readily. Beyond this point it is wise to observe the maxims: "Truck-horse muscles are out of place on a buggy-horse job," and "Why bang around with a five-ton truck when a runabout will do?"

Does exercise increase endurance? The answer is in the affirmative. Your endurance can best be measured by how much work you can do without tiring. It is largely dependent upon how efficiently the heart does its work. This organ must pump blood through the lungs and throughout the entire body. The blood so pumped carries oxygen to the muscles. This oxygen is needed by the muscles to dispose of the waste products of muscle action, such as lactic acid, which, if they did accumulate, would produce fatigue. Thus, it is clear that if plenty of oxygen-bearing blood is pumped out to the muscles they will not tire. In very recent months evidence is accumulating to indicate that no lactic acid need form at all in a muscle if it is continuously supplied with enough oxygen.

Let us digress for a moment to pay our respects to this faithful, hard-working heart, which began its rhythmic contractions long before we were born and will continue them to the very end of our lives. In the average-sized person the heart pumps, each minute, about one gallon of blood to the lungs and an equal amount to the remainder of the body. Thus in the course of a day the heart handles about 11½ tons of blood, and in a lifetime of 65 years over one-quarter of a million tons are pumped by this little organ whose own size is approximately that of a small grapefruit. The blood which is sent out to the muscles of the body leaves the heart under a pressure of 2½ pounds to the square inch. This is from 2 to 3 times the pressure maintained in the steam-heating system which warms our homes. If the work so done by the heart in a single day could be harnessed to a suitable machine, it would be enough to lift a 150-pound man from the sidewalk to the top of New York's Chrysler building, a height of approximately 1000 feet. Stated another way, this is the equivalent of shovelling 25 tons of coal from the floor onto a platform 3 feet high.

All of the figures just mentioned refer to the activity of the heart when its owner is completely at rest. As soon as exercise is begun the figures mount rapidly. I think the world's record for heart performance was measured by my friend, Dr. Christiansen, in Denmark. He found that the heart of a highly trained bicyclist could pump out more than nine gallons of blood per minute to the oxygen-hungry muscles. Since this cyclist, no doubt, had only four or five quarts of blood in all, it means that the equivalent of all his blood must have passed through his heart every nine seconds.

A period of training increases the capacity of the heart in this function of pumping blood. Professor Lindhard, also a Dane, studied an athlete before and after an athletic season and discovered that his heart while at rest was 20 per cent more efficient in this respect at the close of the season. But not only can an athlete's heart pump more blood per minute, it can do so with fewer beats. This is because it puts out almost twice as much blood with each stroke as does the heart of the nonathlete. Herein, it seems, lies the secret of the supremacy of an athlete's heart. Because it can, with fifty or sixty strokes, pump more blood than can another heart with seventy or eighty beats, it has more and longer rests between beats. A heart which beats sixty times a minute works only twenty minutes and rests forty minutes of each hour, while a heart beating eighty times per minute must work twenty-three minutes. A bit of calculation shows that this makes a difference of eighteen days a year.

This difference between the trained and untrained heart becomes even greater when both individuals perform the same task. In fact, the non-athlete's heart, during strenuous exercise, beats so fast that it hardly has time to fill between beats; thus, instead of pumping more and more blood to the active muscles, it soon reaches its maximum beyond which more beats per minute yield no further return in increased heart output. Professor Henderson of Yale has pointed out that the heart of a smoker resembles, in this respect, the heart of a nonathlete, and thus is explained what every athlete knows, namely, that "smoking cuts the wind." . . .

Thus, in summary, exercise—particularly the kind which tends to make you breathless—trains the heart to pump larger quantities of blood with greater ease, and the vasomotor adjustment to direct this blood in more liberal amount to the parts which need it, and because this blood carries the oxygen necessary to dispose of waste products, for this reason exercise helps you to do a bigger day's work without tiring.

Many people are of the opinion that regular exercise will increase their resistance to infectious diseases. In other words, they believe that in some way the disease-fighting powers of the body are strengthened. Unfortunately, there is no good reason for this belief. Scientists have in recent years studied this question most carefully both here and abroad. Experiments have been made on animals and on men. These efforts include statistical studies of large groups of people, blood tests, and experimental inoculation of animals. The conclusion is always the same. An athlete is just as likely to succumb to the poisons of bacteria as is his lazier brother who never visits the gymnasium. Just in one respect may he have a slight edge on him and that is because he does not fatigue as readily. . . .

There are many people who exercise to reduce weight. Some claim success, while others give up in despair after many trials. This is a problem to which I have given much serious thought. Let us get closer to the actual facts with the aid of a simple analogy. The body may be compared to an automobile. The food which we consume is like gasoline in an automobile. If we consume more food than is needed for the day's run, the excess is stored as glycogen in the liver and muscles or as fat in various parts of the body. The Calorie is the unit by which it is possible to express the fuel value of a food or of any other source of energy. Thus, for example, 1 gallon of gasoline is equivalent to 36,124 Calories. The same number of Calories are found in 30 loaves of bread or about 8½ pounds of fat. The average adult needs between 2500 and 3000 Calories per day to perform the functions of the average business man or skilled laborer. If he eats more than this, the excess will be stored as fat. Many people unconsciously adjust their food intake pretty closely to their needs, so that even though they fluctuate a bit from day to day their weight is quite constant over long periods. Some of us, however, are less

fortunate in making this adjustment and therefore vacillate between programs of dieting and exercising in desperate attempts to keep in form.
To help solve this problem let us return to our analogy. If one knows
how much mileage his car will give, under various driving conditions,
on a gallon of gasoline, or shall we say on 36,124 Calories, then it is
possible to calculate just how long or how far it will be necessary to
drive the old bus in order to empty the gas tank.

Exactly the same line of reasoning holds true for the body. Physiologists in all parts of the world have studied the "mileage problem" on the
human motor. They have, of course, had to work with all kind of models
and with what we might call a number of foreign makes—but their
results are surprisingly uniform. From their results, which are expressed
in a number of different ways, I have prepared a table of "human mile-
ages," shall we say, under different driving conditions. Let us now examine the amount of exercise or work, over and above that needed for
just sitting still, which an average-sized man weighing 155 pounds must
perform in order to burn up that extra pound of fat (4320 Calories)
which he has stored, let us say, under his belt.

He may do ordinary office work for eleven 8-hour days.

He may walk 144 miles, at the rate of 2 miles per hour.

If he is a skilled mason, he may lay 14,731 bricks.

He may do a wand drill for 20½ hours; walk 66½ miles, at the rate of
one mile in 17½ minutes; play ping-pong for 17½ hours; shovel 114,739
pounds of sand into a wheelbarrow; saw wood for 10½ hours; fence for 8
hours; parallel-bar work for 7½ hours; walk 34¾ miles, at the rate of 5 miles
an hour; wrestle 5½ hours; play strenuous football for 4 hours and 48 minutes;
run 17.3 miles, at the rate of a mile in 6 minutes; run 129 100-yard dashes
at 10 seconds each; walk to the top of the Washington monument 48 times;
or do 5714 push-ups from the floor.

If he prefers to have the electrical vibrator take off this pound of fat, he
will need to contend with this machine for 375 15-minute periods.

From our study of this list it is no doubt clear that the human motor
is too efficient a machine to make emptying the gas tank by racing the
motor a sensible procedure. The average man has not the time, even if
he had the patience, for this procedure. A further difficulty lies in the
fact that exercise is a great stimulator of the appetite. The individual
whose three-mile constitutional tempts him to consume only one extra
piece of bread and one pat of butter has by that one act already nullified
the weight-reducing value of the entire walk.

It is, of course, true that very heavy people would, because of their
additional weight, expend more energy than would our 155-pound model
man used in the above illustration. On the other hand, it is just as true
that the very heavy person often does not have the strength of muscles,

the feet, or a sufficiently good heart to make the weight reduction by the exercise route at all safe.

Lest I be misunderstood, let me be very specific before leaving this point. I am convinced that it is possible to take weight off by exercise. I have told you how much exercise is necessary. Of course the scales will show a greater loss right after exercise but most of that is the water lost by sweating, and will go on again as soon as one drinks more water. The more sensible way to take off weight is to put less on. . . .

The answer to our question "Why exercise?" is simple to a child and complex to the adult. There are physiological, psychological, and sociological urges, predispositions, effects, and outcomes; there are correlations, predictions, and regression curves; yea, there are cardinal points and objectives. All of these and many others have their place in scientific survey and analysis. Far be it from me to minimize their contributions to our understanding, and at times misunderstandings. But having used them to find for ourselves or others the exercise, game, sport, or activity best suited to the strength, age, temperament, and need of the one concerned, let us forget all else and seek first the joy of the venture; and before you know it the strength, the endurance, the added vitality, and a new outlook on life will be added unto you.

43

What Is Physical Fitness? *

CHARLES H. McCLOY, Ph.D.

Dr. Charles H. McCloy, one of the most capable leaders in American physical education, was an able spokesman on physical fitness. For an account of his professional contributions to physical education, see Document 32.

. . . Physical fitness as defined here is not the same as total fitness, and does not necessarily comprise fitness of the total organism. A moron, for example, might have as high a degree of physical fitness as a genius. An almost totally uneducated person might have as high a degree of physical fitness as a person with two Doctor's degrees. But moron and genius, the ignoramous and the educated person, might be affected as to physical fitness by emotional disturbances via psychosomatic routes.

A second limitation would be that if a certain amount of physical fitness is desirable, it is not necessarily true that a greater degree of physical fitness would be better. For example, insofar as muscular strength may be thought of as a desirable attribute relative to physical fitness, the amount of muscular strength that is desirable may be limited. For example, it may be quite possible (though not proven) that an individual may develop so much muscular strength, with its attendant muscular hypertrophy, as to have the extra amount of muscular tissue act as a parasite on the organism and be, in fact, as much of an overweight detriment as overfatness might be. In other words, strength would not necessarily be synonymous with physical fitness. An adequate amount should be desirable. An excess amount might be a handicap. The same may be true of some other developed qualities or characteristics.

The first thing I would consider would be the hereditary quality of the vital organs. Some people seem to be born with vital organs of a higher quality than those of other persons. For example, it is not uncommon for family physicians to note that almost every member in some families has suffered from chronic nephritis before the age of 40 or 45, and these people usually die of that disease in relatively early middle

* C. H. McCloy, "What is Physical Fitness?" *The Journal of Health, Physical Education and Recreation*, Vol. 27 (September, 1956), pp. 14–15 and 38.

age. These individuals have apparently inherited an inferior quality of kidneys. Those in other families show no deterioration of kidney function throughout a long life.

Some individuals have inherited inferior hearts, and die of what might be thought of as "old age of the heart," not particularly complicated by any other discernable disease of that organ, at a relatively early age. I was at one time talking with a noted scientist, a member of the faculty of a college of medicine. This individual asked me to guess his age. I guessed him as being 55 years of age. The scientist smiled and said, "Mac, you know that you are lying; you know perfectly well that I look as though I were 65. I shall never live to 55 years of age." He then stated that all his family on his father's side for several generations had died of hypertension before they were 50. In other words, this gentleman's heredity relative to his blood vessels and general circulatory system was defective. To summarize this section, inheritance of high-grade organs, both structurally and functionally, is an important aspect of physical fitness.

To push this aspect of physical fitness a little further, let us consider the functioning of some of the glands of internal secretion. As is well known, the "normal" functioning of the thyroid gland is the most desirable. The individual whose thyroid gland functions at too high a rate (hyperthyroidism) and the individual whose gland functions at too low a level (hypothyroidism) are both in the category of those with malfunctioning glands. The same is true of the pituitary and of other glands of internal secretion as well. In other words, it would appear as though the average functioning of these glands represents nature's best experience. Hence, it is certainly not true that the highest degree of functioning of such organs is desirable; it is the normal or average functioning that seems to be the most desirable, to represent that type of heredity, so far as organ functioning is concerned, which is best. The same thing relative to normal hereditary functioning is true of other organs as well. When one's heredity in this respect is good, one is well started on the way towards a potentially good physical fitness.

The next aspect of a good physical fitness is the lack of pathological functioning of the organs; in other words, a person is healthy or, conversely, not ill. He does not suffer from infections, bacterial or virus, that sap his energies. This is particularly important as he becomes older. A 60-year-old man has had three times as much time to accumulate physiological and pathological insults as a 20-year-old person has had. Hence the absence of drains and strains is important. Being healthy is, in a way, only the negative side of physical fitness, but it is nevertheless a prerequisite.

A third necessary aspect is good hygienic habits or, conversely, the absence of bad hygienic habits. It has repeatedly been pointed out by experts in the field of hygiene that bad hygienic habits pile up. For example, it may not be of great detriment that an individual have one mildly detrimental hygienic habit, such as smoking a few cigarettes a day. When, however, to smoking he adds the bad habit of the ingestion of too much alcohol, the chronic ingestion of too much food, the habit of lack of exercise, the habit of worrying, etc., these bad habits pile up in their effects and greatly reduce the individual's physical fitness. . . . So far, we have considered the effects on physical fitnes of what the individual is born with, and of the things that he should not do. Now for the positive aspects.

To be physically fit in the sense of the functioning of the neuromuscular systems, one needs an adequate amount of strength and endurance. This writer thinks that adequate may be defined differently for people whose demands are different. For example, what would be adequate for a furniture mover would be more than adequate for a stenographer—but if either is to be fit, the amount of strength and of endurance should be more than completely adequate for that person's emergency need, for off-the-job work, and for recreation. This may be made a little clearer by two analogies relative to strength.

Suppose the reader were asked, during the colder part of the year, to wear under his clothing a jacket weighted with lead to the point where it weighed approximately 30 pounds, and let us suppose that he were requested to wear this all day long from the time that he arose in the morning until he retired at night. His probable reaction would be, "Don't be silly! If I wore that kind of a 30-pound pack all day, I should be all-in by noon!" His reaction would be a correct one; but if an individual of normal weight were to be "under-muscled" to the extent of 30 pounds and carrying his full normal weight, he would be just as much all-in by noon as he would if he were normally muscled and carrying that much overweight. Hence, it should be clear that the person whose muscular sytem is not up to carrying his weight under normal circumstances is just as much handicapped as is the individual who carries the extra load. . . .

The following is simply my educated guess: I believe, however, that what would be a normal strength for most people would be a Strength Quotient (Physical Fitness Index) of about 115 for the more sedentary persons, to one of about 170 for those with the most active occupations, such as laborers, furniture movers, professional football players, etc.

As to endurance, there are many kinds of endurance. For a discussion of this, see reference given [C. H. McCloy, "Endurance," *The Physical Educator,* May, 1948]. At this point I will mention only four types. One type of endurance is a concomitant of more strength. . . . In other words, the stronger individual uses a smaller proportion of his motor units and hence works more efficiently. A second type of endurance is dependent not only upon strength but upon the degree of training during which training the muscle develops a greater capillary bed. In other words, there may be from 400–600 per cent more capillaries in the muscle per cubic millimeter than in the nondeveloped muscles. . . . Here there is a greater blood supply and hence more oxygen available to the muscles during work.

A third type is that of circulorespiratory endurance, which is a complex. First there is the strength of the muscles used. For example, if the individual is a runner, he must have adequate amounts of strength and adequate amounts of capillary blood supply to the muscles used in running, such as those of the legs. In addition to this, there is an adequate strength and an adequate degree of capillarization of the muscles of the heart. At this point there is some controversy as to the evidence of increased capillarization of the heart muscle. . . . It is as yet unknown what the facts are relative to the human heart.

A fourth type is general autonomic-nervous-system adaptability to fatigue. This is the ability of the autonomic nervous system to cause the splanchnic circulation to adapt to the needs of the peripheral circulation upon demand. The individual whose autonomic nervous system does not stimulate the splanchnic circulation to squeeze out its oversupply of blood into the peripheral circulation when there is a demand, does not respond to overfatigue as does the individual whose autonomic sytem has developed the ability to so respond.

There are other aspects of endurance but it would seem that an adequate development of these four types should, clearly, be seen as important aspects of an adequate amount of physical fitness. For the development of such adequate degrees of strength and endurance, the person must train enough to "get in good shape" and to stay trained to that degree.

It is desirable to have an adequate degree of bodily flexibility, particularly when, as an individual gets older, he tends to become stiffer or less flexible. If he becomes less flexible, he usually has a greater degree or nervous tension than if he remains adequately limber. This lessening of flexibility is not as much a muscular thing as it is a matter of shortening fasciae. This has been discussed rather adequately by Billig. Frequently a feeling of "getting old" is largely waning strength and a greater degree of inflexibility, both of which can usually be kept within the normal range for many years of middle and approaching old age by sensible— and not excessive—exercise programs, appropriately chosen and regularly practiced.

This paper is not a treatise on how to get a high degree of physical fitness and to keep it; it is primarily an attempt to define and to describe physical fitness in simple, understandable terms. There is, in spite of the large amount of health knowledge available at this time, much to be studied as to how best to achieve physical fitness and to retain it. . . .

A SELECT BIBLIOGRAPHY

AINSWORTH, Dorothy, *History of Physical Education in Colleges for Women.* New York, A. S. Barnes and Co., 1930.

American Physical Education Review. The American Association for the Advancement of Physical Education, 1896–1929.

BEECHER, Catherine E., *Physiology and Calisthenics for Schools and Families.* New York, Harper and Brothers, 1856.

BOURNE, H. R. Fox, *The Life of John Locke.* Vol. 2, New York, Harper and Brothers, 1876.

BROWNELL, Clifford Lee, *Principles of Health Education Applied.* New York, McGraw-Hill Book Co., 1949.

BUCHER, Charles A., *Foundations of Physical Education.* St. Louis, The C. V. Mosby Co., 1960.

COULTON, G. G., *Medieval Panorama: The English Scene from Conquest to Reformation.* Cambridge, Cambridge University Press, 1947.

———, *Medieval Village.* Cambridge, Cambridge University Press, 1926.

CREMIN, Lawrence A., *The Transformation of the School: Progressivism in American Education, 1876–1957.* New York, Alfred A. Knopf, 1961.

DANIELS, Arthur S., *Adapted Physical Education: Principles and Practice of Physical Education for Exceptional Students.* New York, Harper and Brothers, 1954.

DAVIES, Godfrey, *Wellington and His Army.* Oxford, Basil Blackwell, 1954. This book was published in co-operation with the Huntington Library, San Marino, California.

DULLES, Foster Rhea, *America Learns to Play: A History of Popular Recreation, 1607–1940.* New York, Appleton-Century Co., 1940.

FERGUSON, Wallace K., and BRUNN, Geoffrey, *A Survey of European Civilization.* Boston, Houghton Mifflin Co., 1958.

FRANKLIN, Benjamin, *Proposals Relating to the Education of Youth in Pennsylvania.* Facsimile Reprint with an introduction by William Pepper, Philadelphia, University of Pennsylvania Press, 1931.

GULICK, Luther H., *A Philosophy of Play.* New York, Charles Scribner's Sons, 1920.

HAYES, Carlton J. H., *A Political and Cultural History of Modern Europe,* Vol. 1. New York, The Macmillan Co., 1932.

HETHERINGTON, Clark, *School Program in Physical Education.* Yonkers-on-Hudson, World Book Co., 1922.

HITCHCOCK, Edward, *A Report of Twenty Years Experience in the Department of Physical Education and Hygiene in Amherst College to the Board of Trustees.* Amherst, Massachusetts, Press of C. A. Bangs and Co., 1881.

Journal of the American Association for Health, Physical Education, and

Recreation. The American Association for Health, Physical Education, and Recreation, 1948–1954.

Journal of Health and Physical Education. American Physical Education Association, 1930–1948.

Journal of Health, Physical Education and Recreation. The American Association for Health, Physical Education and Recreation, 1955–.

Journal of Higher Education. Columbus, Ohio, The Ohio State University Press, January, 1930–.

KROUT, John L., *Annals of American Sport, The Pageant of America,* Vol. 15, Ralph Henry Gabriel, ed. New Haven, Yale University Press, 1929.

LEONARD, Fred Eugene, *A Guide to The History of Physical Education,* 3d ed., revised and enlarged by George B. Affleck. Philadelphia, Lea and Febiger, 1947.

———, *Pioneers of Modern Physical Training.* New York, Association Press, 1919.

LEWIS, Dio, *New Gymnastics.* Boston, Ticknor and Fields, 1862.

LUCAS, Henry S., *The Renaissance and the Reformation.* New York, Harper and Brothers, 1934.

McCLOY, Charles H., *Philosophical Bases for Physical Education.* New York, F. S. Crofts, 1940.

Mind and Body. New Ulm, Minnesota, Mind and Body Publishing Co., 1894–1936.

MITCHELL, Elmer D., *Intramural Sports.* New York, A. S. Barnes and Co., 1939.

NASH, Jay B., *Physical Education: Interpretations and Objectives.* New York, A. S. Barnes and Co., 1948.

National Education Association Journal of Proceedings and Addresses. Winona, Minnesota, The National Education Association, 1908.

National Society for the Study of Education, *Yearbook.* Chicago, 1895–.

NYE, R. B. and MORPURGO, J. E., *A History of the United States.* Baltimore, Penguin Books, 1955.

Physical Training: A Full Report of the Papers and Discussions of the Conference held in Boston in November, 1889, reported and edited by Isabel C. Barrows. Boston, Press of George H. Ellis, 1890.

PRENTICE, William Kelly, *The Ancient Greeks.* Princeton, Princeton University Press, 1940.

Research Quarterly of the American Physical Education Association, 1930–.

RICE, Emmett A., HUTCHISON, John L., and LEE, Mabel, *A Brief History of Physical Education.* New York, Ronald Press, fourth edition, 1958.

SARGENT, Dudley A., *Autobiography.* Philadelphia, Lea and Febiger, 1927.

School Athletics in Modern Education, Wingate Memorial Lectures, E. Dana Caulkins, ed. New York, Wingate Memorial Foundation, 1931.

School Review. Chicago, University of Chicago Press, January, 1908, Vol. 16.

SCHWENDENER, Norma, *A History of Physical Education in the United States.* New York, A. S. Barnes, 1942.

SCOTT, Harry A., *Competitive Sports in Schools and Colleges.* New York, Harper and Brothers, 1951.

Selections from the Addresses of Thomas D. Wood. New York, Teachers College, Columbia University, 1932.

Teachers College Record, Vol. 58. New York, Teachers College, Columbia University, October–May, 1957.

THOMPSON, James Westfall, ROWLEY, George, SCHEVILL, Ferdinand, and SARTON, George, *The Civilization of the Renaissance.* Chicago, University of Chicago Press, 1929.

VAN DALEN, Deobold B., MITCHELL, Elmer D., and BENNETT, Bruce L., *A World History of Physical Education.* New York, Prentice-Hall, Inc., 1953.

WILLIAMS, Jesse F., *The Principles of Physical Education.* Philadelphia, W. B. Saunders Co., 1948.

INDEX

317